JUMP MANGA EDITION

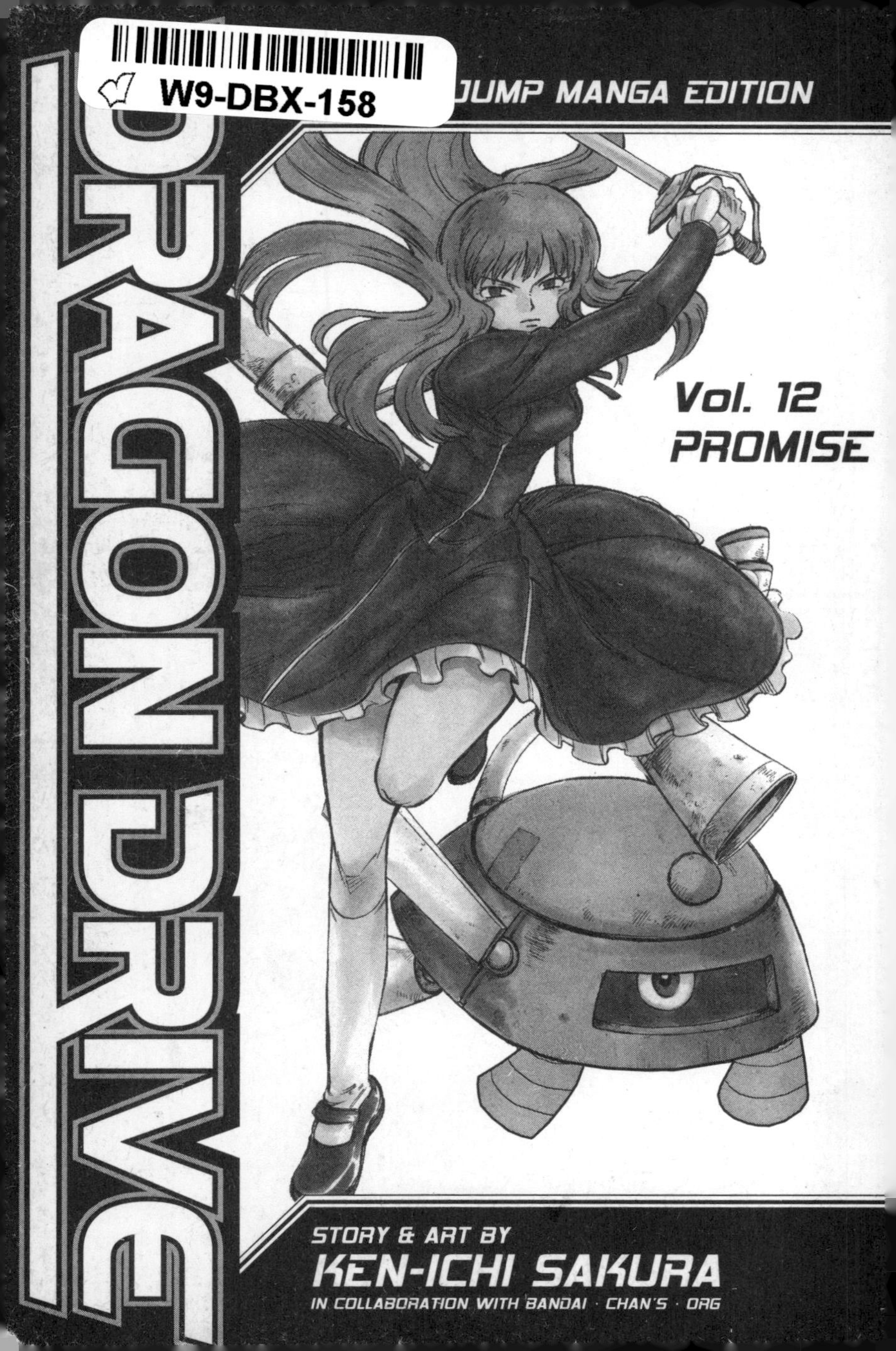

Vol. 12 PROMISE

STORY & ART BY
KEN-ICHI SAKURA
IN COLLABORATION WITH BANDAI · CHAN'S · ORG

CHARACTERS

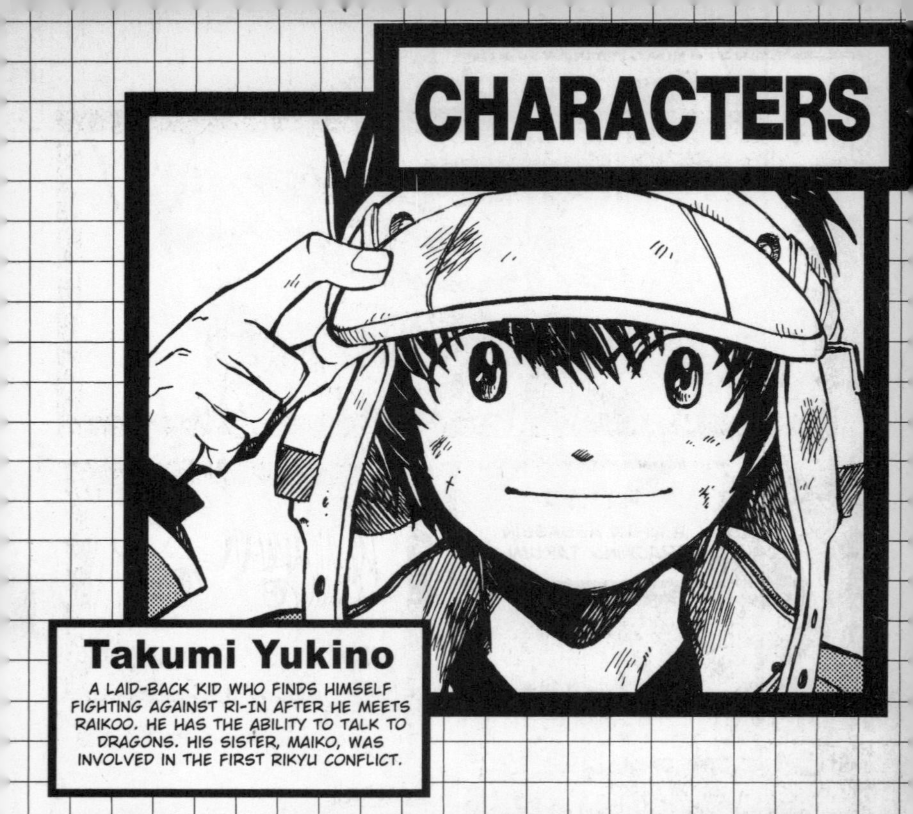

Takumi Yukino

A LAID-BACK KID WHO FINDS HIMSELF FIGHTING AGAINST RI-IN AFTER HE MEETS RAIKOO. HE HAS THE ABILITY TO TALK TO DRAGONS. HIS SISTER, MAIKO, WAS INVOLVED IN THE FIRST RIKYU CONFLICT.

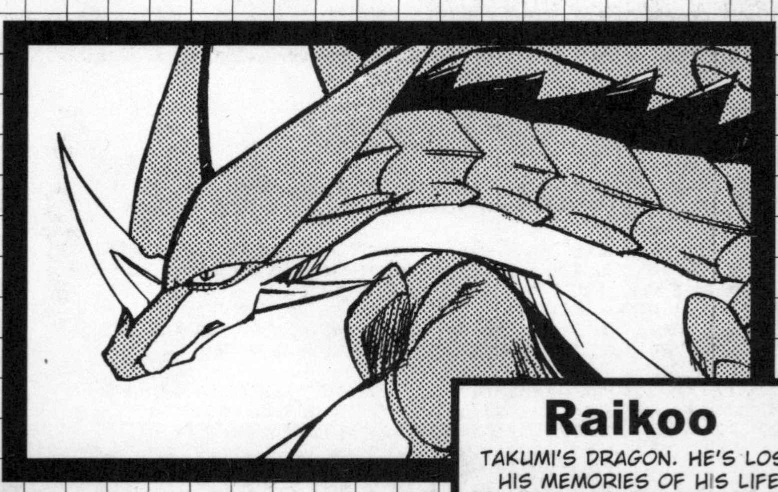

Raikoo

TAKUMI'S DRAGON. HE'S LOST HIS MEMORIES OF HIS LIFE BEFORE HE MET TAKUMI.

Bug

A GUIDE TO THE WORLD OF RAIKOO'S CONSCIOUSNESS. IS HE TRYING TO TRICK TAKUMI?

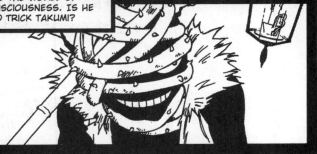

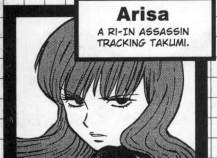

Neko Chihoda

A GIRL WHO WAS LEFT BEHIND ON EARTH.

Arisa

A RI-IN ASSASSIN TRACKING TAKUMI.

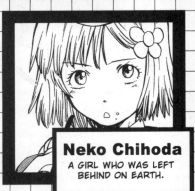

STORY

A GAME CALLED DRAGON DRIVE IS WILDLY POPULAR WITH KIDS ALL OVER THE WORLD. ONE DAY, TAKUMI YUKINO RECEIVES A DECK OF D.D. CARDS FROM AGENT A AND JOINS A TOURNAMENT. EVEN THOUGH HE'S NEVER PLAYED BEFORE, HE MANAGES TO MAKE IT TO THE NATIONAL FINALS WITH THE HELP OF HIS DRAGON, RAIKOO. TAKUMI TURNS OUT TO BE A TRANSLATOR, A PERSON WITH THE RARE ABILITY TO TALK TO DRAGONS.

BEFORE THE FINALS, TAKUMI HAS A STRANGE DREAM. HE'S TOLD THAT TO AWAKEN THE TRUE RAIKOO FROM AMONG THE 99 RAIKOO CARDS, ALL THE RAIKOOS MUST FIGHT EACH OTHER. A WEEK LATER, AN ORGANIZATION CALLED RI-IN HACKS INTO THE D.D. COMPUTER SYSTEM. THE D-ZONE DRAGONS TRADE PLACES WITH THE PEOPLE OF EARTH. ONLY THE PEOPLE WHO WERE INSIDE A D.D. CENTER AT THE TIME ARE LEFT BEHIND.

TAKUMI AND HIS FRIENDS SET OUT ON A QUEST TO RESTORE THE EARTH AND ITS PEOPLE. IN A BATTLE WITH THE POWERFUL ASSASSIN ARISA, RAIKOO IS DELETED. TO SAVE RAIKOO, TAKUMI AND NEKO ENTER THE WORLD OF RAIKOO'S CONSCIOUSNESS...

Vol. 12 PROMISE
CONTENTS

DRAGON DRIVE

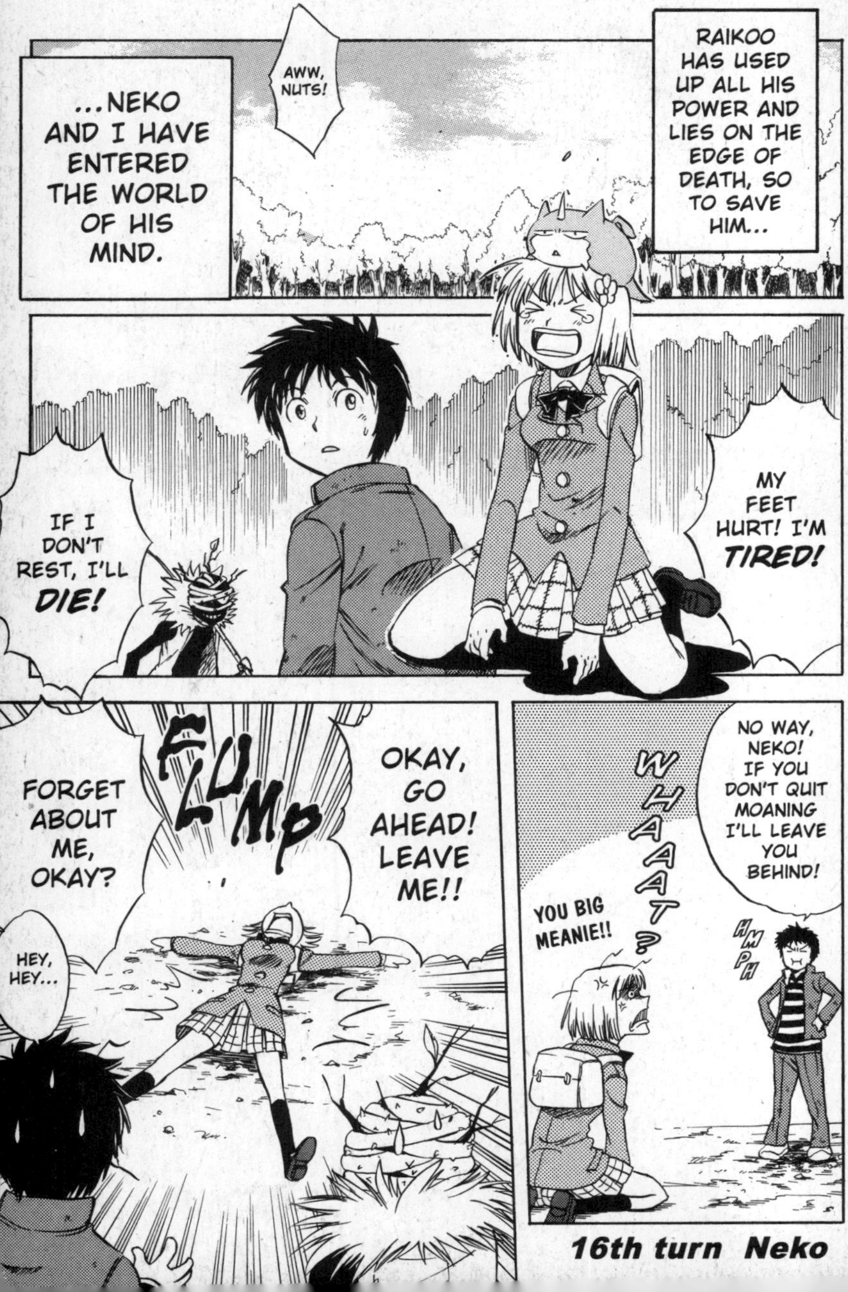
RAIKOO HAS USED UP ALL HIS POWER AND LIES ON THE EDGE OF DEATH, SO TO SAVE HIM...
AWW, NUTS!
...NEKO AND I HAVE ENTERED THE WORLD OF HIS MIND.
MY FEET HURT! I'M TIRED!
IF I DON'T REST, I'LL DIE!
NO WAY, NEKO! IF YOU DON'T QUIT MOANING I'LL LEAVE YOU BEHIND!
HMPH
WHAAAT?
YOU BIG MEANIE!!
OKAY, GO AHEAD! LEAVE ME!!
FLUMP
FORGET ABOUT ME, OKAY?
HEY, HEY...

16th turn Neko

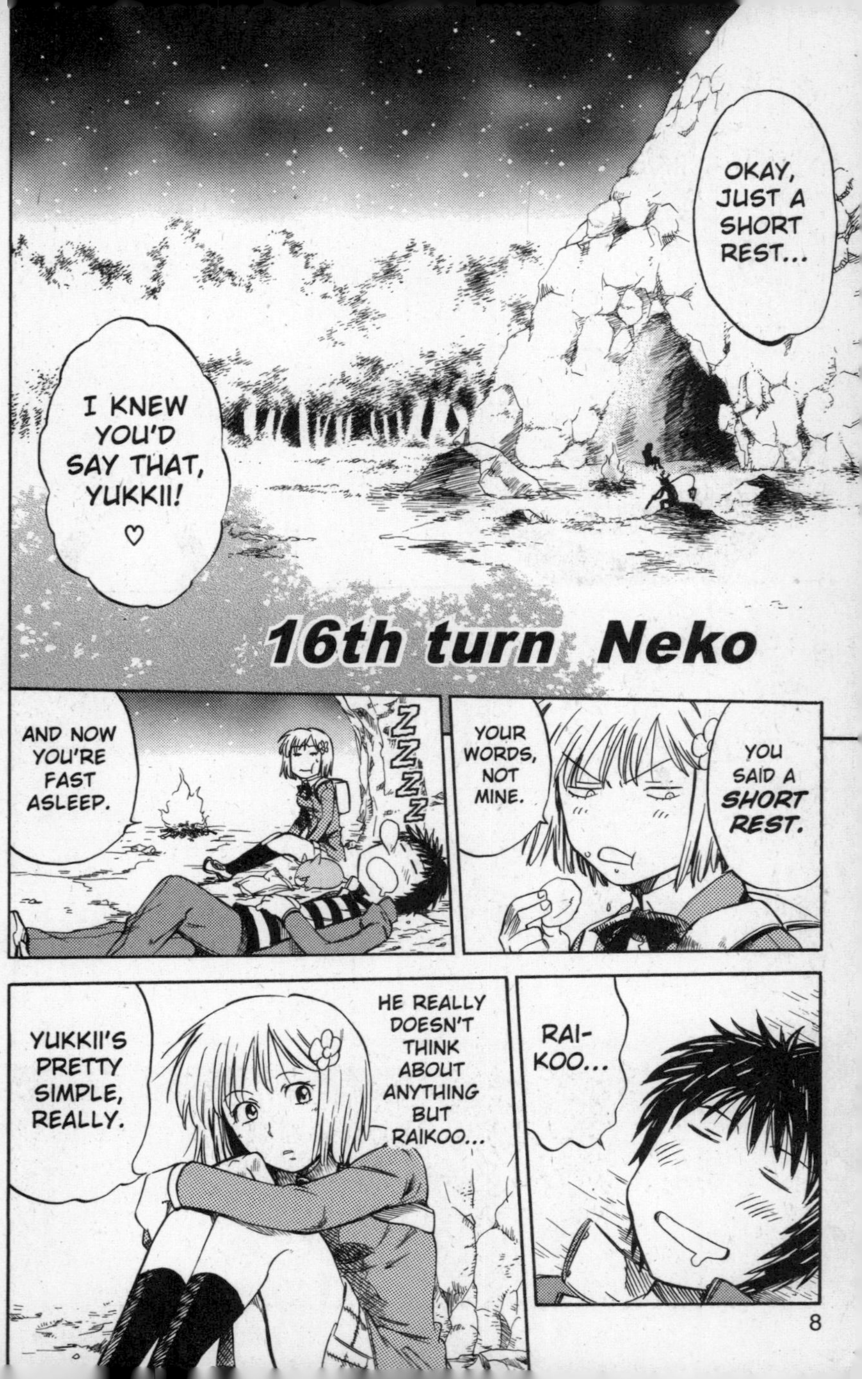
OKAY, JUST A SHORT REST...
I KNEW YOU'D SAY THAT, YUKKII! ♡
16th turn Neko
YOU SAID A *SHORT REST.*
YOUR WORDS, NOT MINE.
ZZZZ
AND NOW YOU'RE FAST ASLEEP.
RAI-KOO...
HE REALLY DOESN'T THINK ABOUT ANYTHING BUT RAIKOO...
YUKKII'S PRETTY SIMPLE, REALLY.

READ THIS WAY

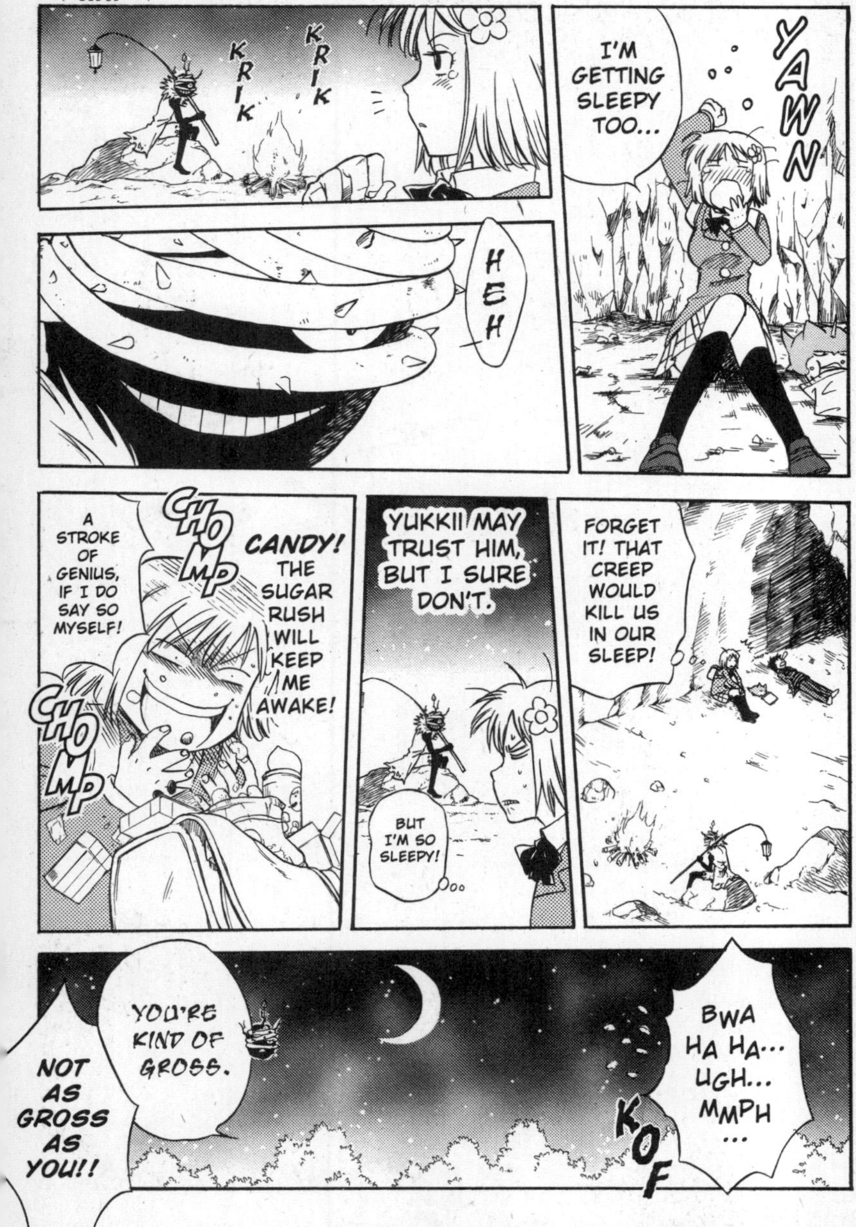
YAWN
I'M GETTING SLEEPY TOO...
KRIK KRIK
HEH
FORGET IT! THAT CREEP WOULD KILL US IN OUR SLEEP!
YUKKII MAY TRUST HIM, BUT I SURE DON'T.
BUT I'M SO SLEEPY!
CANDY! THE SUGAR RUSH WILL KEEP ME AWAKE!
CHOMP
A STROKE OF GENIUS, IF I DO SAY SO MYSELF!
CHOMP
BWA HA HA... UGH... MMPH...
KOF
YOU'RE KIND OF GROSS.
NOT AS GROSS AS YOU!!

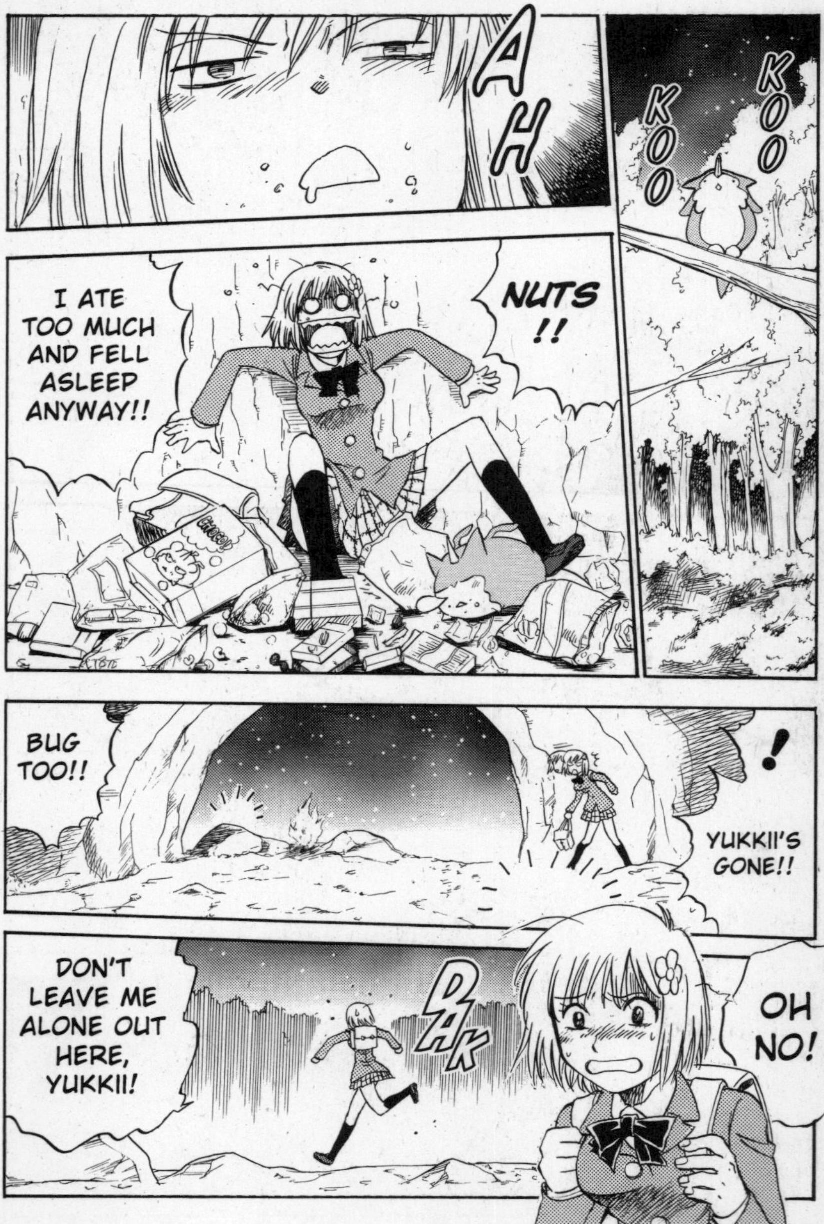

KOO
KOO
AH
NUTS !!
I ATE TOO MUCH AND FELL ASLEEP ANYWAY!!
!
YUKKII'S GONE!!
BUG TOO!!
OH NO!
DAK
DON'T LEAVE ME ALONE OUT HERE, YUKKII!

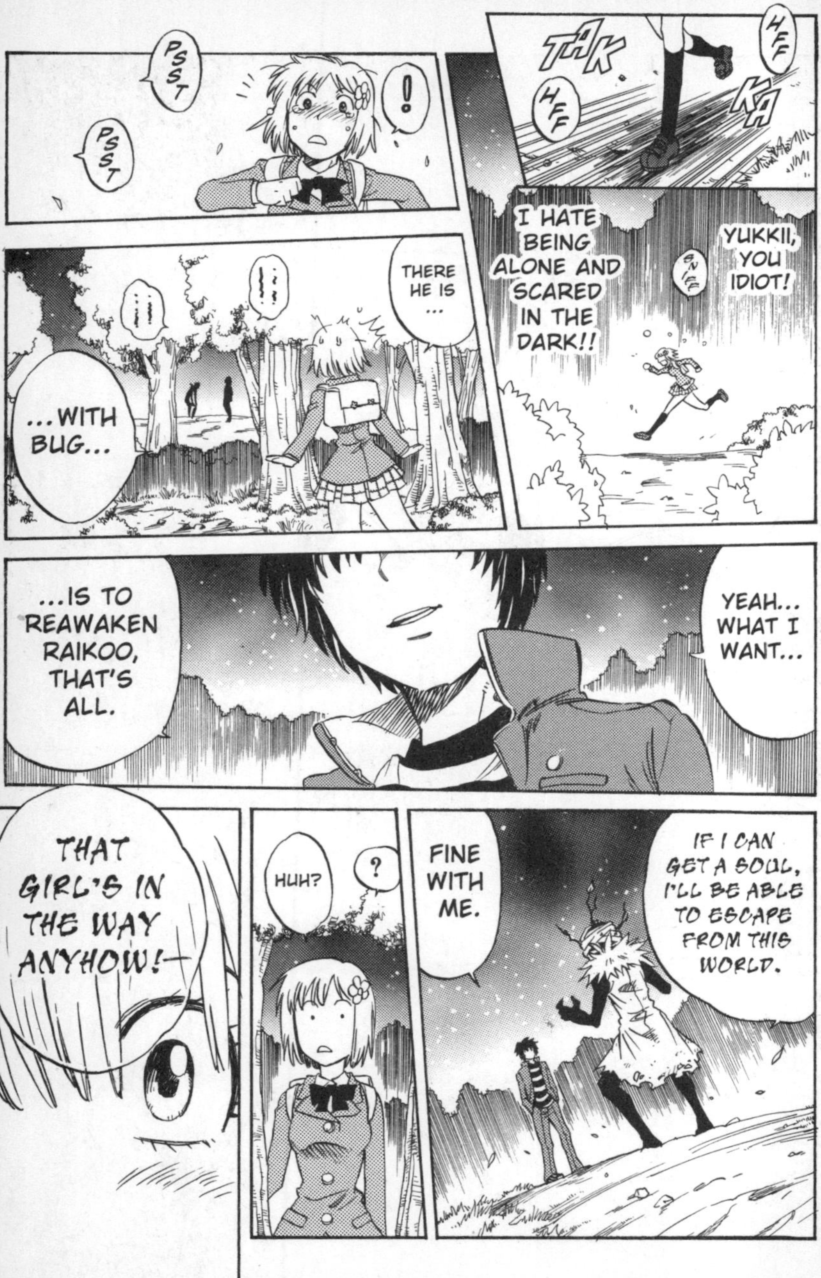
HEFF
KA
TAK
HEFF
!
PSST
PSST
YUKKII, YOU IDIOT!
SNIFF
I HATE BEING ALONE AND SCARED IN THE DARK!!
THERE HE IS...
...WITH BUG...
YEAH... WHAT I WANT...
...IS TO REAWAKEN RAIKOO, THAT'S ALL.
IF I CAN GET A SOUL, I'LL BE ABLE TO ESCAPE FROM THIS WORLD.
FINE WITH ME.
?
HUH?
THAT GIRL'S IN THE WAY ANYHOW!

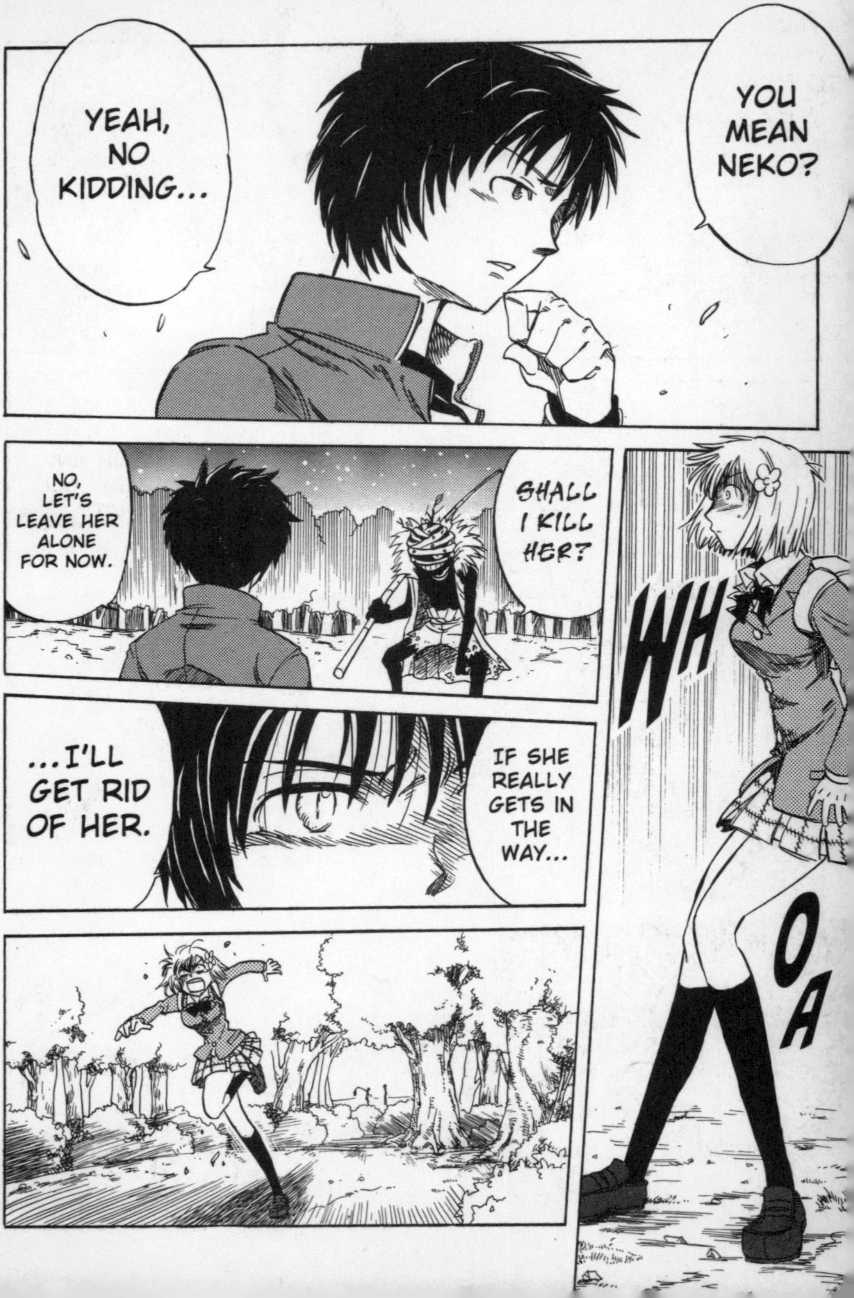
YOU MEAN NEKO?
YEAH, NO KIDDING...
WHOA
SHALL I KILL HER?
NO, LET'S LEAVE HER ALONE FOR NOW.
IF SHE REALLY GETS IN THE WAY...
...I'LL GET RID OF HER.

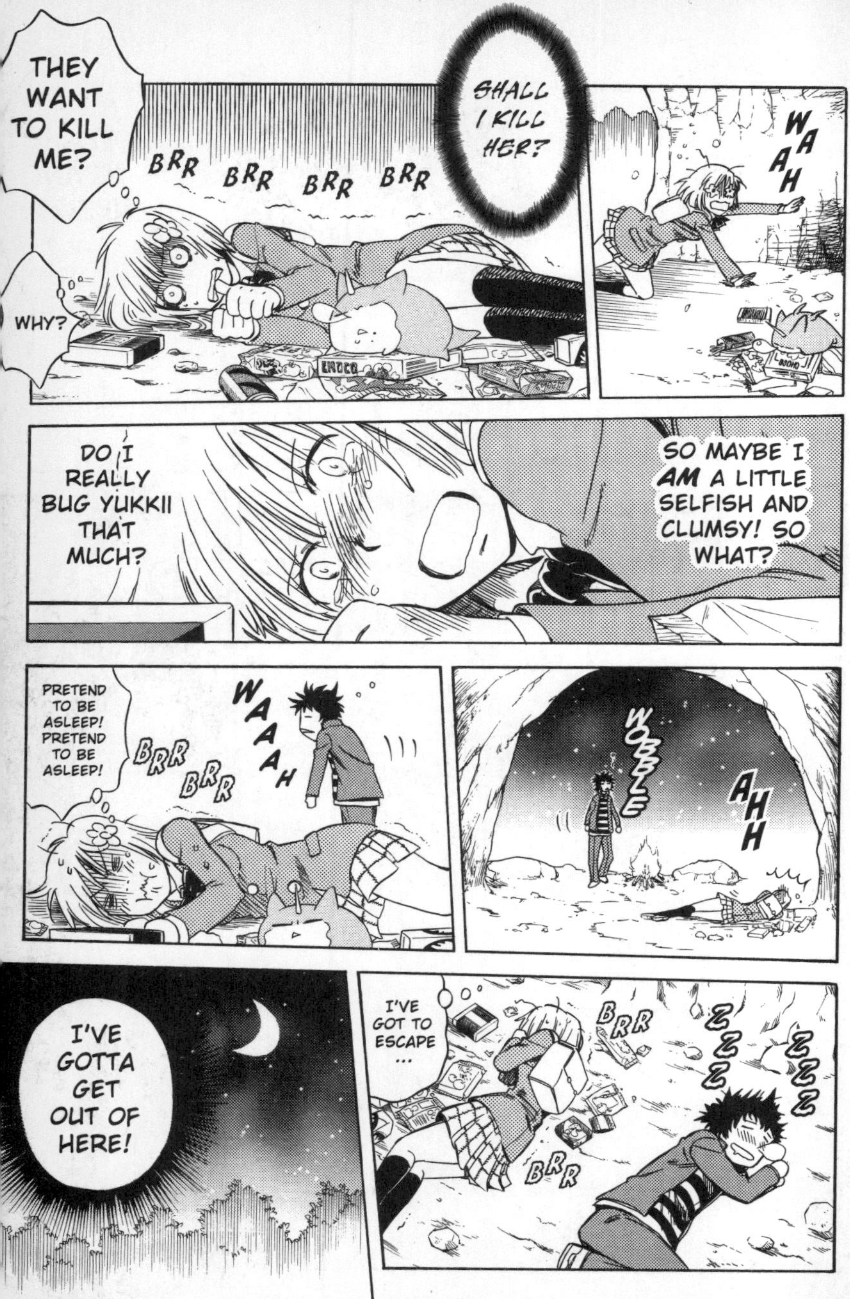
SHALL I KILL HER?
WAAH
THEY WANT TO KILL ME?
BRR BRR BRR BRR
WHY?
SO MAYBE I AM A LITTLE SELFISH AND CLUMSY! SO WHAT?
DO I REALLY BUG YUKKII THAT MUCH?
WOBBLE
AHH
WAAAH
PRETEND TO BE ASLEEP! PRETEND TO BE ASLEEP!
BRR BRR
I'VE GOT TO ESCAPE ...
BRR
ZZZ ZZZ
BRR
I'VE GOTTA GET OUT OF HERE!

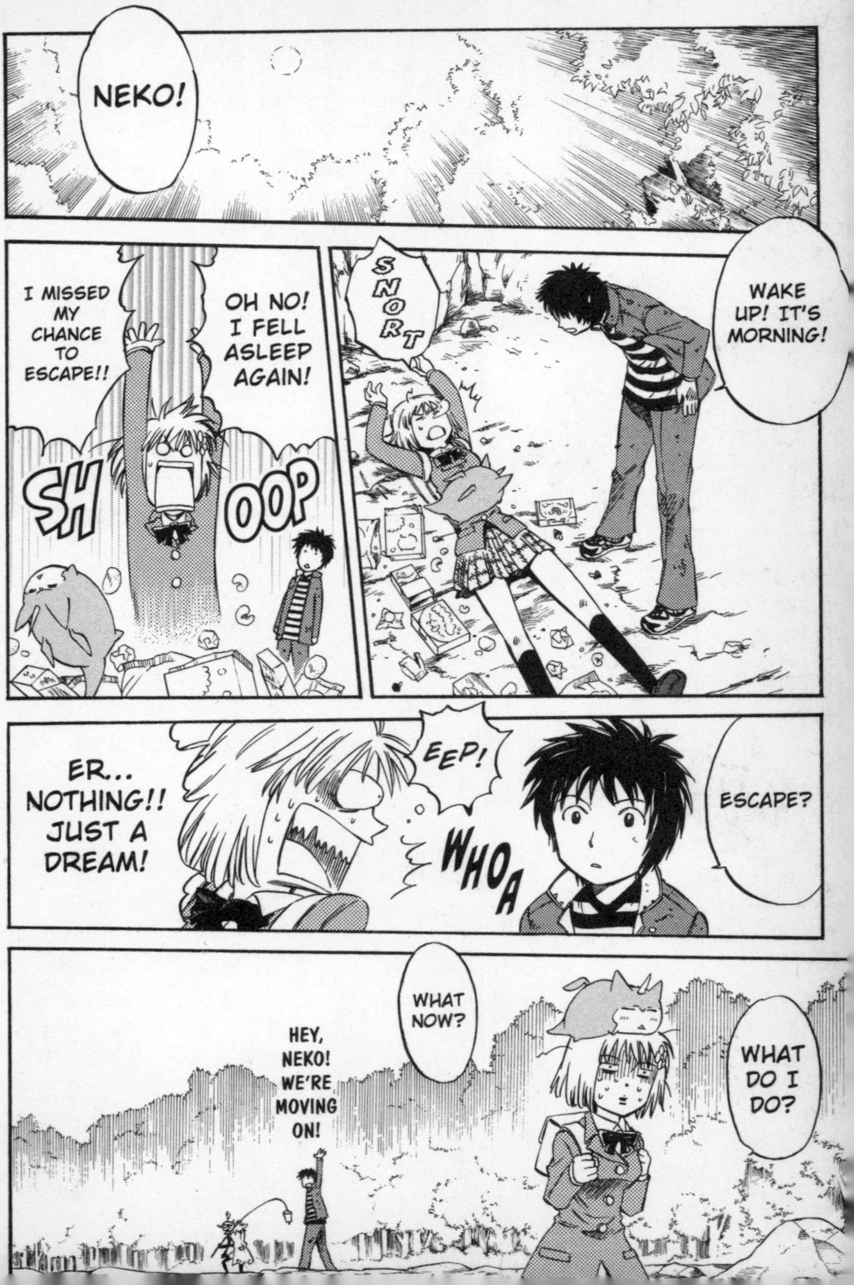
NEKO!
WAKE UP! IT'S MORNING!
SNORT
OH NO! I FELL ASLEEP AGAIN!
I MISSED MY CHANCE TO ESCAPE!!
SHOOP
ESCAPE?
WHOA
EEP!
ER... NOTHING!! JUST A DREAM!
WHAT DO I DO?
WHAT NOW?
HEY, NEKO! WE'RE MOVING ON!

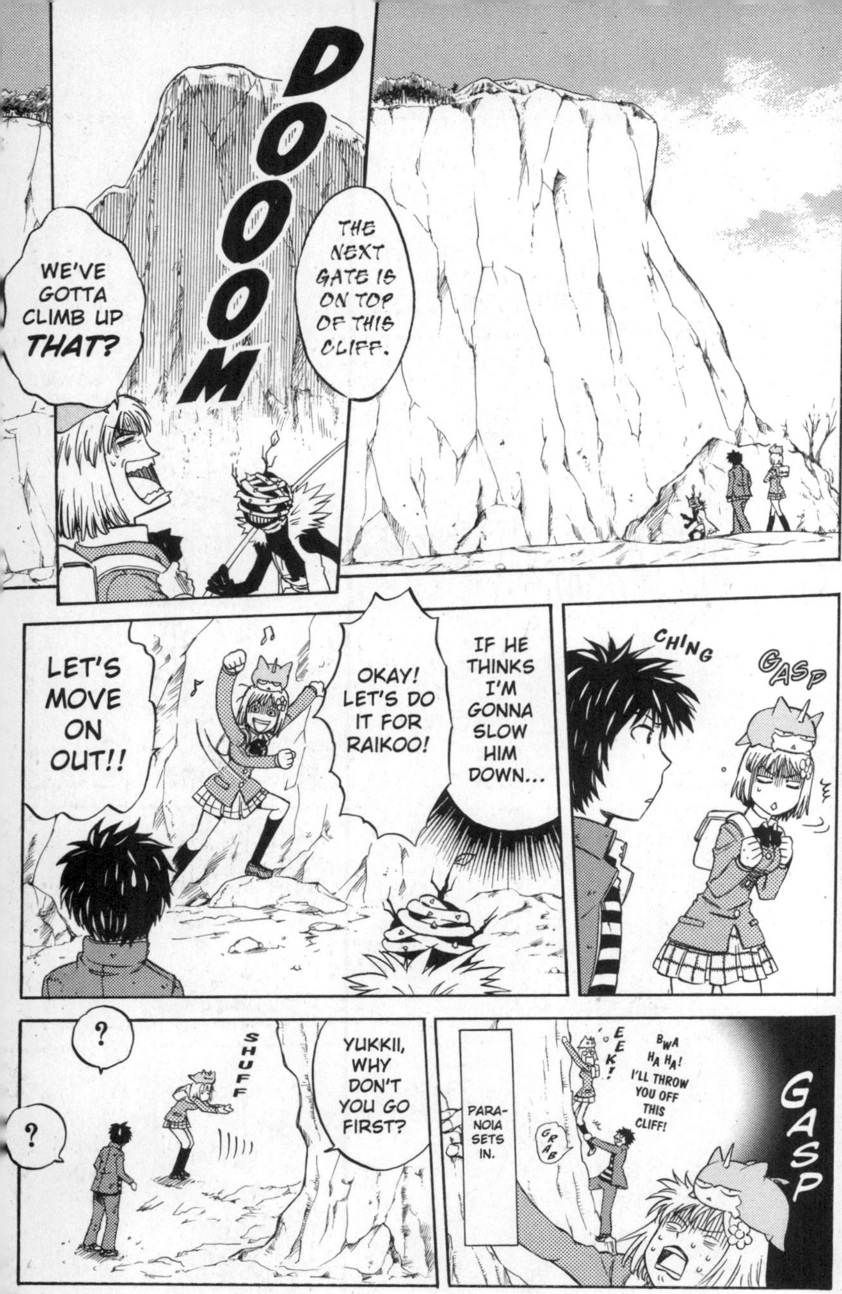
DOOOOM
THE NEXT GATE IS ON TOP OF THIS CLIFF.
WE'VE GOTTA CLIMB UP *THAT?*
CHING
GASP
IF HE THINKS I'M GONNA SLOW HIM DOWN...
OKAY! LET'S DO IT FOR RAIKOO!
LET'S MOVE ON OUT!!
GASP
BWA HA HA! I'LL THROW YOU OFF THIS CLIFF!
EEK!
PARA-NOIA SETS IN.
GRAB
YUKKII, WHY DON'T YOU GO FIRST?
SHUFF
?
?

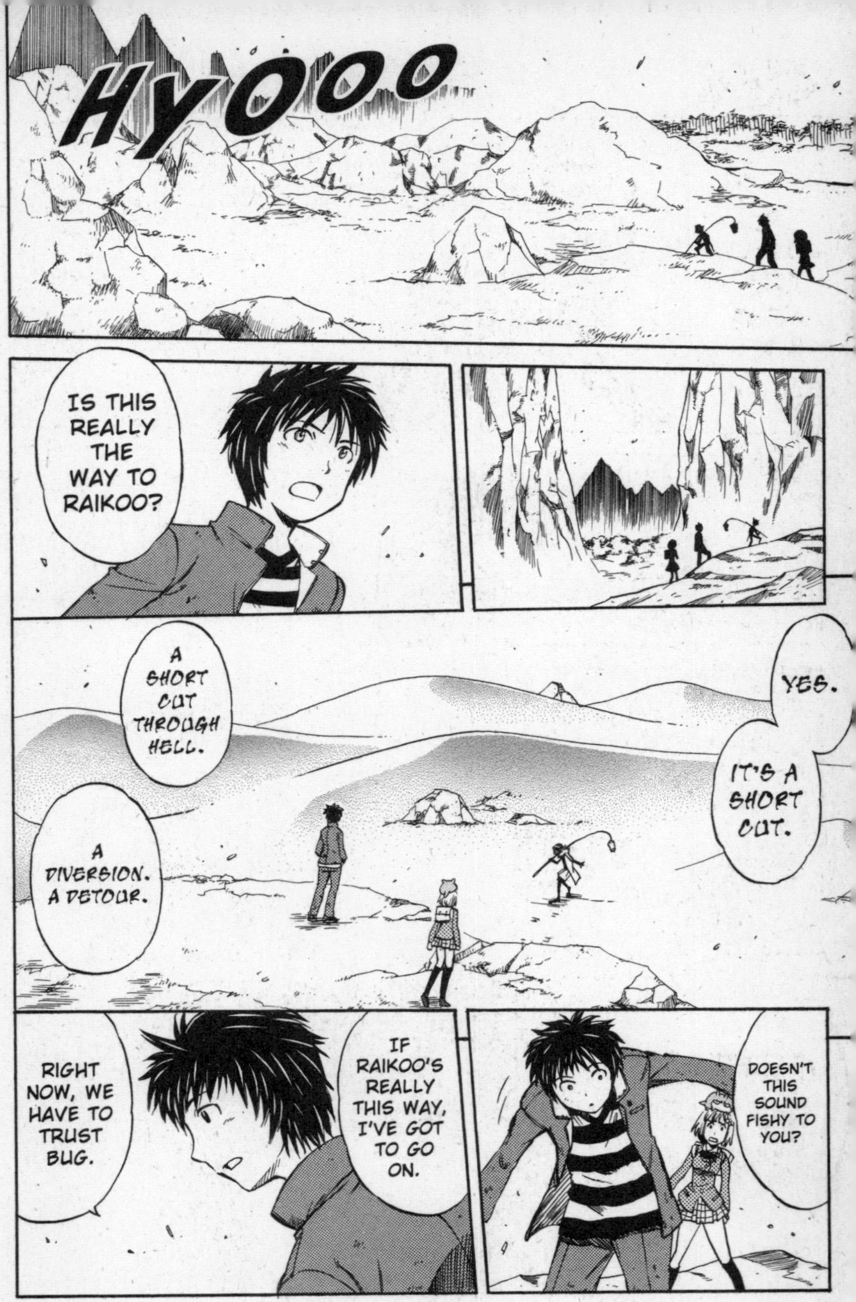
HYOOO
IS THIS REALLY THE WAY TO RAIKOO?
YES.
IT'S A SHORT CUT.
A SHORT CUT THROUGH HELL.
A DIVERSION. A DETOUR.
DOESN'T THIS SOUND FISHY TO YOU?
IF RAIKOO'S REALLY THIS WAY, I'VE GOT TO GO ON.
RIGHT NOW, WE HAVE TO TRUST BUG.

READ THIS WAY

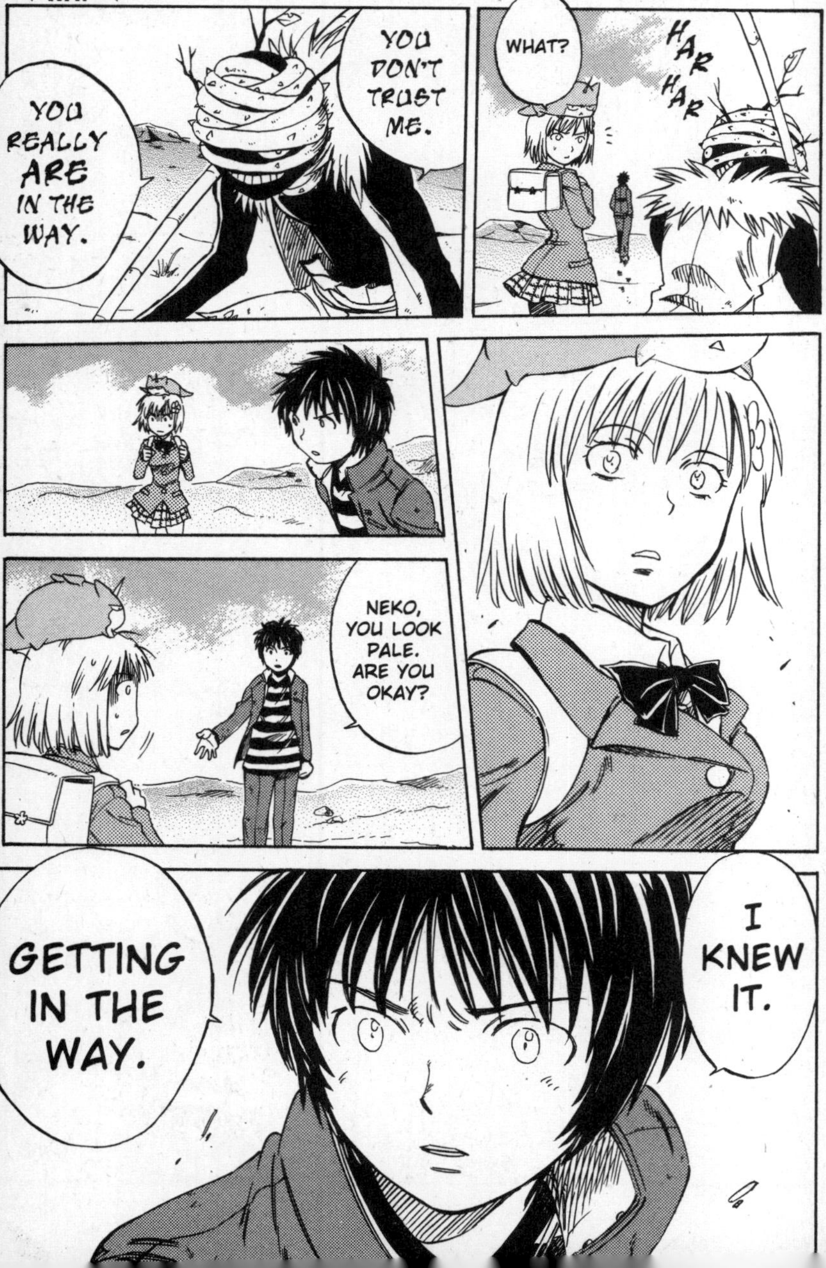
WHAT?
HAR HAR
YOU DON'T TRUST ME.
YOU REALLY ARE IN THE WAY.
NEKO, YOU LOOK PALE. ARE YOU OKAY?
I KNEW IT.
GETTING IN THE WAY.

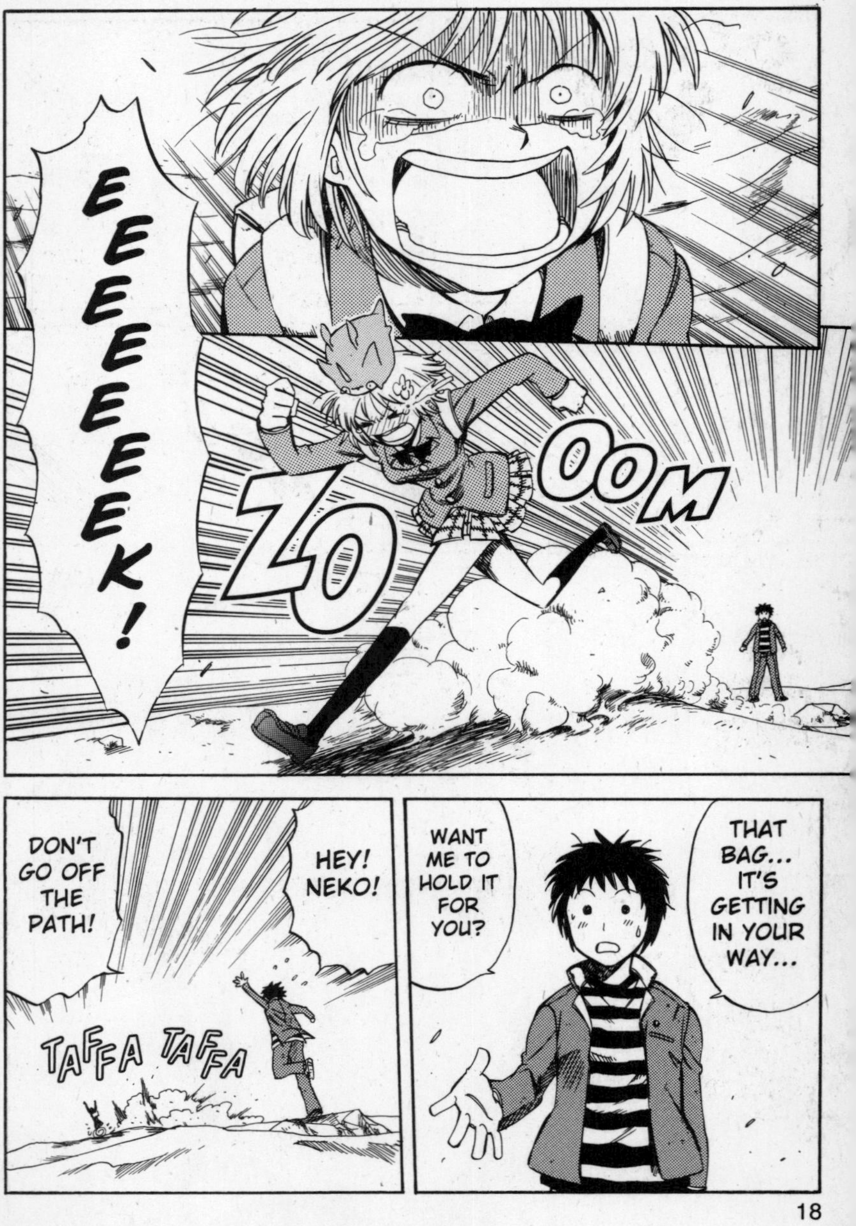
EEEEEEEK!
ZOOOOM
THAT BAG... IT'S GETTING IN YOUR WAY...
WANT ME TO HOLD IT FOR YOU?
HEY! NEKO!
DON'T GO OFF THE PATH!
TAFFA TAFFA

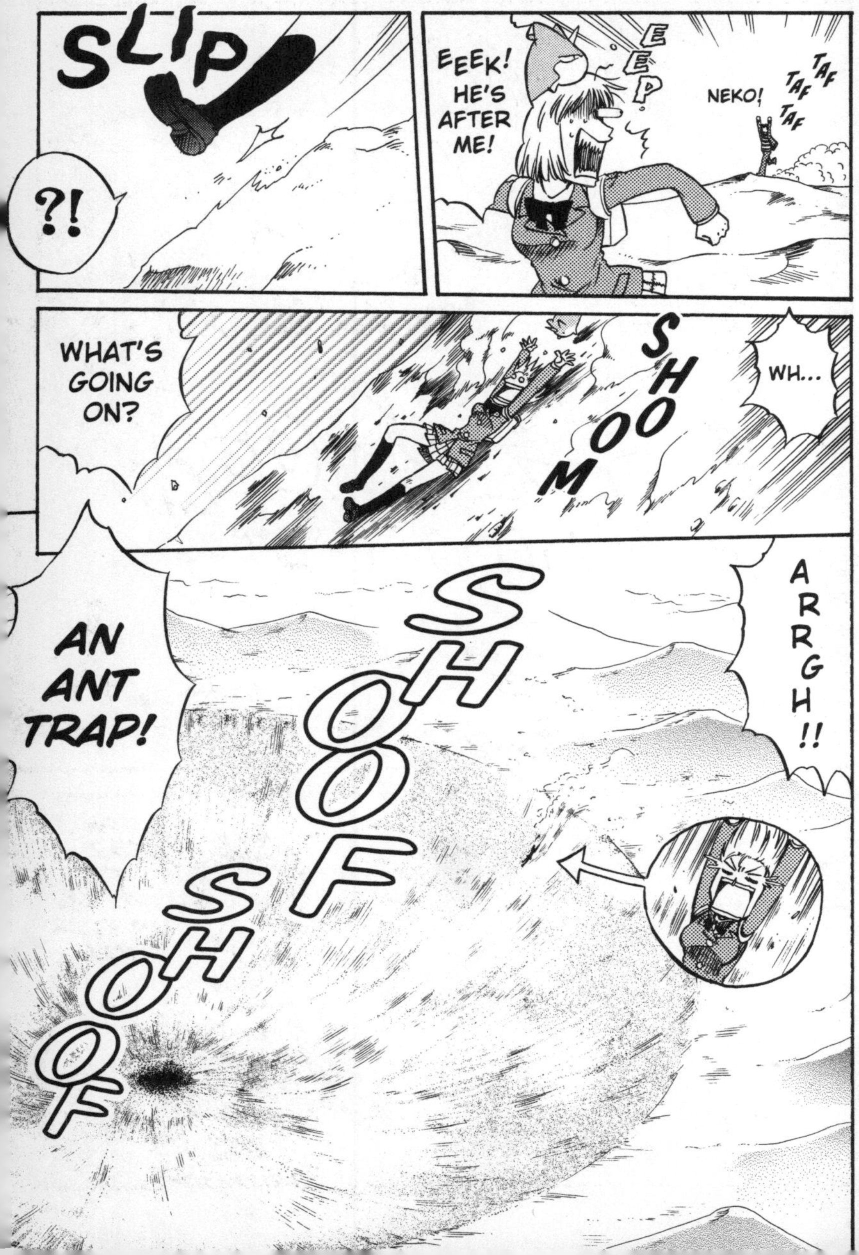
TAF TAF TAF TAF
NEKO!
EEP
EEEK! HE'S AFTER ME!
SLIP
?!
WH...
SHOOOM
WHAT'S GOING ON?
ARRGH!!
SHOOF
AN ANT TRAP!
SHOOF

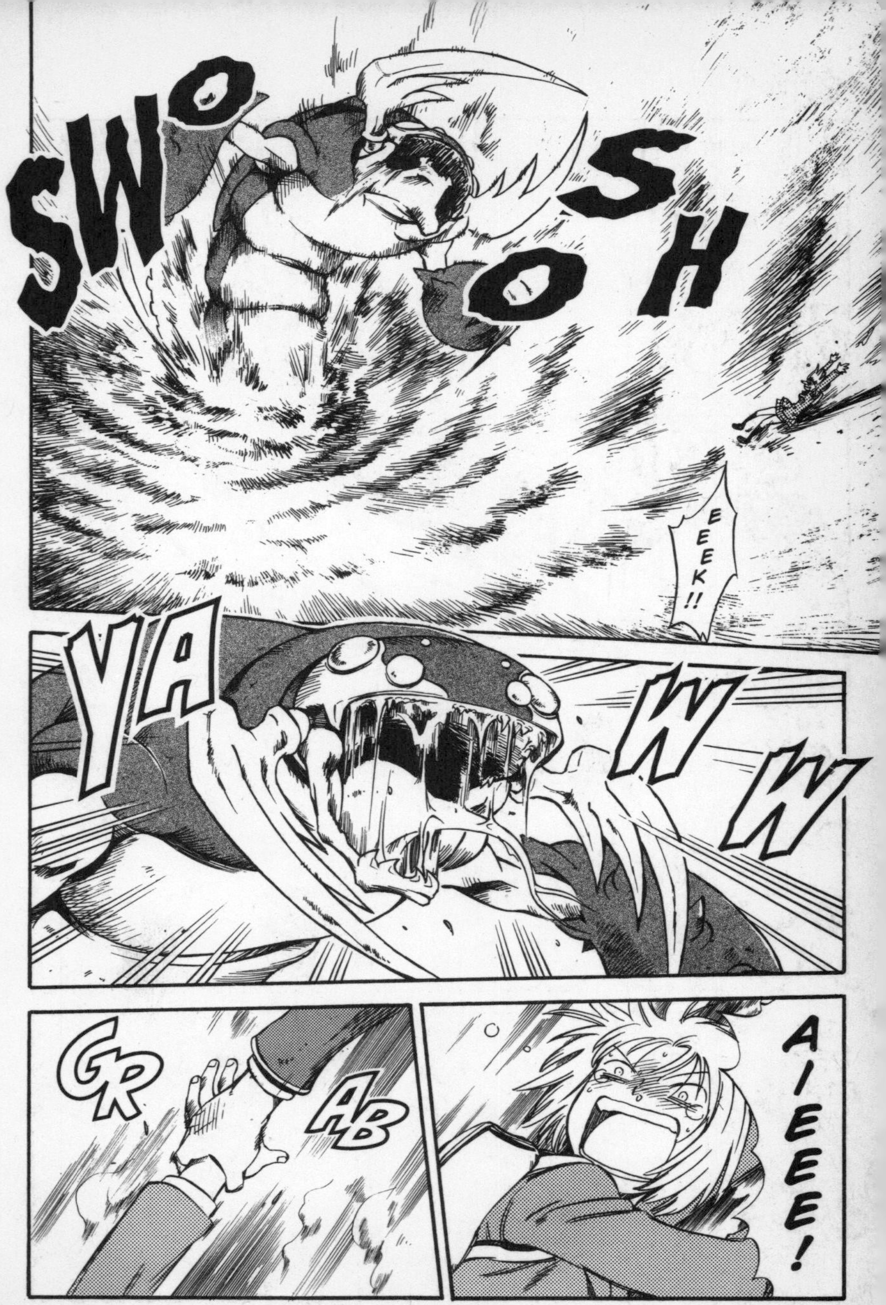
SWOOSH
EEEK!!
YAWWN
AIEEEE!
GRAB

READ THIS WAY

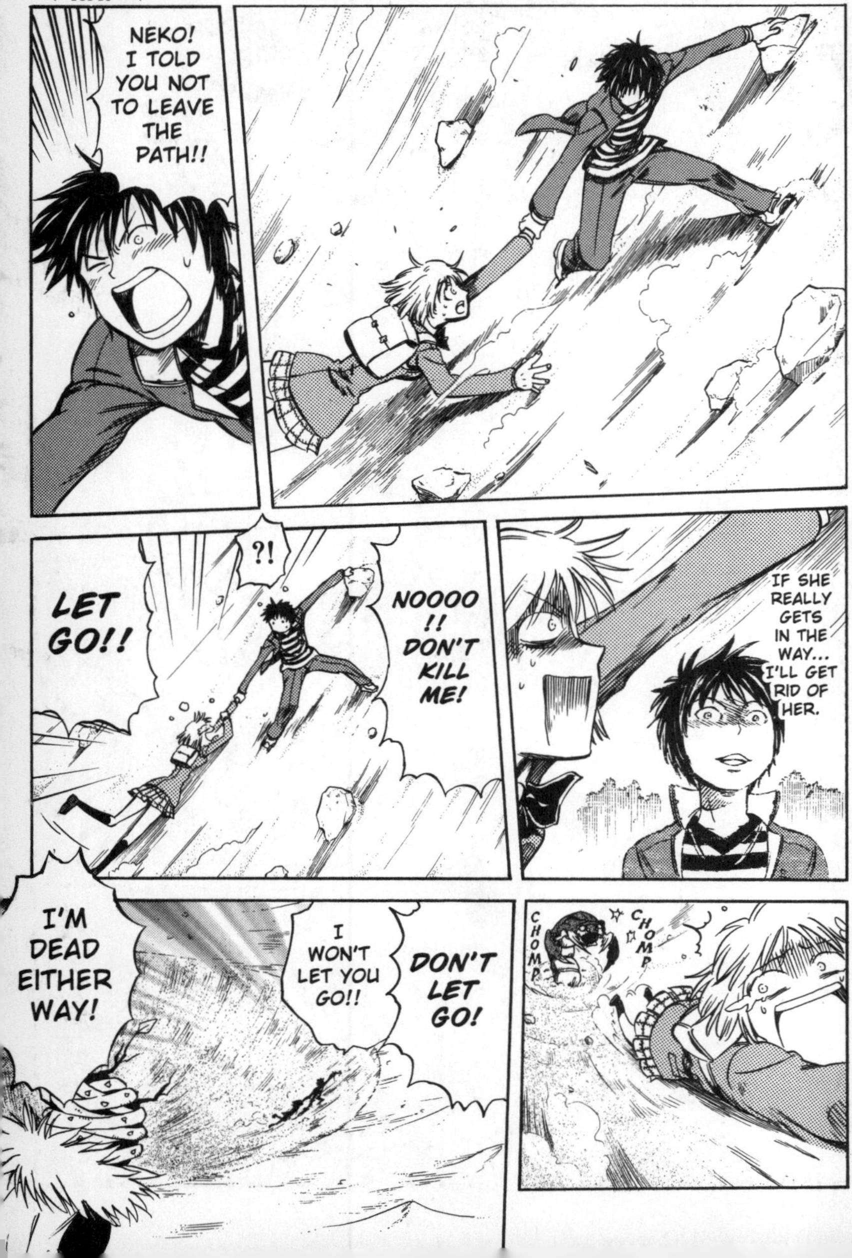
NEKO! I TOLD YOU NOT TO LEAVE THE PATH!!
IF SHE REALLY GETS IN THE WAY... I'LL GET RID OF HER.
NOOOO!! DON'T KILL ME!
?!
LET GO!!
CHOMP
CHOMP
DON'T LET GO!
I WON'T LET YOU GO!!
I'M DEAD EITHER WAY!

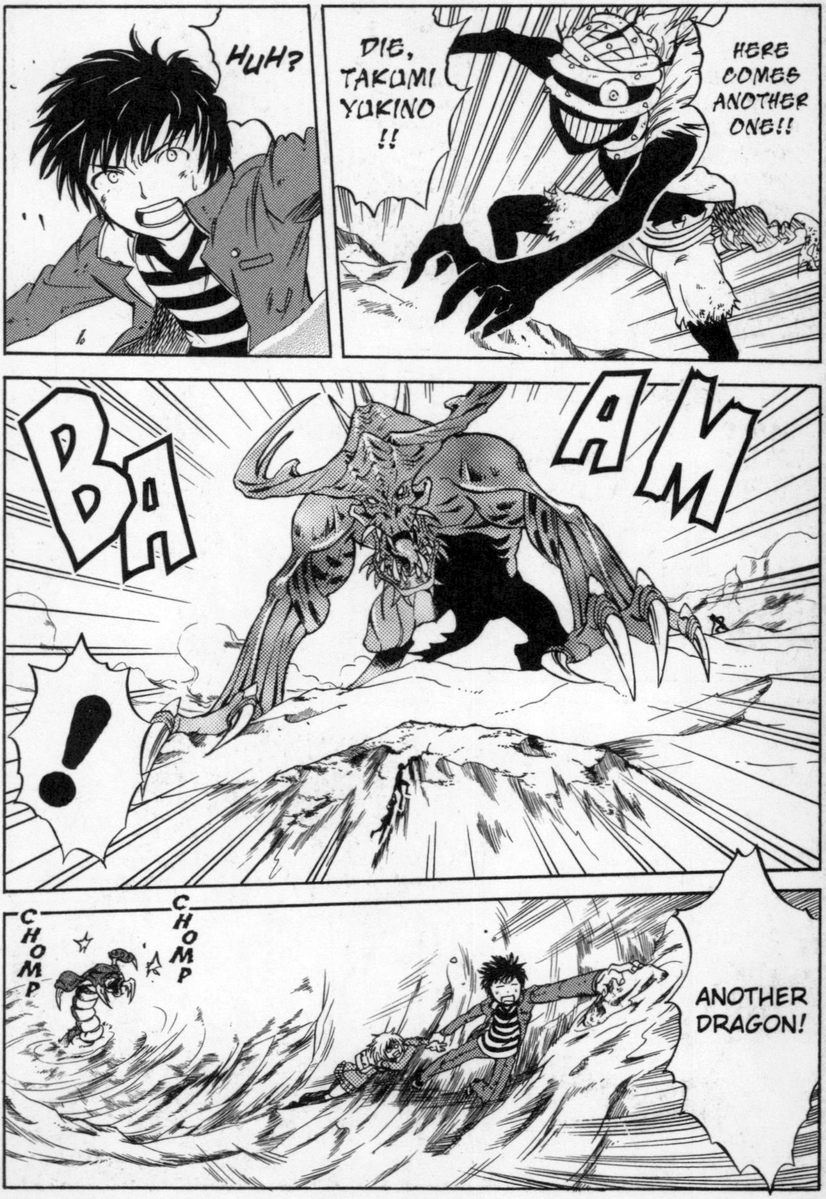
HERE COMES ANOTHER ONE!!
DIE, TAKUMI YUKINO!!
HUH?
BAAM
!
ANOTHER DRAGON!
CHOMP
CHOMP

READ THIS WAY

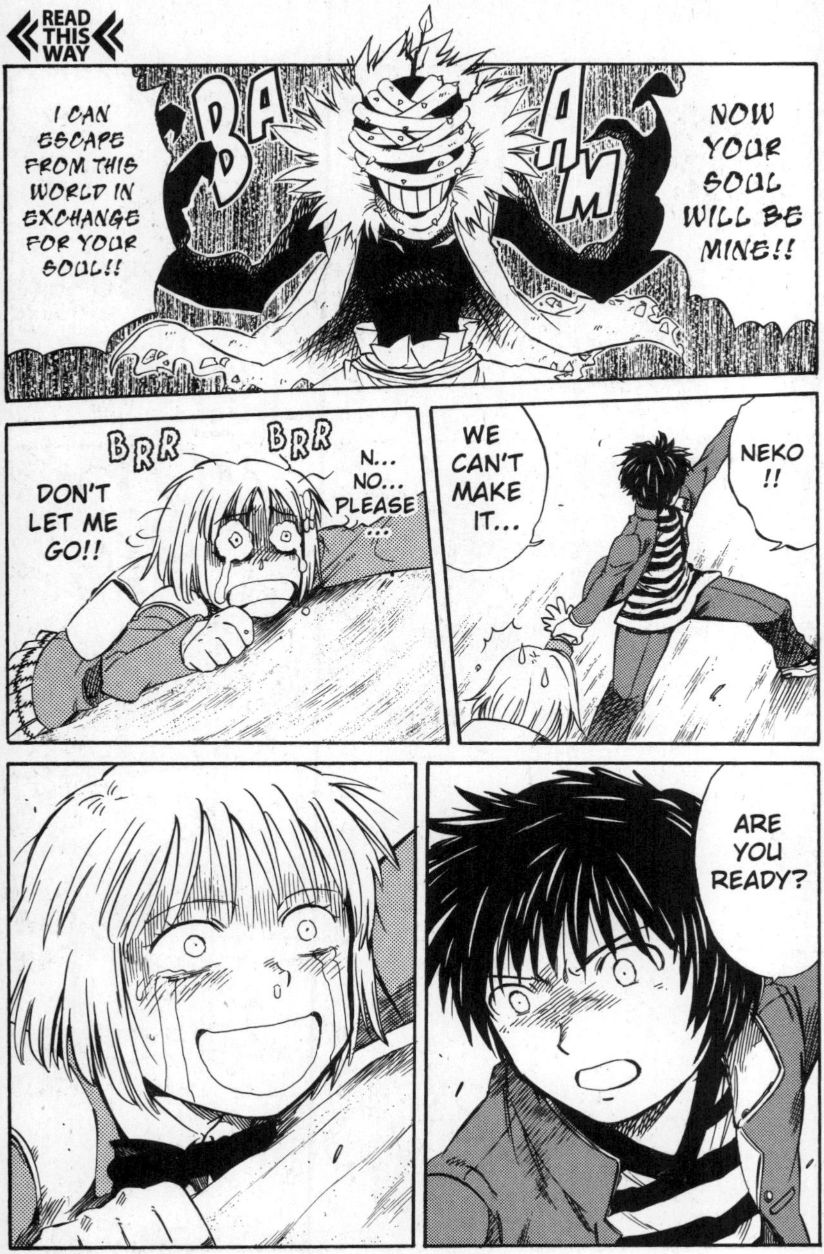
NOW YOUR SOUL WILL BE MINE!!
BAAM
I CAN ESCAPE FROM THIS WORLD IN EXCHANGE FOR YOUR SOUL!!
NEKO !!
WE CAN'T MAKE IT...
N... NO... PLEASE ...
BRR
BRR
DON'T LET ME GO!!
ARE YOU READY?

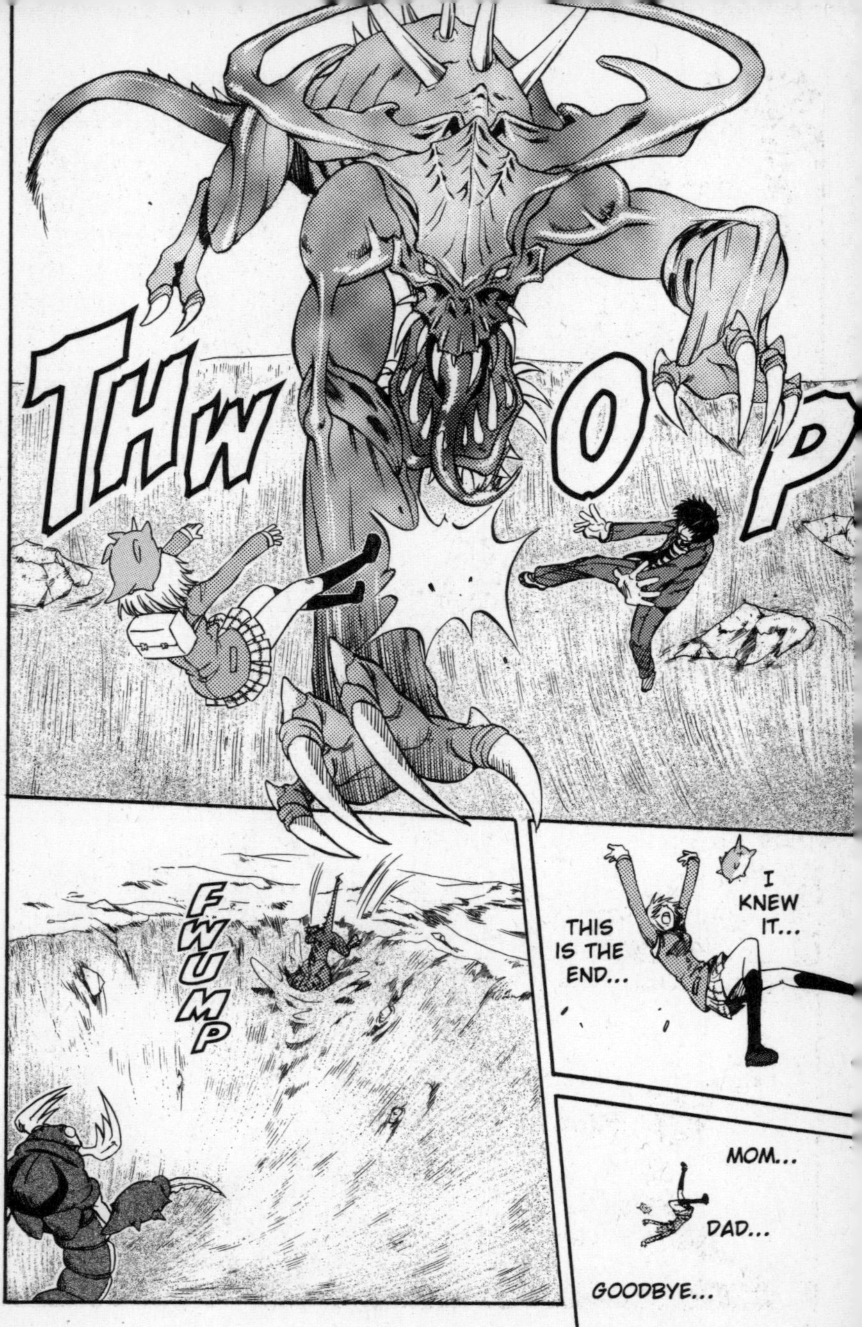
THWOOP
I KNEW IT...
THIS IS THE END...
MOM...
DAD...
GOODBYE...
FWUMP

READ THIS WAY

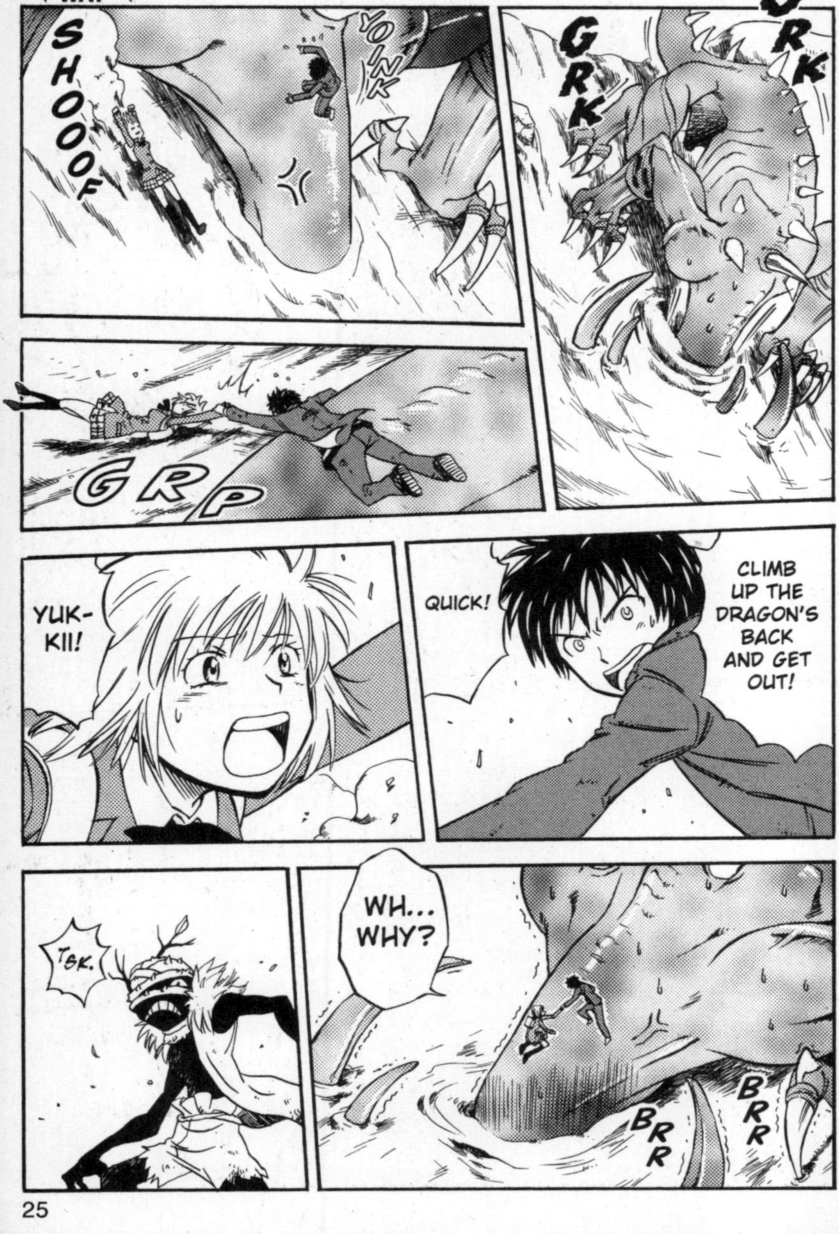
GRK
GRK
YOINK
SHOOOOF
GRP
CLIMB UP THE DRAGON'S BACK AND GET OUT!
QUICK!
YUK-KII!
WH... WHY?
BRR
BRR
TSK.

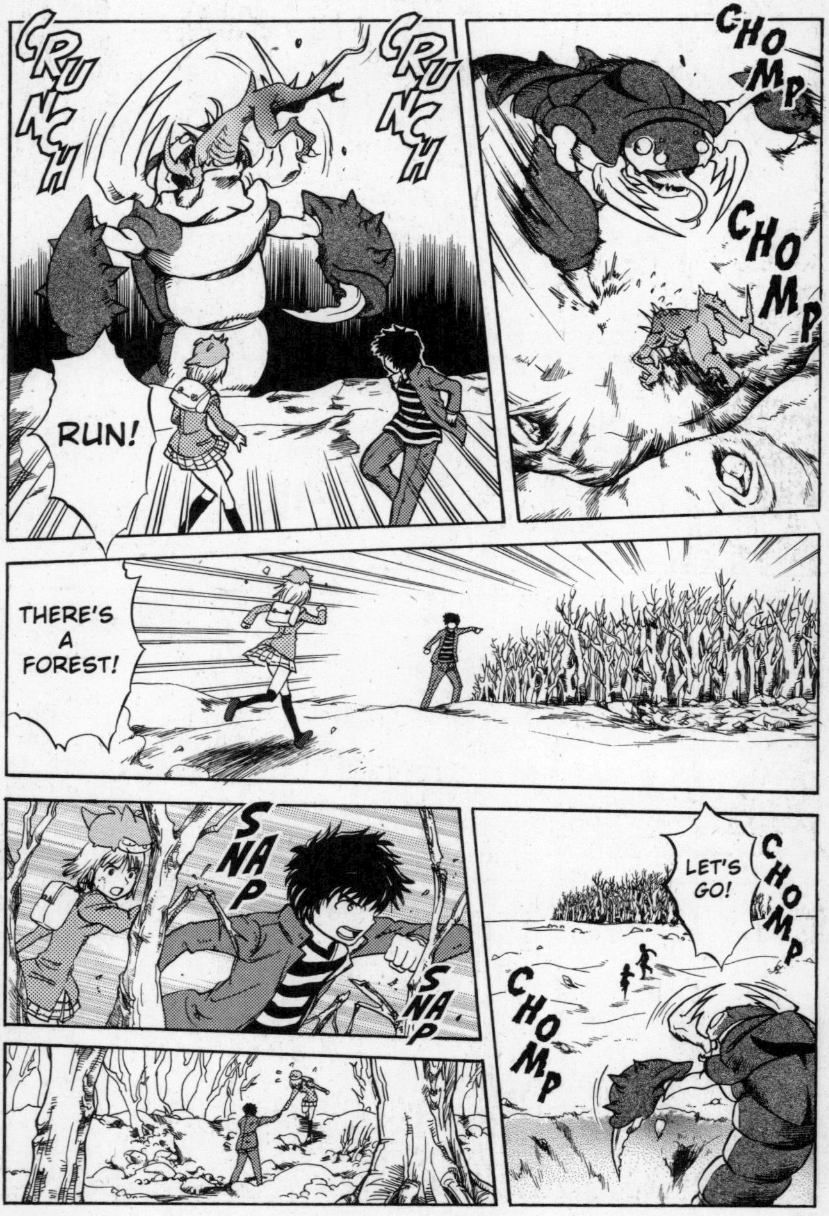
CHOMP
CHOMP
CRUNCH
CRUNCH
RUN!
THERE'S A FOREST!
CHOMP
LET'S GO!
CHOMP
SNAP
SNAP

READ THIS WAY

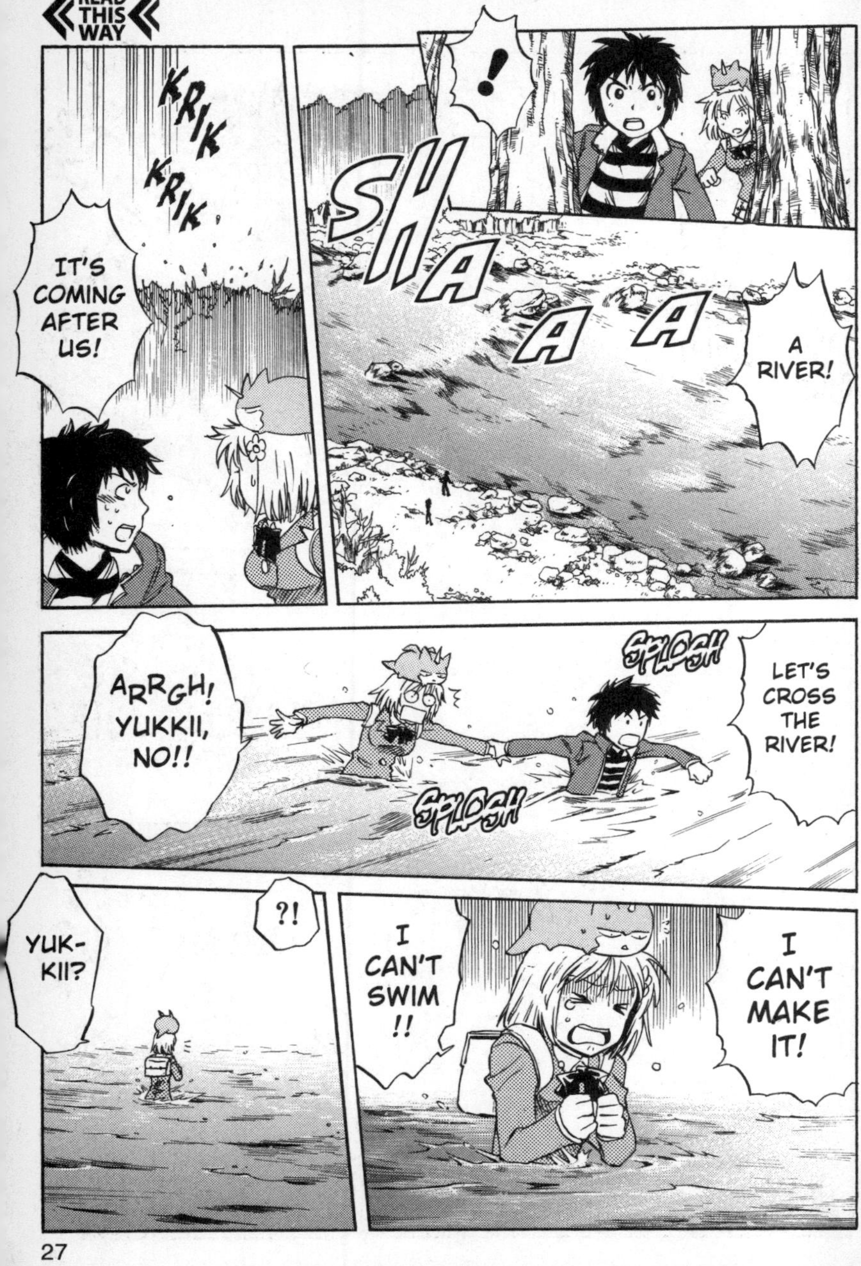

!
SHAAA
A RIVER!
KRIK KRIK
IT'S COMING AFTER US!
SPLOSH
LET'S CROSS THE RIVER!
SPLOSH
ARRGH! YUKKII, NO!!
I CAN'T MAKE IT!
I CAN'T SWIM!!
?!
YUK-KII?

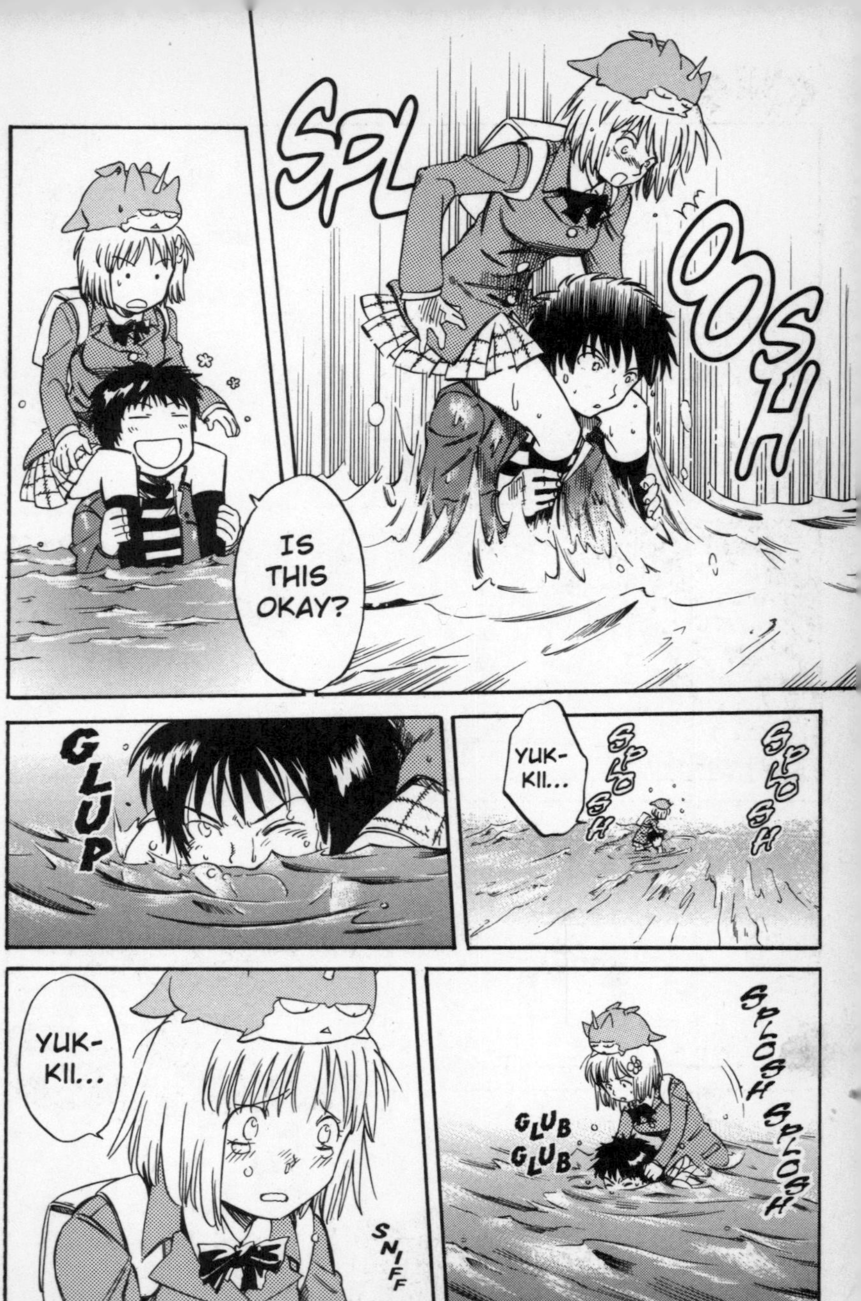
SPLOOSH
IS THIS OKAY?
YUK-KII...
SPLOSH
SPLOSH
GLUP
SPLOSH SPLOSH
GLUB GLUB
YUK-KII...
SNIFF

READ THIS WAY

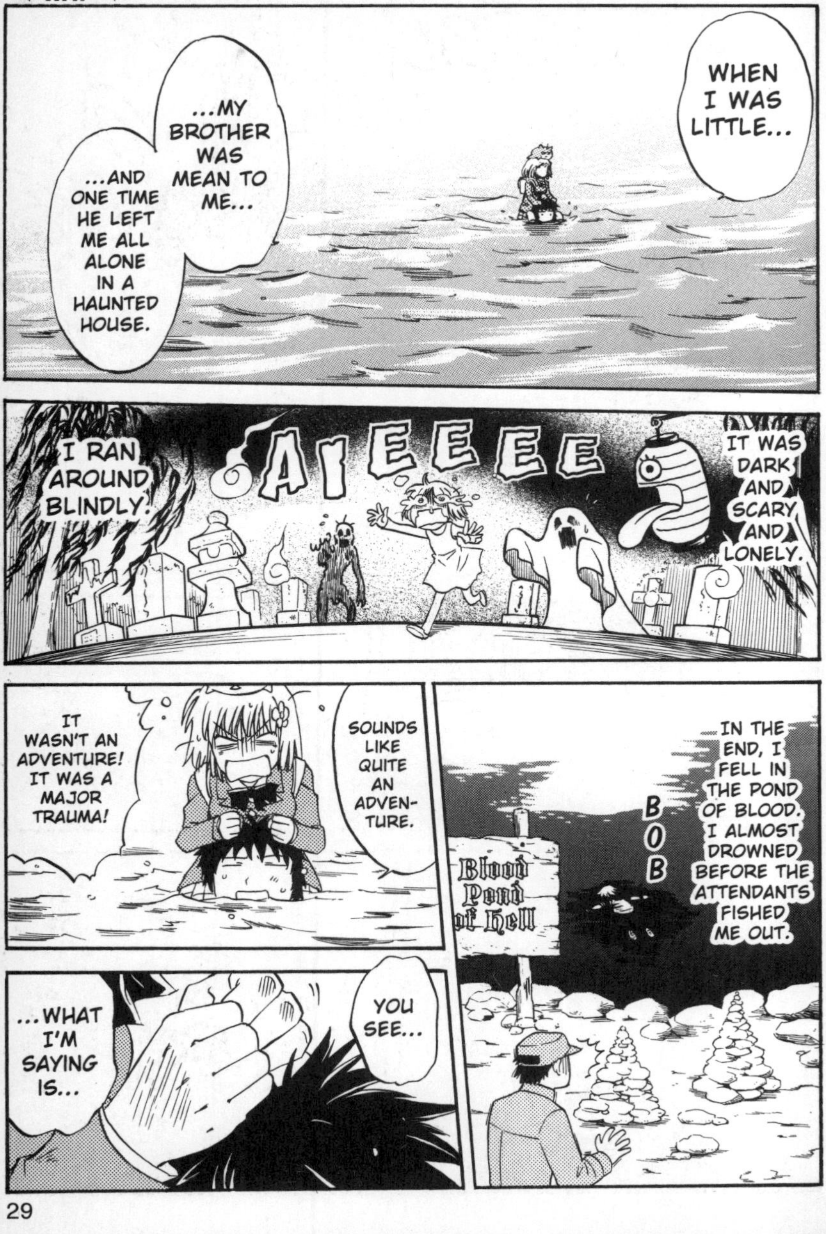
WHEN I WAS LITTLE...
...MY BROTHER WAS MEAN TO ME...
...AND ONE TIME HE LEFT ME ALL ALONE IN A HAUNTED HOUSE.
IT WAS DARK AND SCARY AND LONELY.
AIEEEE
I RAN AROUND BLINDLY.
IN THE END, I FELL IN THE POND OF BLOOD. I ALMOST DROWNED BEFORE THE ATTENDANTS FISHED ME OUT.
BOB
Blood Pond of Hell
SOUNDS LIKE QUITE AN ADVEN-TURE.
IT WASN'T AN ADVENTURE! IT WAS A MAJOR TRAUMA!
YOU SEE...
...WHAT I'M SAYING IS...

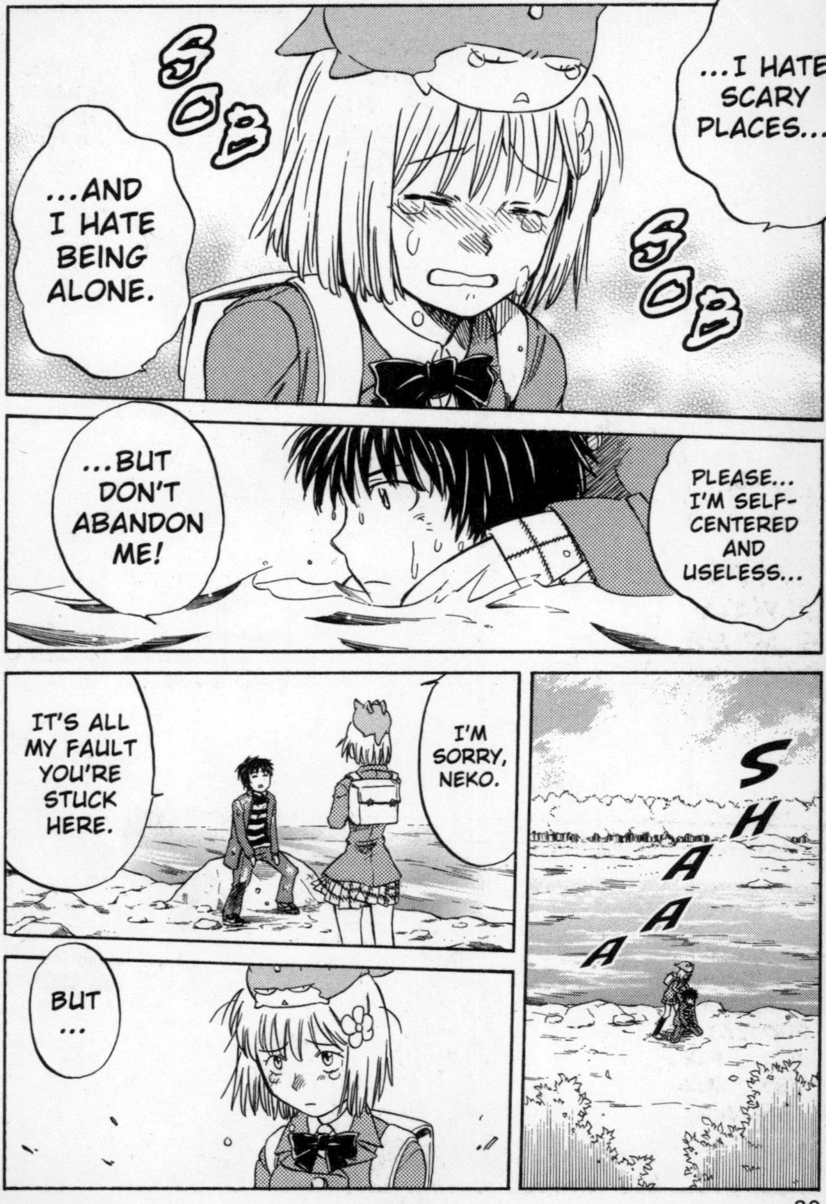
...I HATE SCARY PLACES...
SOB
SOB
...AND I HATE BEING ALONE.
PLEASE... I'M SELF-CENTERED AND USELESS...
...BUT DON'T ABANDON ME!
SHAAAA
I'M SORRY, NEKO.
IT'S ALL MY FAULT YOU'RE STUCK HERE.
BUT...

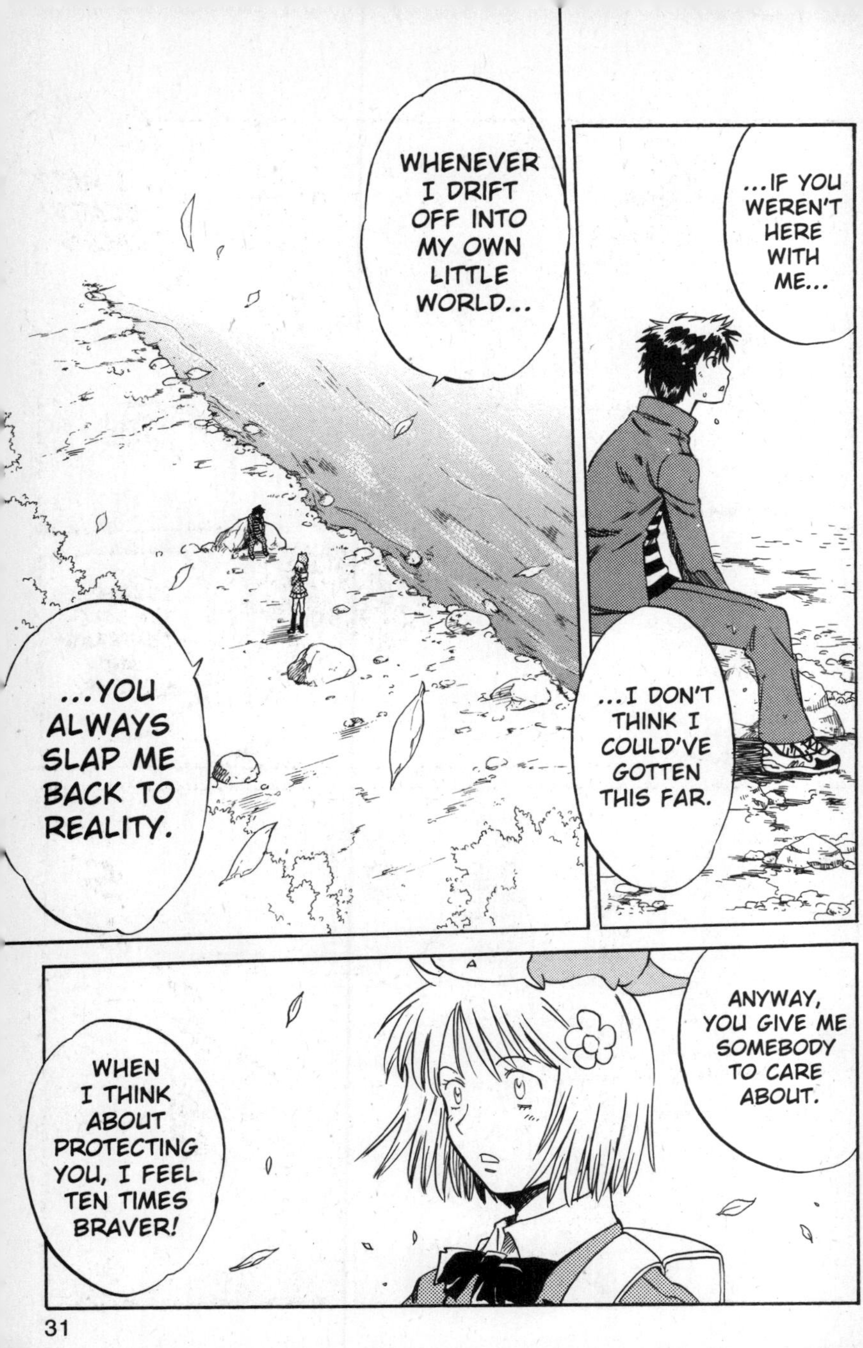
...IF YOU WEREN'T HERE WITH ME...
...I DON'T THINK I COULD'VE GOTTEN THIS FAR.
WHENEVER I DRIFT OFF INTO MY OWN LITTLE WORLD...
...YOU ALWAYS SLAP ME BACK TO REALITY.
ANYWAY, YOU GIVE ME SOMEBODY TO CARE ABOUT.
WHEN I THINK ABOUT PROTECTING YOU, I FEEL TEN TIMES BRAVER!

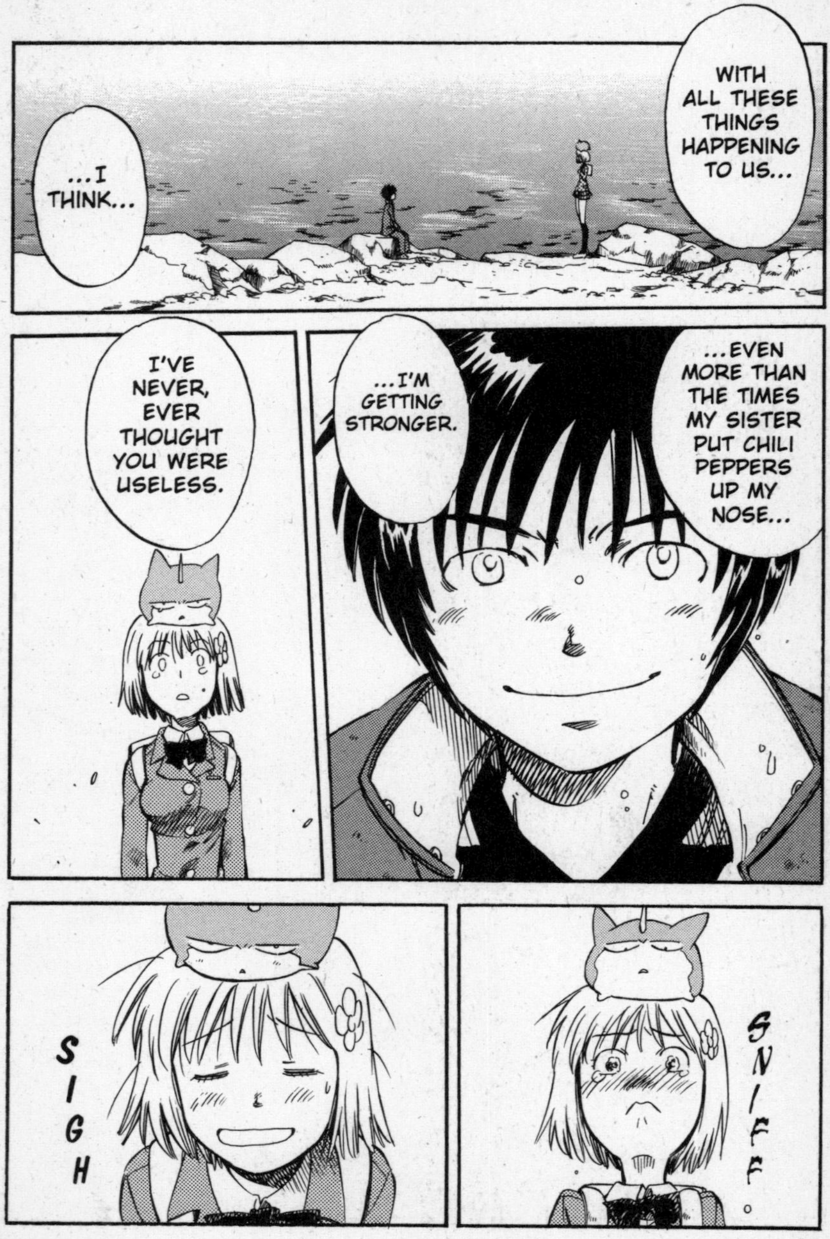
WITH ALL THESE THINGS HAPPENING TO US...
...I THINK...
...EVEN MORE THAN THE TIMES MY SISTER PUT CHILI PEPPERS UP MY NOSE...
...I'M GETTING STRONGER.
I'VE NEVER, EVER THOUGHT YOU WERE USELESS.
SNIFF
SIGH

READ THIS WAY

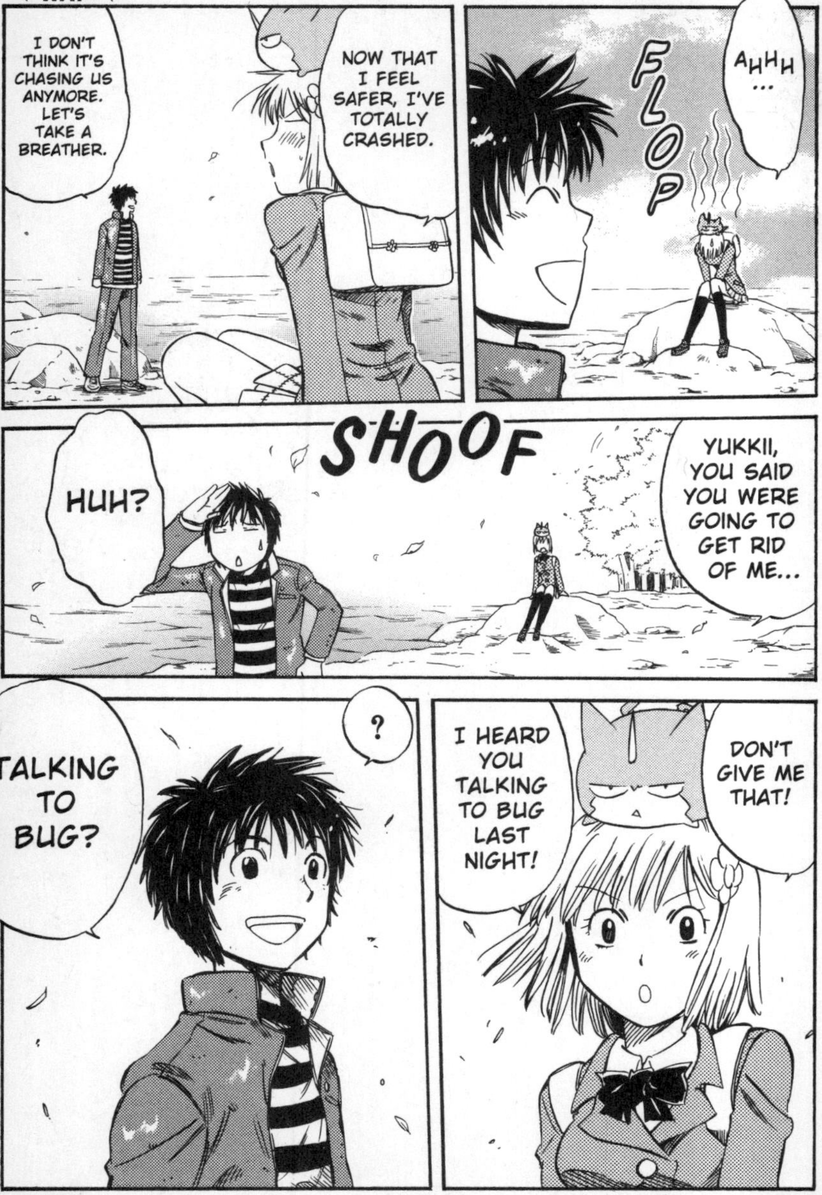
AHHH...
FLOP
NOW THAT I FEEL SAFER, I'VE TOTALLY CRASHED.
I DON'T THINK IT'S CHASING US ANYMORE. LET'S TAKE A BREATHER.
YUKKII, YOU SAID YOU WERE GOING TO GET RID OF ME...
SHOOF
HUH?
DON'T GIVE ME THAT!
I HEARD YOU TALKING TO BUG LAST NIGHT!
?
TALKING TO BUG?

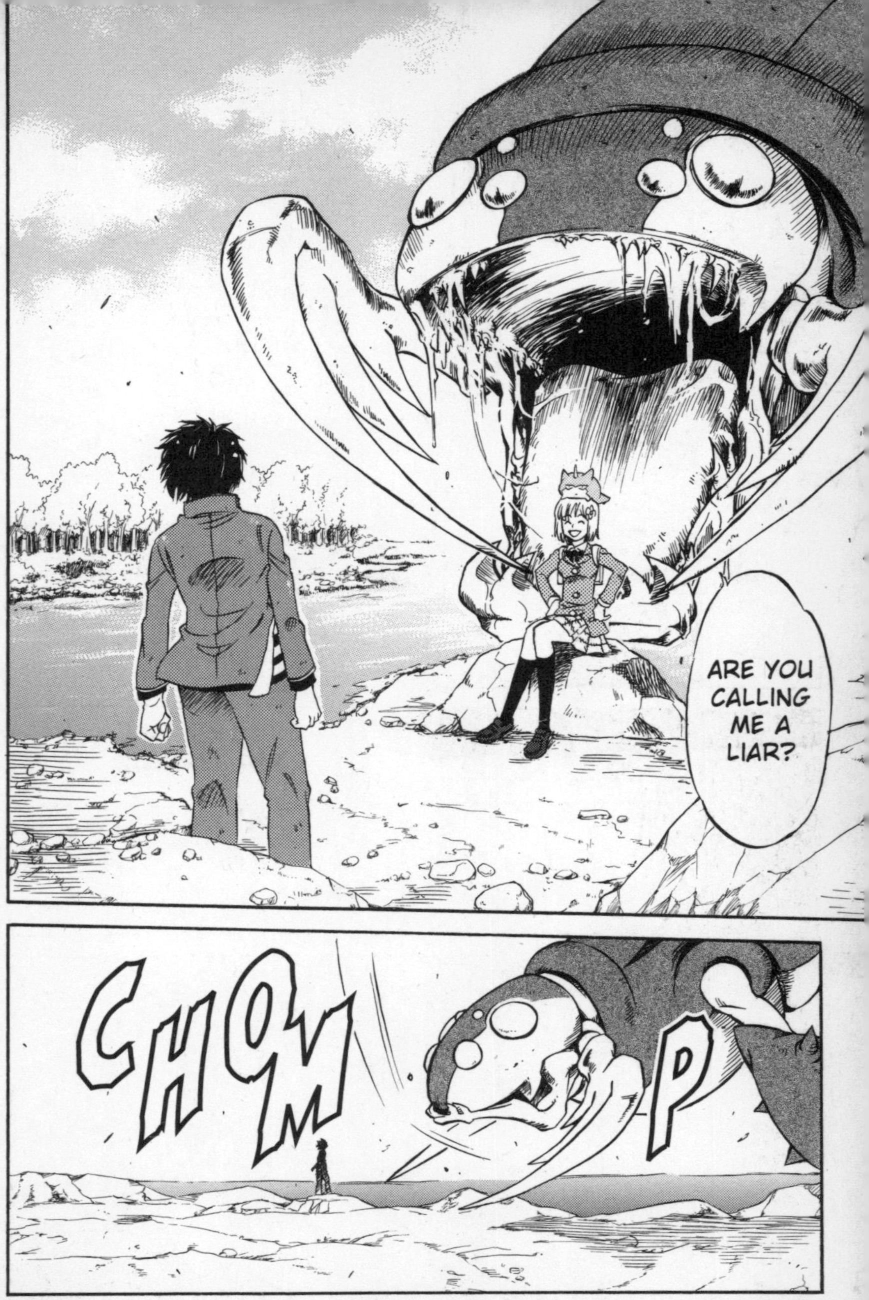
ARE YOU CALLING ME A LIAR?
CHOMP

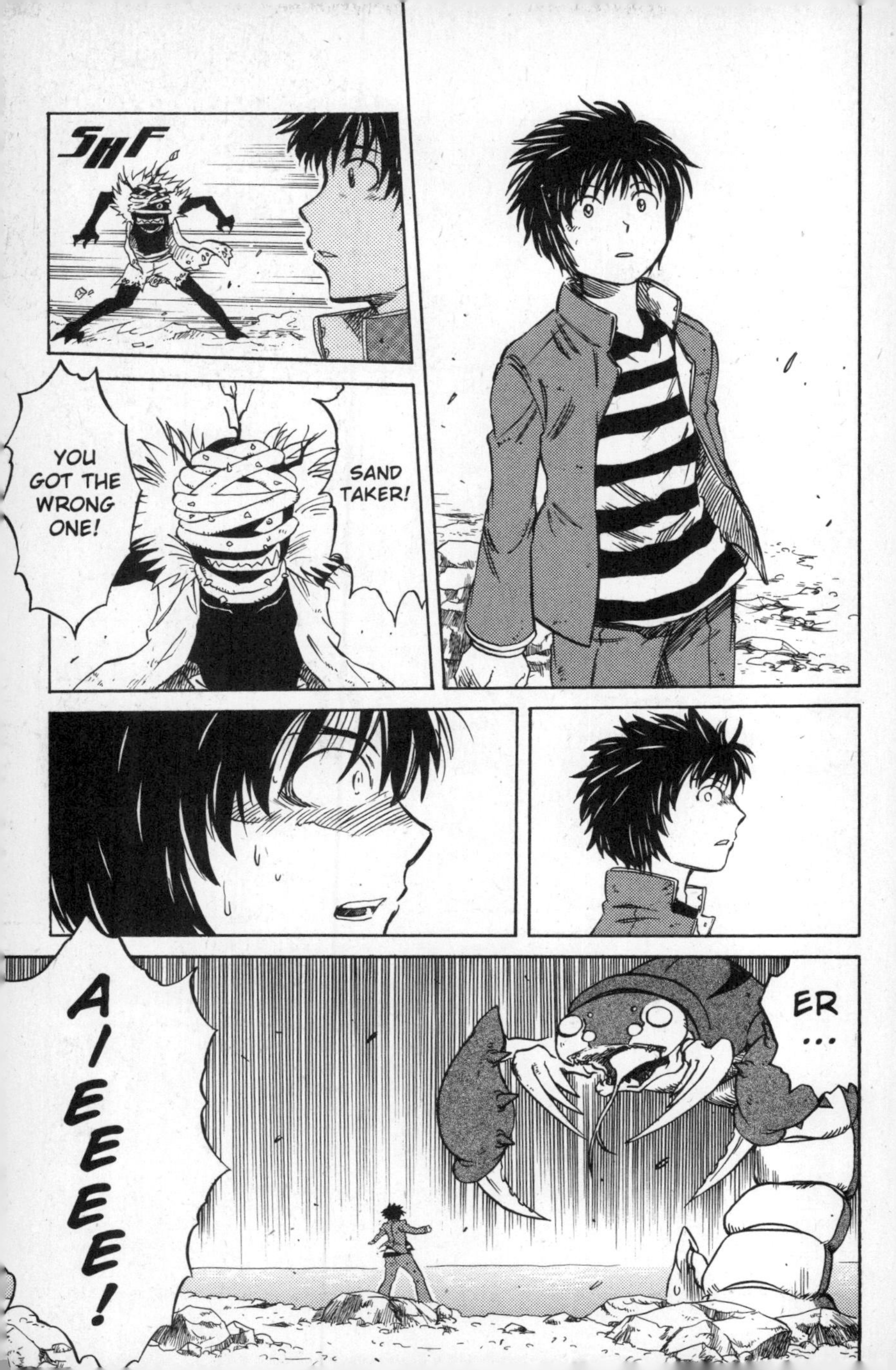
SHF
SAND TAKER!
YOU GOT THE WRONG ONE!
ER ...
AIEEEEE!

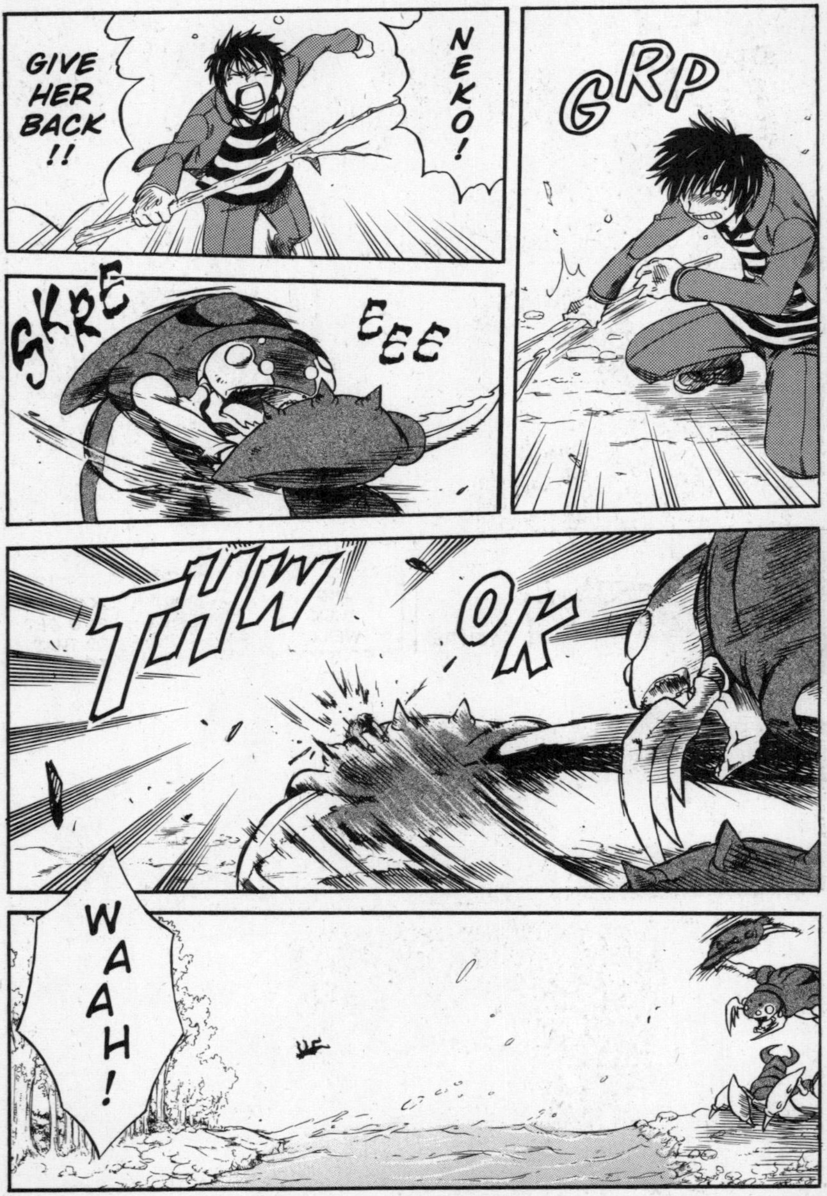
GRP
NEKO!
GIVE HER BACK!!
SKREEEE
THWOK
WAAH!

READ THIS WAY

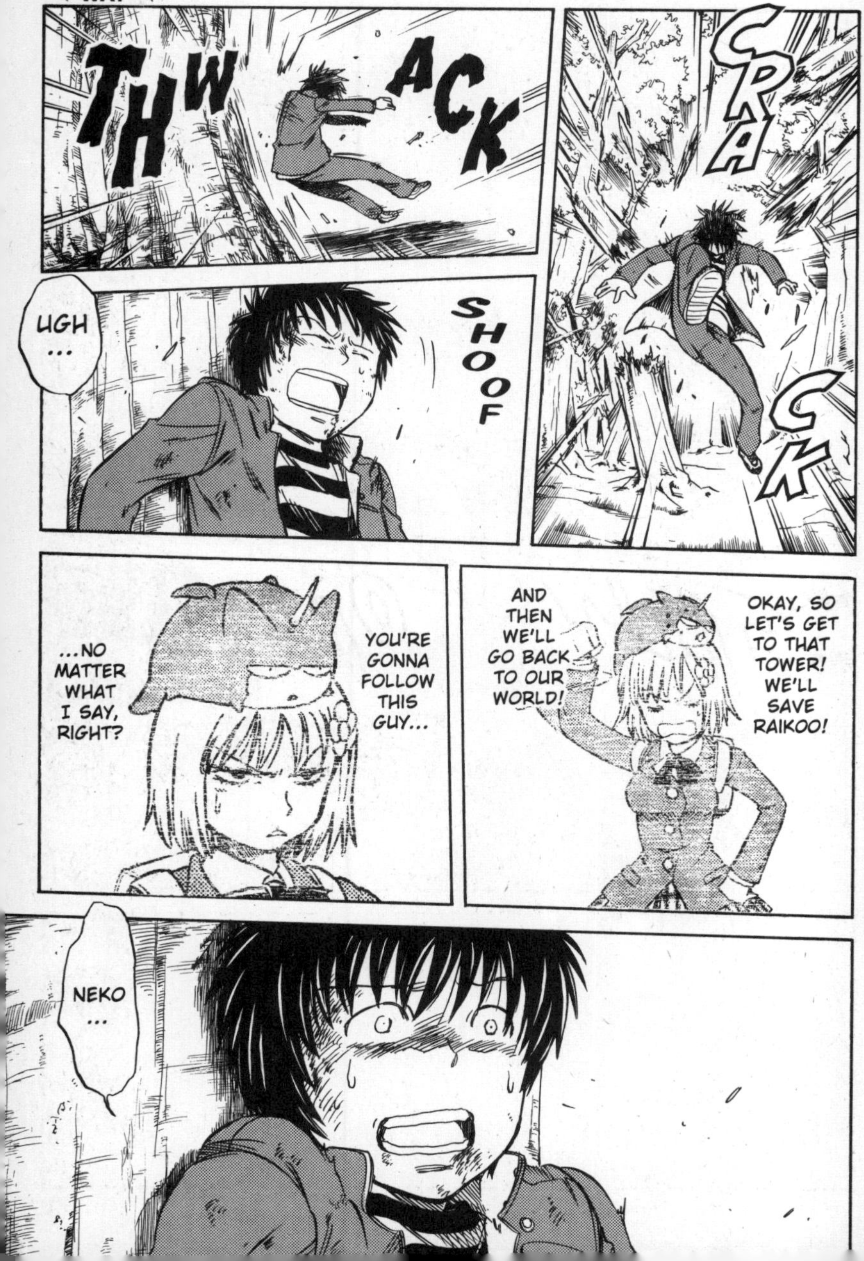
CRACK
THWACK
SHOOF
UGH...
OKAY, SO LET'S GET TO THAT TOWER! WE'LL SAVE RAIKOO!
AND THEN WE'LL GO BACK TO OUR WORLD!
YOU'RE GONNA FOLLOW THIS GUY...
...NO MATTER WHAT I SAY, RIGHT?
NEKO...

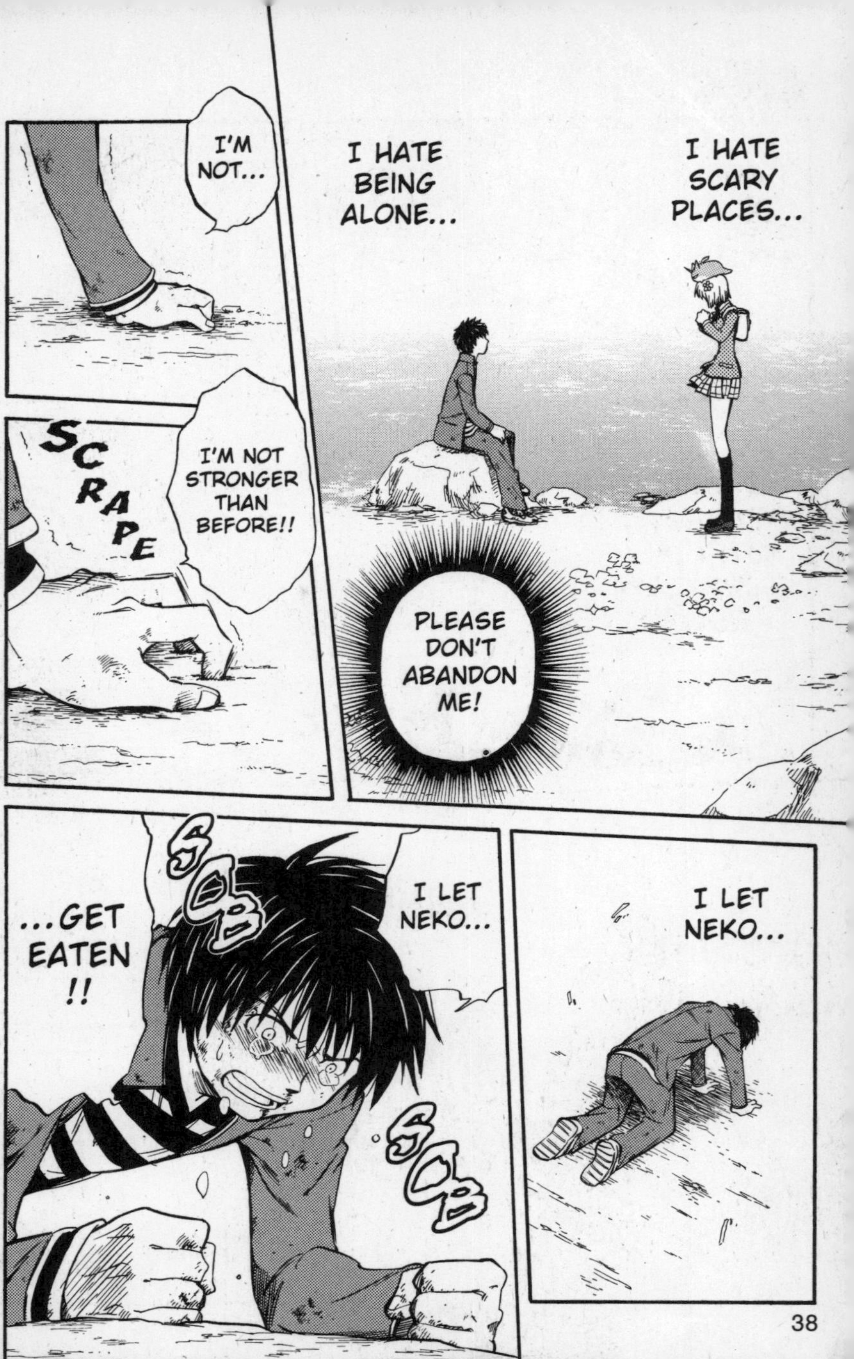
I HATE SCARY PLACES...
I HATE BEING ALONE...
PLEASE DON'T ABANDON ME!
I'M NOT...
SCRAPE
I'M NOT STRONGER THAN BEFORE!!
I LET NEKO...
I LET NEKO...
SOB
...GET EATEN!!
SOB

READ THIS WAY

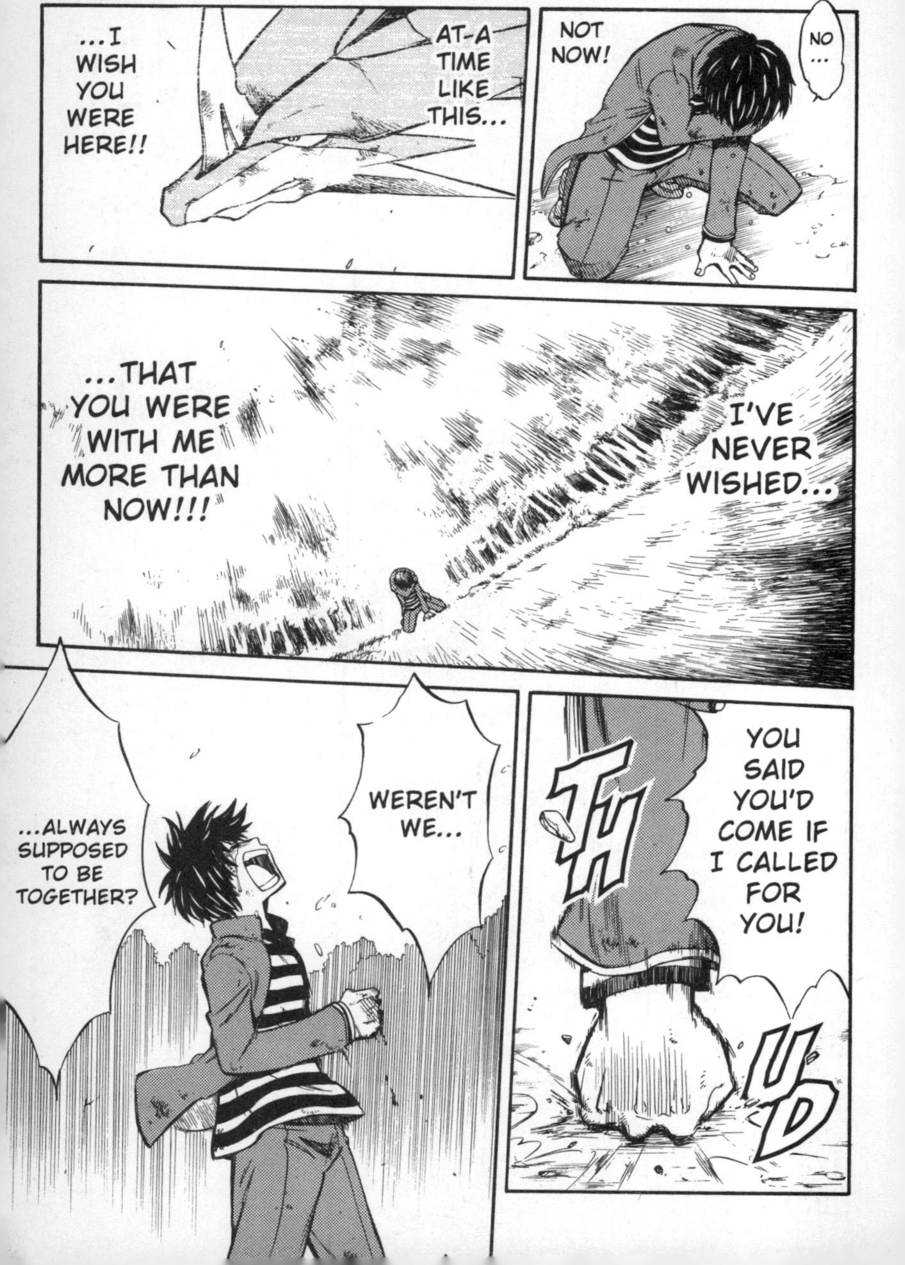
NO ...
NOT NOW!
AT-A TIME LIKE THIS...
...I WISH YOU WERE HERE!!
I'VE NEVER WISHED...
...THAT YOU WERE WITH ME MORE THAN NOW!!!
YOU SAID YOU'D COME IF I CALLED FOR YOU!
THUD
WEREN'T WE...
...ALWAYS SUPPOSED TO BE TOGETHER?

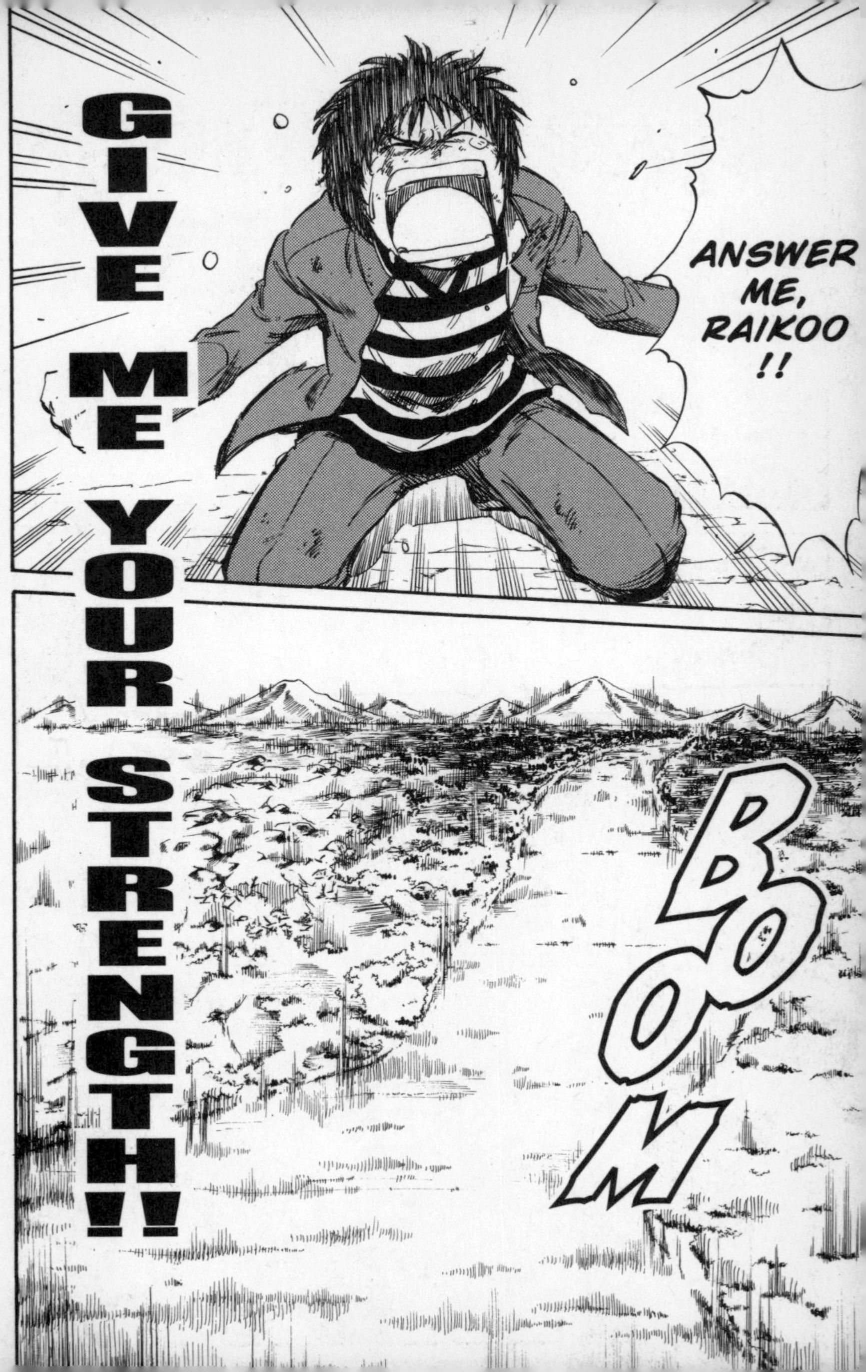
ANSWER ME, RAIKOO !!
GIVE ME YOUR STRENGTH!!
BOOM

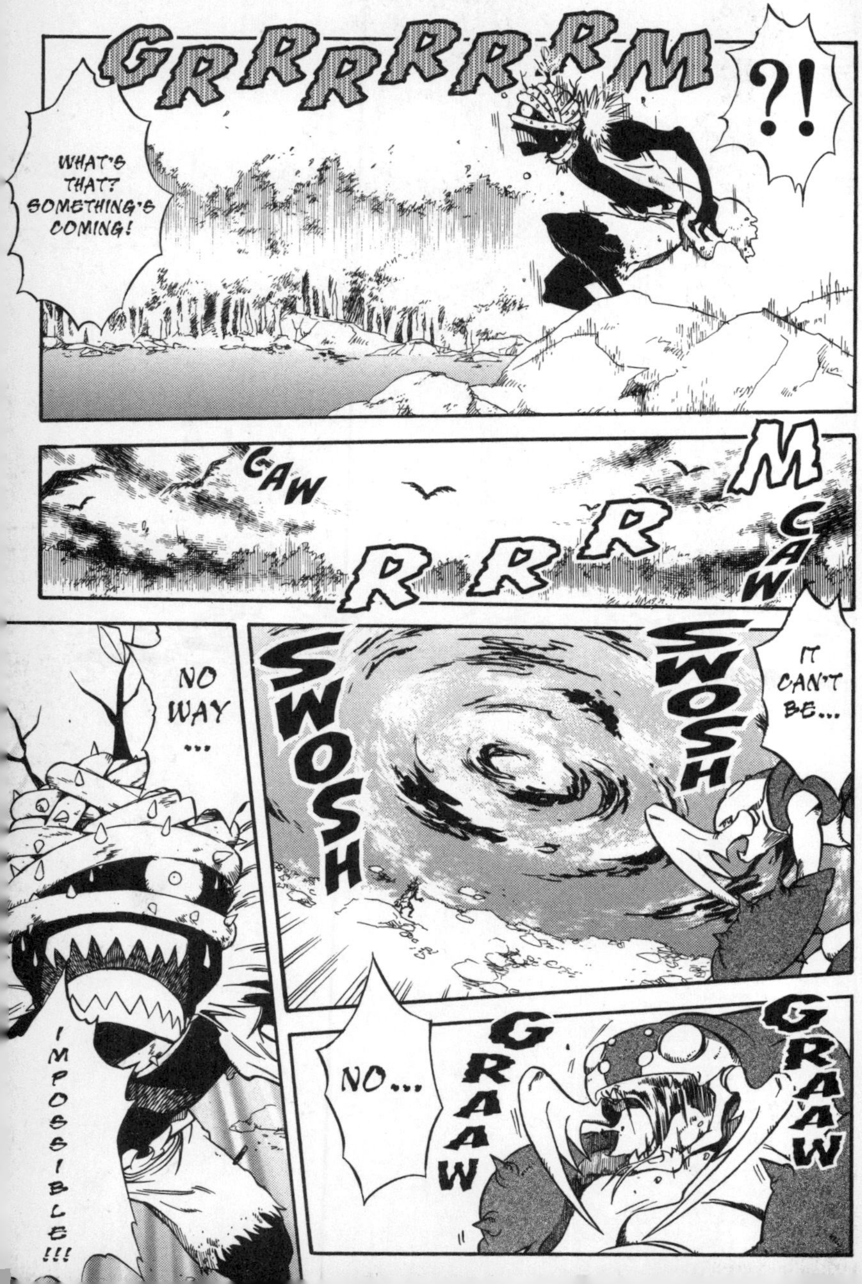
GRRRRRM
?!
WHAT'S THAT? SOMETHING'S COMING!
MRRRR
CAW
CAW
IT CAN'T BE...
SWOSH
SWOSH
GRAAW
GRAAW
NO...
NO WAY...
IMPOSSIBLE!!!

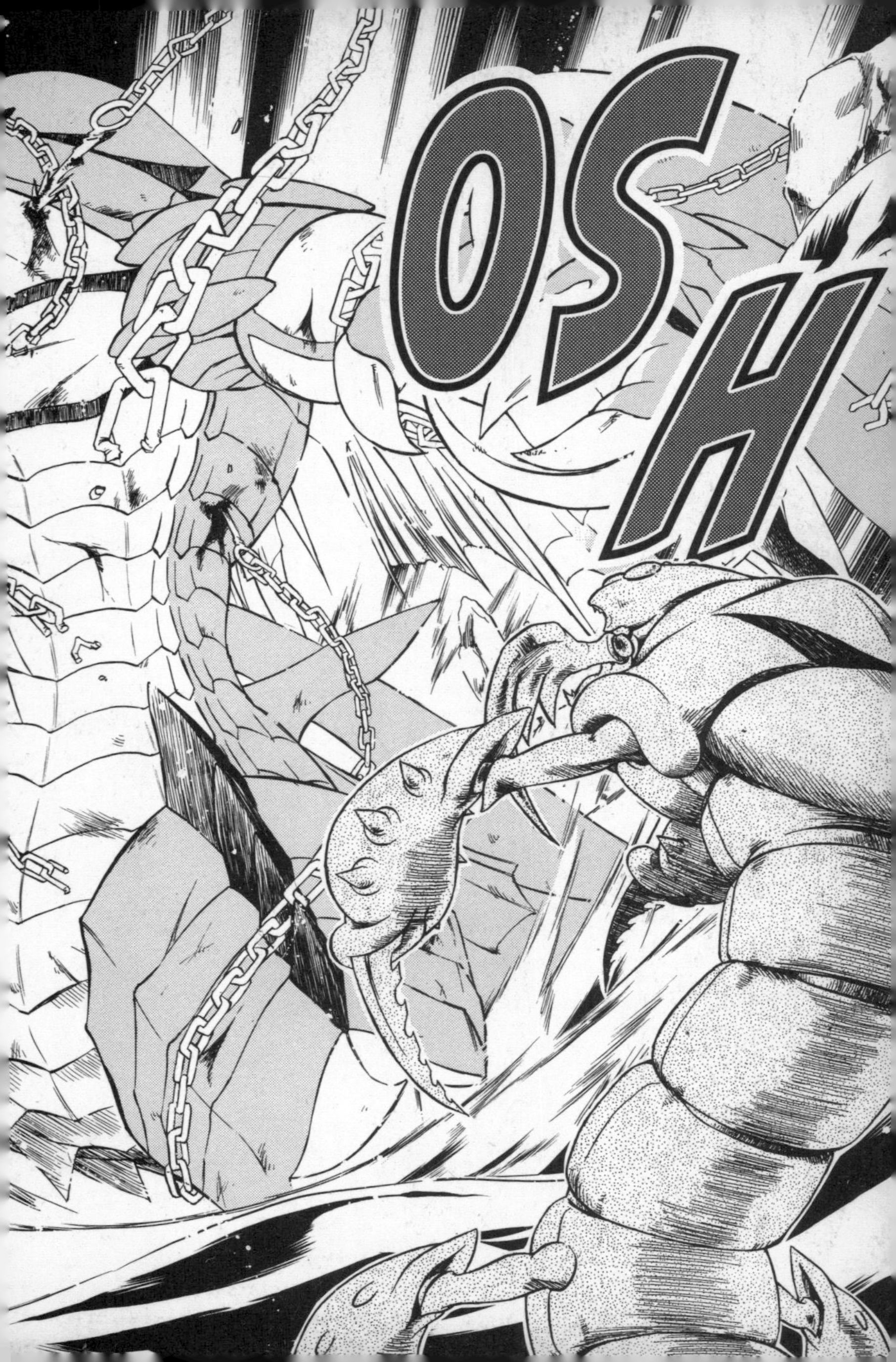
OSH

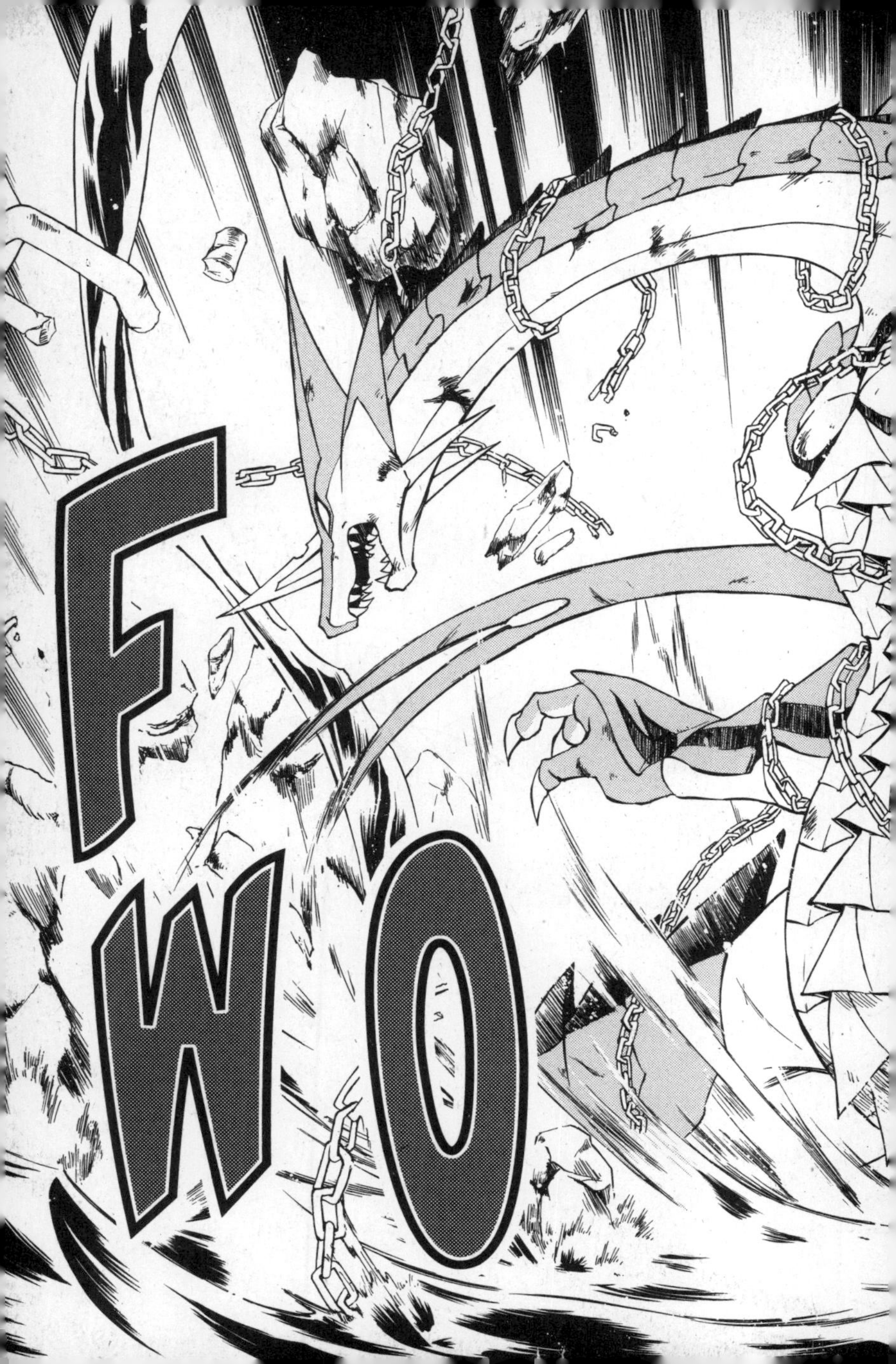
FWO

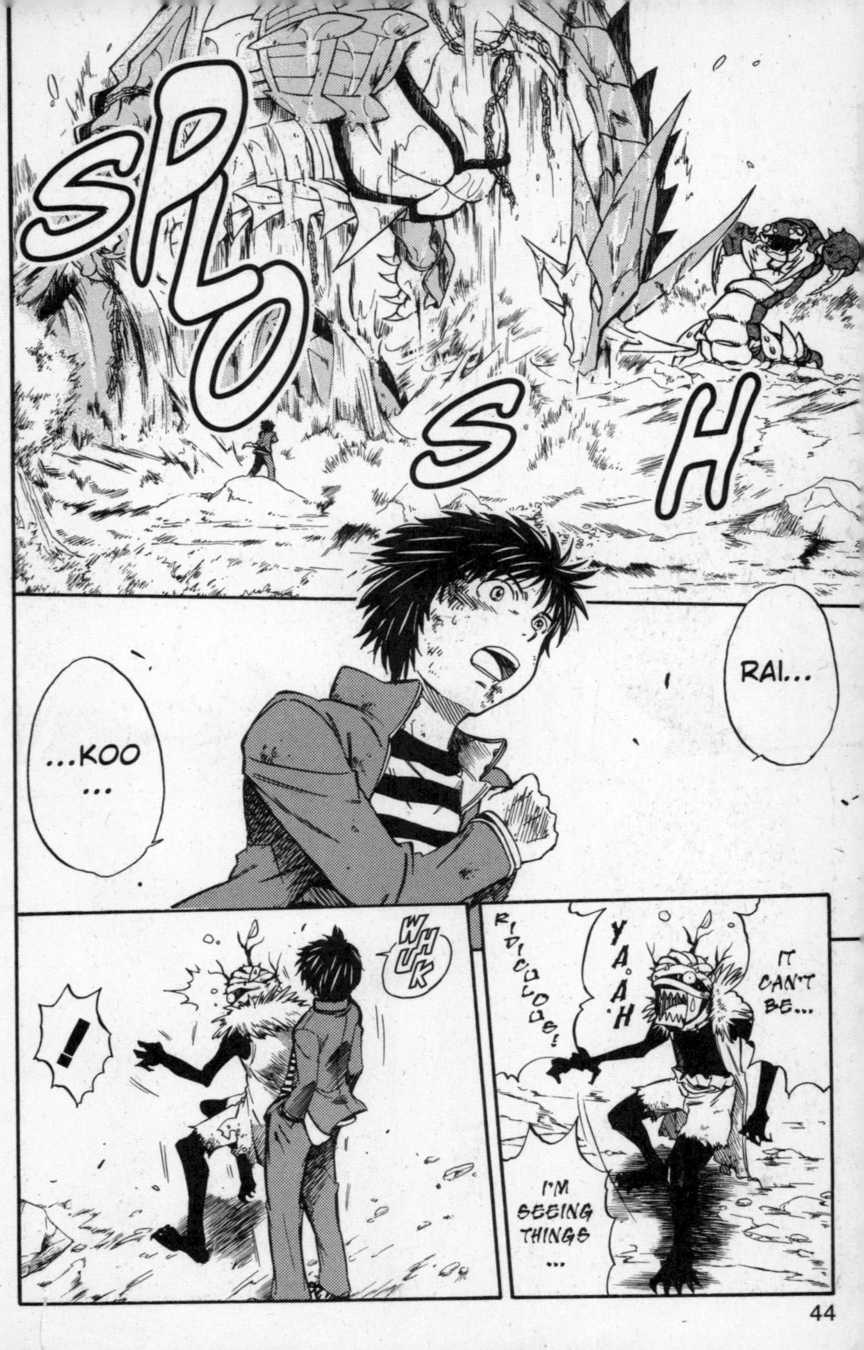
SPLOSH
RAI...
...KOO ...
IT CAN'T BE...
YAAH
RIDICULOUS!
I'M SEEING THINGS ...
WHUK
!

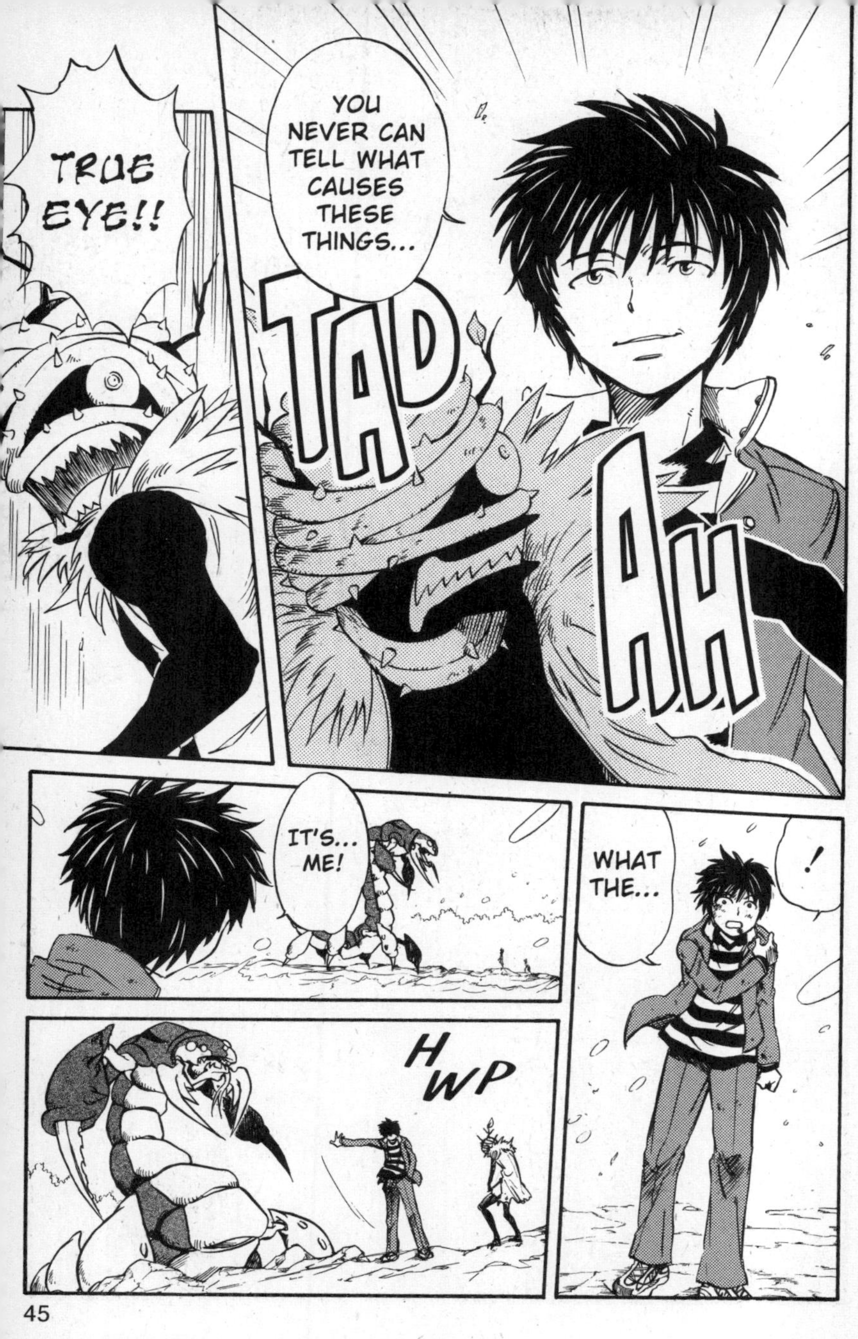
YOU NEVER CAN TELL WHAT CAUSES THESE THINGS...
TAD
AH
TRUE EYE!!
!
WHAT THE...
IT'S... ME!
HWP

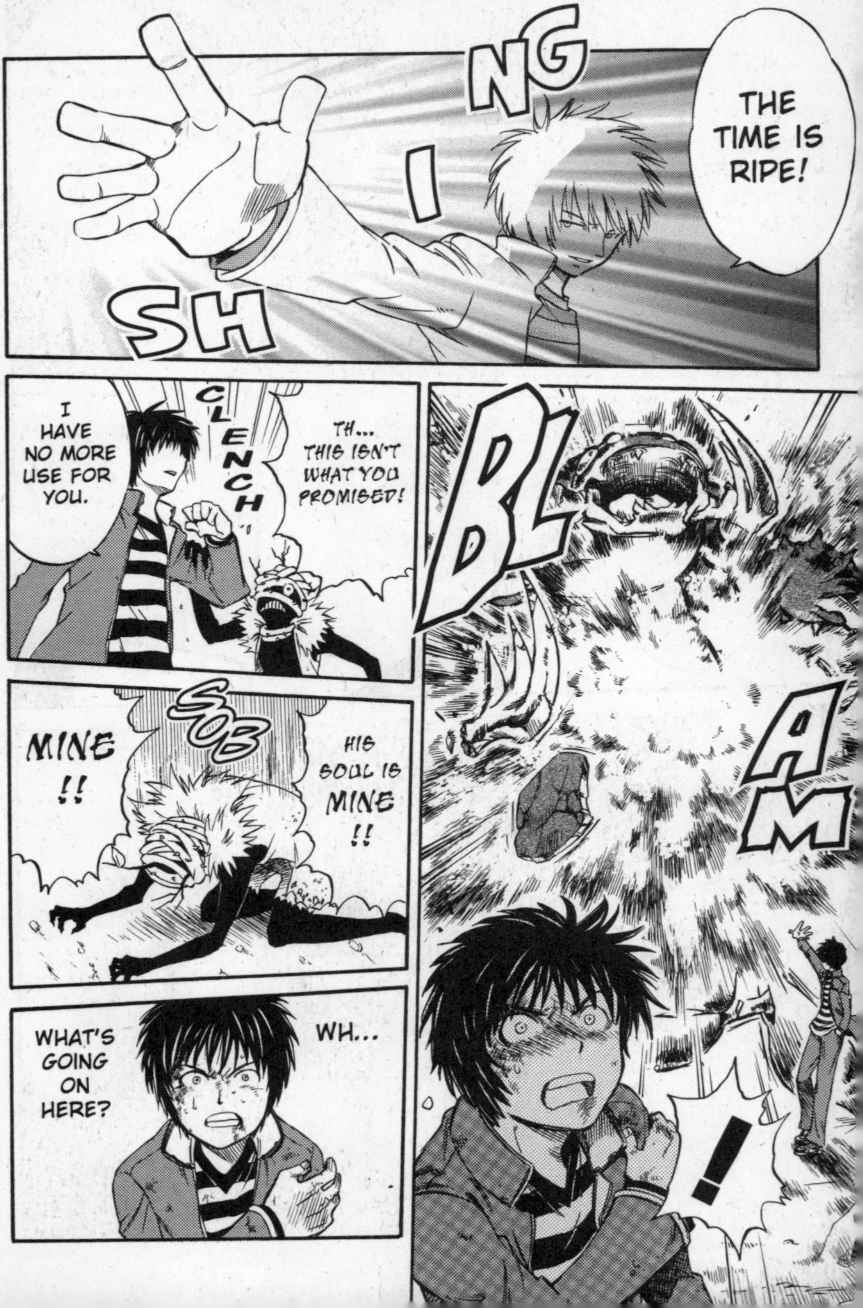
THE TIME IS RIPE!
SH I NG
BLAM
TH... THIS ISN'T WHAT YOU PROMISED!
CLENCH
I HAVE NO MORE USE FOR YOU.
HIS SOUL IS MINE !!
SOB
MINE !!
!
WH...
WHAT'S GOING ON HERE?

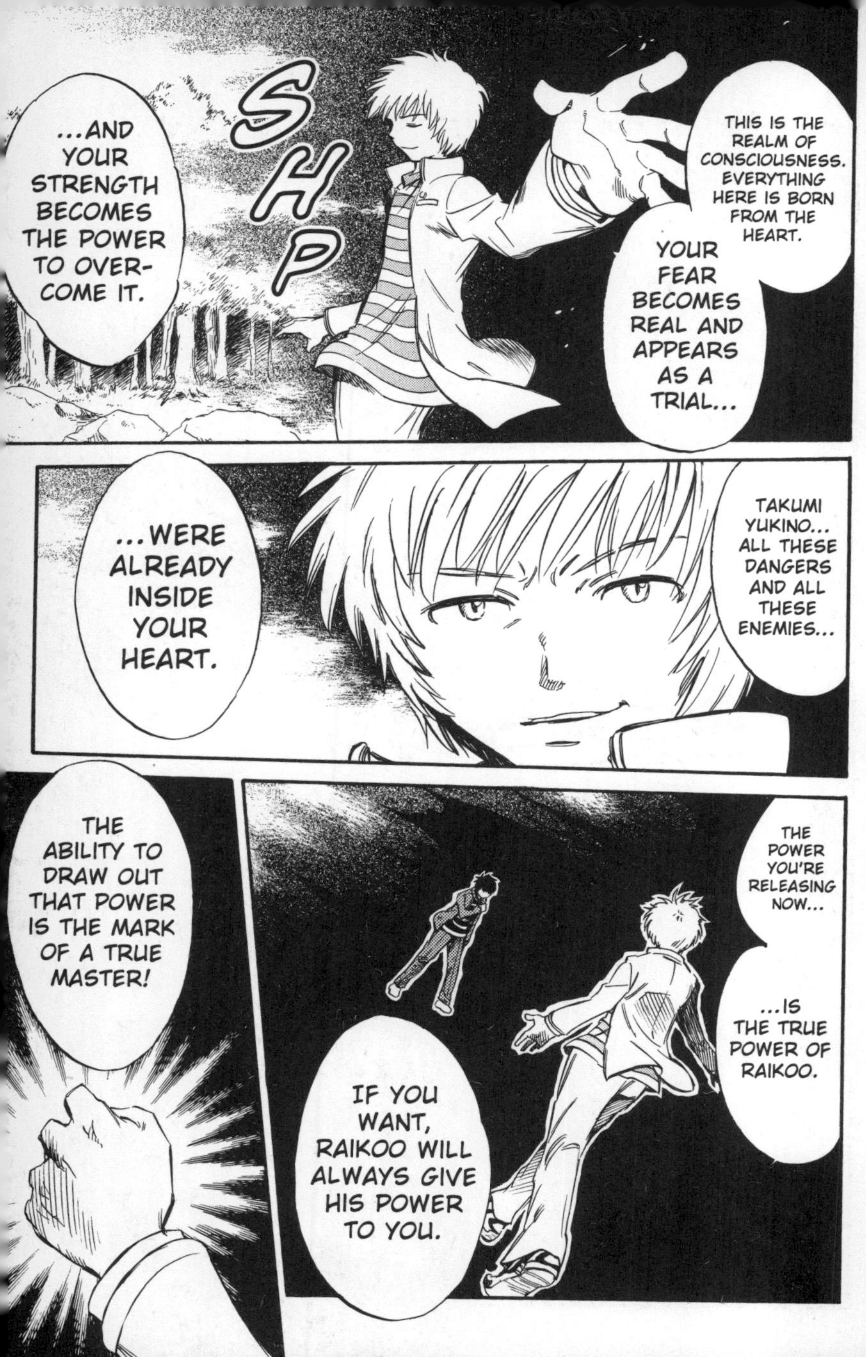
THIS IS THE REALM OF CONSCIOUSNESS. EVERYTHING HERE IS BORN FROM THE HEART.
YOUR FEAR BECOMES REAL AND APPEARS AS A TRIAL...
SHP
...AND YOUR STRENGTH BECOMES THE POWER TO OVER-COME IT.
TAKUMI YUKINO... ALL THESE DANGERS AND ALL THESE ENEMIES...
...WERE ALREADY INSIDE YOUR HEART.
THE POWER YOU'RE RELEASING NOW...
...IS THE TRUE POWER OF RAIKOO.
IF YOU WANT, RAIKOO WILL ALWAYS GIVE HIS POWER TO YOU.
THE ABILITY TO DRAW OUT THAT POWER IS THE MARK OF A TRUE MASTER!

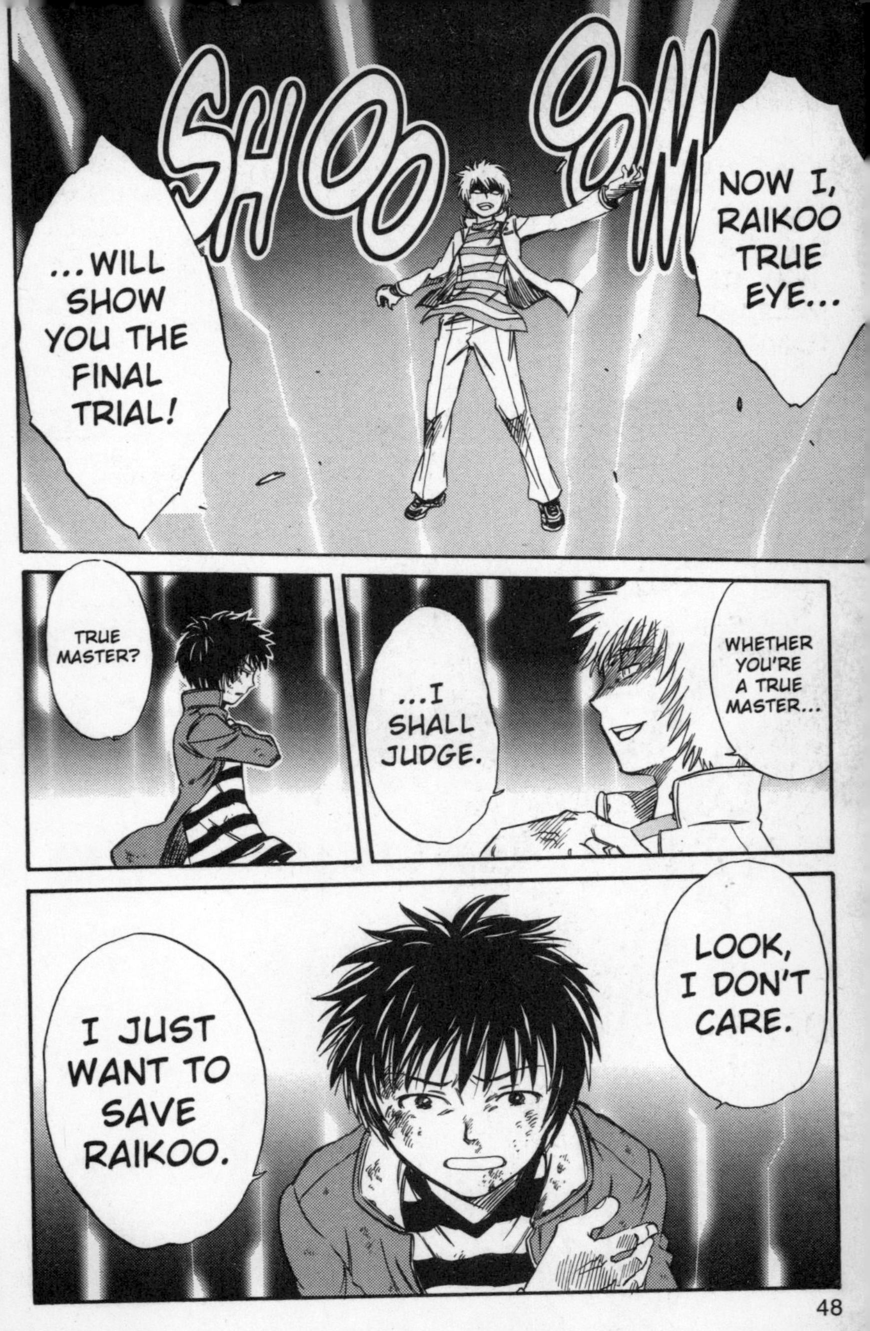
SHOOOOM
NOW I, RAIKOO TRUE EYE...
...WILL SHOW YOU THE FINAL TRIAL!
WHETHER YOU'RE A TRUE MASTER...
...I SHALL JUDGE.
TRUE MASTER?
LOOK, I DON'T CARE.
I JUST WANT TO SAVE RAIKOO.

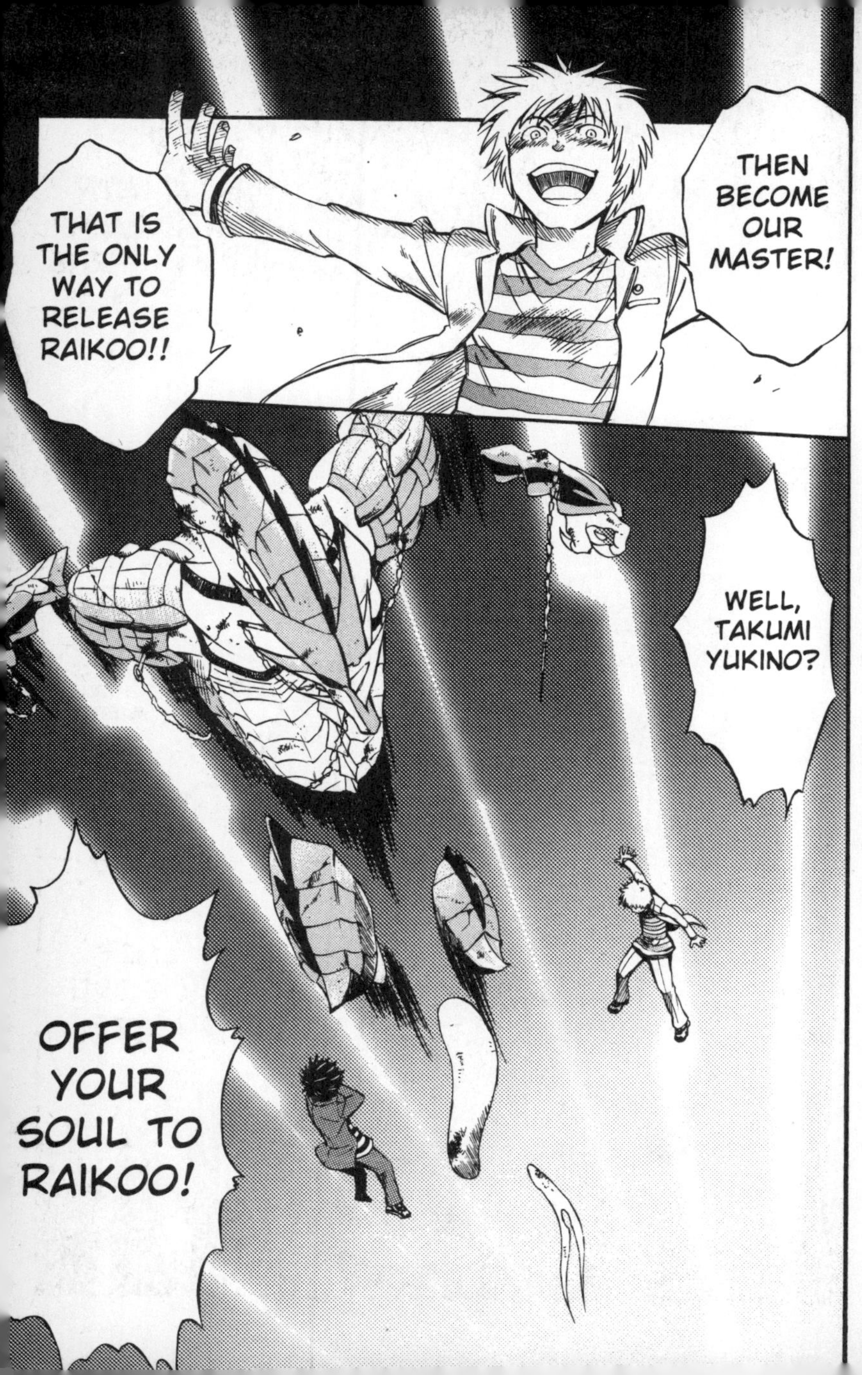
THEN BECOME OUR MASTER!
THAT IS THE ONLY WAY TO RELEASE RAIKOO!!
WELL, TAKUMI YUKINO?
OFFER YOUR SOUL TO RAIKOO!

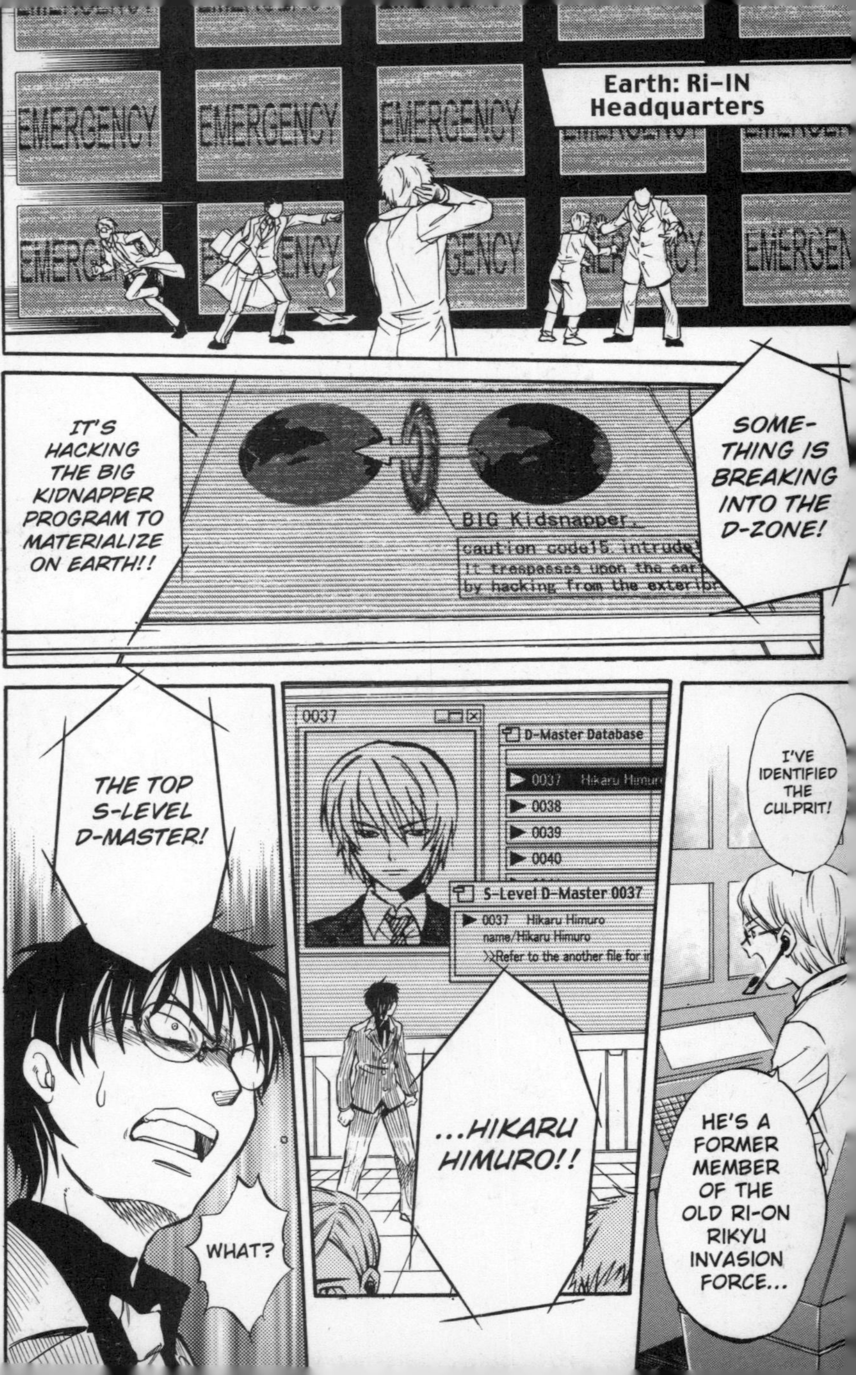Earth: Ri-IN Headquarters
EMERGENCY
EMERGENCY
EMERGENCY
SOMETHING IS BREAKING INTO THE D-ZONE!
BIG Kidsnapper.
IT'S HACKING THE BIG KIDNAPPER PROGRAM TO MATERIALIZE ON EARTH!!
I'VE IDENTIFIED THE CULPRIT!
HE'S A FORMER MEMBER OF THE OLD RI-ON RIKYU INVASION FORCE...
0037
D-Master Database
0038
0039
0040
S-Level D-Master 0037
0037 Hikaru Himuro
name/Hikaru Himuro
...HIKARU HIMURO!!
THE TOP S-LEVEL D-MASTER!
WHAT?

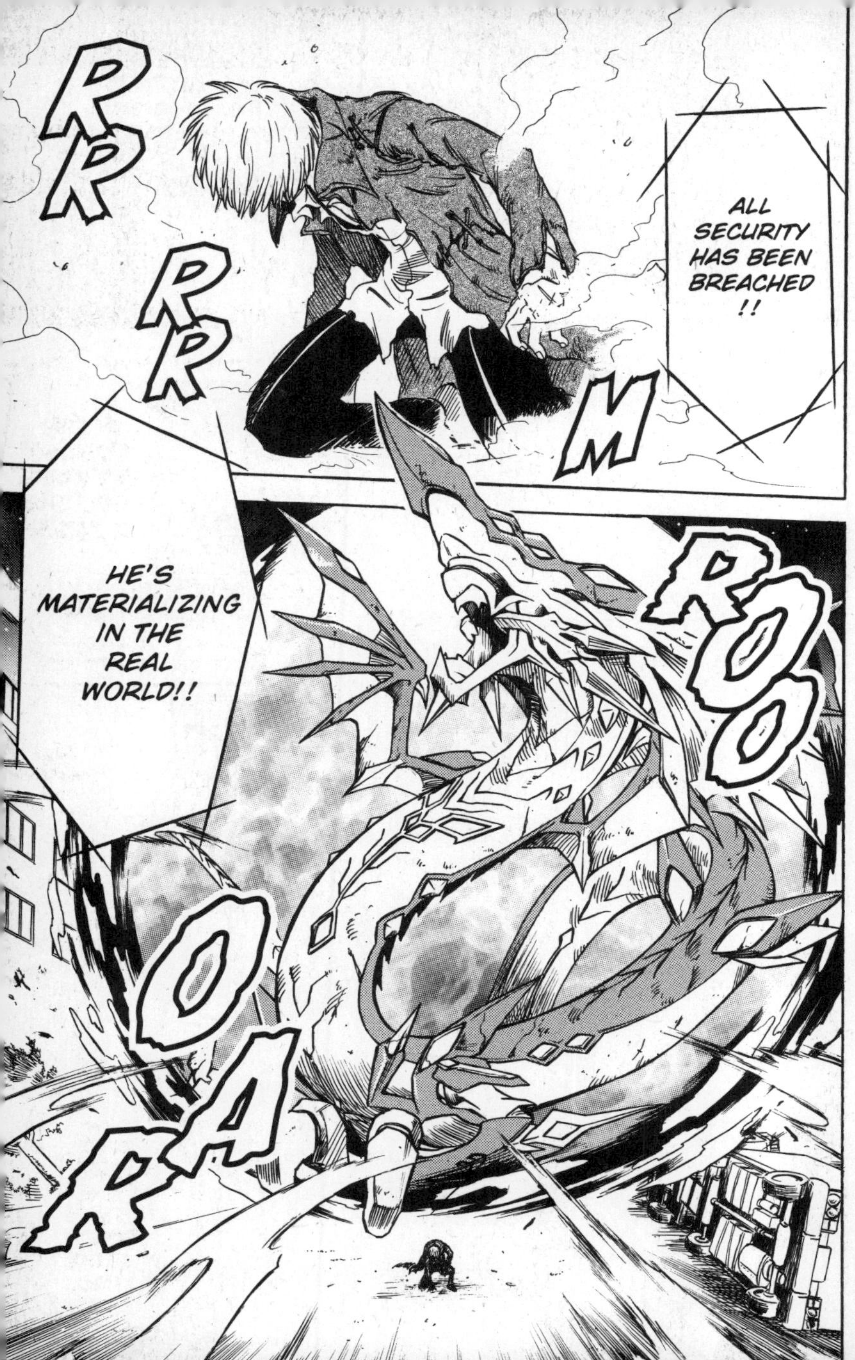
ALL SECURITY HAS BEEN BREACHED!!
RRRRM
ROOOAR
HE'S MATERIALIZING IN THE REAL WORLD!!

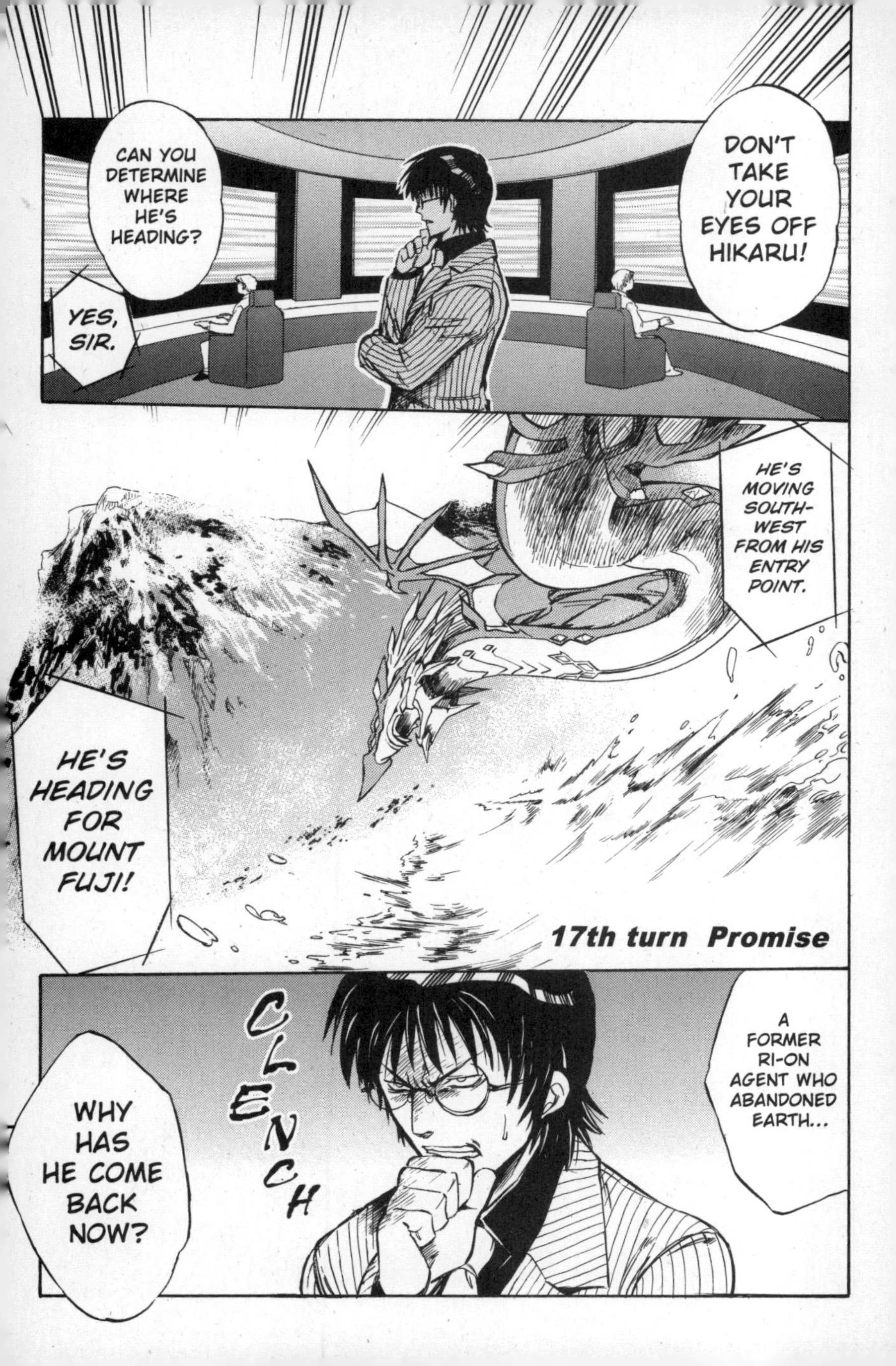
DON'T TAKE YOUR EYES OFF HIKARU!
CAN YOU DETERMINE WHERE HE'S HEADING?
YES, SIR.
HE'S MOVING SOUTH-WEST FROM HIS ENTRY POINT.
HE'S HEADING FOR MOUNT FUJI!
17th turn Promise
A FORMER RI-ON AGENT WHO ABANDONED EARTH...
CLENCH
WHY HAS HE COME BACK NOW?

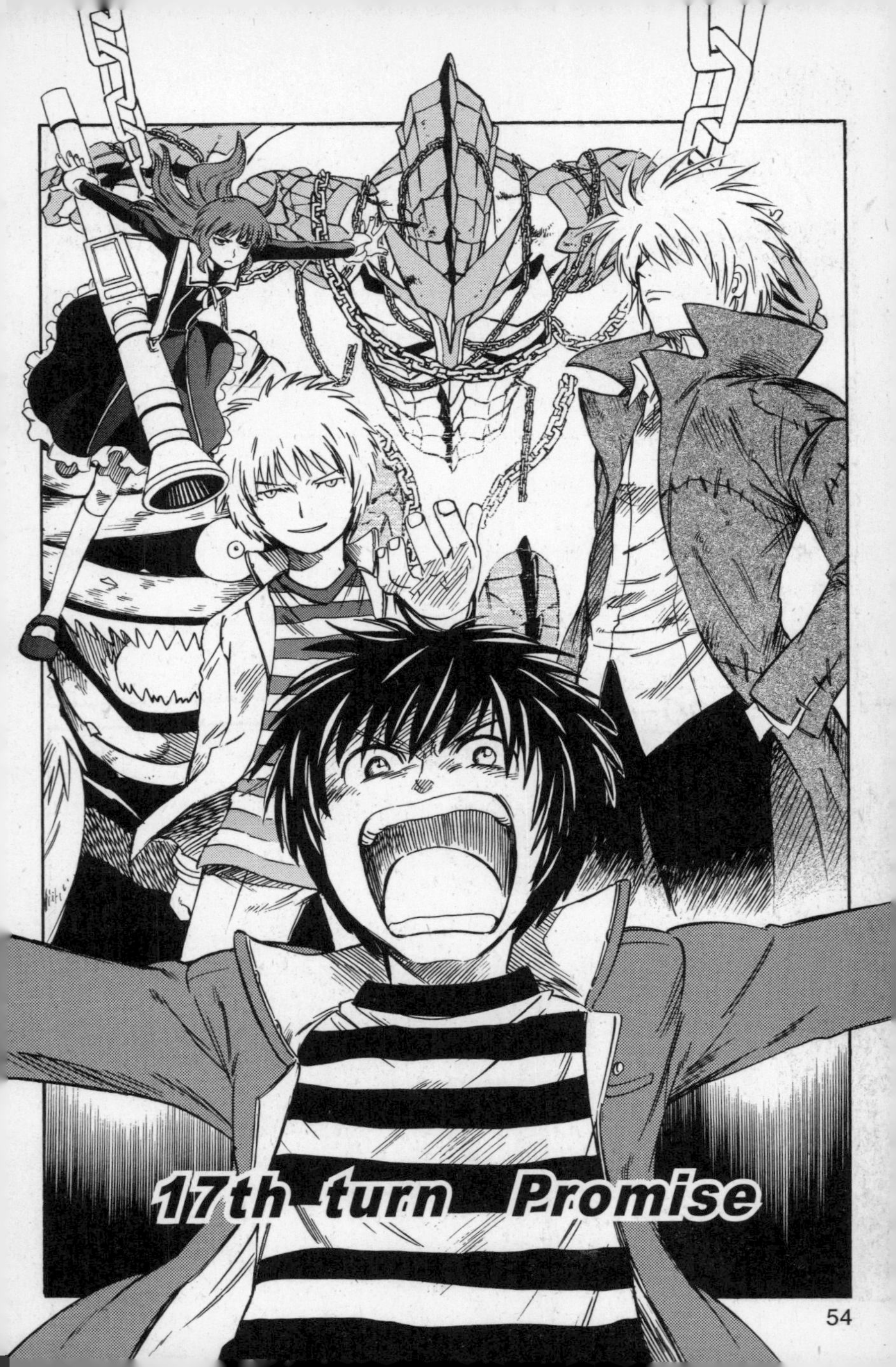
17th turn Promise

READ THIS WAY

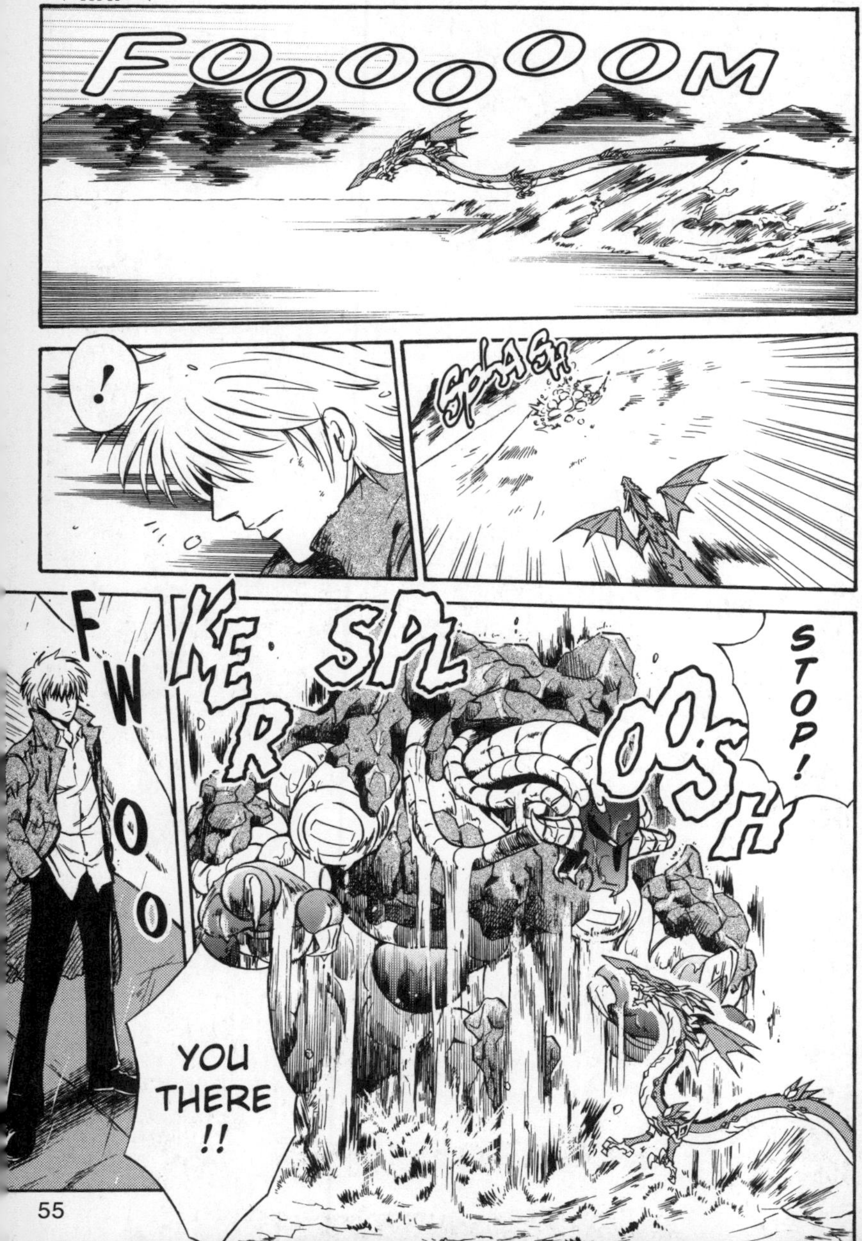
FOOOOOOM
SPLASH
!
STOP!
KERSPLOOSH
FWOOO
YOU THERE!!

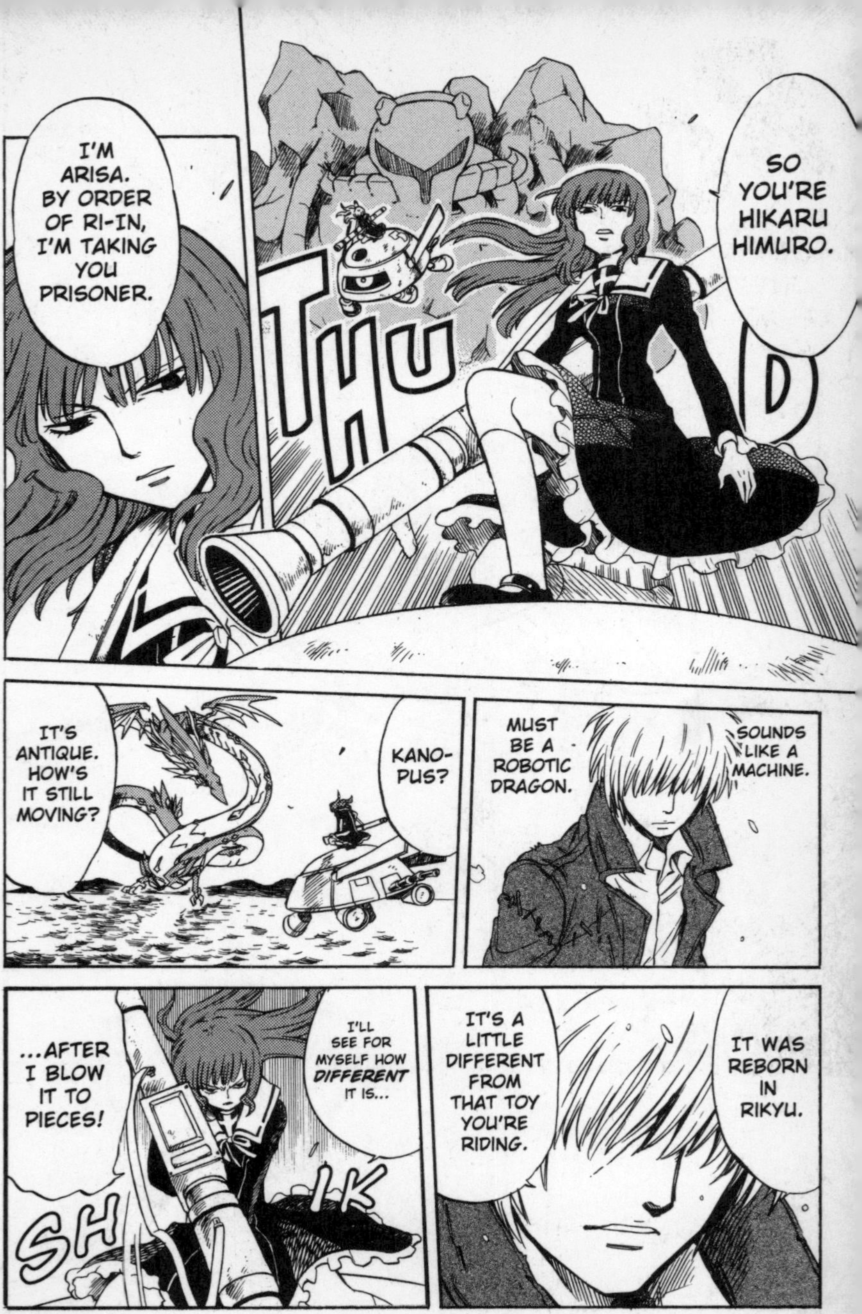
SO YOU'RE HIKARU HIMURO.
THUD
I'M ARISA. BY ORDER OF RI-IN, I'M TAKING YOU PRISONER.
SOUNDS LIKE A MACHINE.
MUST BE A ROBOTIC DRAGON.
KANO-PUS?
IT'S ANTIQUE. HOW'S IT STILL MOVING?
IT WAS REBORN IN RIKYU.
IT'S A LITTLE DIFFERENT FROM THAT TOY YOU'RE RIDING.
I'LL SEE FOR MYSELF HOW *DIFFERENT* IT IS...
...AFTER I BLOW IT TO PIECES!
SHIK

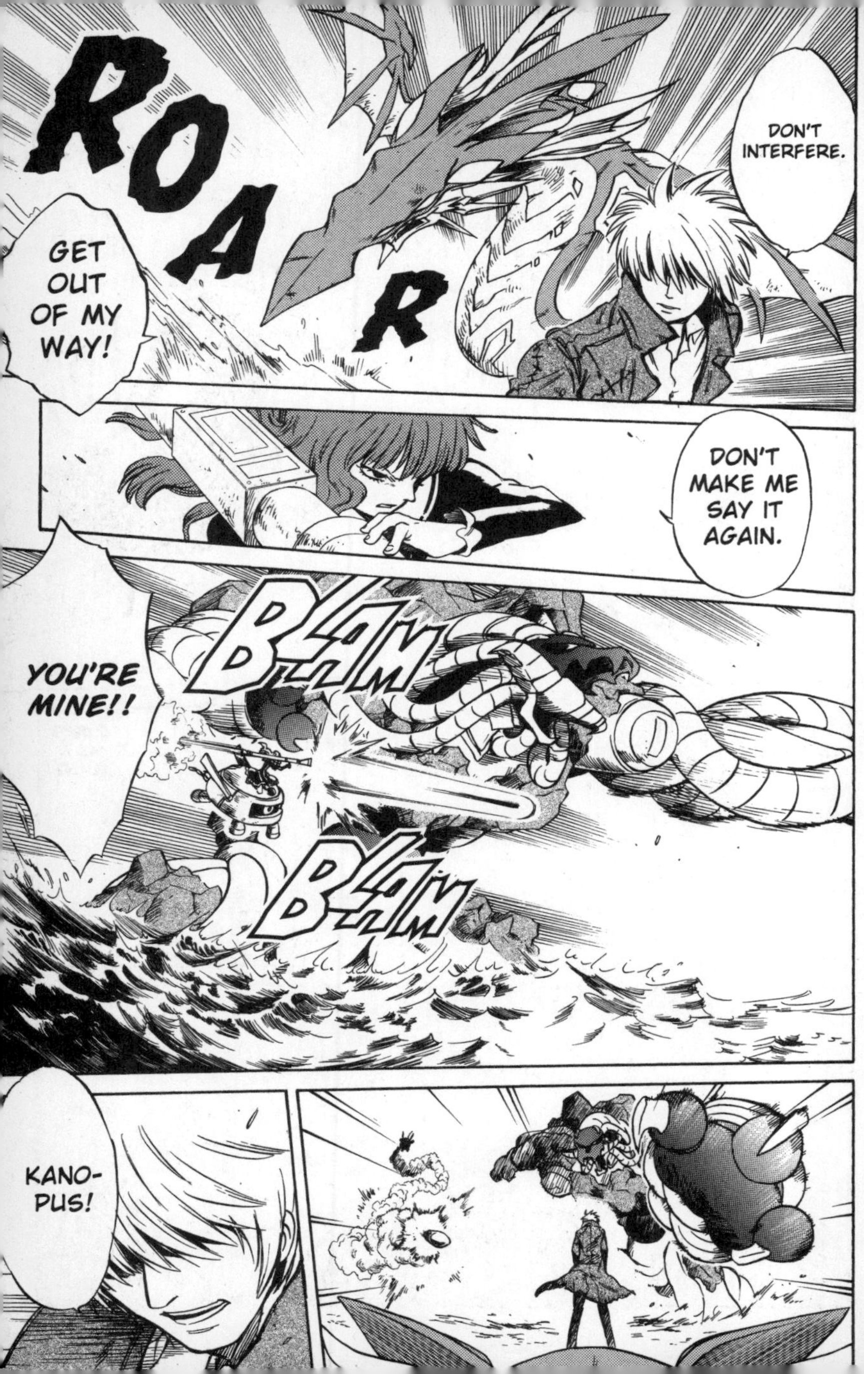
DON'T INTERFERE.
ROAR
GET OUT OF MY WAY!
DON'T MAKE ME SAY IT AGAIN.
BLAM
YOU'RE MINE!!
BLAM
KANO-PUS!

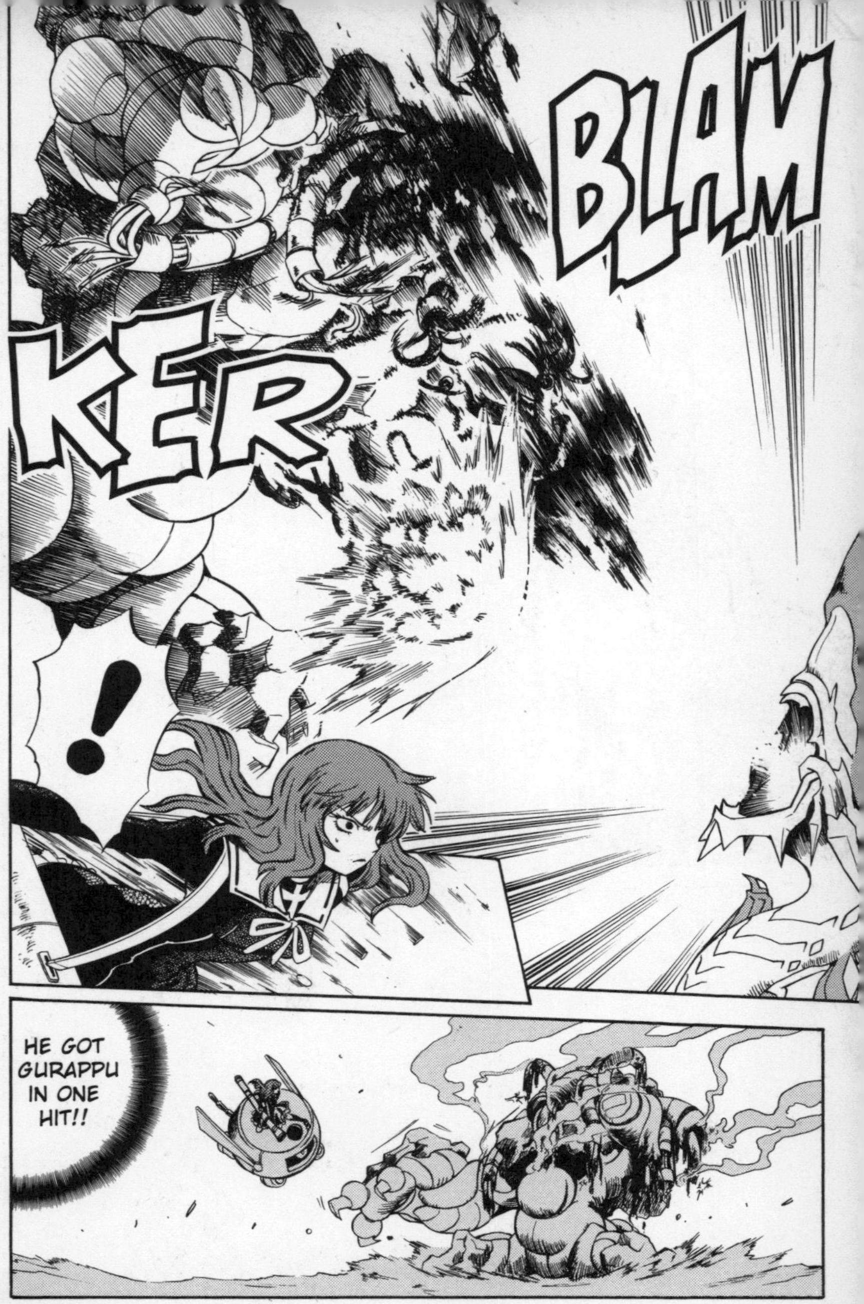
BLAM
KER
!
HE GOT GURAPPU IN ONE HIT!!

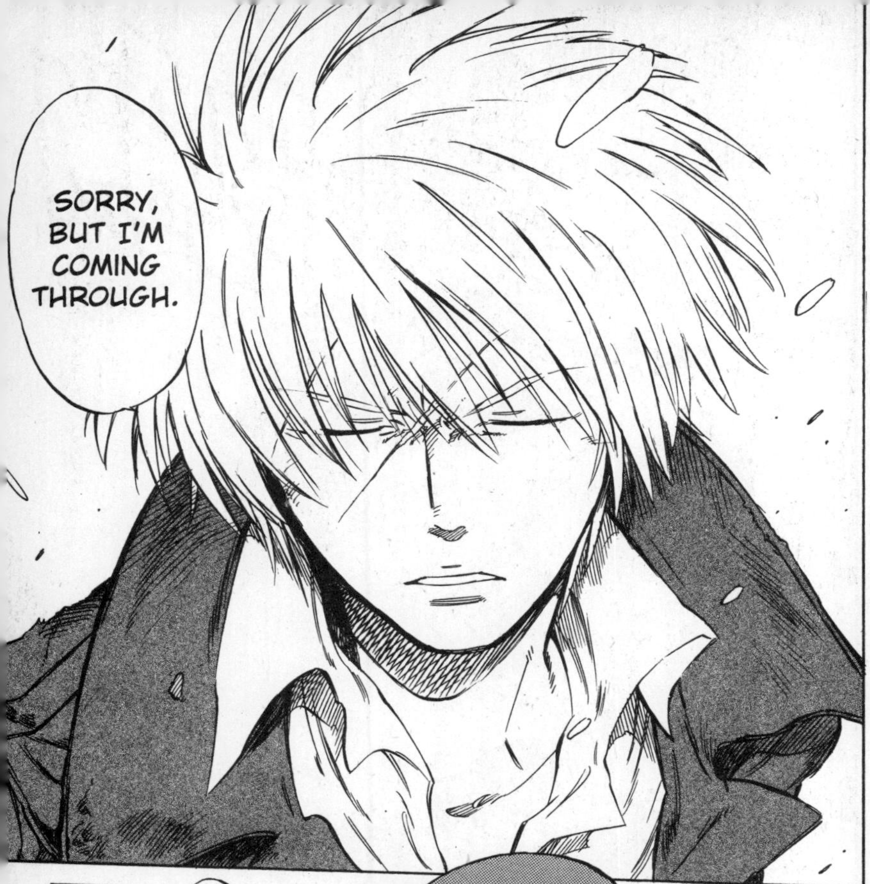
SORRY, BUT I'M COMING THROUGH.

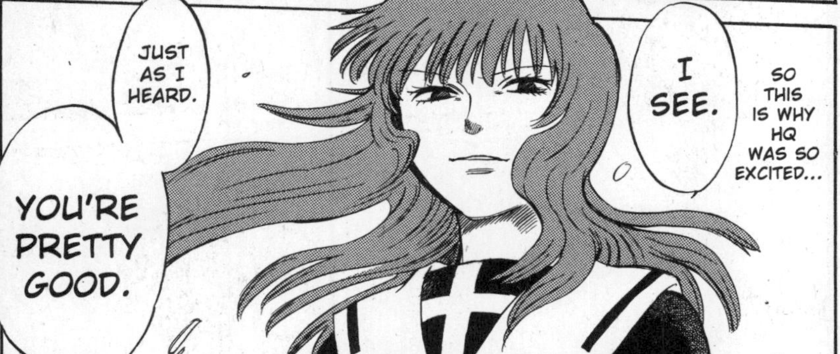
I SEE.
SO THIS IS WHY HQ WAS SO EXCITED...
JUST AS I HEARD.
YOU'RE PRETTY GOOD.

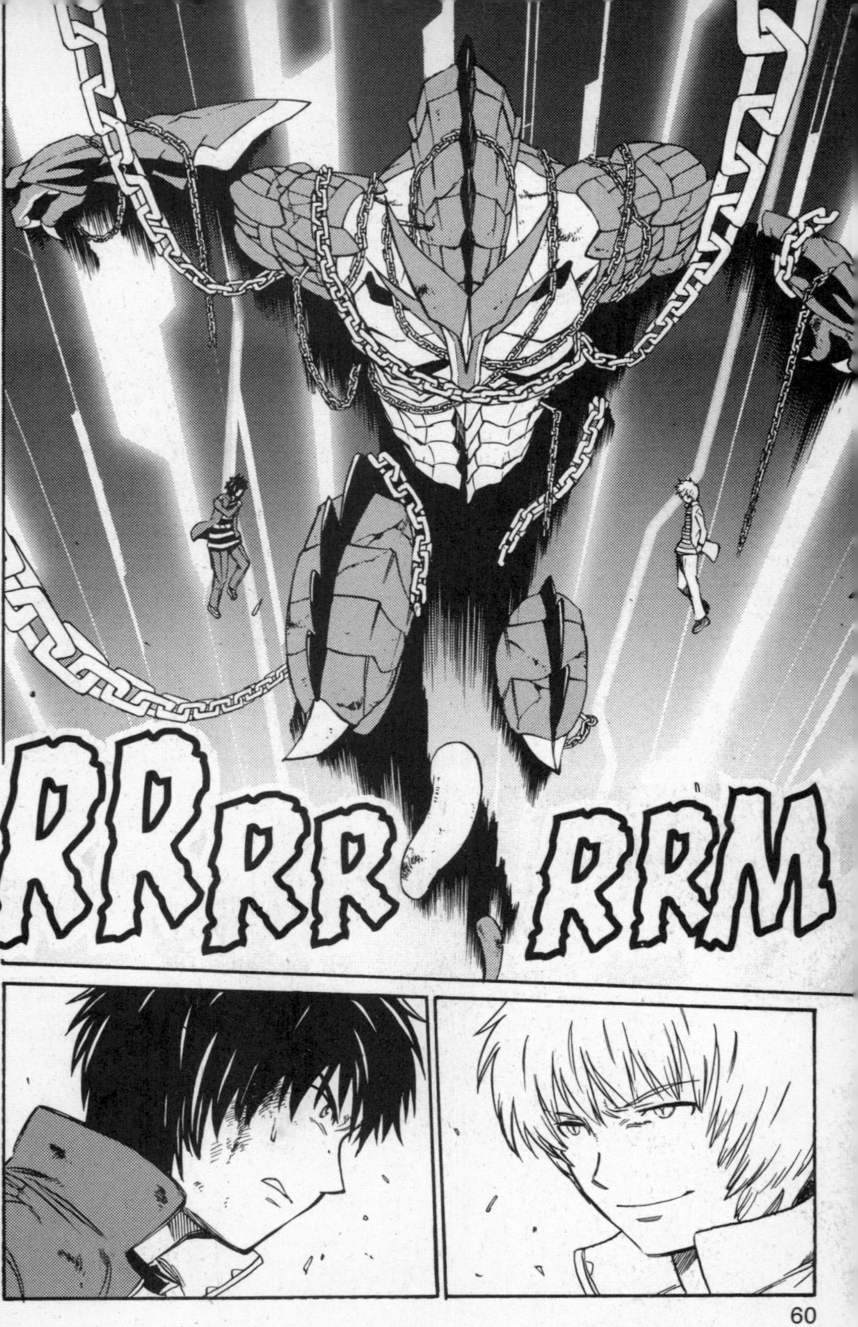
RRRR RRM

READ THIS WAY

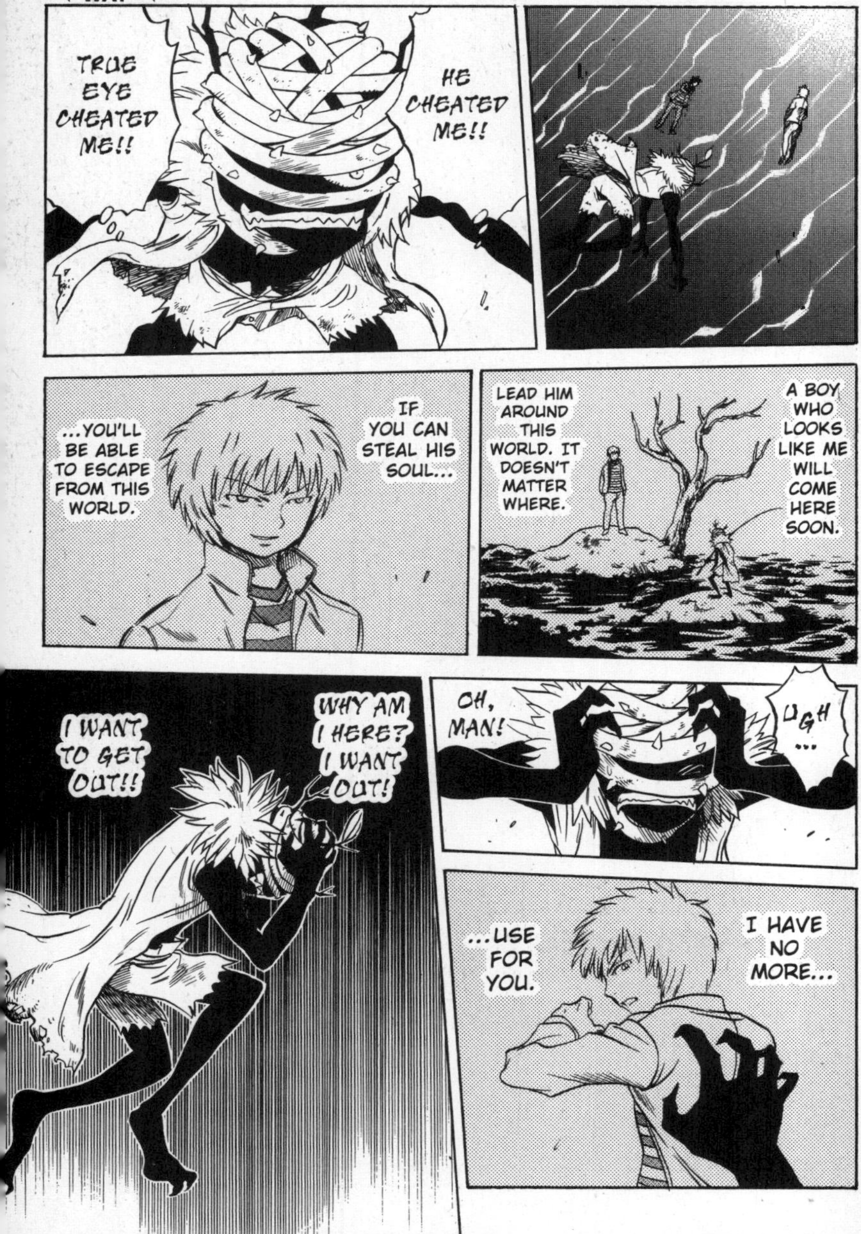

HE CHEATED ME!!
TRUE EYE CHEATED ME!!
A BOY WHO LOOKS LIKE ME WILL COME HERE SOON.
LEAD HIM AROUND THIS WORLD. IT DOESN'T MATTER WHERE.
IF YOU CAN STEAL HIS SOUL...
...YOU'LL BE ABLE TO ESCAPE FROM THIS WORLD.
UGH...
OH, MAN!
I HAVE NO MORE...
...USE FOR YOU.
WHY AM I HERE? I WANT OUT!
I WANT TO GET OUT!!

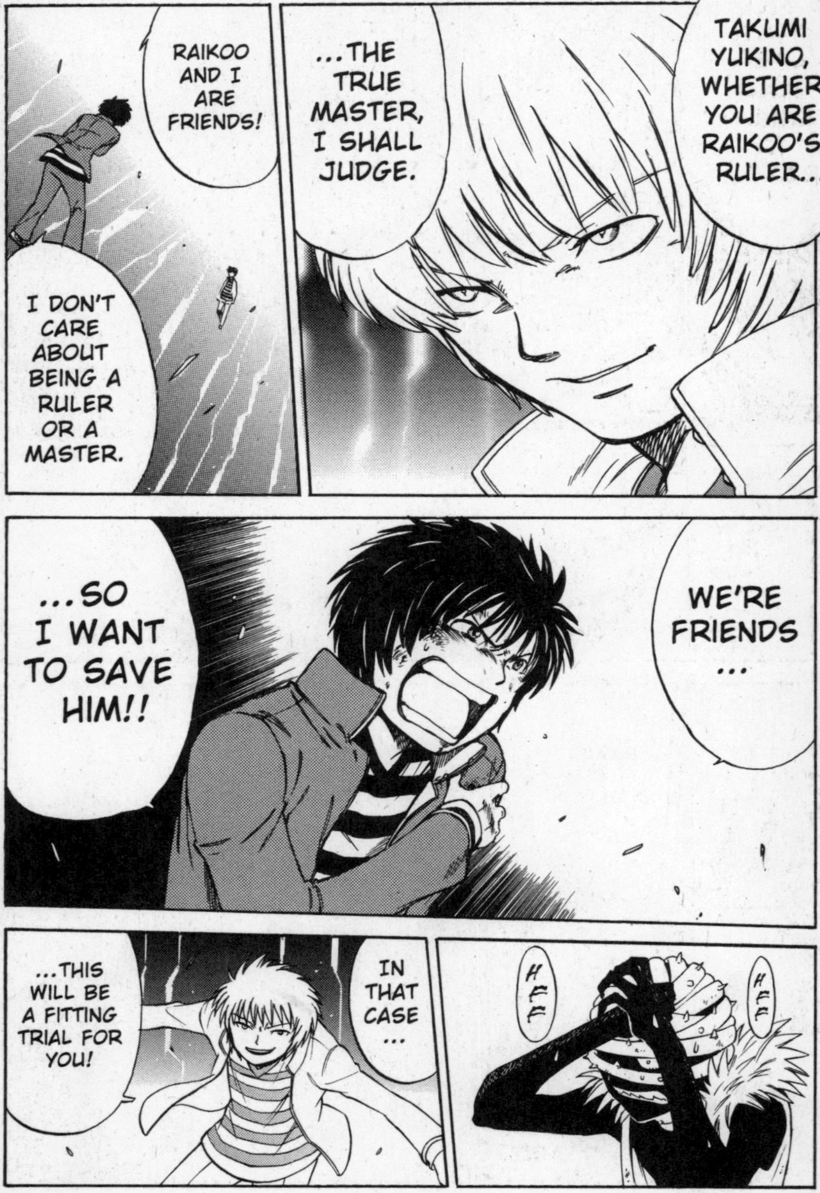
TAKUMI YUKINO, WHETHER YOU ARE RAIKOO'S RULER...
...THE TRUE MASTER, I SHALL JUDGE.
RAIKOO AND I ARE FRIENDS!
I DON'T CARE ABOUT BEING A RULER OR A MASTER.
WE'RE FRIENDS...
...SO I WANT TO SAVE HIM!!
HFF
HFF
IN THAT CASE...
...THIS WILL BE A FITTING TRIAL FOR YOU!

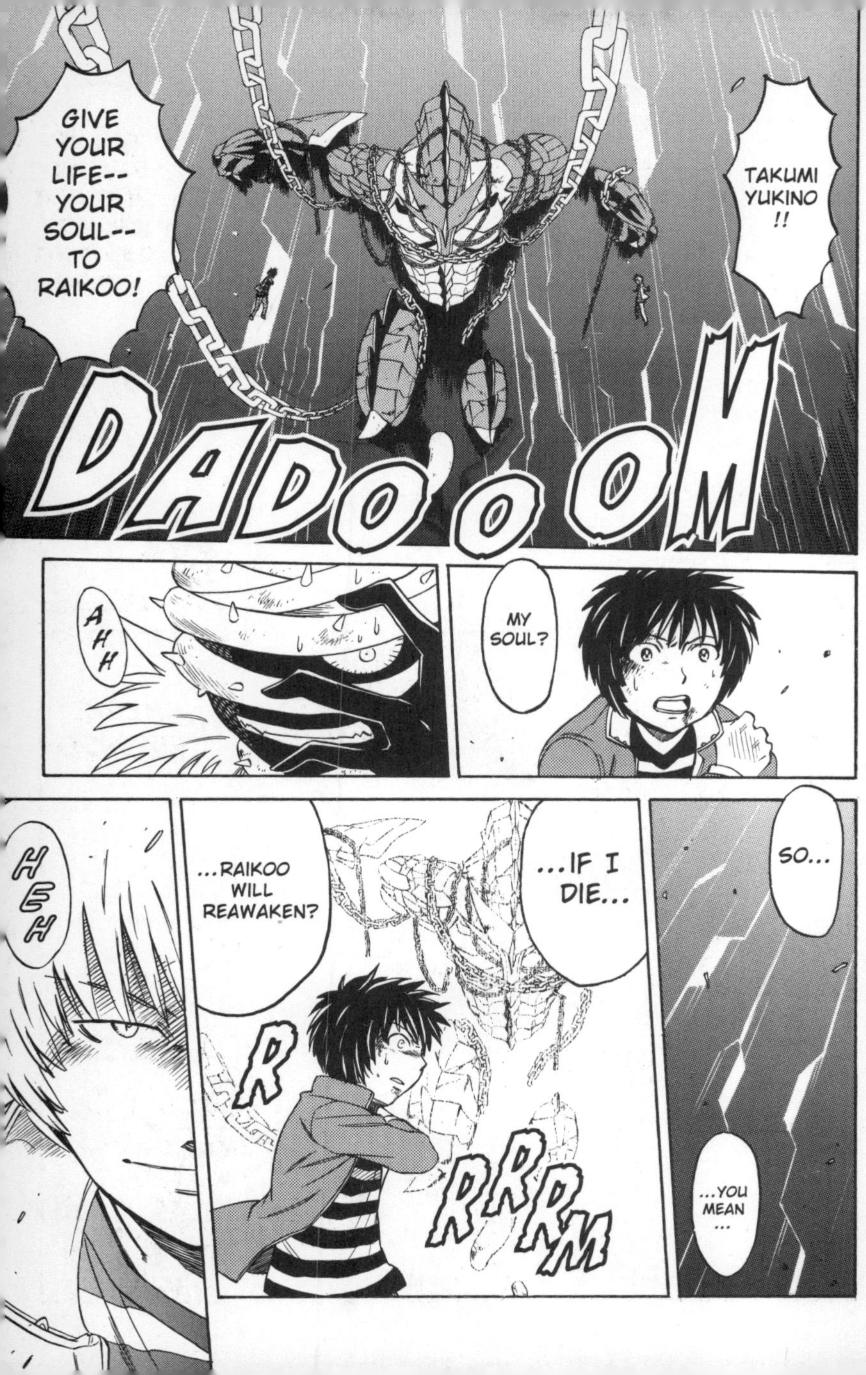
TAKUMI YUKINO !!
GIVE YOUR LIFE-- YOUR SOUL-- TO RAIKOO!
DADOOOM
MY SOUL?
AHH
SO...
...YOU MEAN ...
...IF I DIE...
...RAIKOO WILL REAWAKEN?
RRRRM
HEHEH

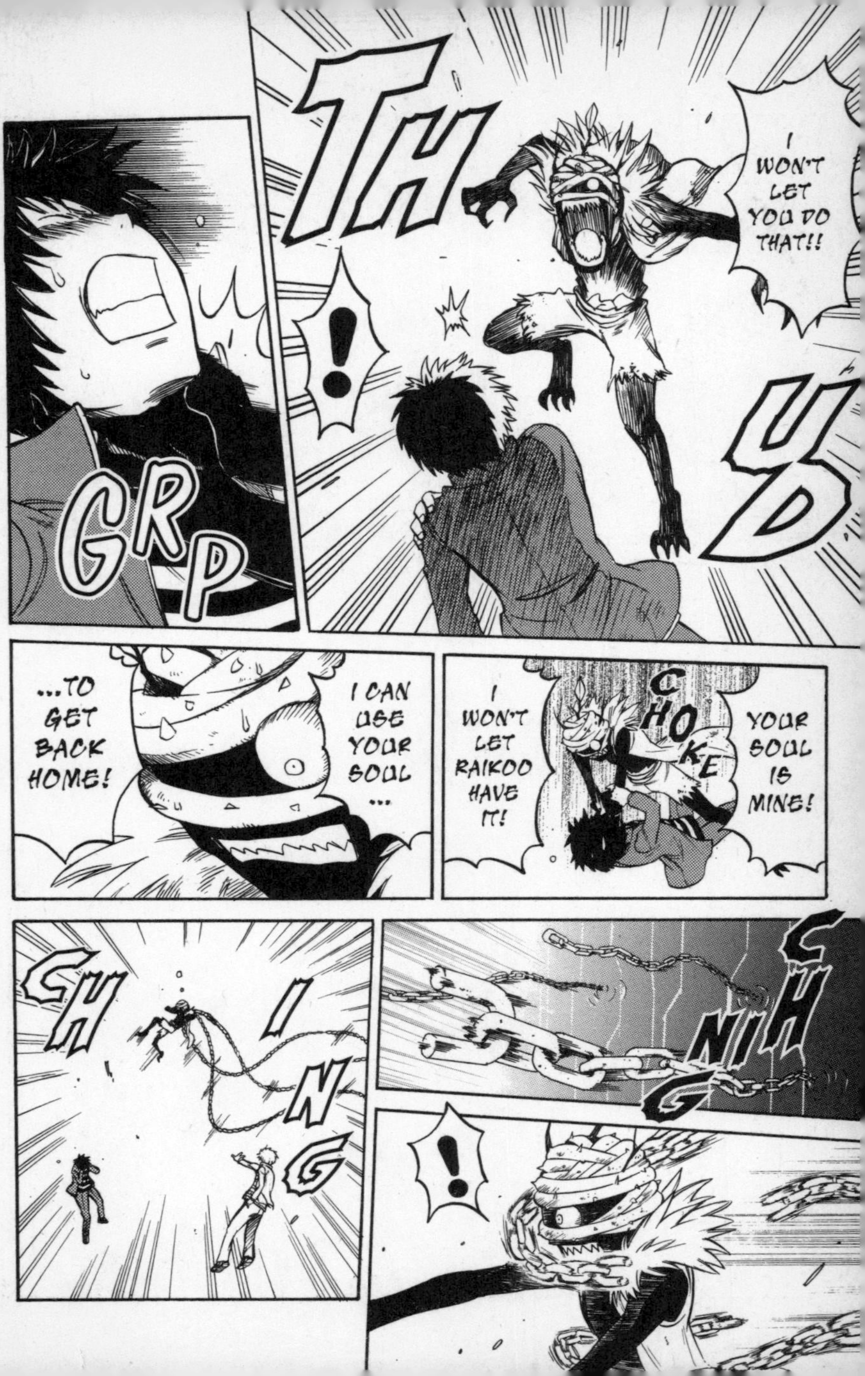
I WON'T LET YOU DO THAT!!
THUD
!
GRP
YOUR SOUL IS MINE!
CHOKE
I WON'T LET RAIKOO HAVE IT!
I CAN USE YOUR SOUL...
...TO GET BACK HOME!
CHING
!
CHING

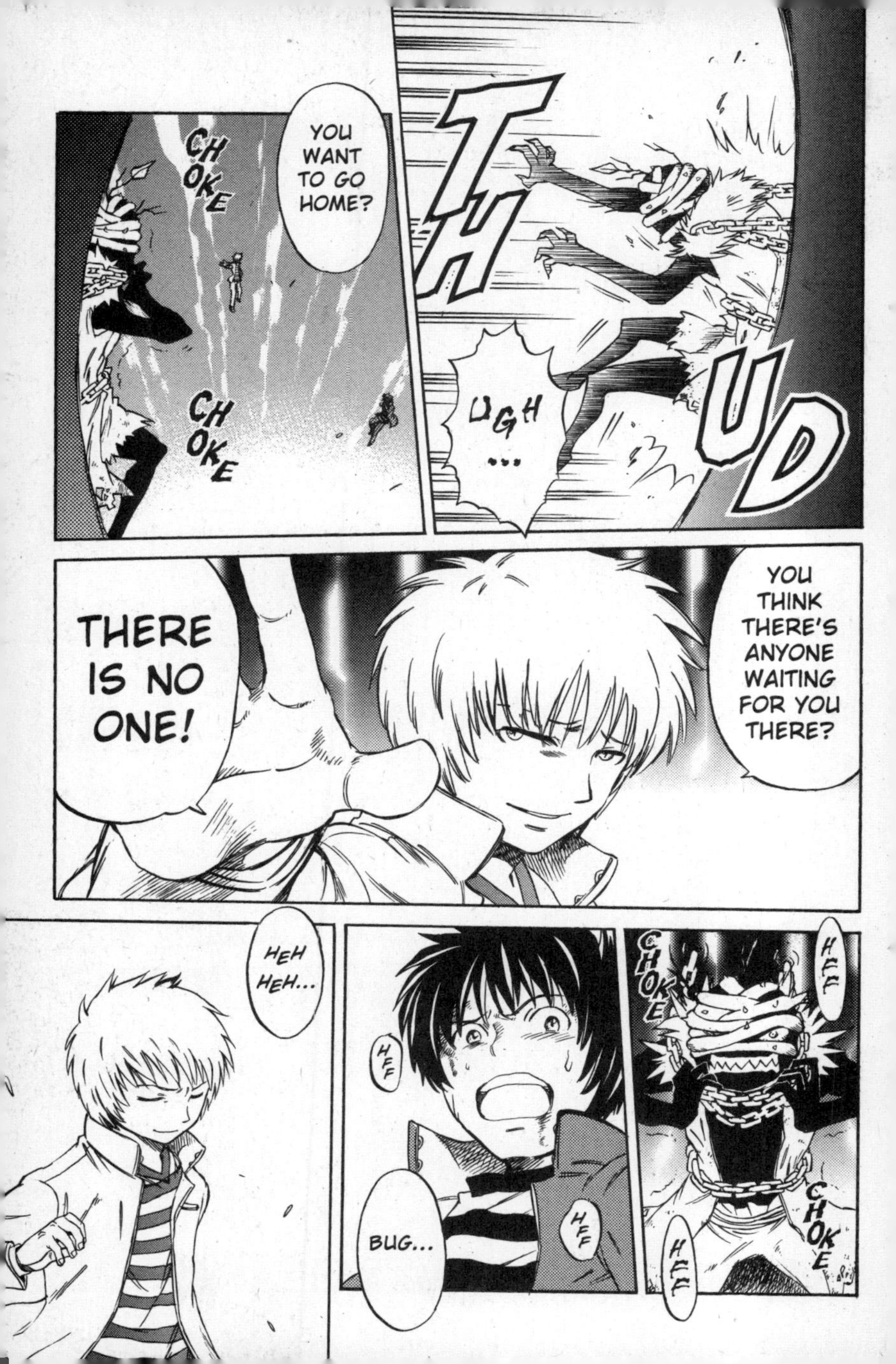
THUD
UGH...
YOU WANT TO GO HOME?
CHOKE
CHOKE
YOU THINK THERE'S ANYONE WAITING FOR YOU THERE?
THERE IS NO ONE!
HEF
CHOKE
CHOKE
HEF
HEF
HEF
BUG...
HEH HEH...

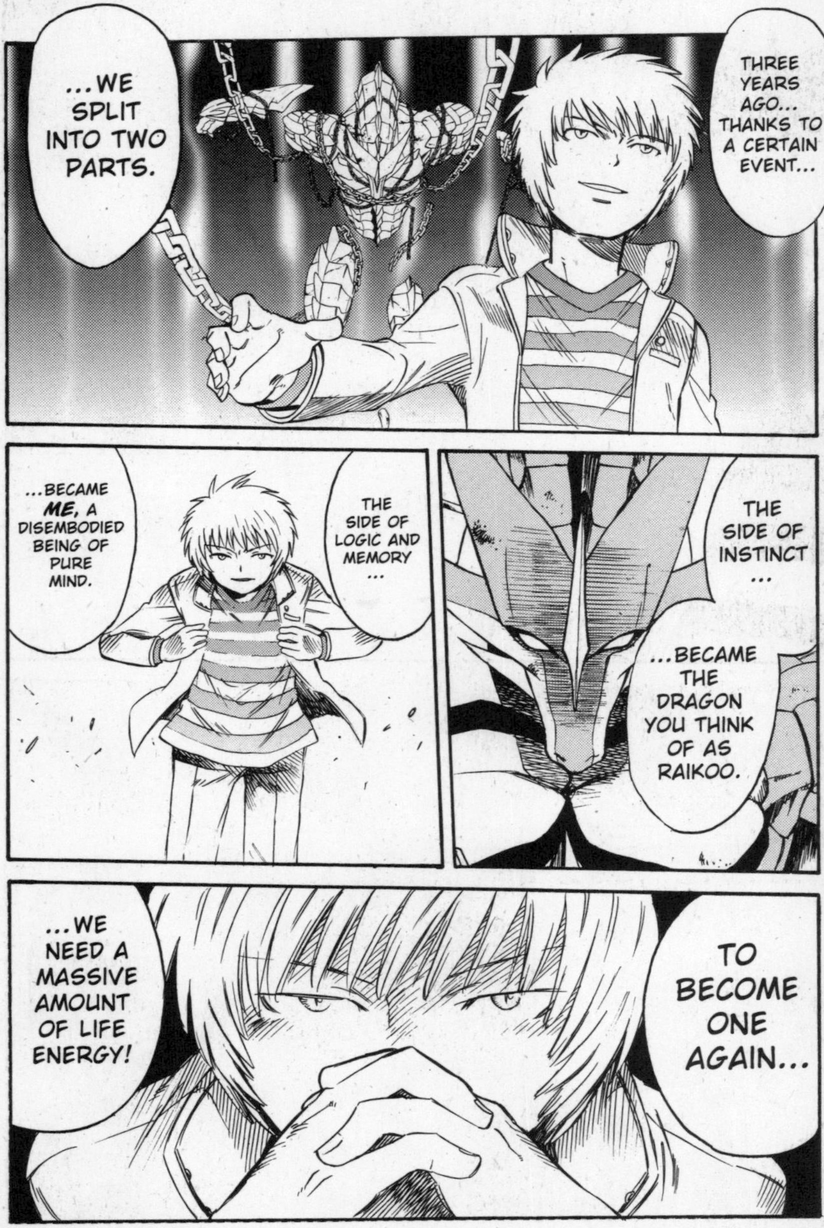
THREE YEARS AGO... THANKS TO A CERTAIN EVENT...
...WE SPLIT INTO TWO PARTS.
THE SIDE OF INSTINCT...
...BECAME THE DRAGON YOU THINK OF AS RAIKOO.
THE SIDE OF LOGIC AND MEMORY...
...BECAME *ME*, A DISEMBODIED BEING OF PURE MIND.
TO BECOME ONE AGAIN...
...WE NEED A MASSIVE AMOUNT OF LIFE ENERGY!

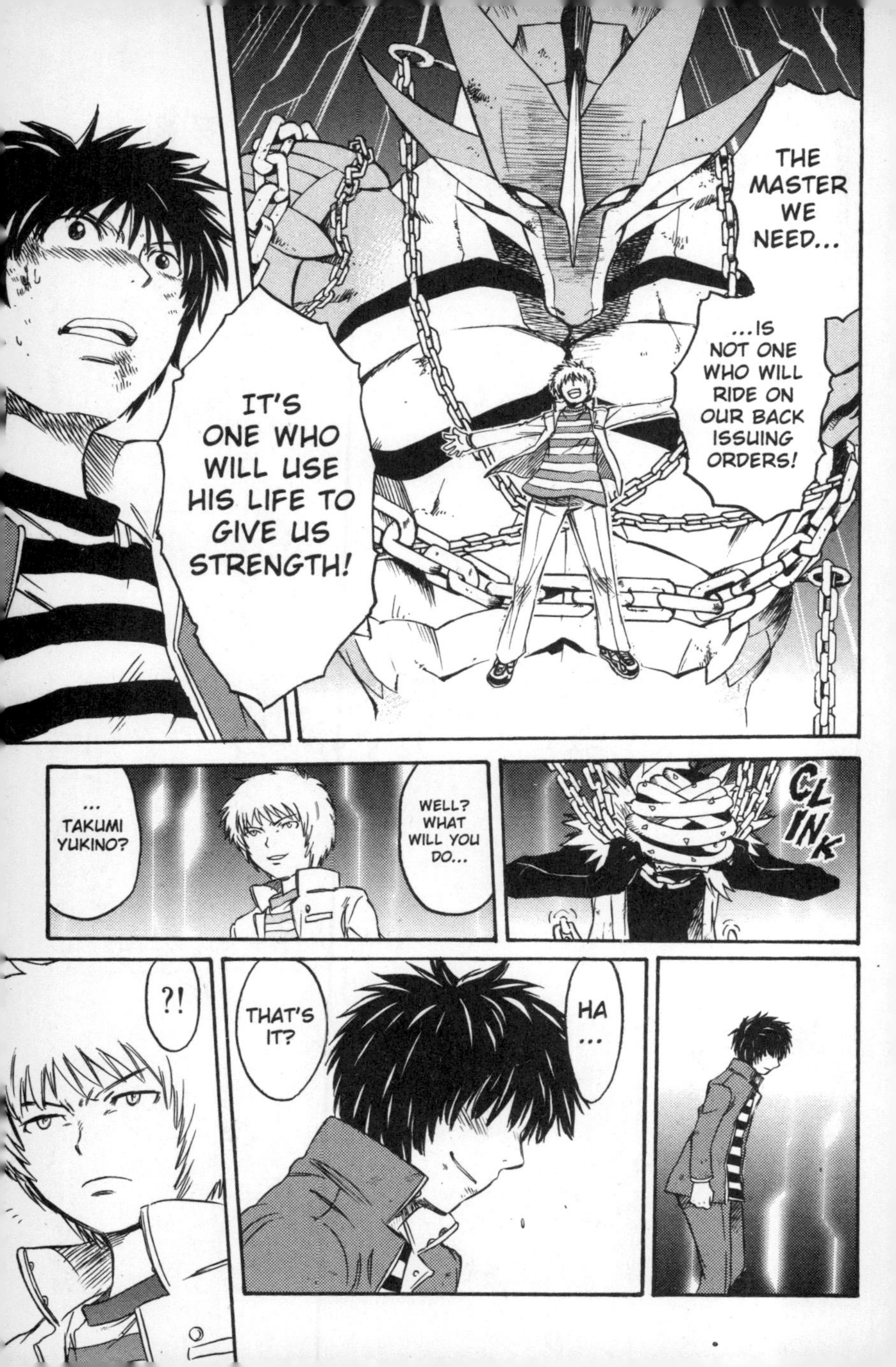
THE MASTER WE NEED...
...IS NOT ONE WHO WILL RIDE ON OUR BACK ISSUING ORDERS!
IT'S ONE WHO WILL USE HIS LIFE TO GIVE US STRENGTH!
CLINK
WELL? WHAT WILL YOU DO...
... TAKUMI YUKINO?
HA ...
THAT'S IT?
?!

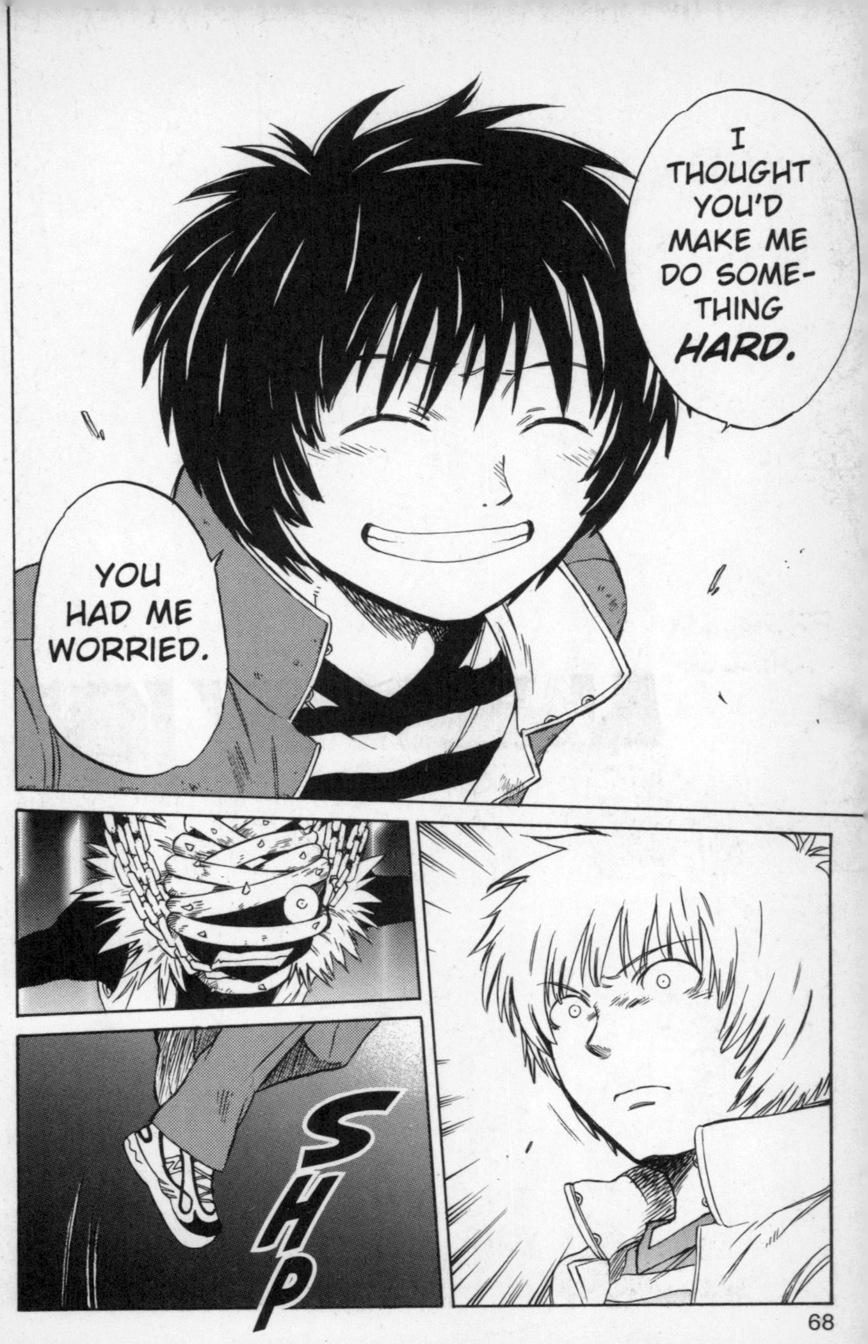
I THOUGHT YOU'D MAKE ME DO SOME-THING HARD.
YOU HAD ME WORRIED.
SHP

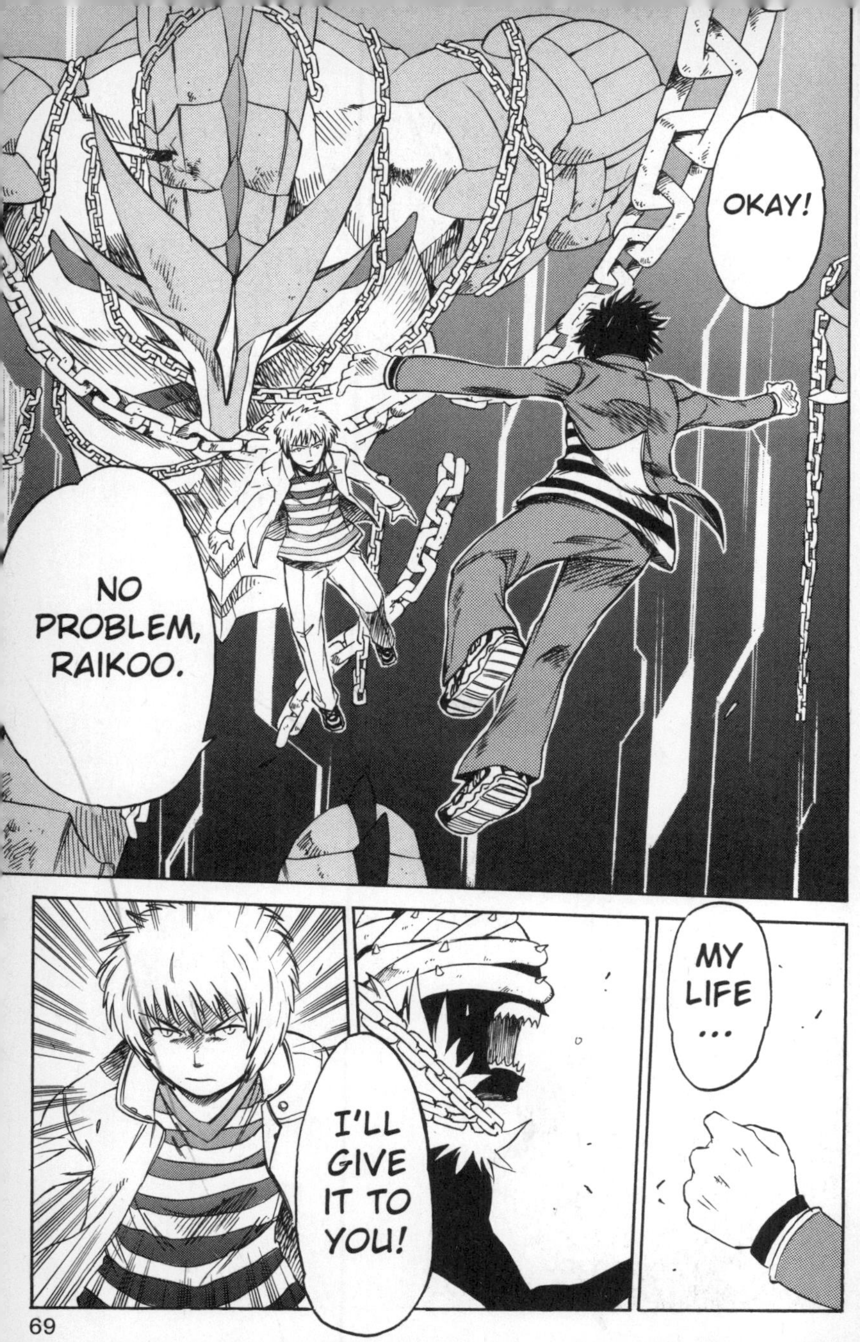
OKAY!
NO PROBLEM, RAIKOO.
MY LIFE ...
I'LL GIVE IT TO YOU!

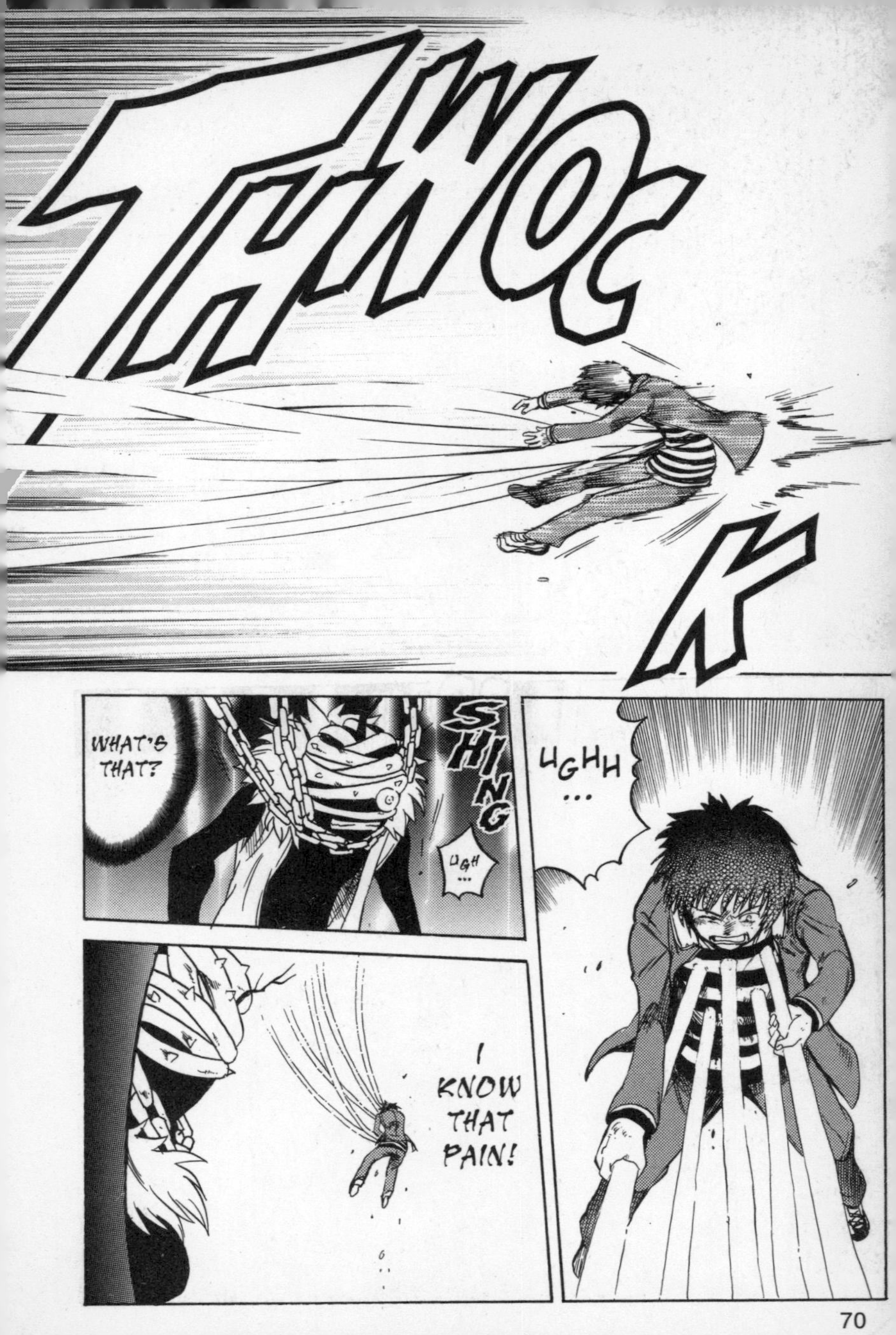
THWOCK
UGHH ...
SHING
UGH ...
WHAT'S THAT?
I KNOW THAT PAIN!

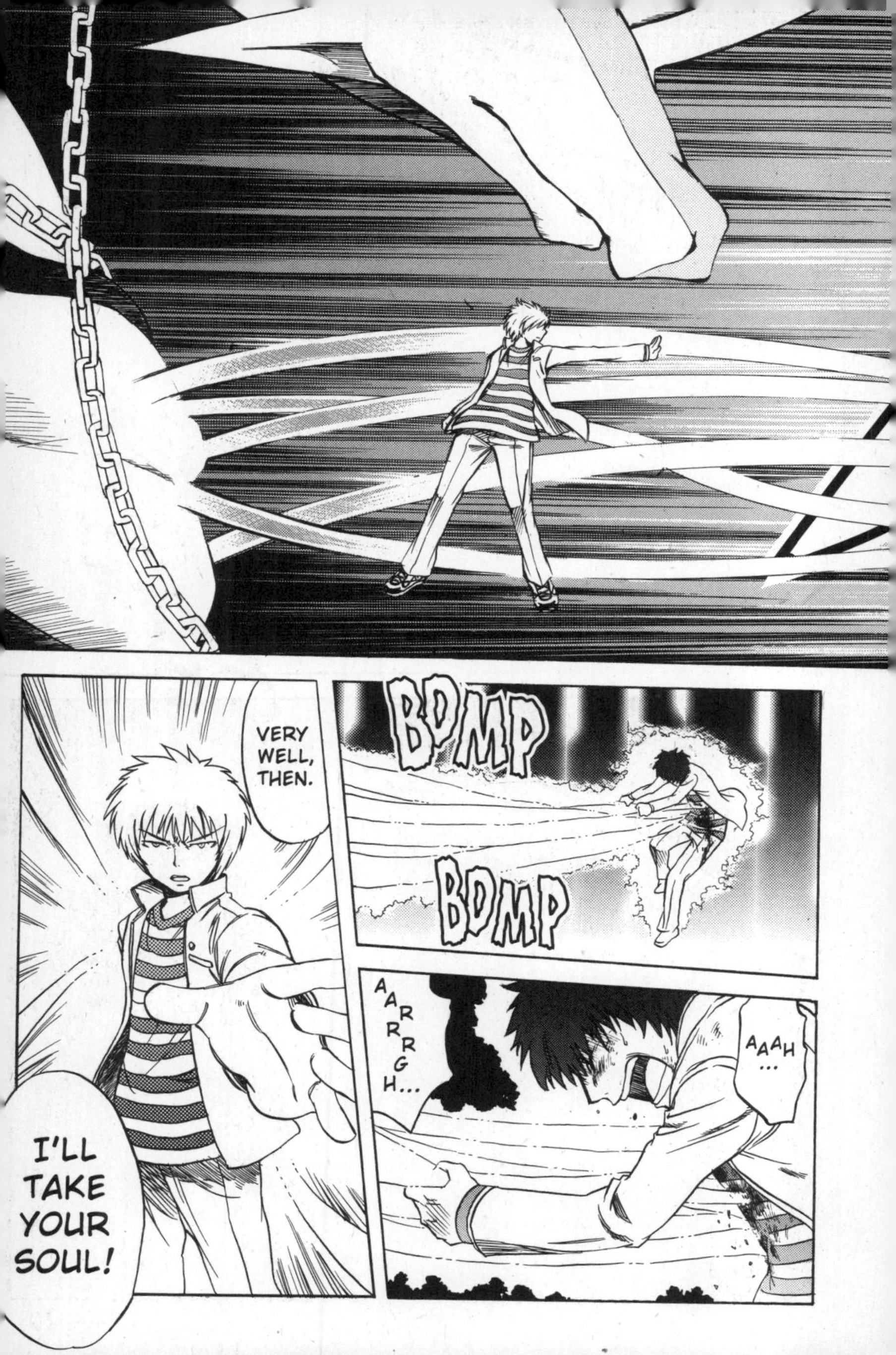
BDMP
BDMP
AAAH...
AARRRGH...
VERY WELL, THEN.
I'LL TAKE YOUR SOUL!

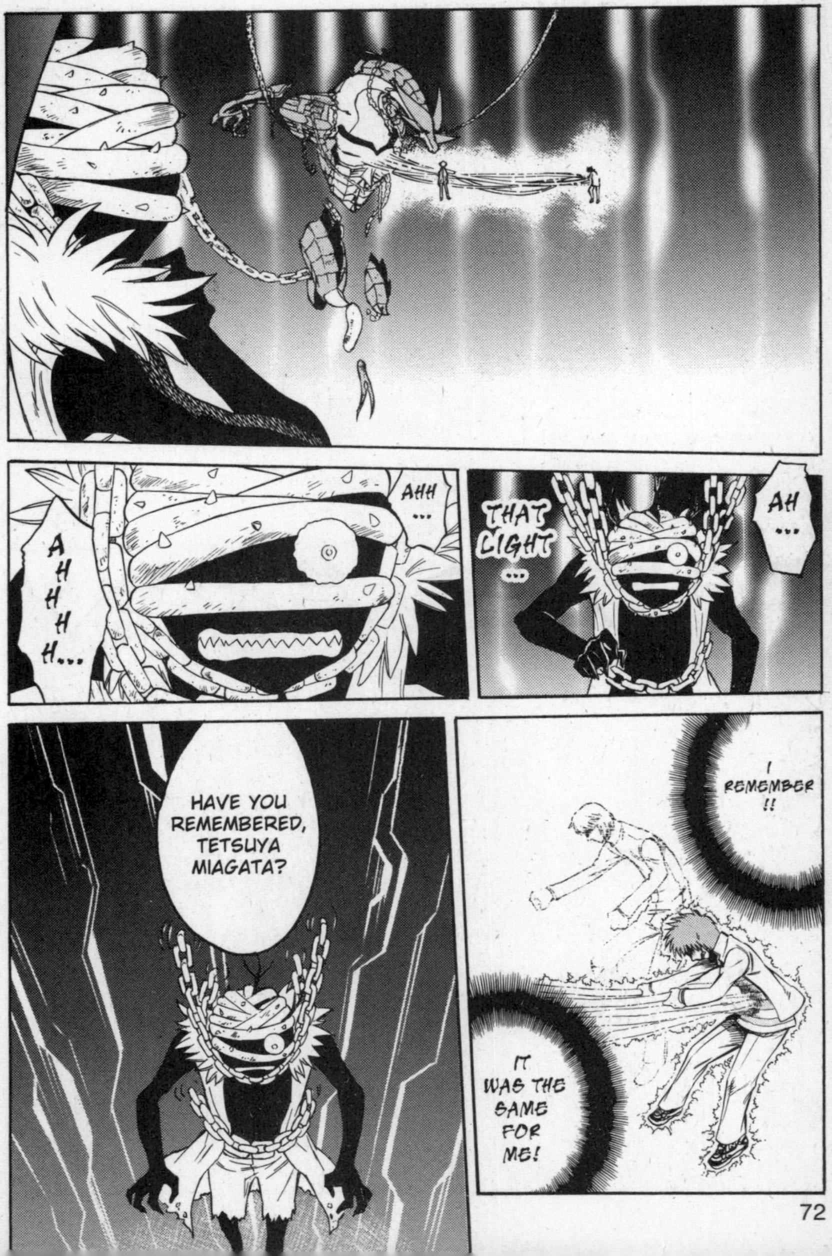
AH ...
THAT LIGHT ...
AHH ...
AHHHH...
I REMEMBER !!
IT WAS THE SAME FOR ME!
HAVE YOU REMEMBERED, TETSUYA MIAGATA?

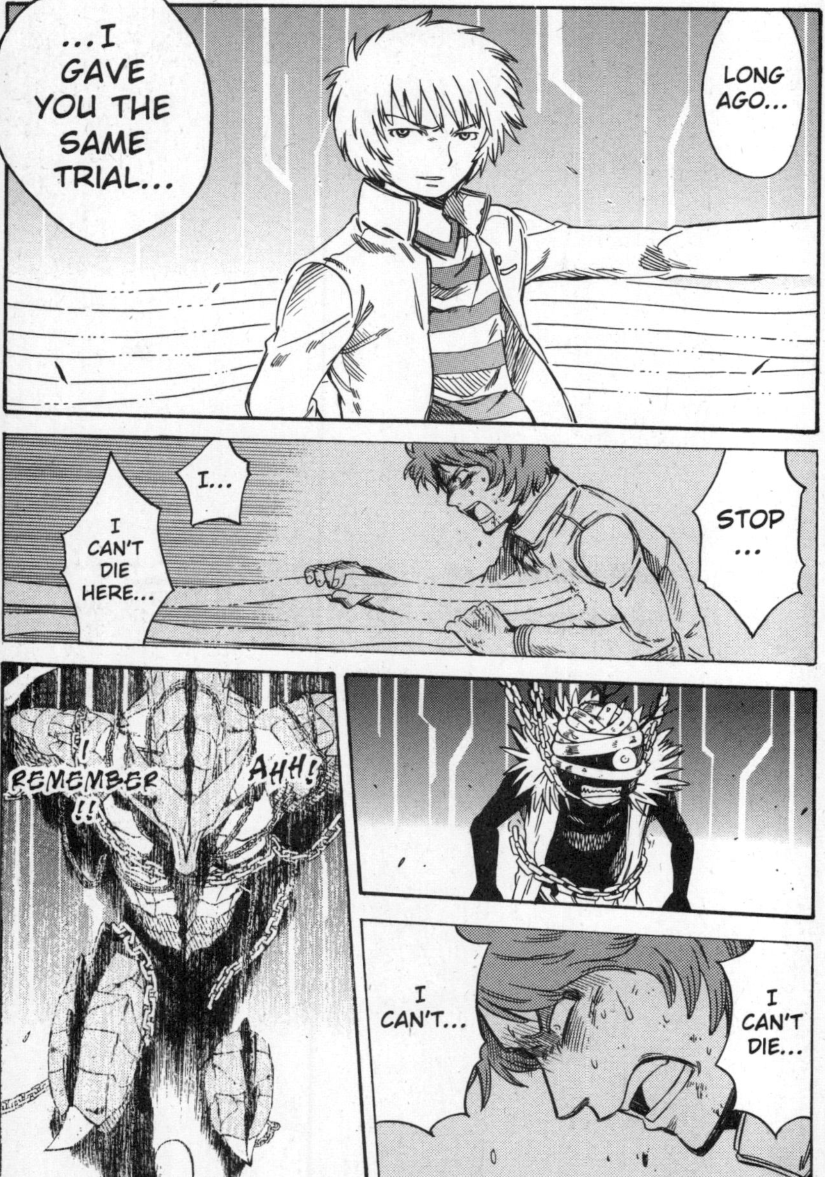

LONG AGO...
...I GAVE YOU THE SAME TRIAL...
STOP ...
I...
I CAN'T DIE HERE...
I CAN'T DIE...
I CAN'T...
AHH!
I REMEMBER!!

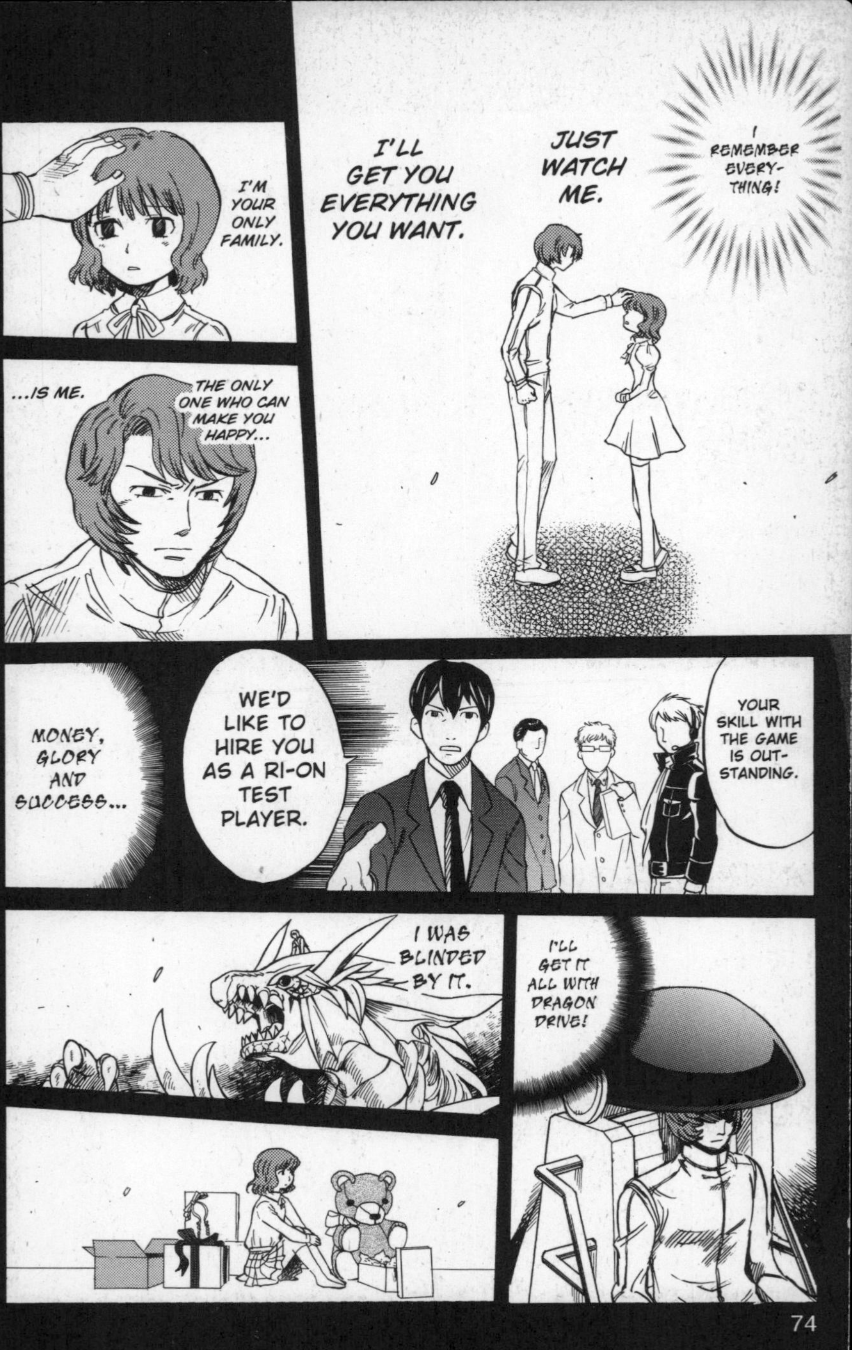
I REMEMBER EVERY-THING!
JUST WATCH ME.
I'LL GET YOU EVERYTHING YOU WANT.
I'M YOUR ONLY FAMILY.
THE ONLY ONE WHO CAN MAKE YOU HAPPY...
...IS ME.
YOUR SKILL WITH THE GAME IS OUT-STANDING.
WE'D LIKE TO HIRE YOU AS A RI-ON TEST PLAYER.
MONEY, GLORY AND SUCCESS...
I'LL GET IT ALL WITH DRAGON DRIVE!
I WAS BLINDED BY IT.

READ THIS WAY

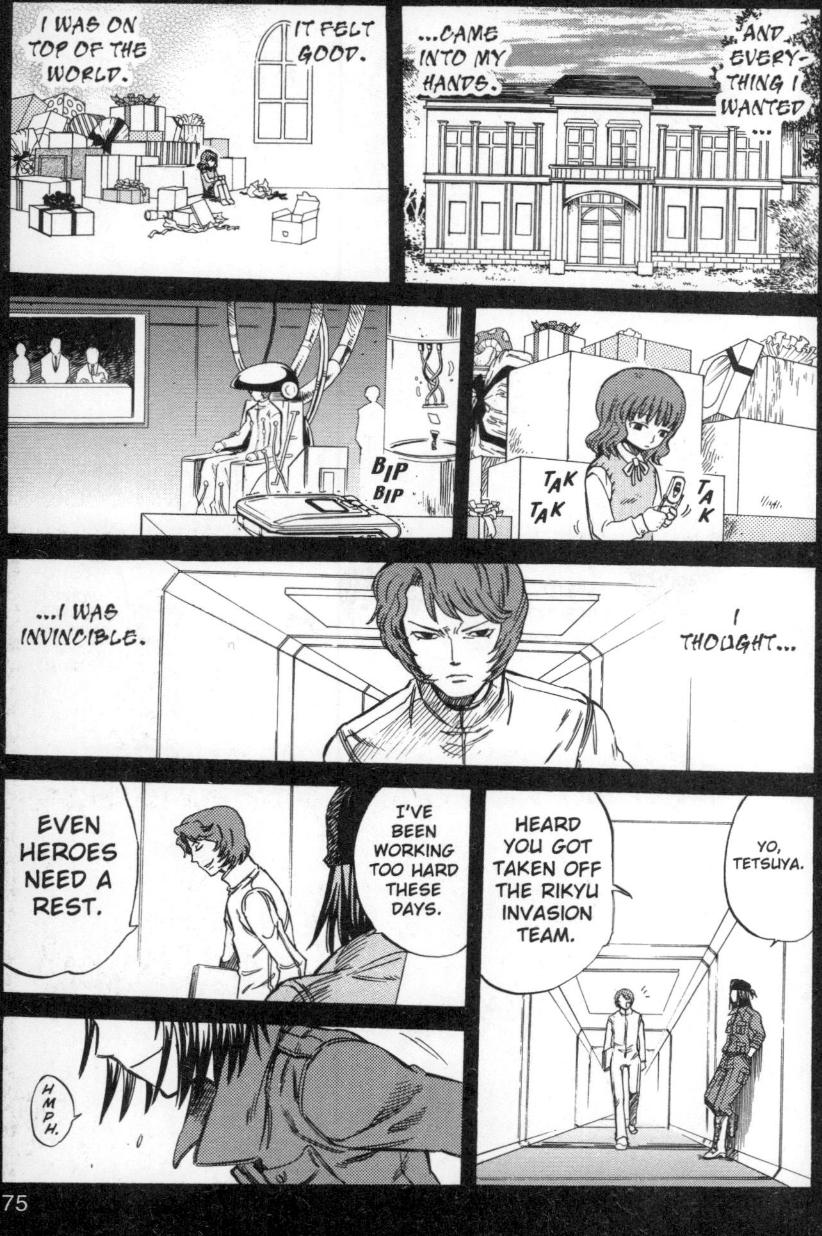
AND EVERYTHING I WANTED...
...CAME INTO MY HANDS.
IT FELT GOOD.
I WAS ON TOP OF THE WORLD.
TAK TAK
TAK TAK
BIP BIP
I THOUGHT...
...I WAS INVINCIBLE.
YO, TETSUYA.
HEARD YOU GOT TAKEN OFF THE RIKYU INVASION TEAM.
I'VE BEEN WORKING TOO HARD THESE DAYS.
EVEN HEROES NEED A REST.
HMPH.

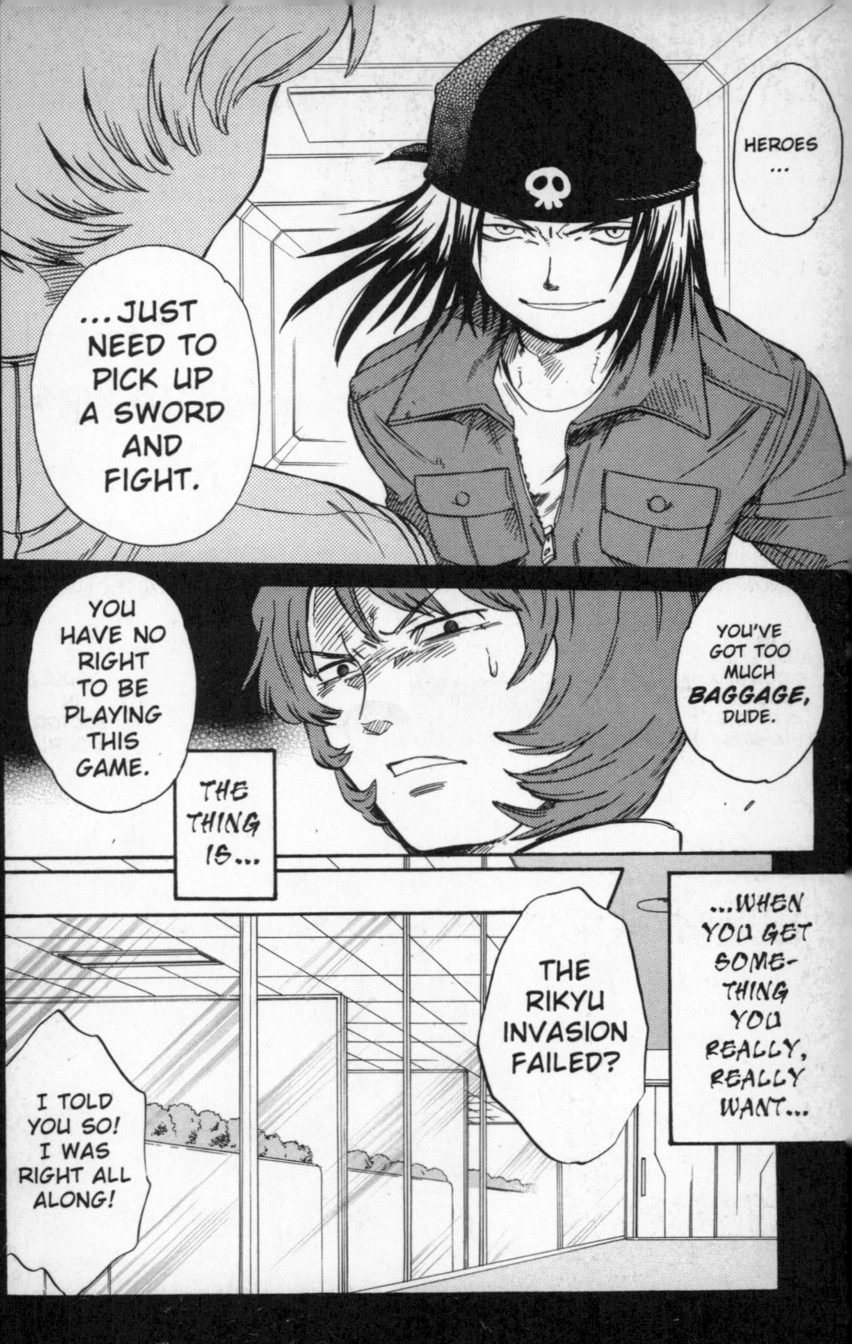
HEROES...
...JUST NEED TO PICK UP A SWORD AND FIGHT.
YOU'VE GOT TOO MUCH BAGGAGE, DUDE.
YOU HAVE NO RIGHT TO BE PLAYING THIS GAME.
THE THING IS...
...WHEN YOU GET SOME-THING YOU REALLY, REALLY WANT...
THE RIKYU INVASION FAILED?
I TOLD YOU SO! I WAS RIGHT ALL ALONG!

READ THIS WAY

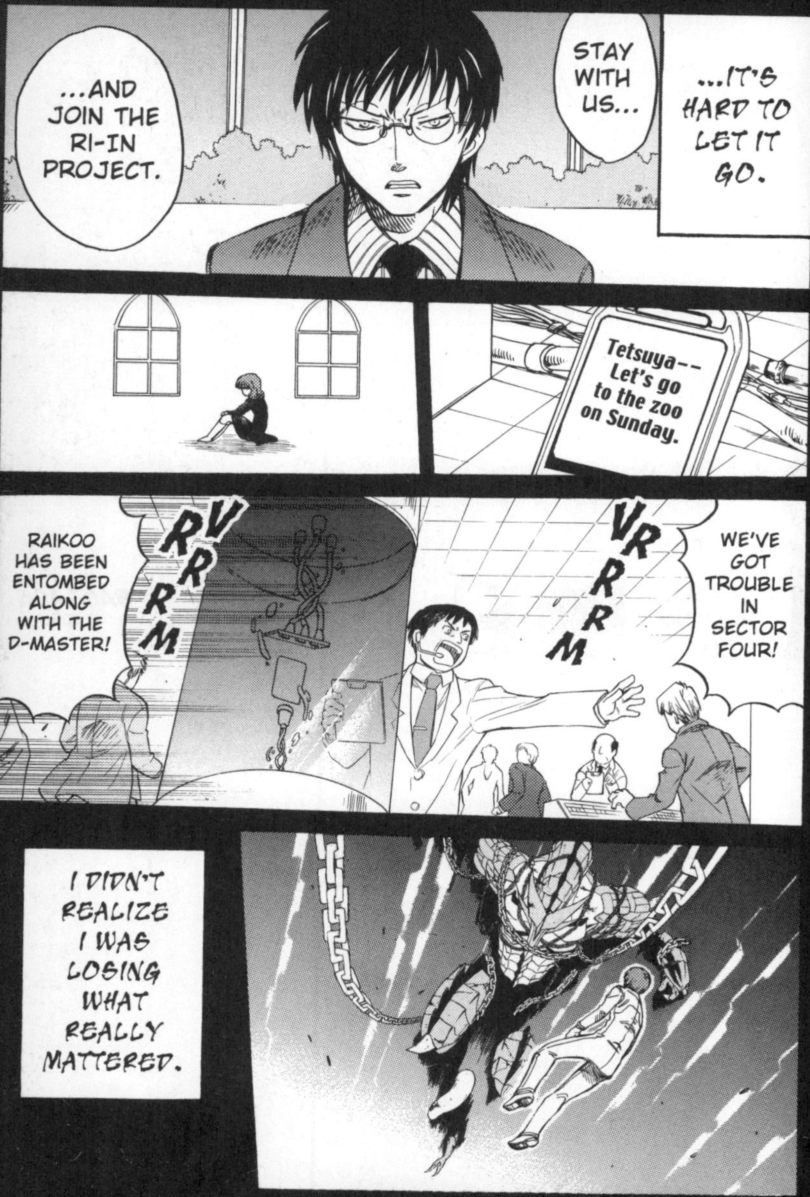

...IT'S HARD TO LET IT GO.
STAY WITH US...
...AND JOIN THE RI-IN PROJECT.
Tetsuya-- Let's go to the zoo on Sunday.
WE'VE GOT TROUBLE IN SECTOR FOUR!
VRRRRM
RVRRRM
RAIKOO HAS BEEN ENTOMBED ALONG WITH THE D-MASTER!
I DIDN'T REALIZE I WAS LOSING WHAT REALLY MATTERED.

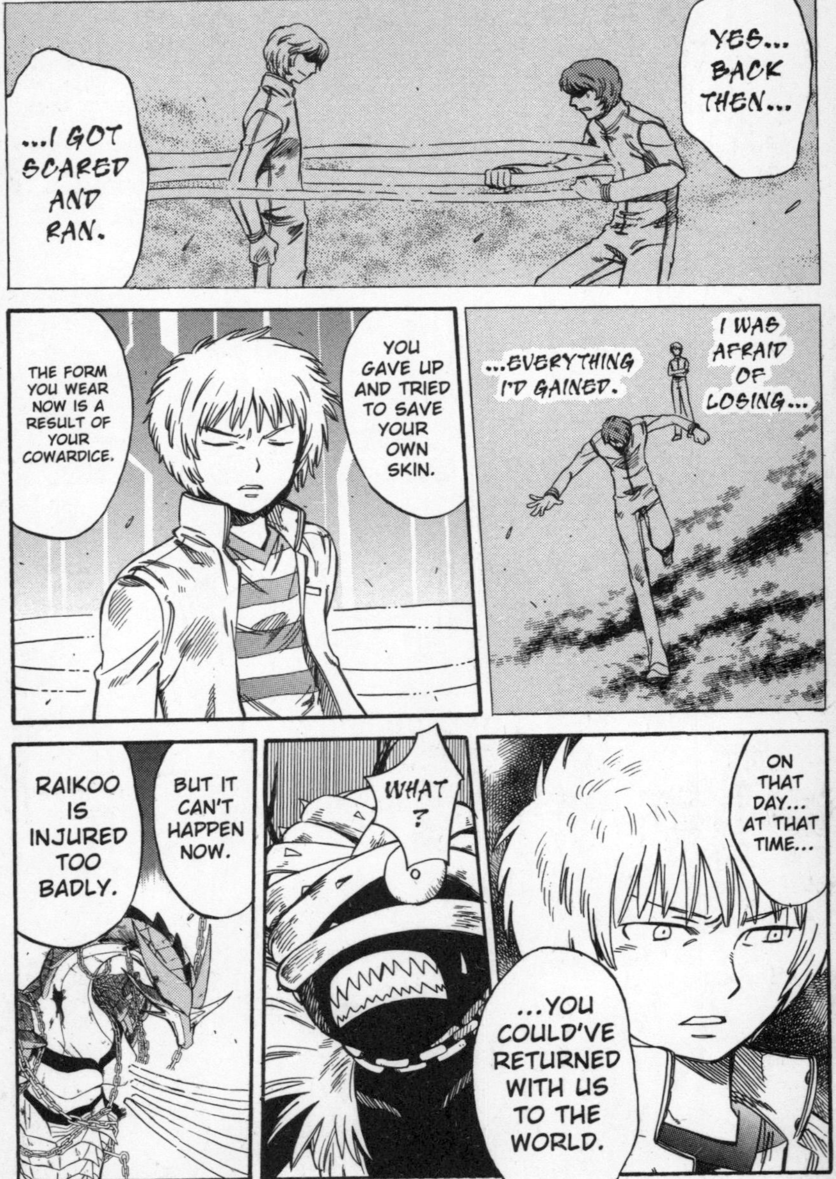
YES... BACK THEN...
...I GOT SCARED AND RAN.
I WAS AFRAID OF LOSING...
...EVERYTHING I'D GAINED.
YOU GAVE UP AND TRIED TO SAVE YOUR OWN SKIN.
THE FORM YOU WEAR NOW IS A RESULT OF YOUR COWARDICE.
ON THAT DAY... AT THAT TIME...
...YOU COULD'VE RETURNED WITH US TO THE WORLD.
WHAT?
BUT IT CAN'T HAPPEN NOW.
RAIKOO IS INJURED TOO BADLY.

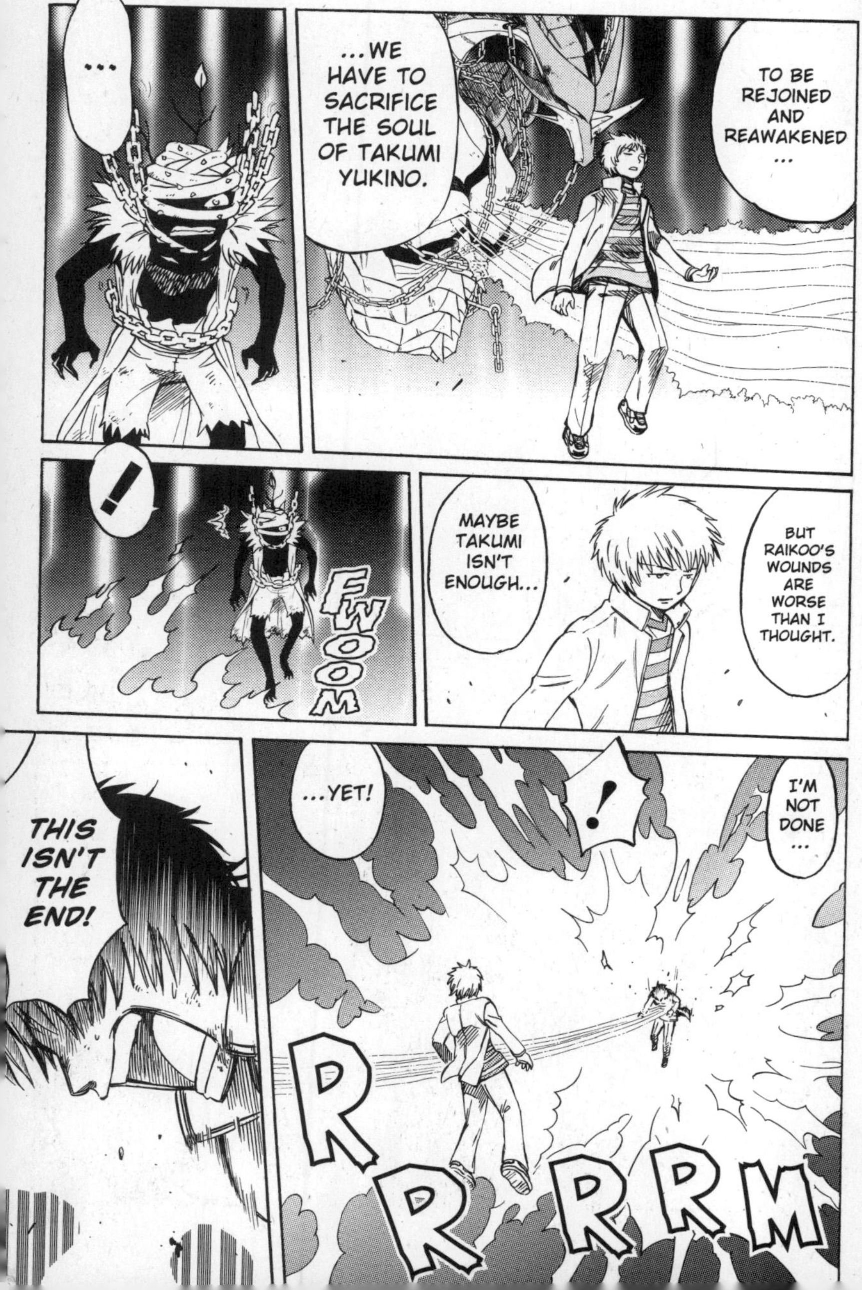
TO BE REJOINED AND REAWAKENED ...
...WE HAVE TO SACRIFICE THE SOUL OF TAKUMI YUKINO.
...
BUT RAIKOO'S WOUNDS ARE WORSE THAN I THOUGHT.
MAYBE TAKUMI ISN'T ENOUGH...
!
FWOOM
I'M NOT DONE ...
!
...YET!
RRRRM
THIS ISN'T THE END!

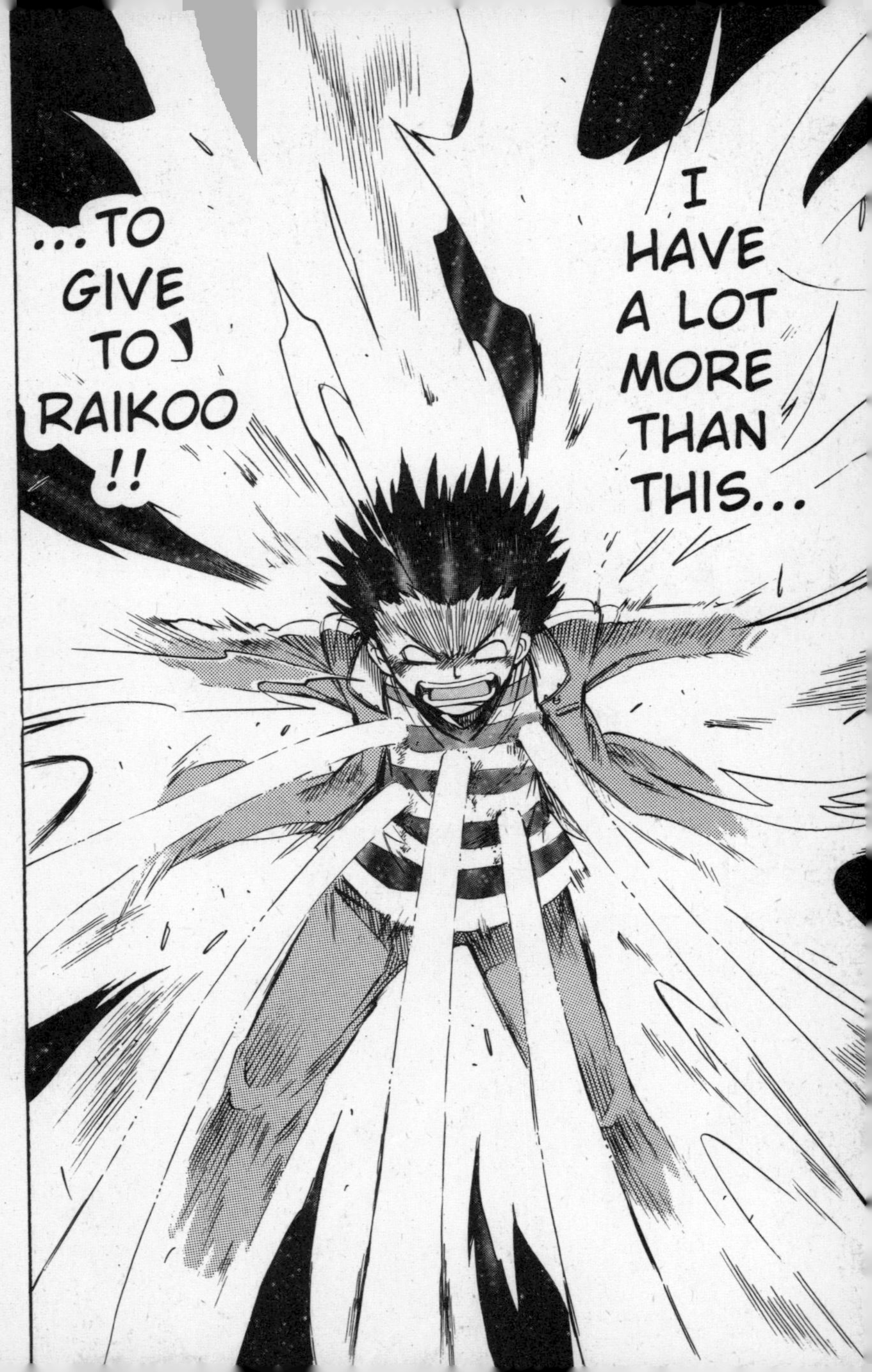
I HAVE A LOT MORE THAN THIS...
...TO GIVE TO RAIKOO!!

READ THIS WAY

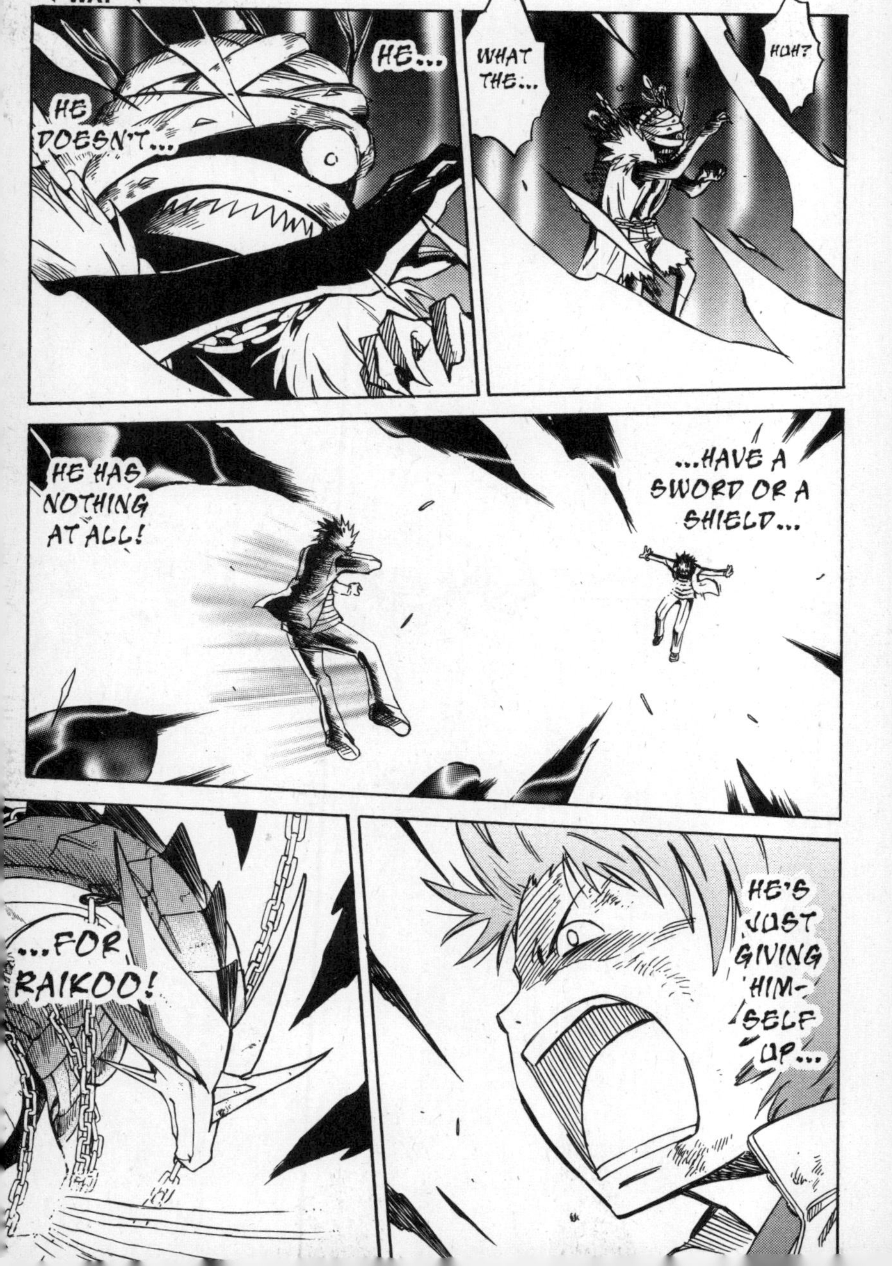
HUH?
WHAT THE...
HE...
HE DOESN'T...
...HAVE A SWORD OR A SHIELD...
HE HAS NOTHING AT ALL!
HE'S JUST GIVING HIM-SELF UP...
...FOR RAIKOO!

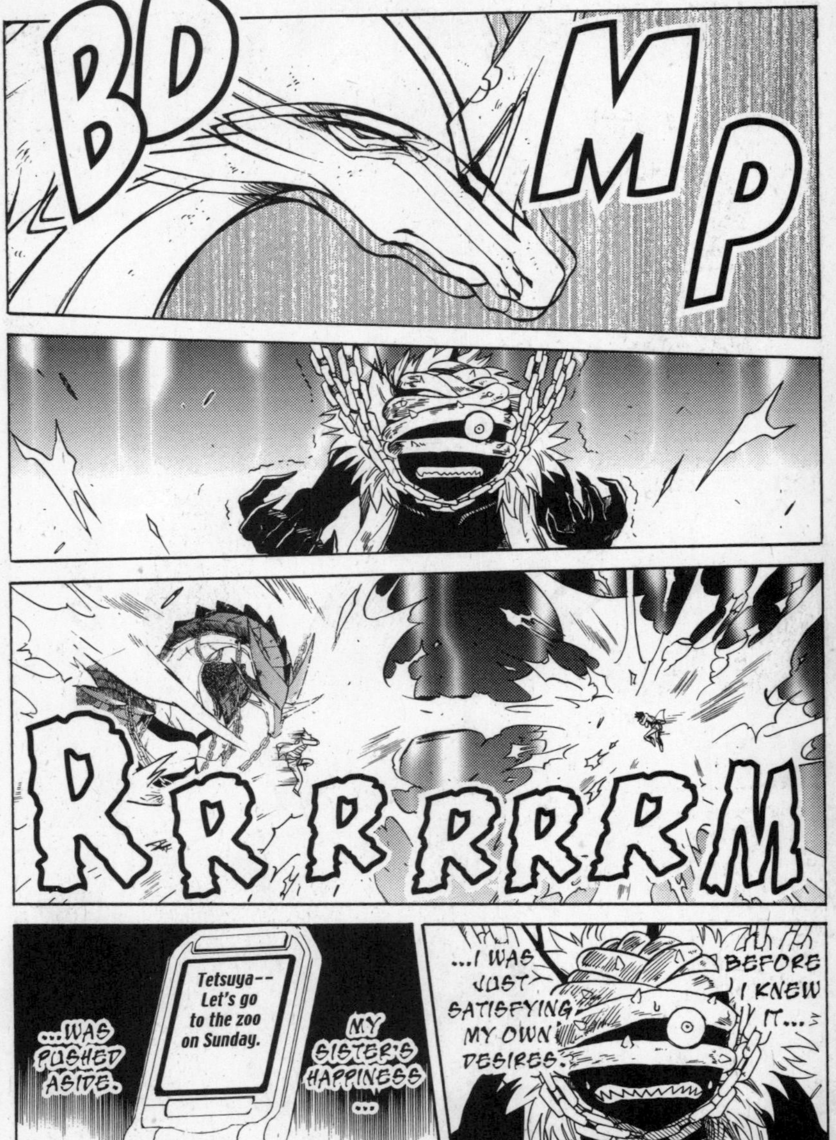
BDMP
RRRRRRM
BEFORE I KNEW IT...
...I WAS JUST SATISFYING MY OWN DESIRES.
MY SISTER'S HAPPINESS...
Tetsuya-- Let's go to the zoo on Sunday.
...WAS PUSHED ASIDE.

READ THIS WAY

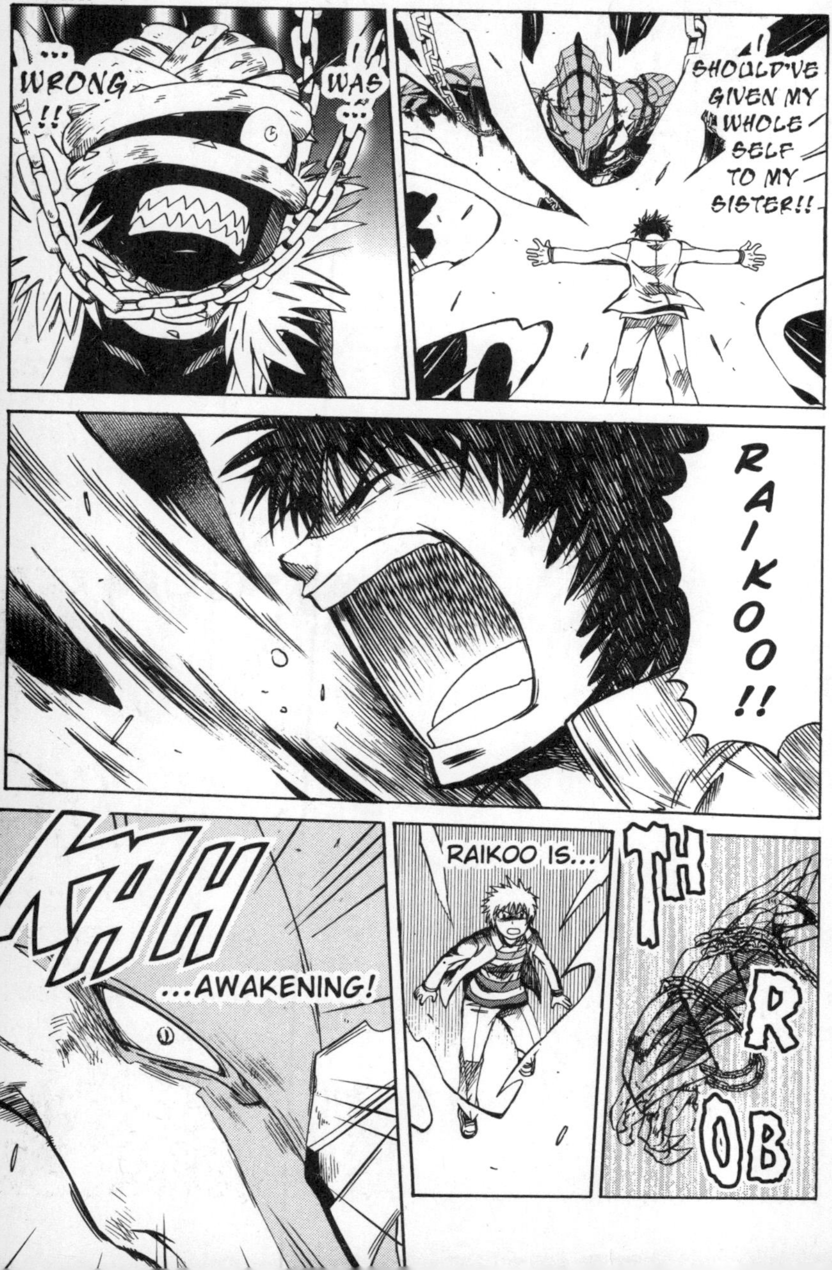

I SHOULD'VE GIVEN MY WHOLE SELF TO MY SISTER!!
WAS...
...WRONG!!
RAIKOO!!
THROB
RAIKOO IS...
KAH
...AWAKENING!

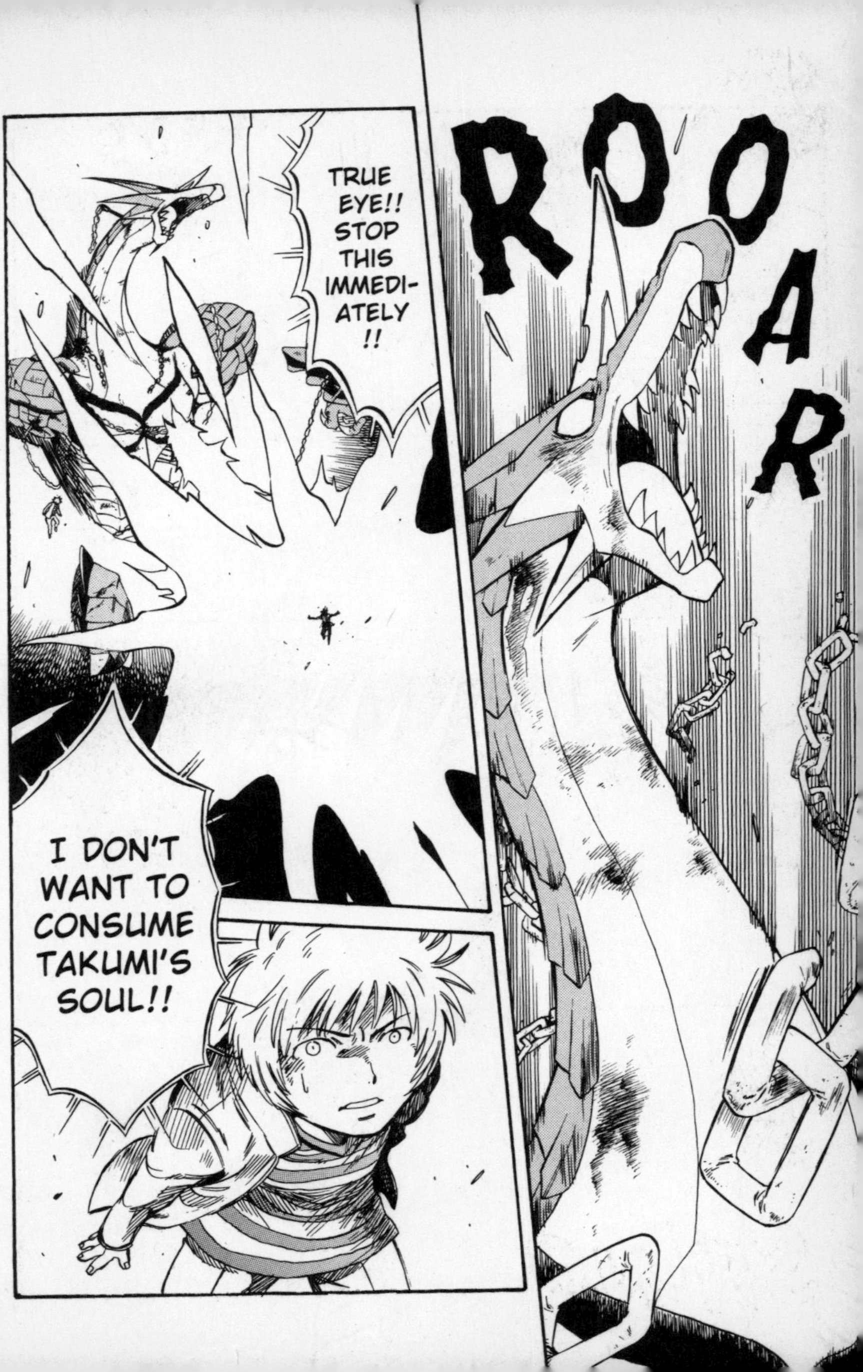
ROOOAR
TRUE EYE!! STOP THIS IMMEDIATELY!!
I DON'T WANT TO CONSUME TAKUMI'S SOUL!!

READ THIS WAY

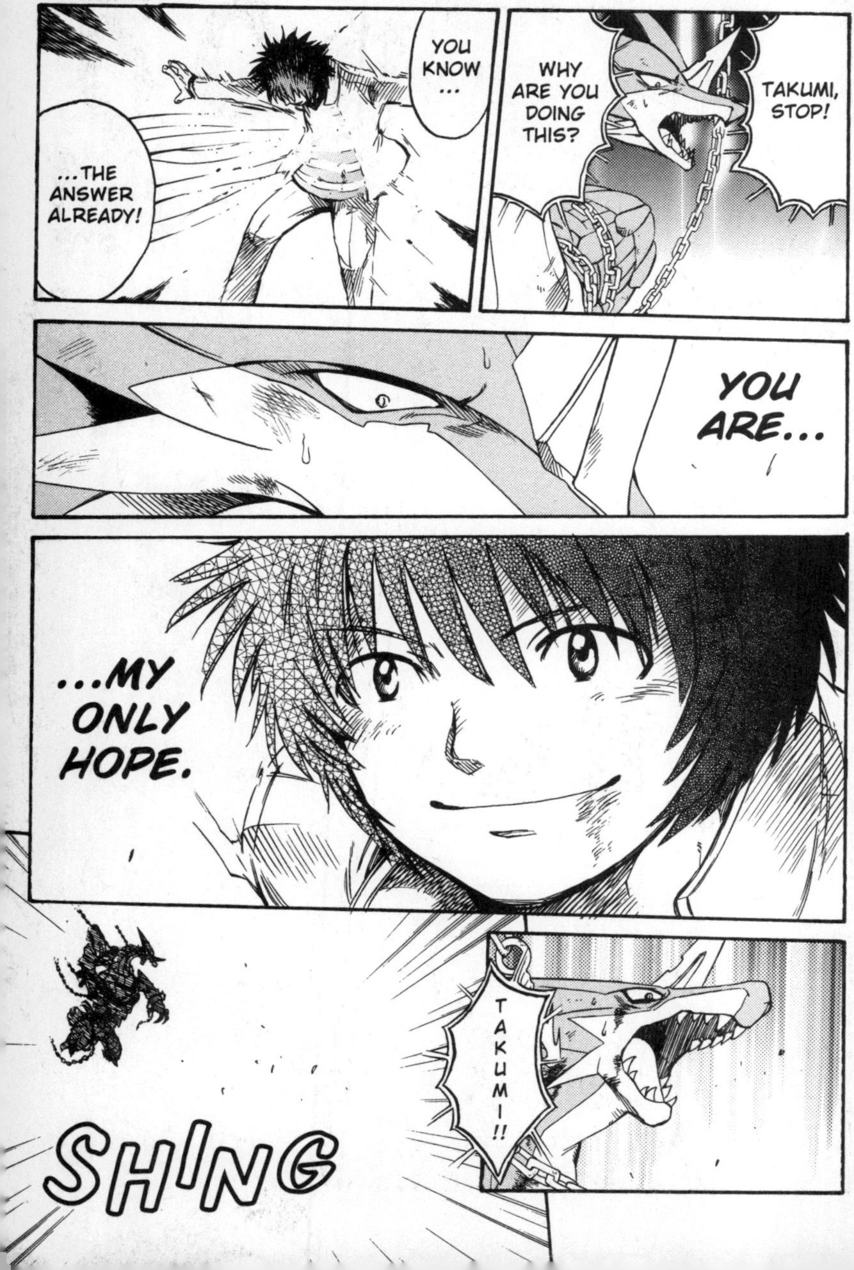
TAKUMI, STOP!
WHY ARE YOU DOING THIS?
YOU KNOW...
...THE ANSWER ALREADY!
YOU ARE...
...MY ONLY HOPE.
TAKUMI!!
SHING

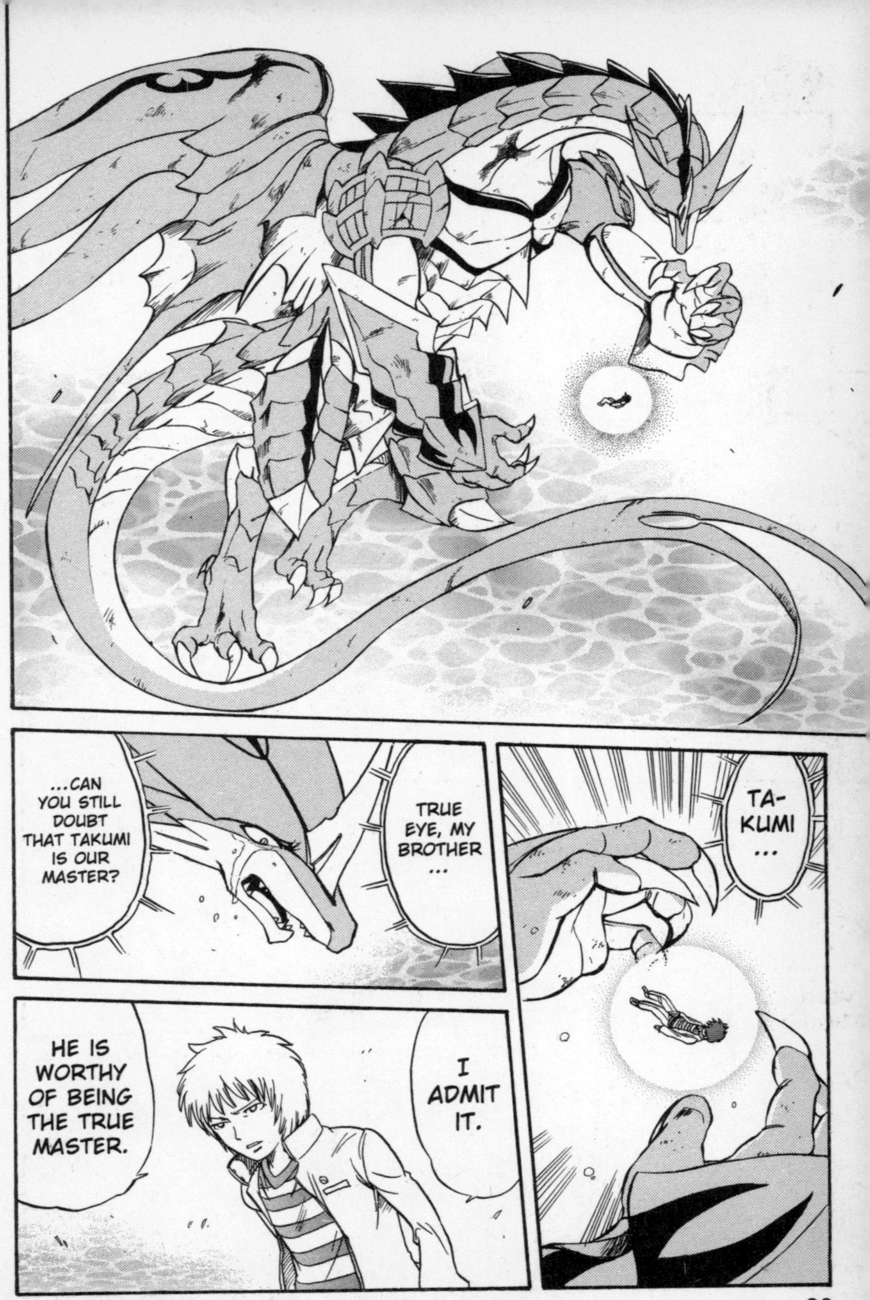
TA-KUMI ...
TRUE EYE, MY BROTHER ...
...CAN YOU STILL DOUBT THAT TAKUMI IS OUR MASTER?
I ADMIT IT.
HE IS WORTHY OF BEING THE TRUE MASTER.

READ THIS WAY

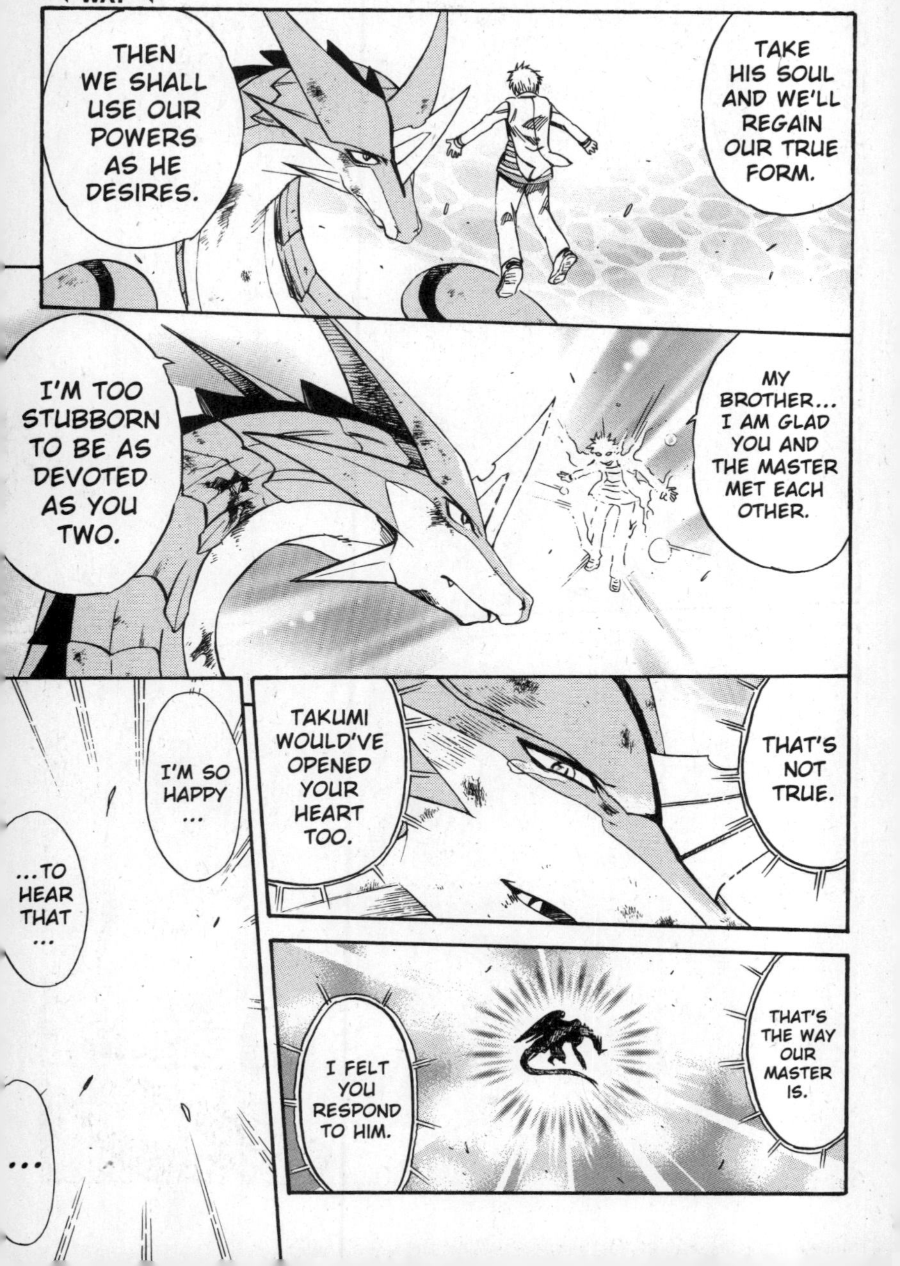

TAKE HIS SOUL AND WE'LL REGAIN OUR TRUE FORM.
THEN WE SHALL USE OUR POWERS AS HE DESIRES.
MY BROTHER... I AM GLAD YOU AND THE MASTER MET EACH OTHER.
I'M TOO STUBBORN TO BE AS DEVOTED AS YOU TWO.
THAT'S NOT TRUE.
TAKUMI WOULD'VE OPENED YOUR HEART TOO.
THAT'S THE WAY OUR MASTER IS.
I FELT YOU RESPOND TO HIM.
I'M SO HAPPY ...
...TO HEAR THAT ...
...

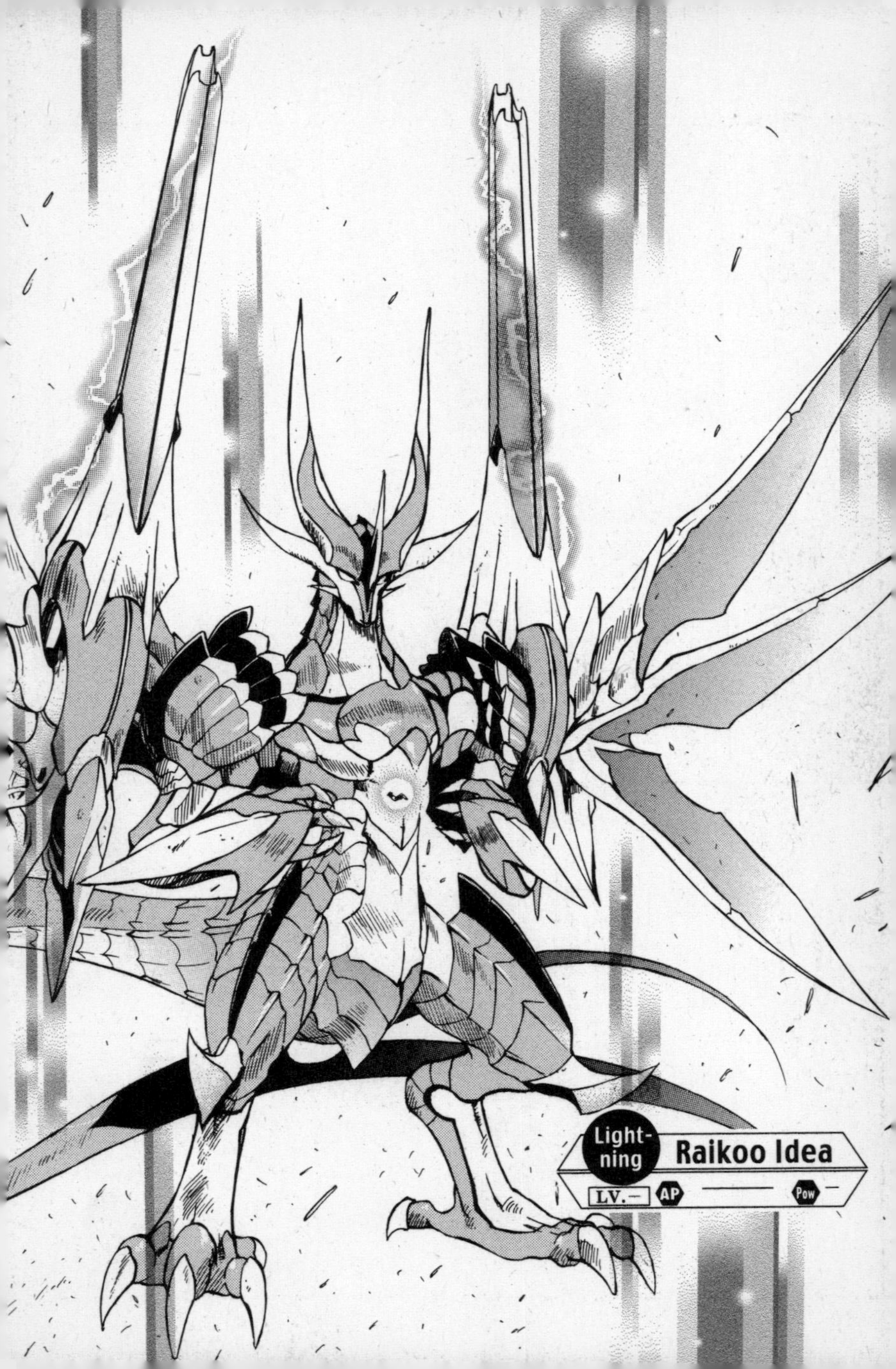
Light-ning
Raikoo Idea
LV. –
AP –
Pow –

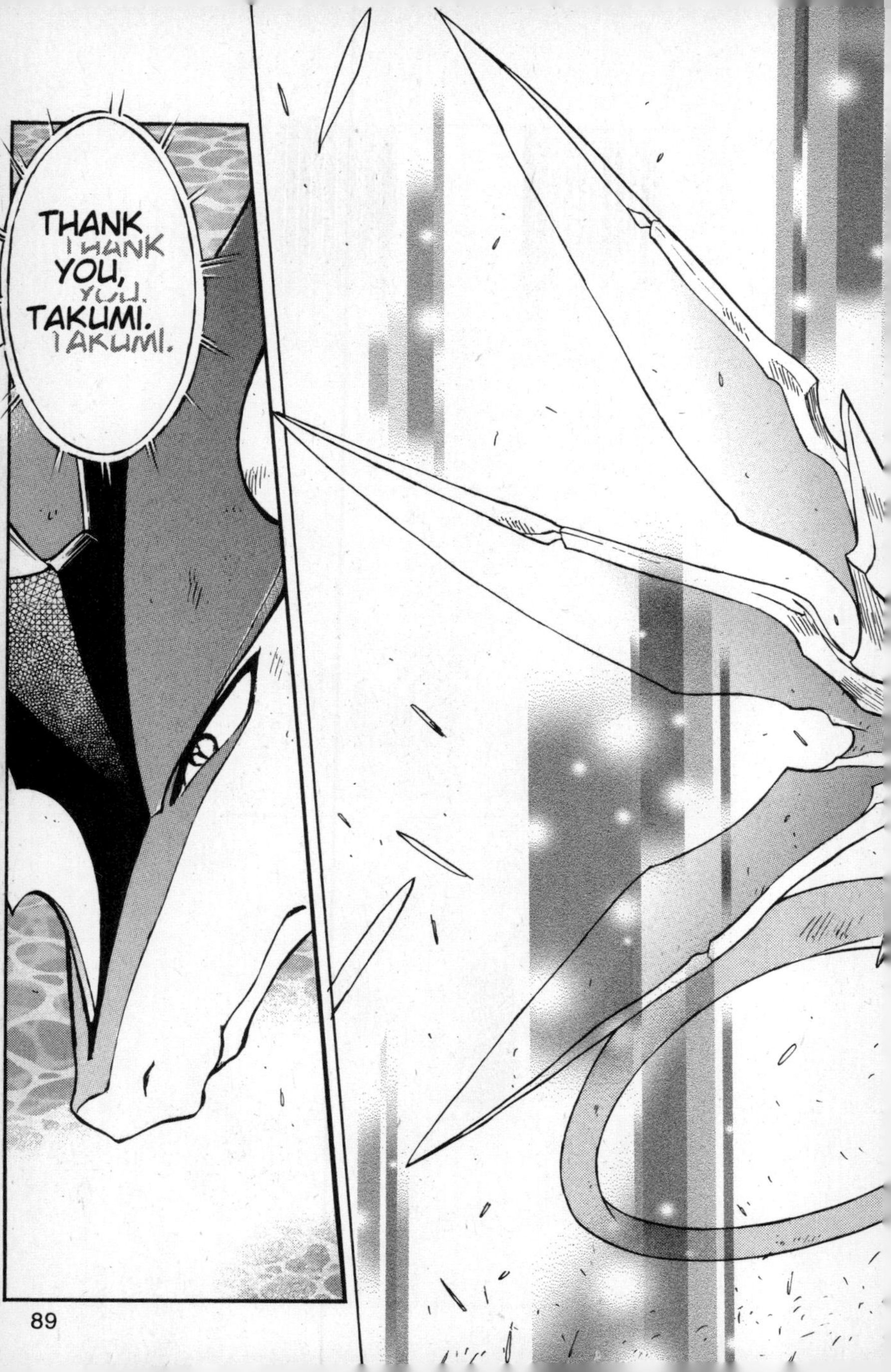
THANK YOU, TAKUMI.

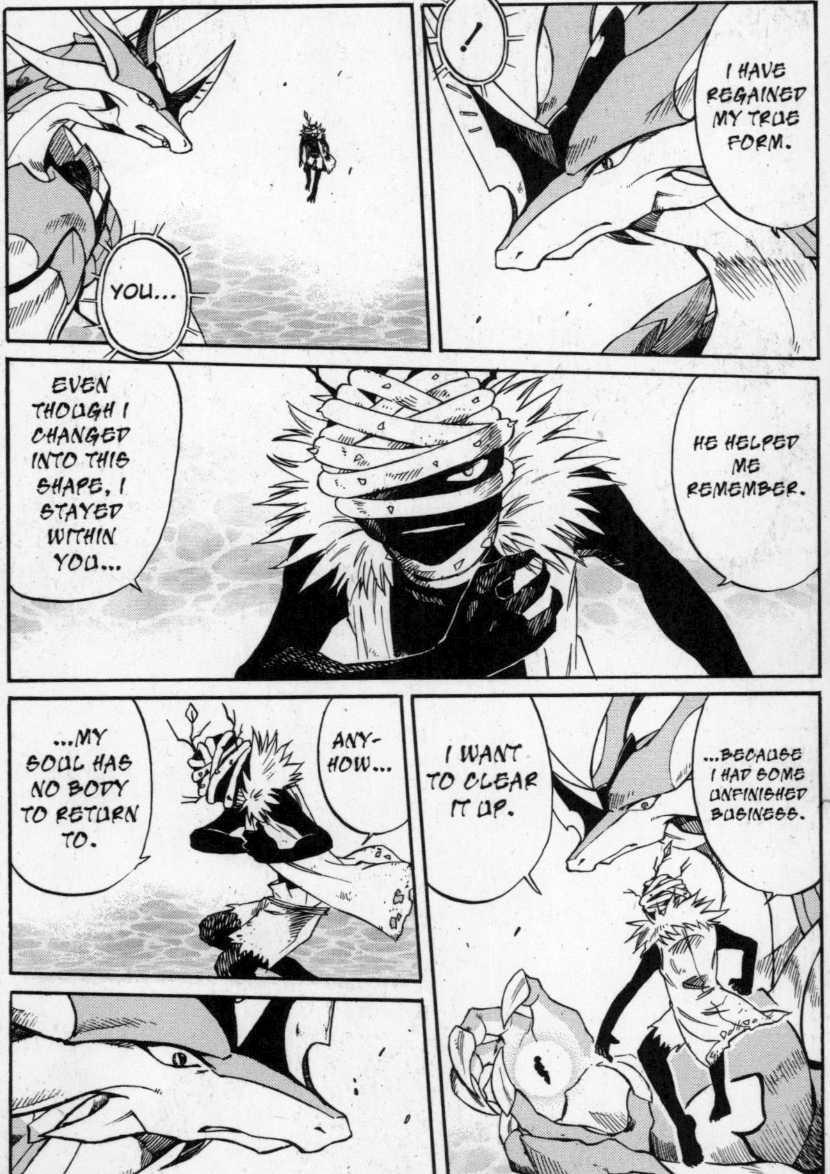
!
I HAVE REGAINED MY TRUE FORM.
YOU...
HE HELPED ME REMEMBER.
EVEN THOUGH I CHANGED INTO THIS SHAPE, I STAYED WITHIN YOU...
...BECAUSE I HAD SOME UNFINISHED BUSINESS.
I WANT TO CLEAR IT UP.
ANY-HOW...
...MY SOUL HAS NO BODY TO RETURN TO.

READ THIS WAY

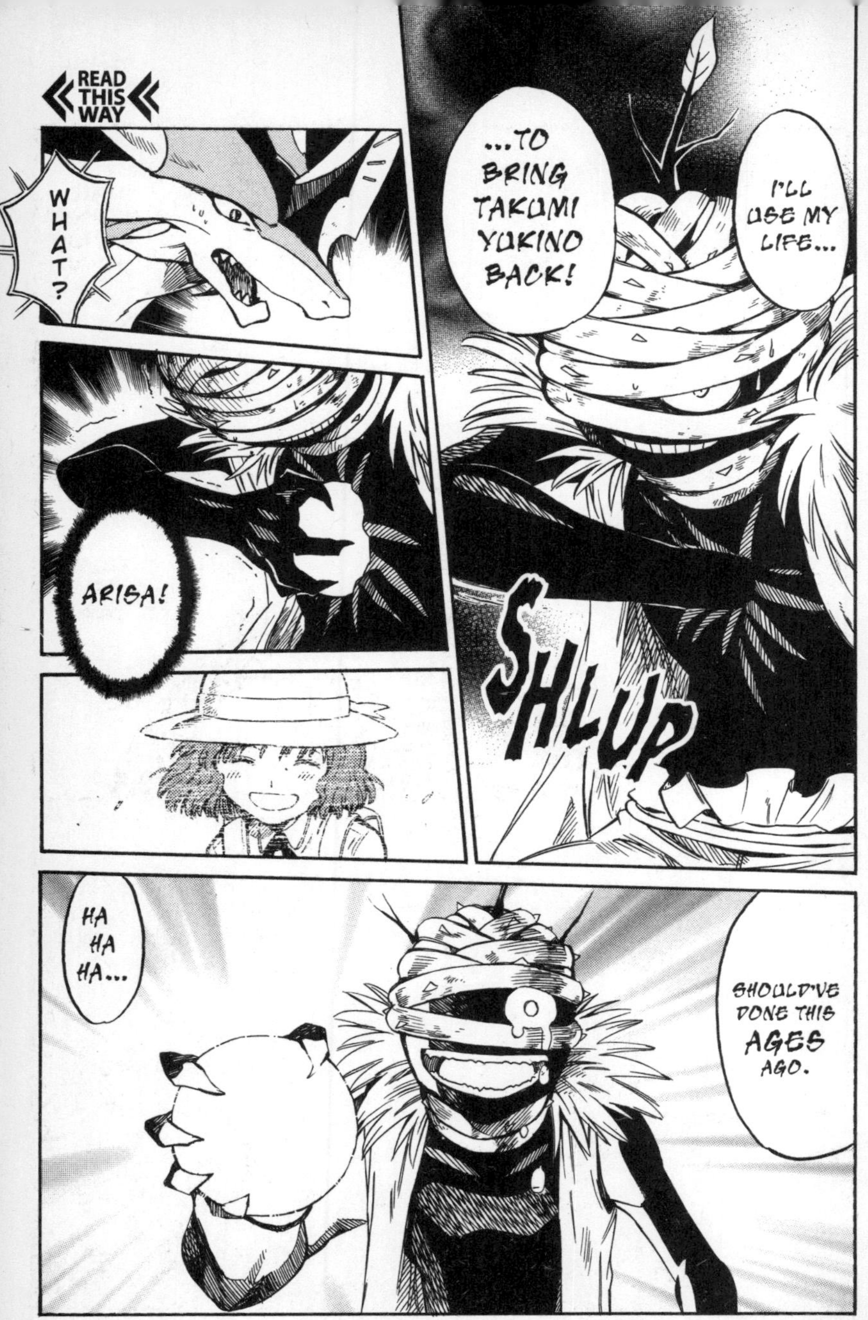
I'LL USE MY LIFE...
...TO BRING TAKUMI YUKINO BACK!
SHLUP
WHAT?
ARISA!
SHOULD'VE DONE THIS AGES AGO.
HA HA HA...

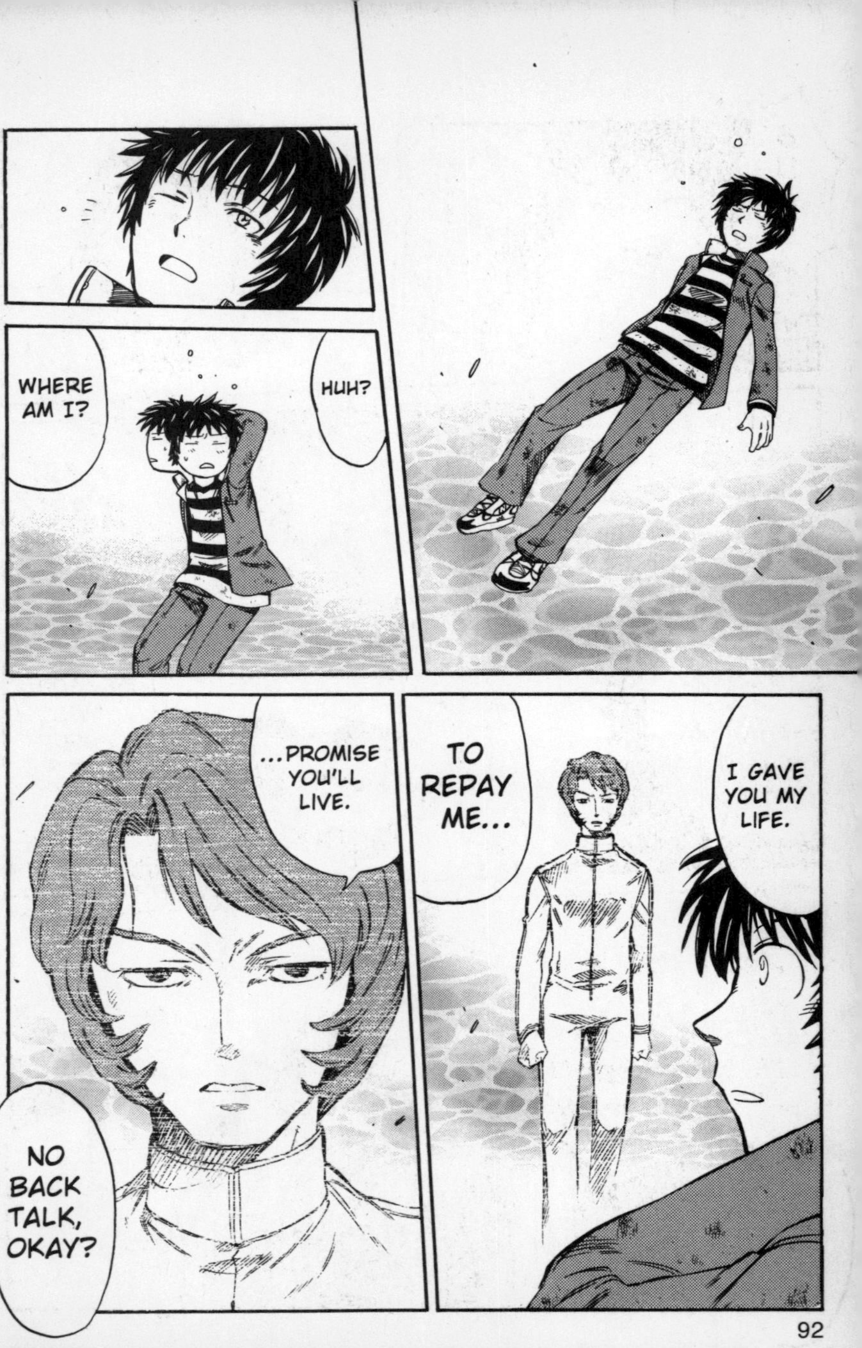
HUH?
WHERE AM I?
I GAVE YOU MY LIFE.
TO REPAY ME...
...PROMISE YOU'LL LIVE.
NO BACK TALK, OKAY?

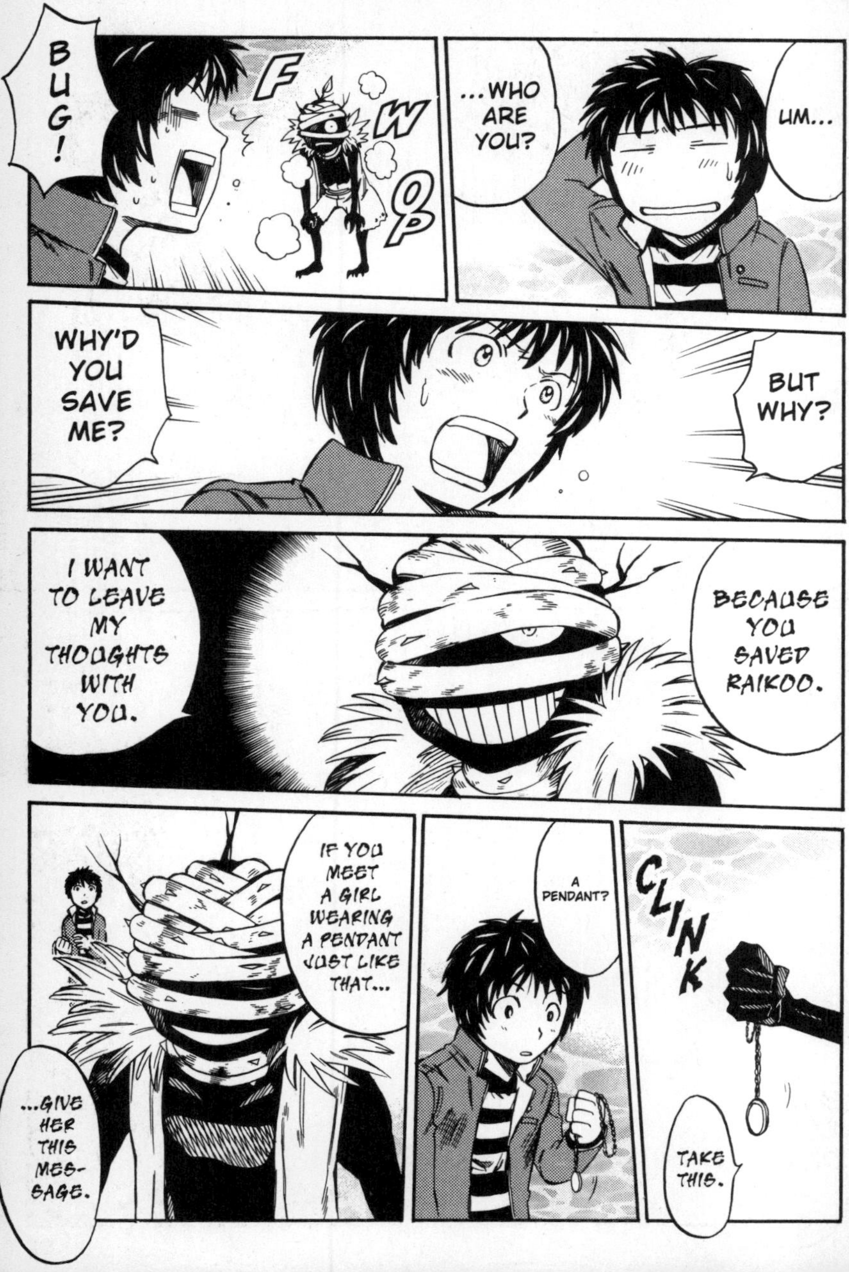
UM...
...WHO ARE YOU?
F WOP
BUG!
BUT WHY?
WHY'D YOU SAVE ME?
BECAUSE YOU SAVED RAIKOO.
I WANT TO LEAVE MY THOUGHTS WITH YOU.
CLINK
TAKE THIS.
A PENDANT?
IF YOU MEET A GIRL WEARING A PENDANT JUST LIKE THAT...
...GIVE HER THIS MES-SAGE.

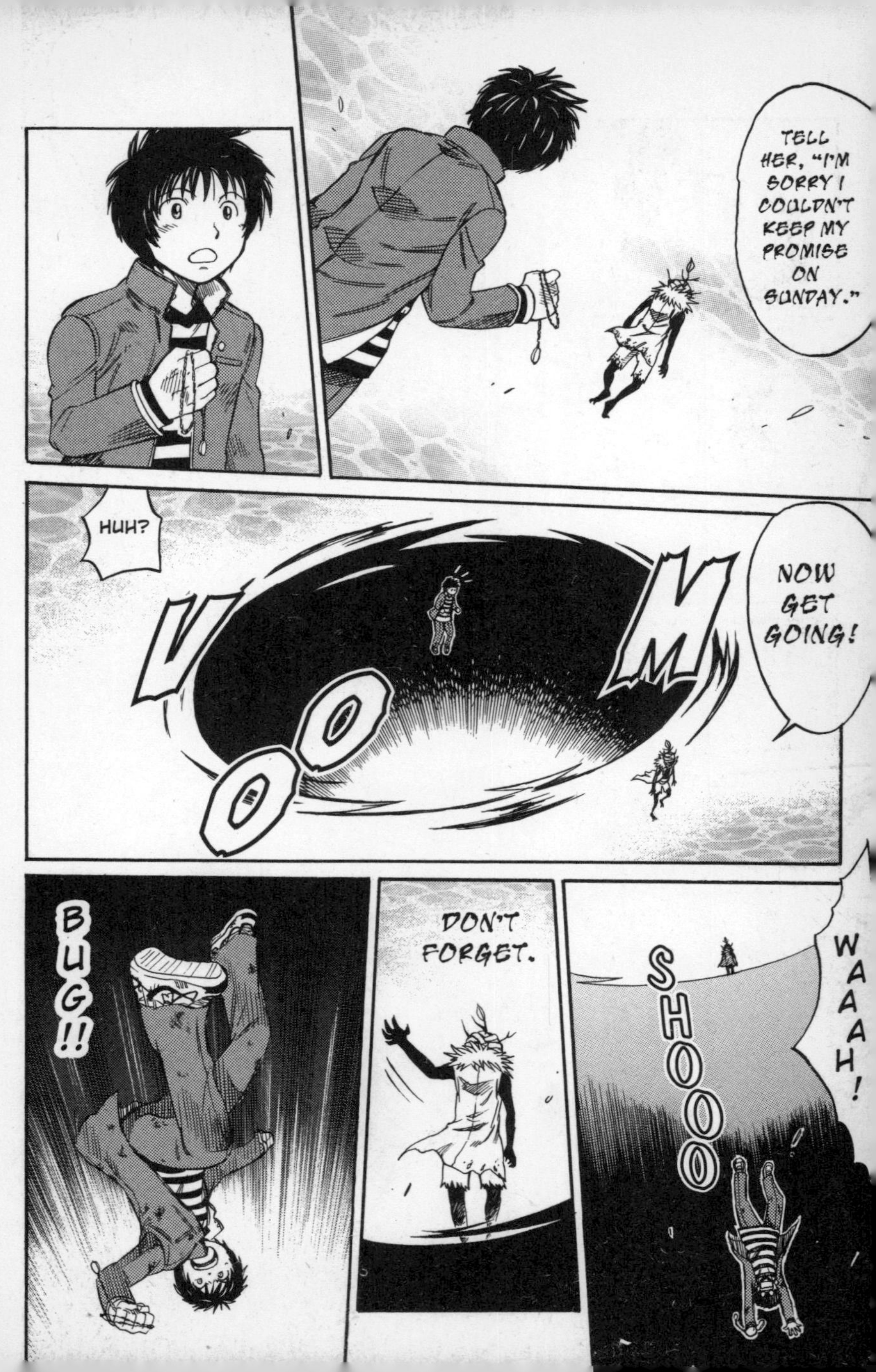
TELL HER, "I'M SORRY I COULDN'T KEEP MY PROMISE ON SUNDAY."
NOW GET GOING!
VOOOOM
HUH?
WAAAH!
SHOOOO
DON'T FORGET.
BUG!!

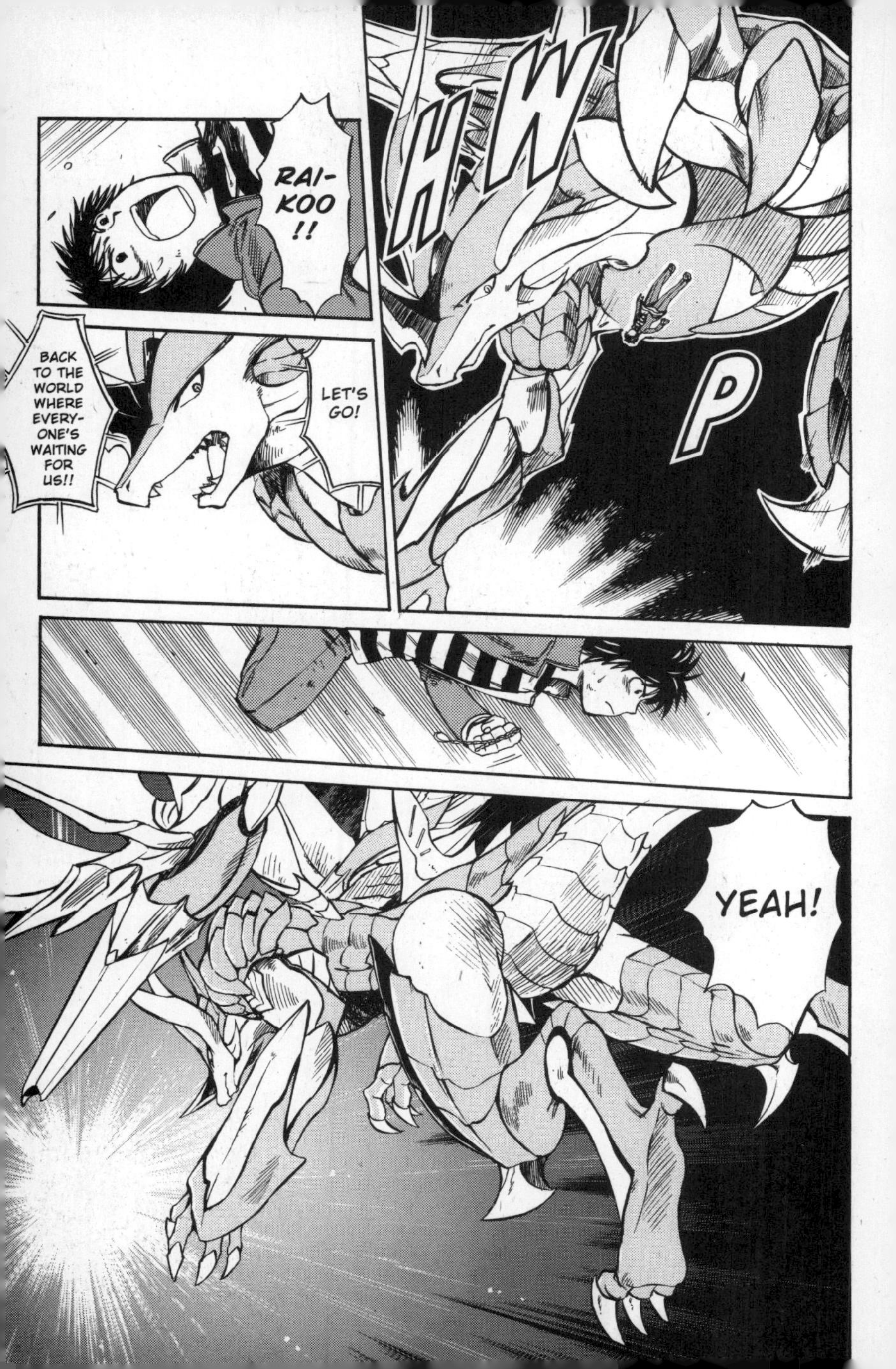
RAI-KOO!!
LET'S GO!
BACK TO THE WORLD WHERE EVERYONE'S WAITING FOR US!!
YEAH!

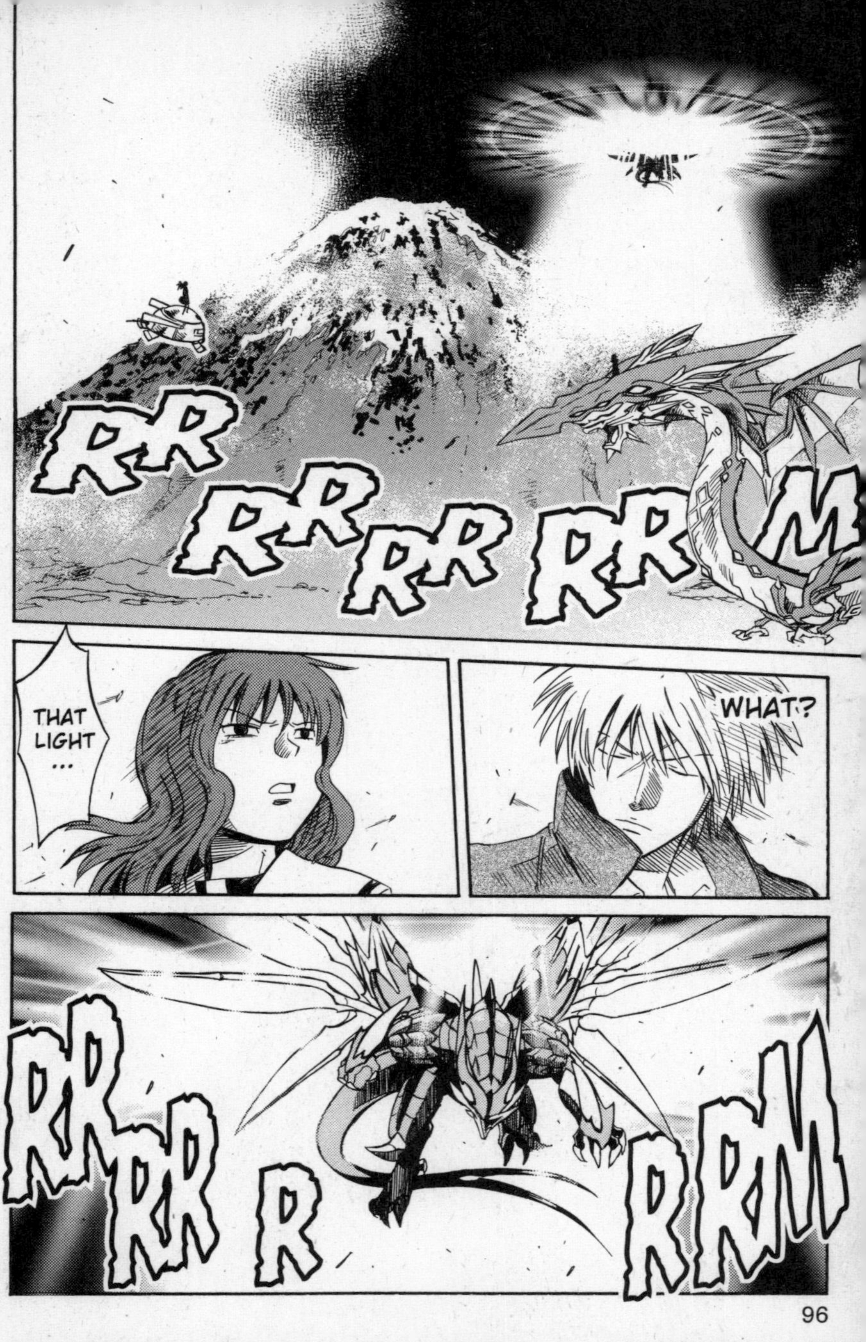
RRRRRRRRM
WHAT?
THAT LIGHT ...
RRRRRRRM

READ THIS WAY

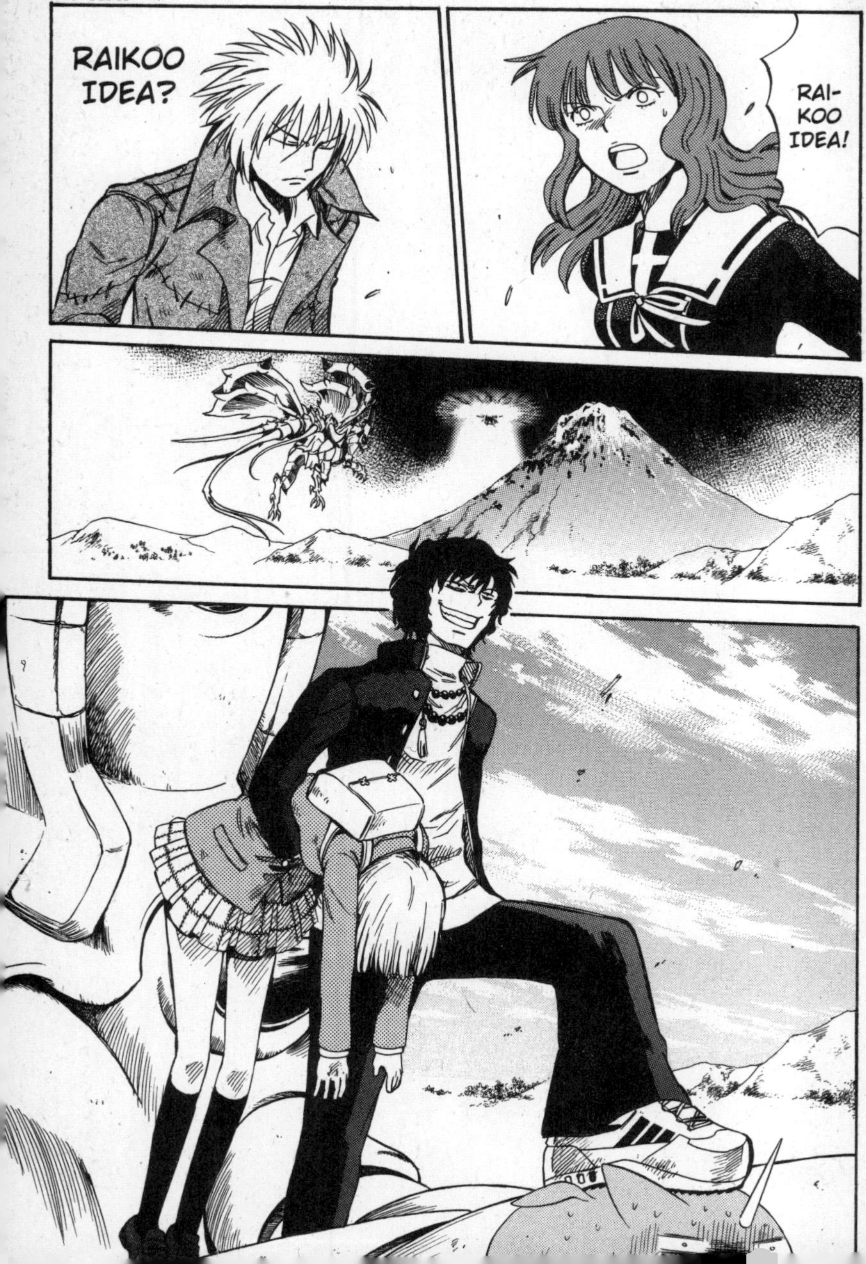
RAI-KOO IDEA!
RAIKOO IDEA?

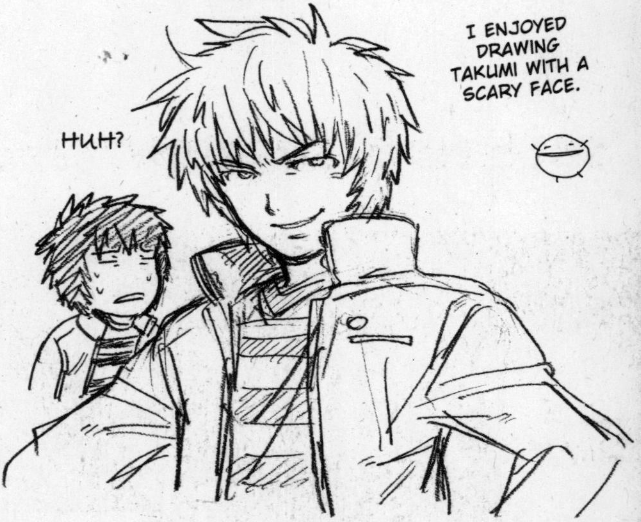
I ENJOYED DRAWING TAKUMI WITH A SCARY FACE.
HUH?

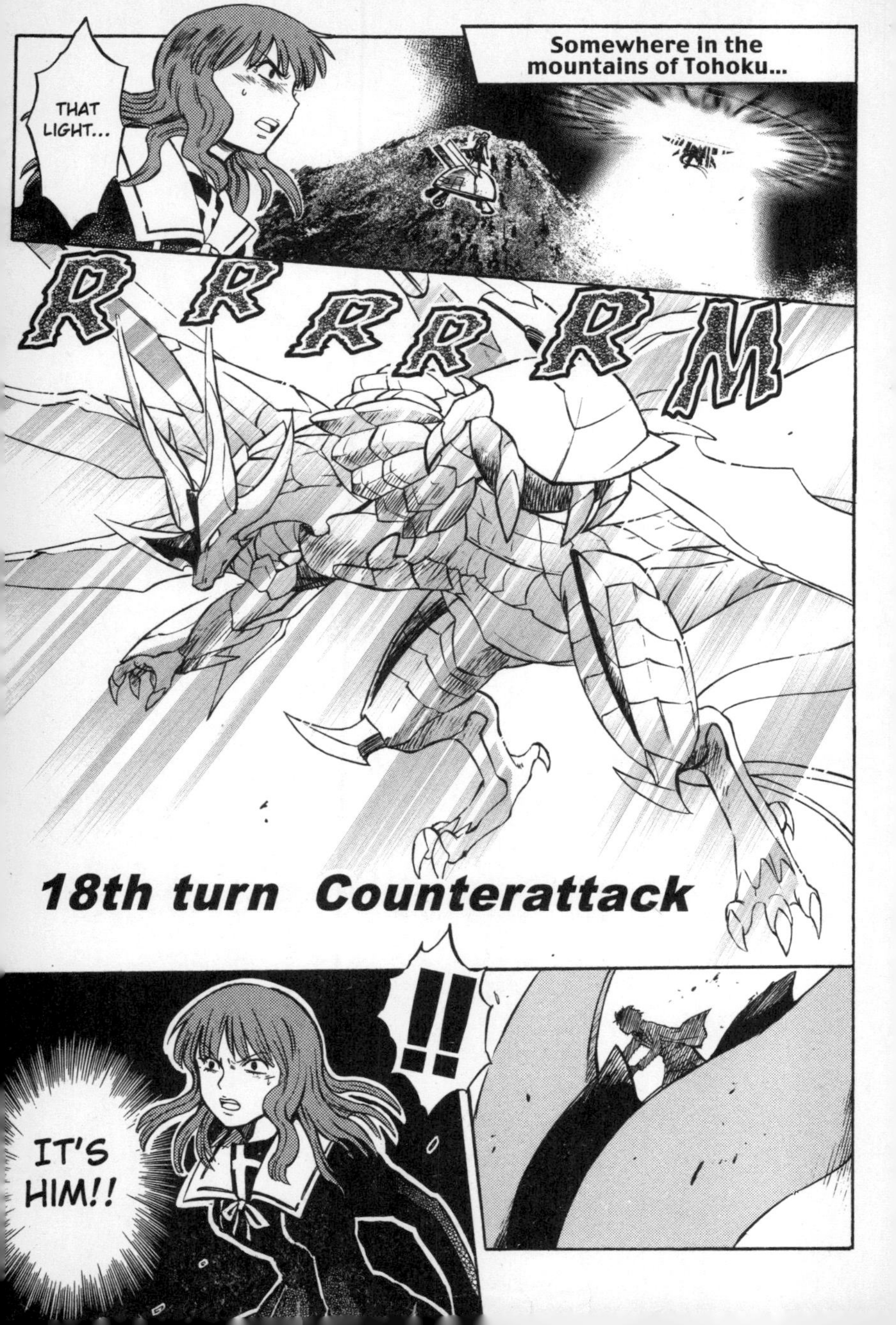
Somewhere in the mountains of Tohoku...
THAT LIGHT...
RRRRRM
18th turn Counterattack
!!
IT'S HIM!!

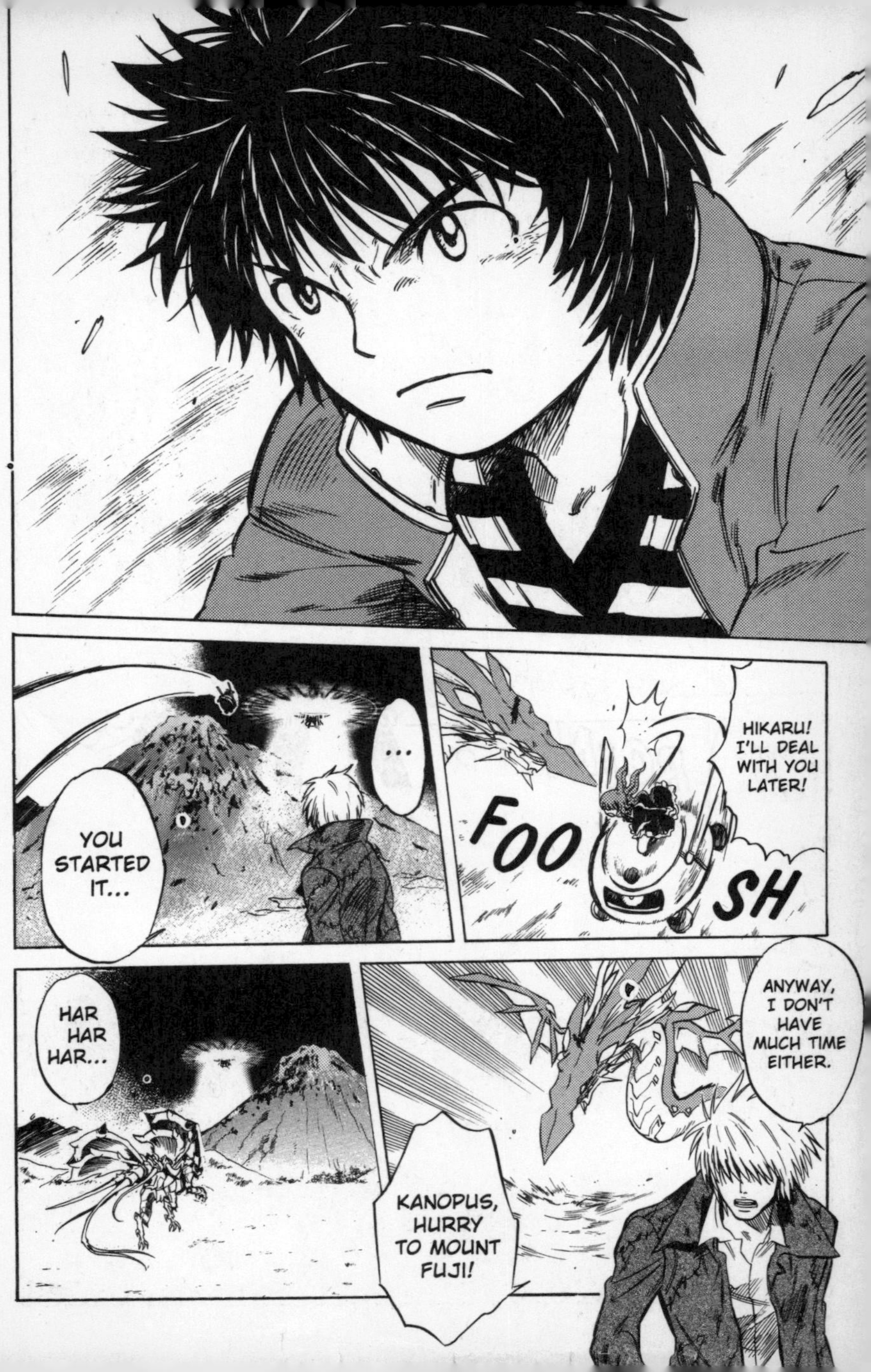
HIKARU! I'LL DEAL WITH YOU LATER!
FOOSH
...
YOU STARTED IT...
ANYWAY, I DON'T HAVE MUCH TIME EITHER.
KANOPUS, HURRY TO MOUNT FUJI!
HAR HAR HAR...

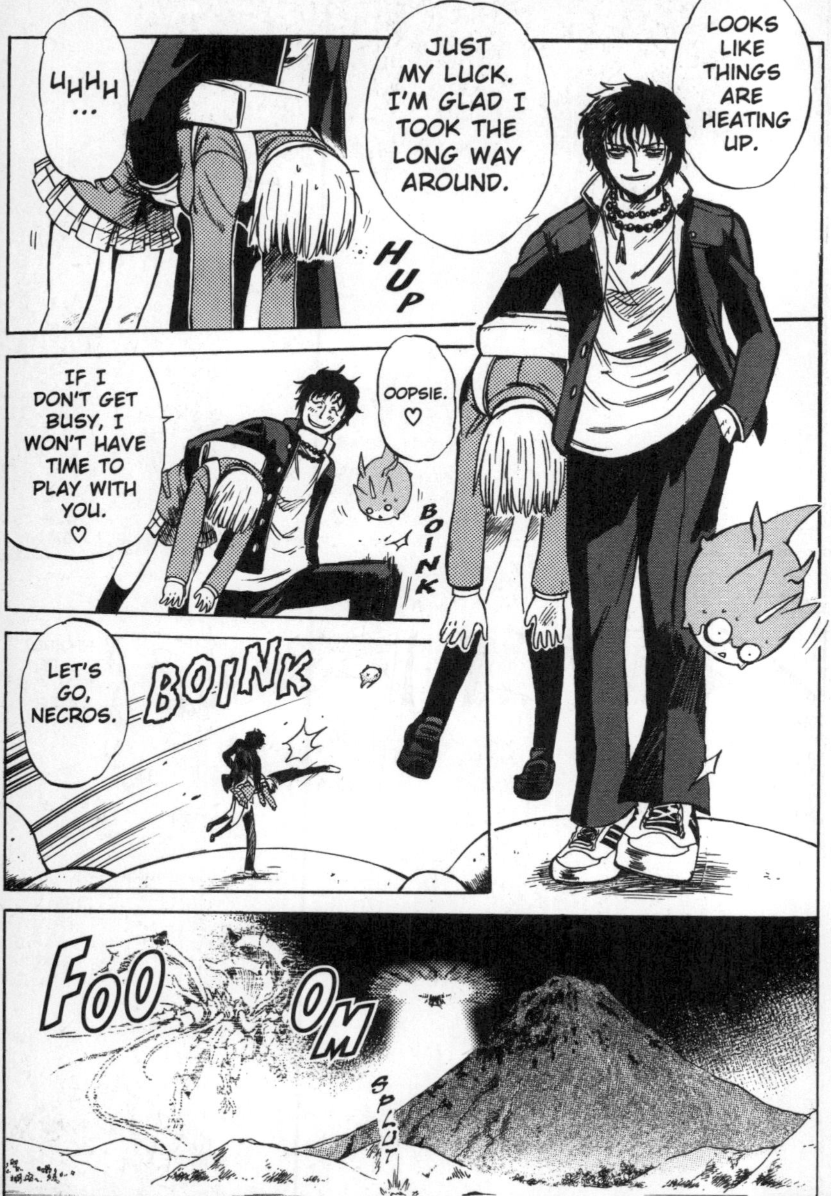
LOOKS LIKE THINGS ARE HEATING UP.
JUST MY LUCK. I'M GLAD I TOOK THE LONG WAY AROUND.
UHHH...
HUP
OOPSIE. ♡
BOINK
IF I DON'T GET BUSY, I WON'T HAVE TIME TO PLAY WITH YOU. ♡
BOINK
LET'S GO, NECROS.
FOO OM
SPLUT

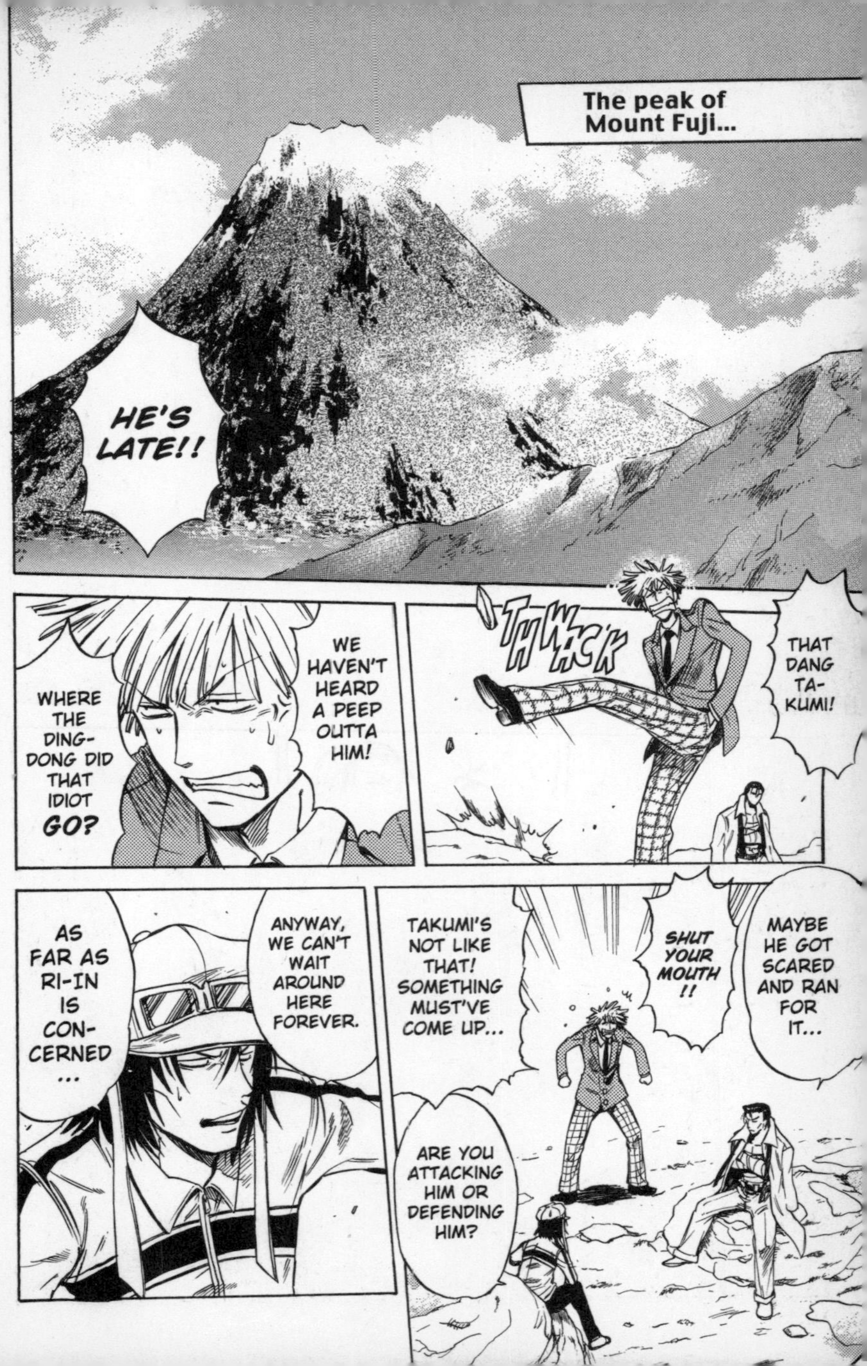
The peak of Mount Fuji...
HE'S LATE!!
THAT DANG TAKUMI!
THWACK
WE HAVEN'T HEARD A PEEP OUTTA HIM!
WHERE THE DING-DONG DID THAT IDIOT GO?
MAYBE HE GOT SCARED AND RAN FOR IT...
SHUT YOUR MOUTH!!
TAKUMI'S NOT LIKE THAT! SOMETHING MUST'VE COME UP...
ARE YOU ATTACKING HIM OR DEFENDING HIM?
ANYWAY, WE CAN'T WAIT AROUND HERE FOREVER.
AS FAR AS RI-IN IS CONCERNED...

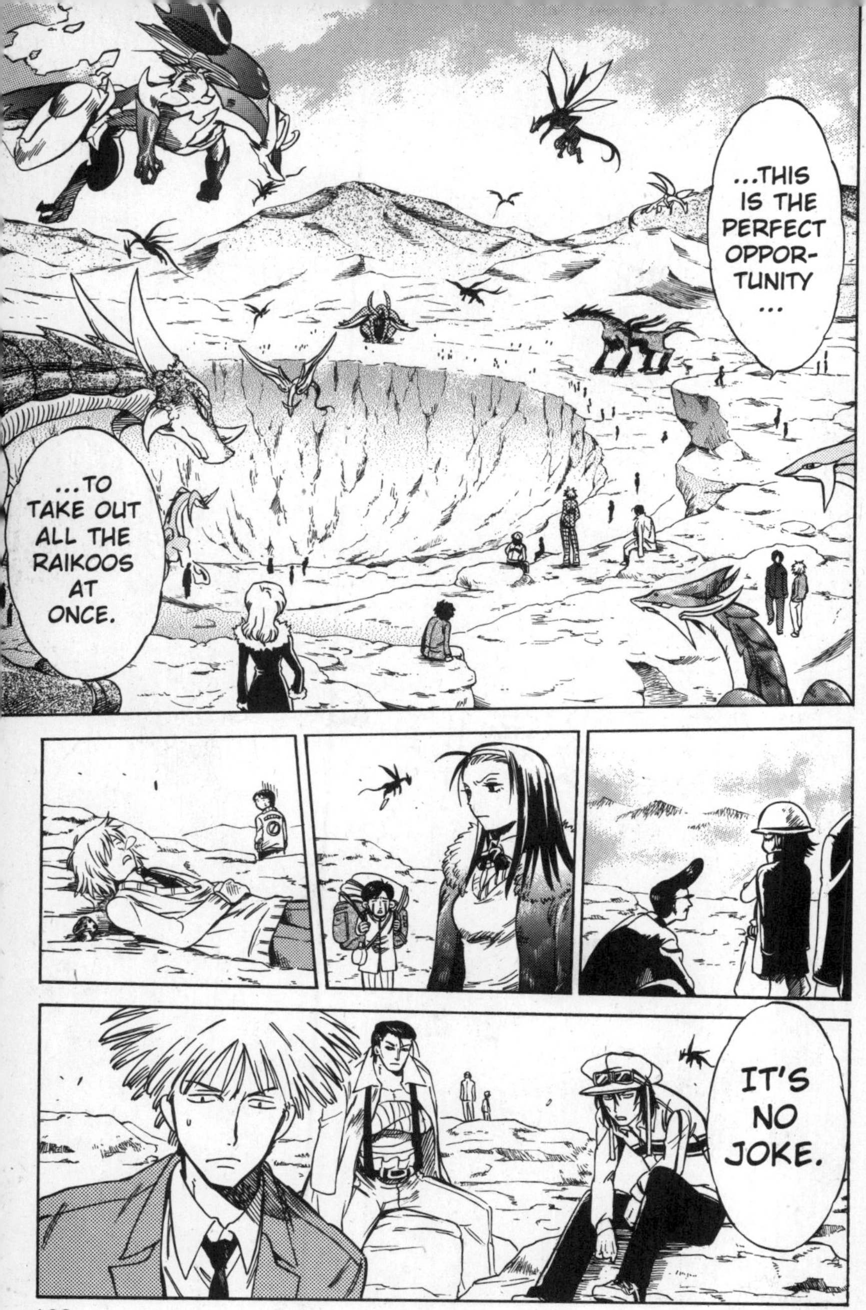
...THIS IS THE PERFECT OPPOR-TUNITY ...
...TO TAKE OUT ALL THE RAIKOOS AT ONCE.
IT'S NO JOKE.

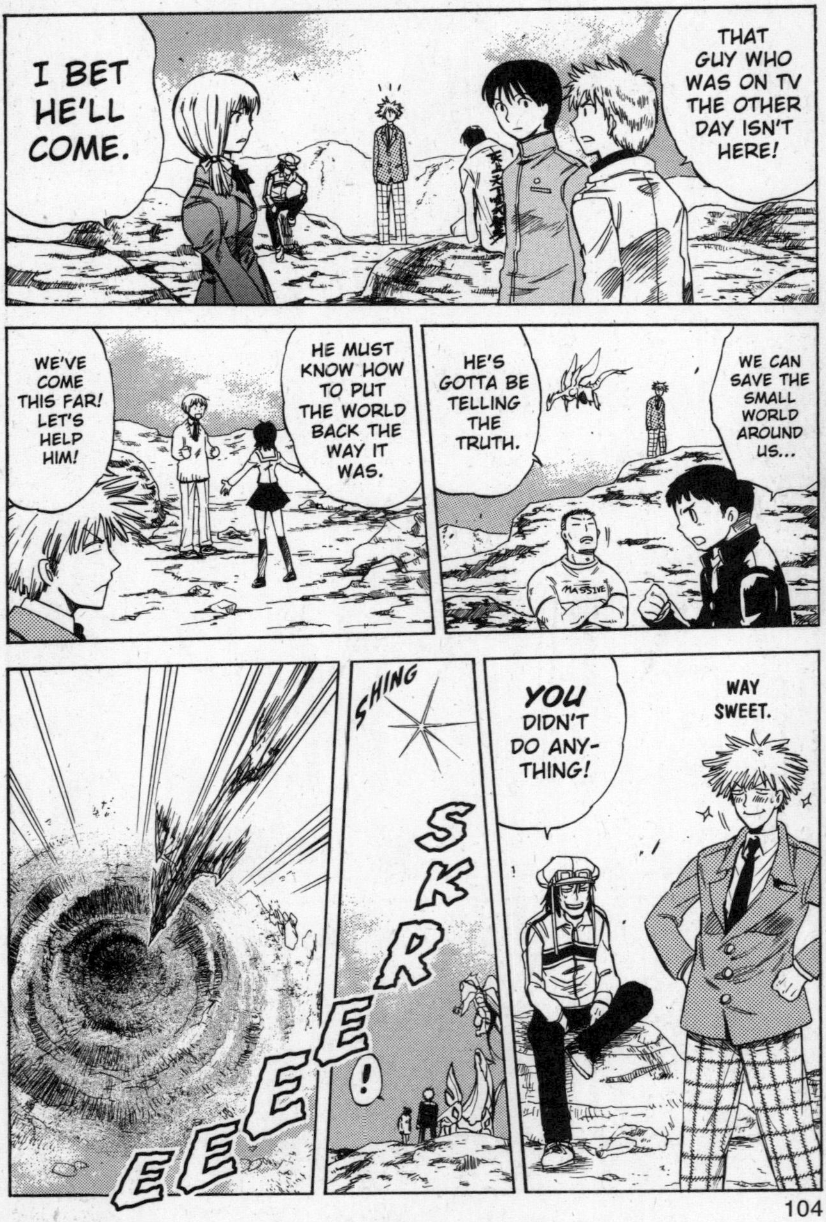
THAT GUY WHO WAS ON TV THE OTHER DAY ISN'T HERE!
I BET HE'LL COME.
WE CAN SAVE THE SMALL WORLD AROUND US...
HE'S GOTTA BE TELLING THE TRUTH.
MASSIVE
HE MUST KNOW HOW TO PUT THE WORLD BACK THE WAY IT WAS.
WE'VE COME THIS FAR! LET'S HELP HIM!
WAY SWEET.
YOU DIDN'T DO ANY-THING!
SHING
SKREEEEE!

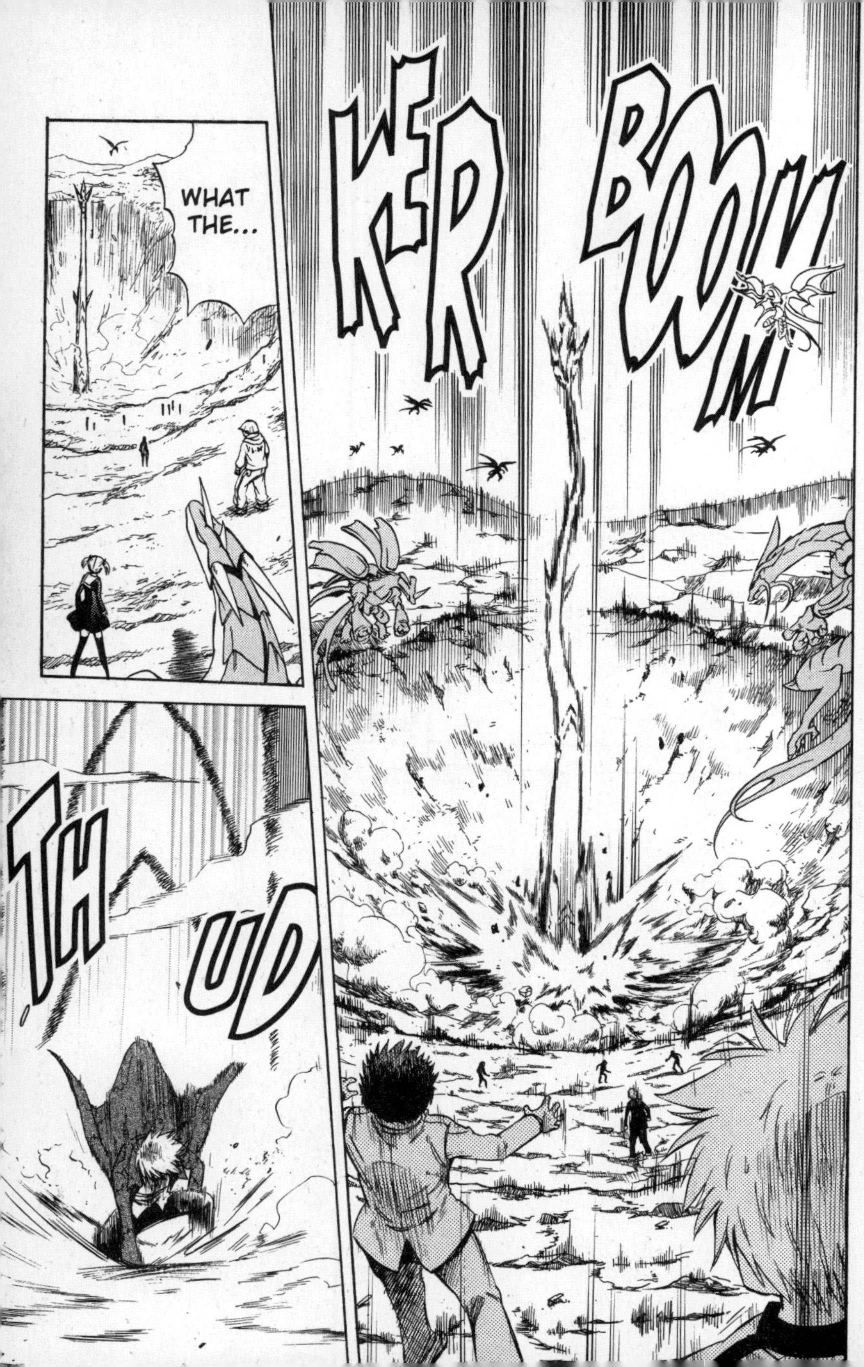
KER BOOM
WHAT THE...
THUD

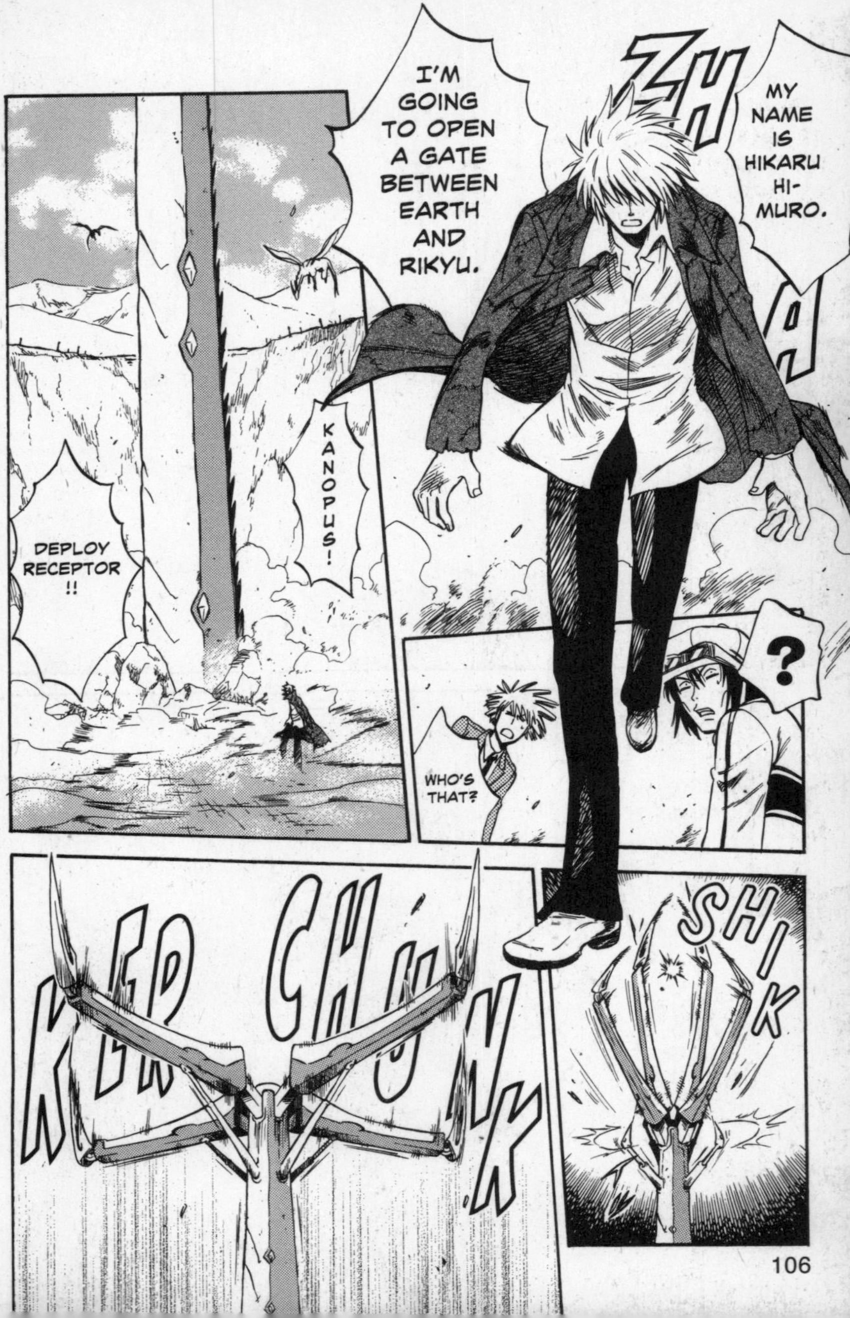
ZHA
MY NAME IS HIKARU HI-MURO.
I'M GOING TO OPEN A GATE BETWEEN EARTH AND RIKYU.
?
WHO'S THAT?
KANOPUS!
DEPLOY RECEPTOR!!
SHIK
KER CHUNK

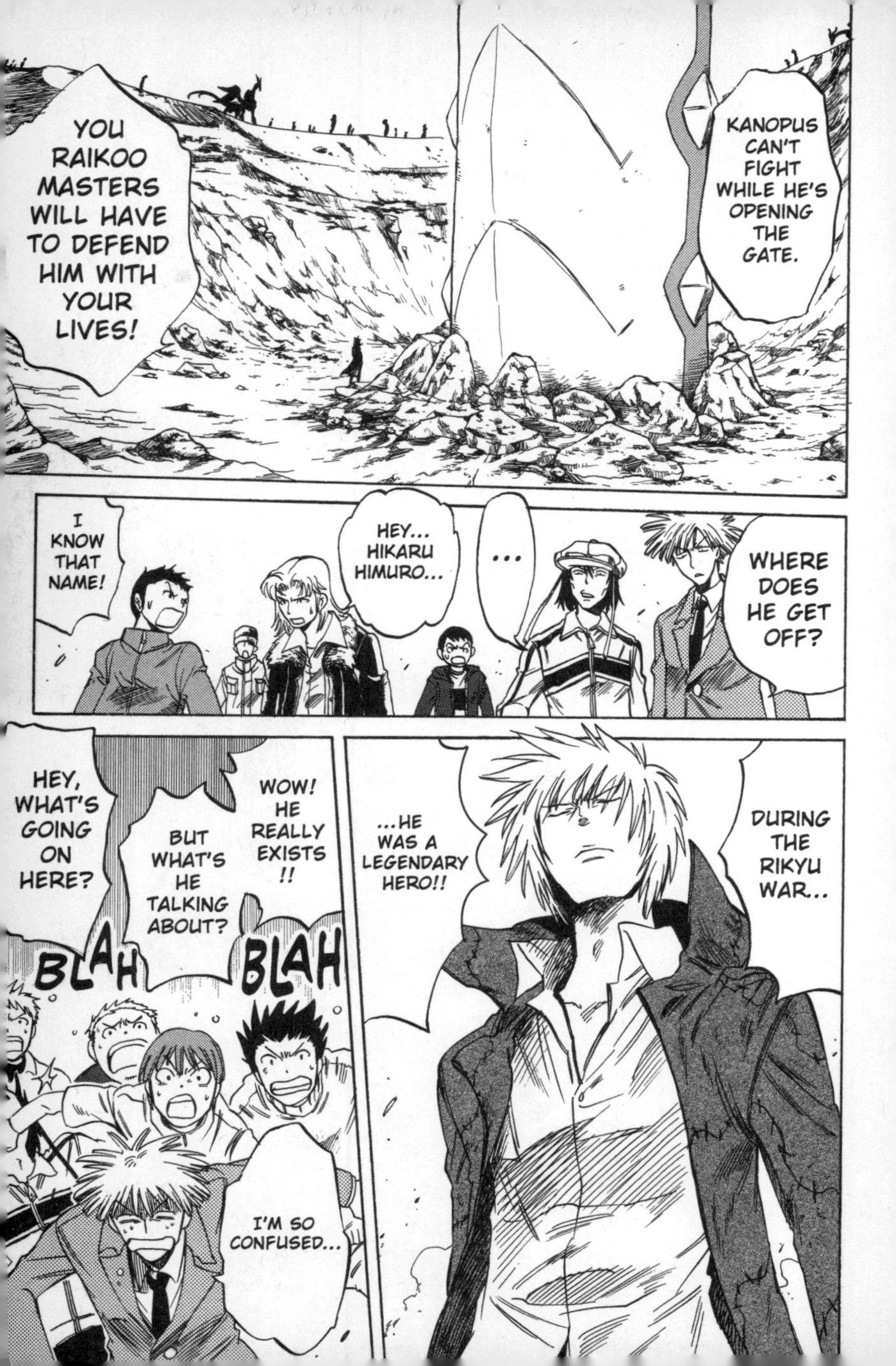
KANOPUS CAN'T FIGHT WHILE HE'S OPENING THE GATE.
YOU RAIKOO MASTERS WILL HAVE TO DEFEND HIM WITH YOUR LIVES!
WHERE DOES HE GET OFF?
...
HEY... HIKARU HIMURO...
I KNOW THAT NAME!
DURING THE RIKYU WAR...
...HE WAS A LEGENDARY HERO!!
WOW! HE REALLY EXISTS!!
BUT WHAT'S HE TALKING ABOUT?
HEY, WHAT'S GOING ON HERE?
BLAH
BLAH
I'M SO CONFUSED...

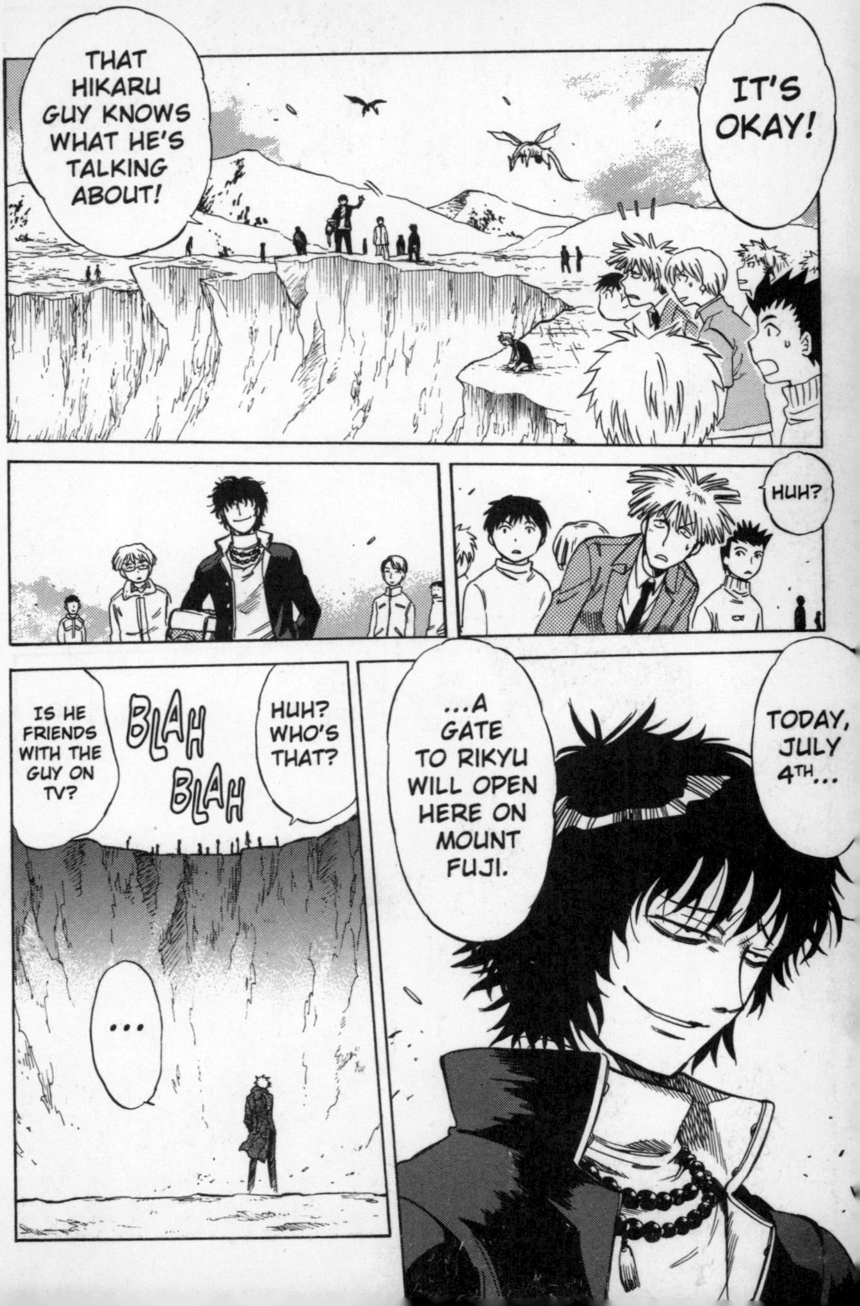
IT'S OKAY!
THAT HIKARU GUY KNOWS WHAT HE'S TALKING ABOUT!
HUH?
TODAY, JULY 4TH...
...A GATE TO RIKYU WILL OPEN HERE ON MOUNT FUJI.
HUH? WHO'S THAT?
BLAH BLAH
IS HE FRIENDS WITH THE GUY ON TV?
...

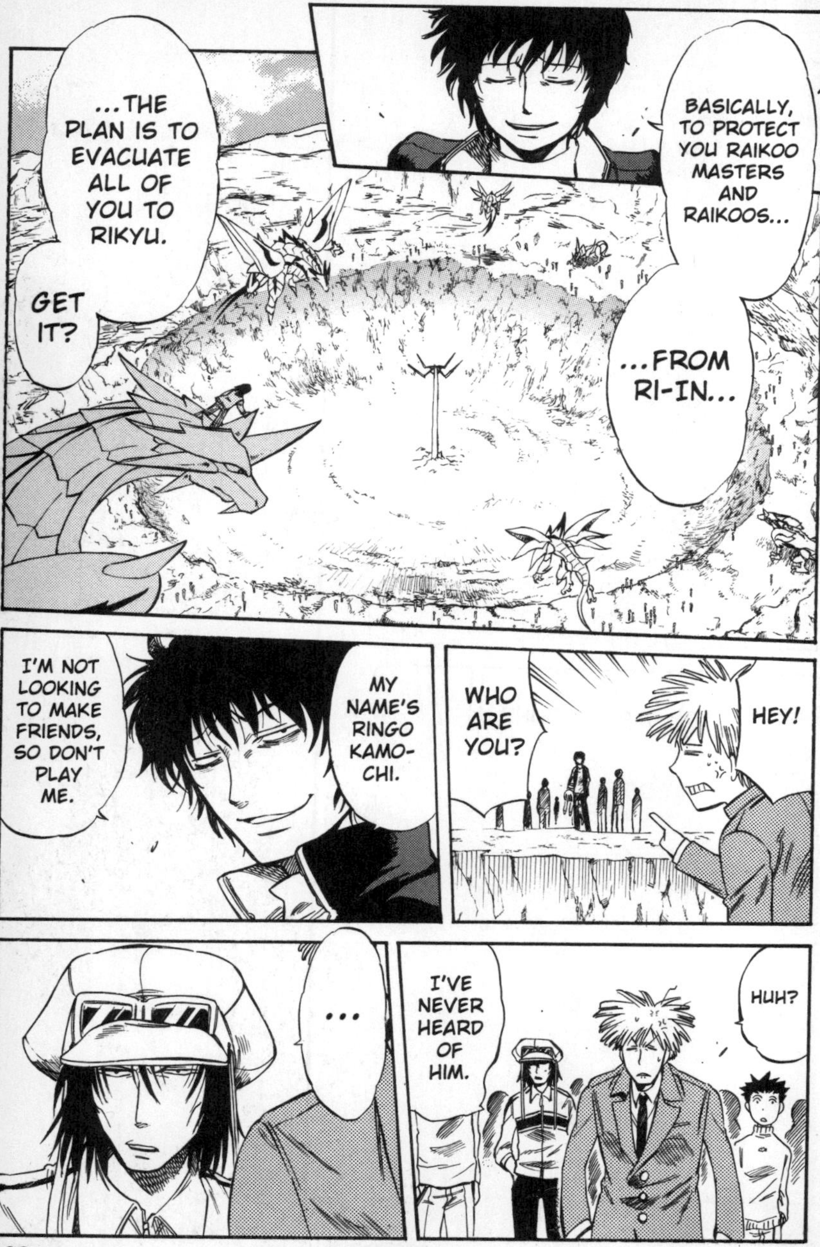
BASICALLY, TO PROTECT YOU RAIKOO MASTERS AND RAIKOOS...
...FROM RI-IN...
...THE PLAN IS TO EVACUATE ALL OF YOU TO RIKYU.
GET IT?
HEY!
WHO ARE YOU?
MY NAME'S RINGO KAMO-CHI.
I'M NOT LOOKING TO MAKE FRIENDS, SO DON'T PLAY ME.
HUH?
I'VE NEVER HEARD OF HIM.
...

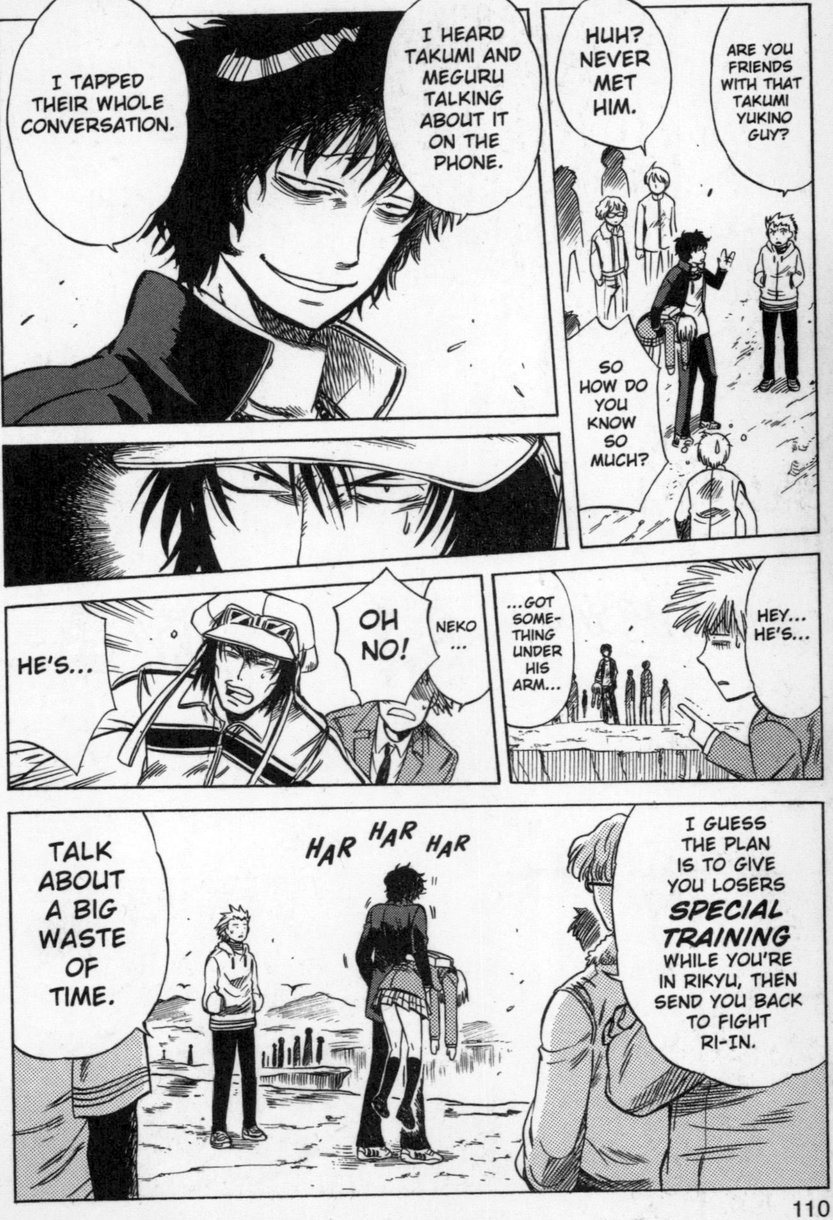
ARE YOU FRIENDS WITH THAT TAKUMI YUKINO GUY?
HUH? NEVER MET HIM.
SO HOW DO YOU KNOW SO MUCH?
I HEARD TAKUMI AND MEGURU TALKING ABOUT IT ON THE PHONE.
I TAPPED THEIR WHOLE CONVERSATION.
HEY... HE'S...
...GOT SOMETHING UNDER HIS ARM...
NEKO ...
OH NO!
HE'S...
I GUESS THE PLAN IS TO GIVE YOU LOSERS **SPECIAL TRAINING** WHILE YOU'RE IN RIKYU, THEN SEND YOU BACK TO FIGHT RI-IN.
HAR HAR HAR
TALK ABOUT A BIG WASTE OF TIME.

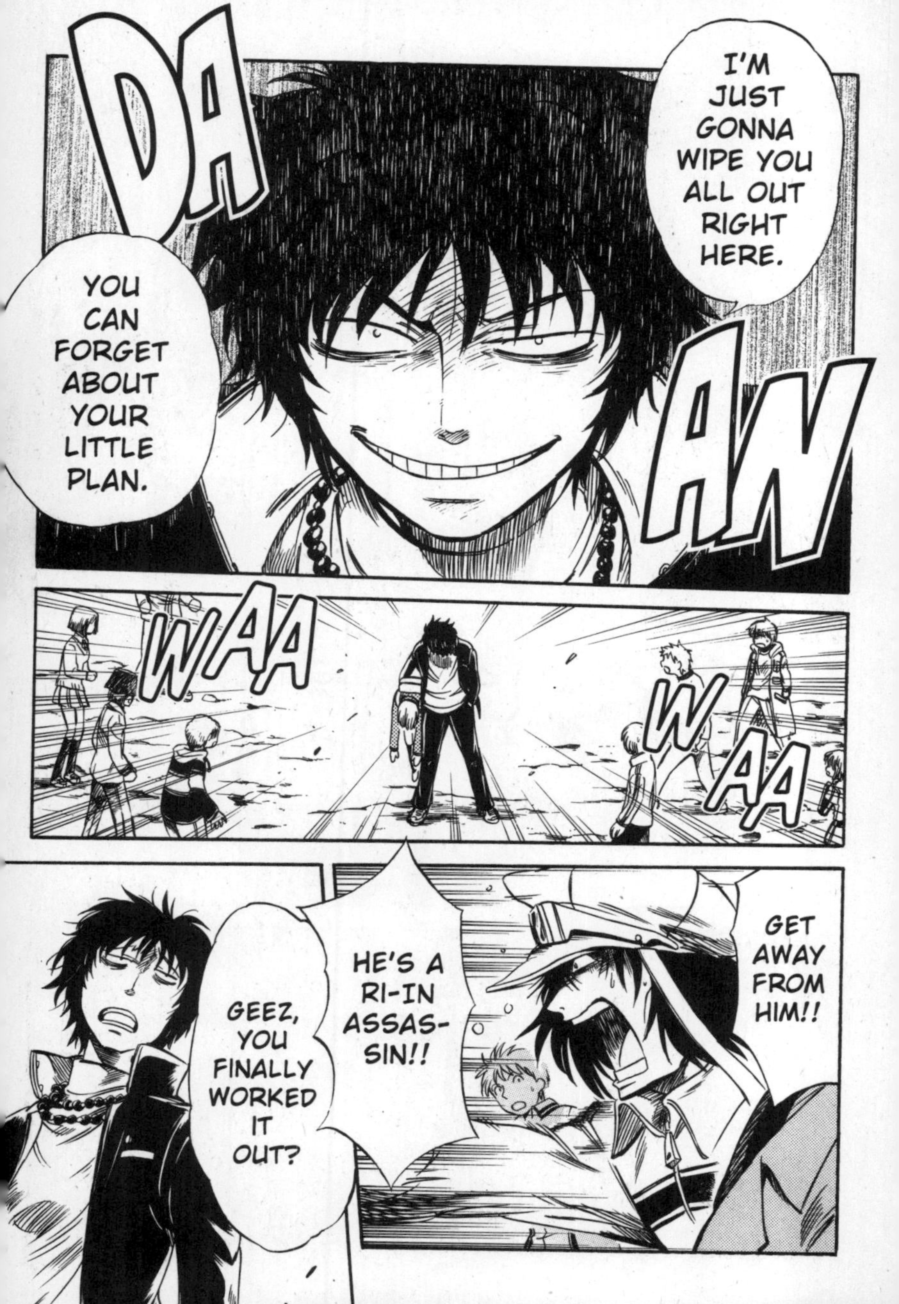
I'M JUST GONNA WIPE YOU ALL OUT RIGHT HERE.
DA
YOU CAN FORGET ABOUT YOUR LITTLE PLAN.
AN
WAA
WAA
GET AWAY FROM HIM!!
HE'S A RI-IN ASSAS-SIN!!
GEEZ, YOU FINALLY WORKED IT OUT?

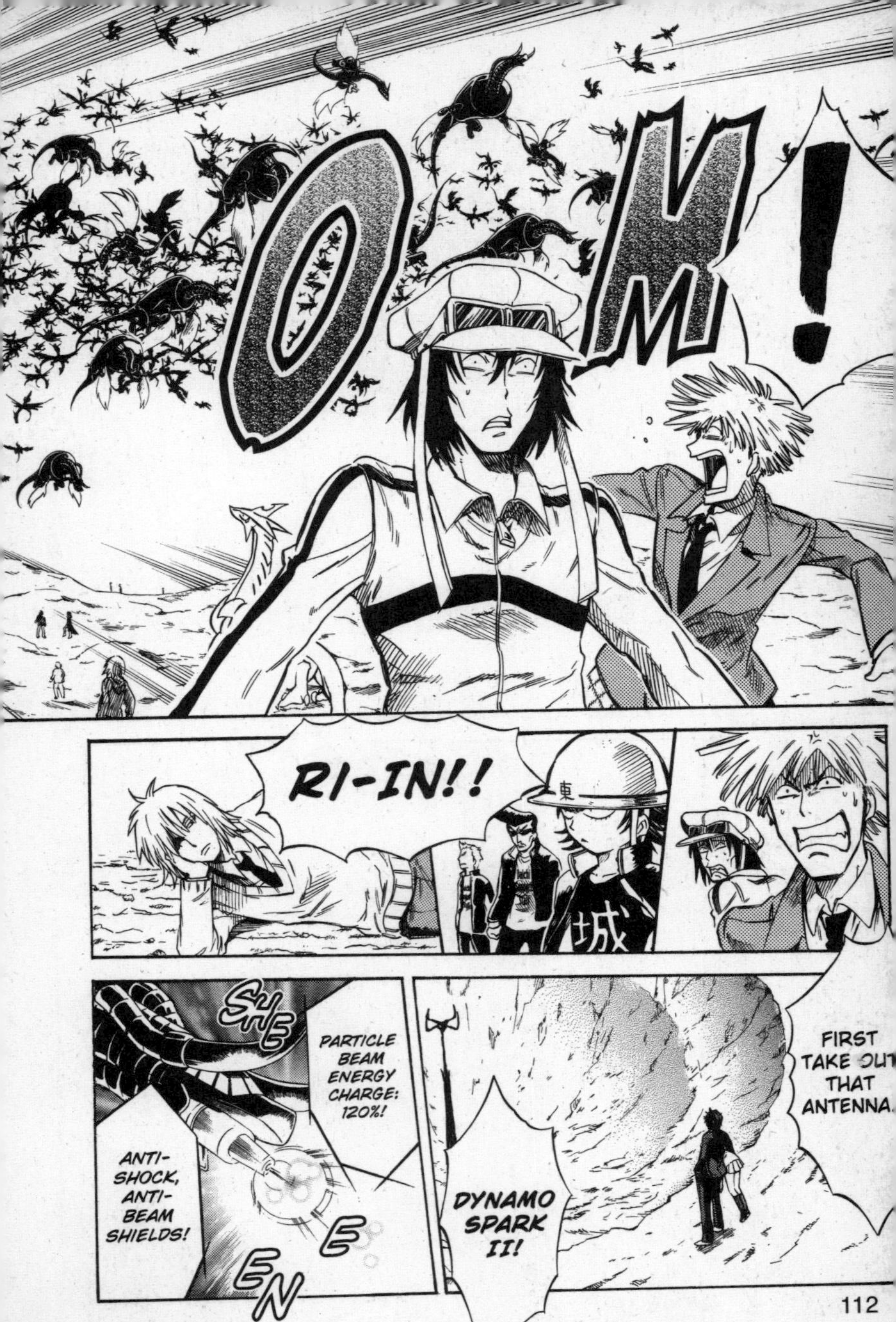
OM!
RI-IN!!
FIRST TAKE OUT THAT ANTENNA.
DYNAMO SPARK II!
SHE
PARTICLE BEAM ENERGY CHARGE: 120%!
ANTI-SHOCK, ANTI-BEAM SHIELDS!
EEN

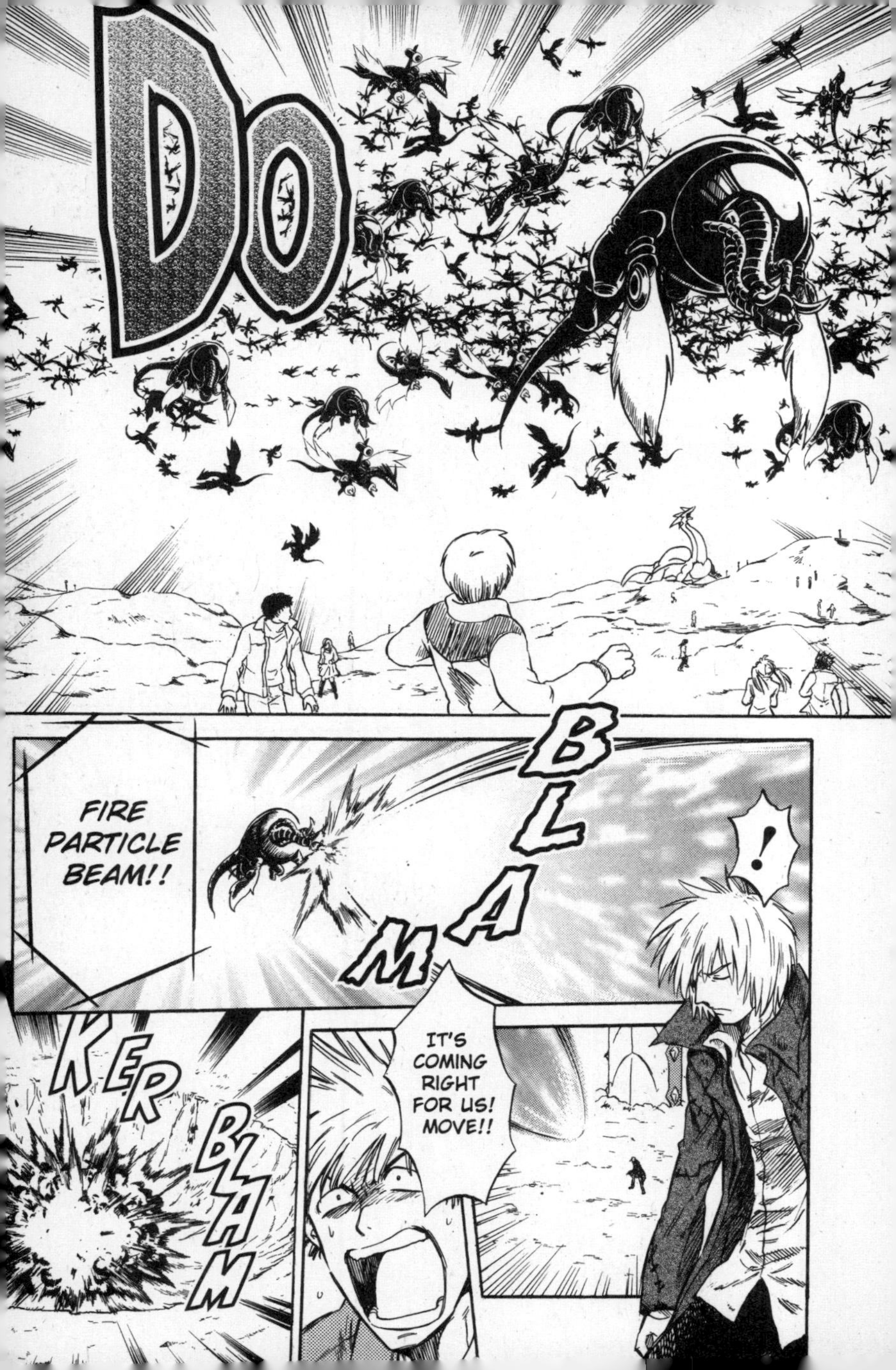
DO
!
BLAM
FIRE PARTICLE BEAM!!
IT'S COMING RIGHT FOR US! MOVE!!
KERBLAM

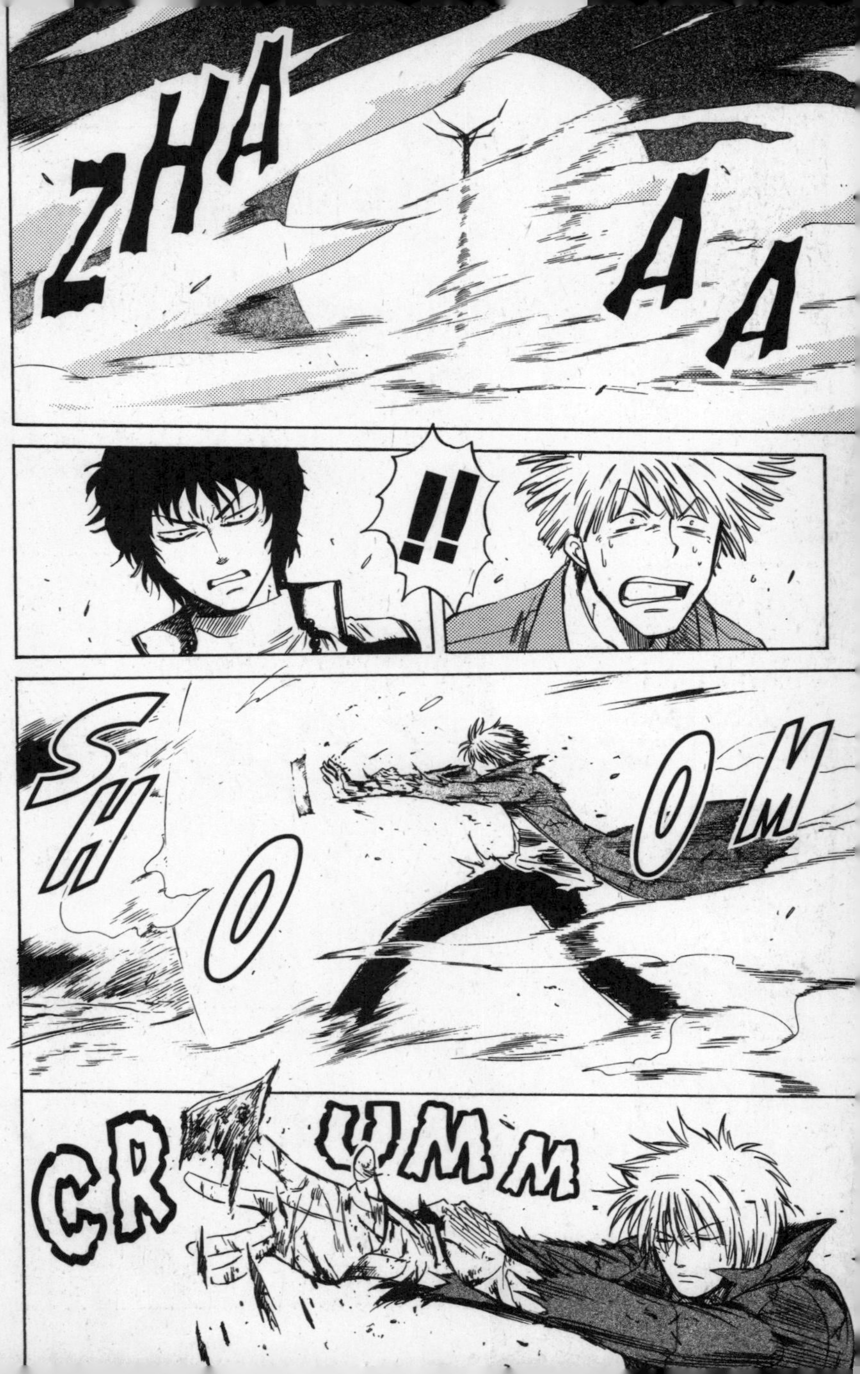
ZHAAA
!!
SHOOOM
CRUMM

READ THIS WAY

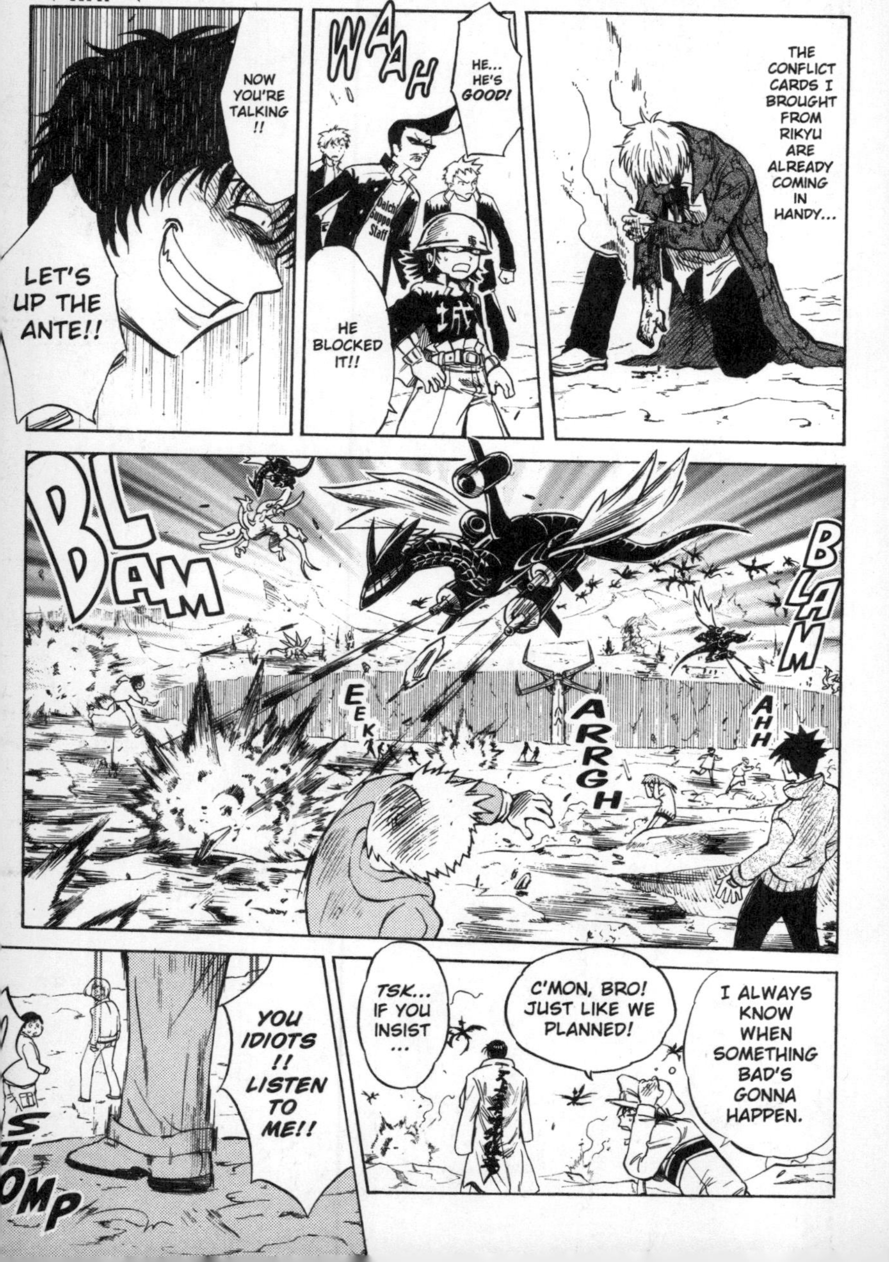
THE CONFLICT CARDS I BROUGHT FROM RIKYU ARE ALREADY COMING IN HANDY...
WAAH
HE... HE'S GOOD!
HE BLOCKED IT!!
NOW YOU'RE TALKING!!
LET'S UP THE ANTE!!
BLAM
BLAM
AHH
ARRGH
EEK
I ALWAYS KNOW WHEN SOMETHING BAD'S GONNA HAPPEN.
C'MON, BRO! JUST LIKE WE PLANNED!
TSK... IF YOU INSIST...
YOU IDIOTS!! LISTEN TO ME!!
STOMP

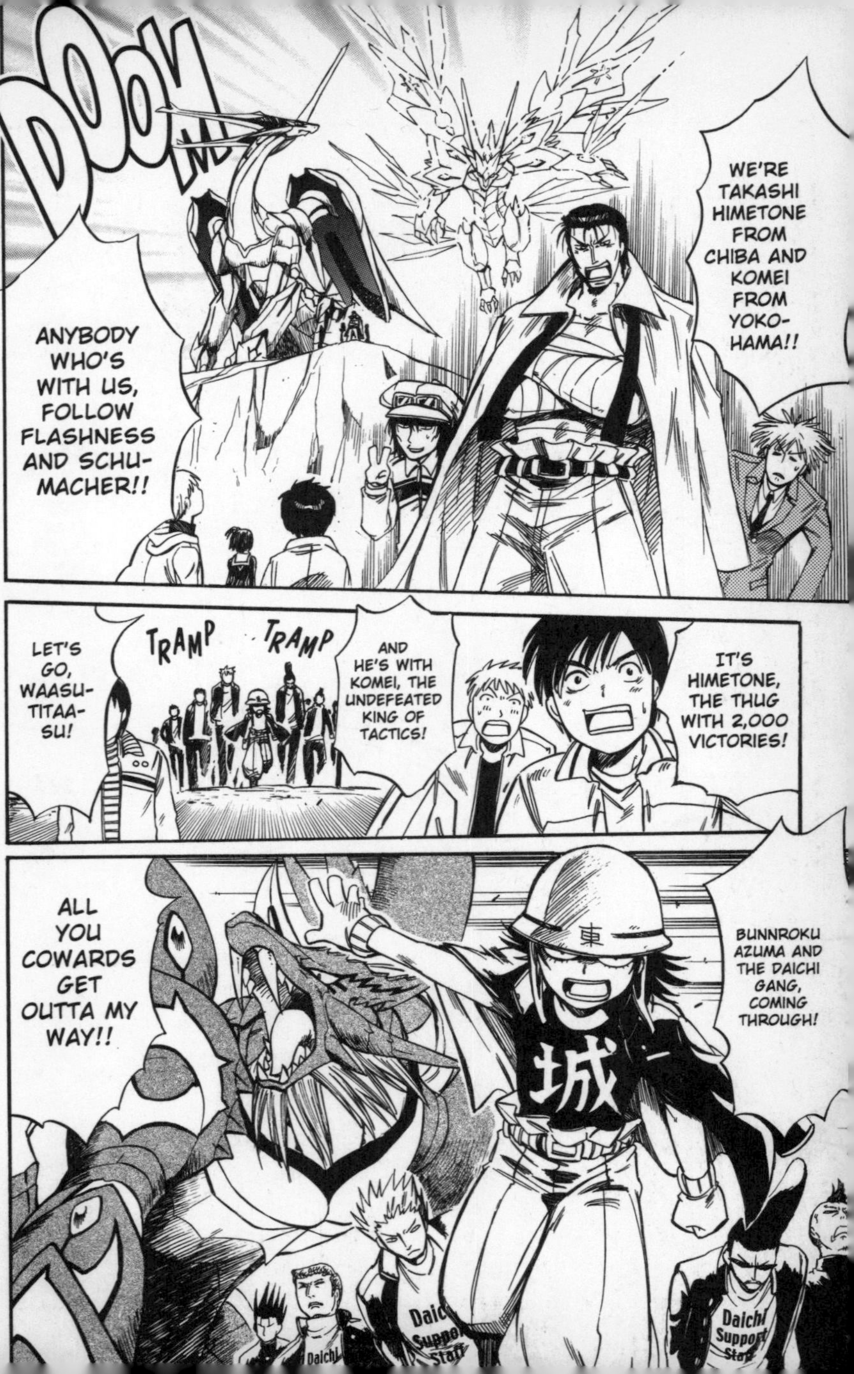
WE'RE TAKASHI HIMETONE FROM CHIBA AND KOMEI FROM YOKO-HAMA!!
DOOOM
ANYBODY WHO'S WITH US, FOLLOW FLASHNESS AND SCHU-MACHER!!
IT'S HIMETONE, THE THUG WITH 2,000 VICTORIES!
AND HE'S WITH KOMEI, THE UNDEFEATED KING OF TACTICS!
TRAMP TRAMP
LET'S GO, WAASU-TITAA-SU!
BUNNROKU AZUMA AND THE DAICHI GANG, COMING THROUGH!
東
城
ALL YOU COWARDS GET OUTTA MY WAY!!
Daichi Support Staff

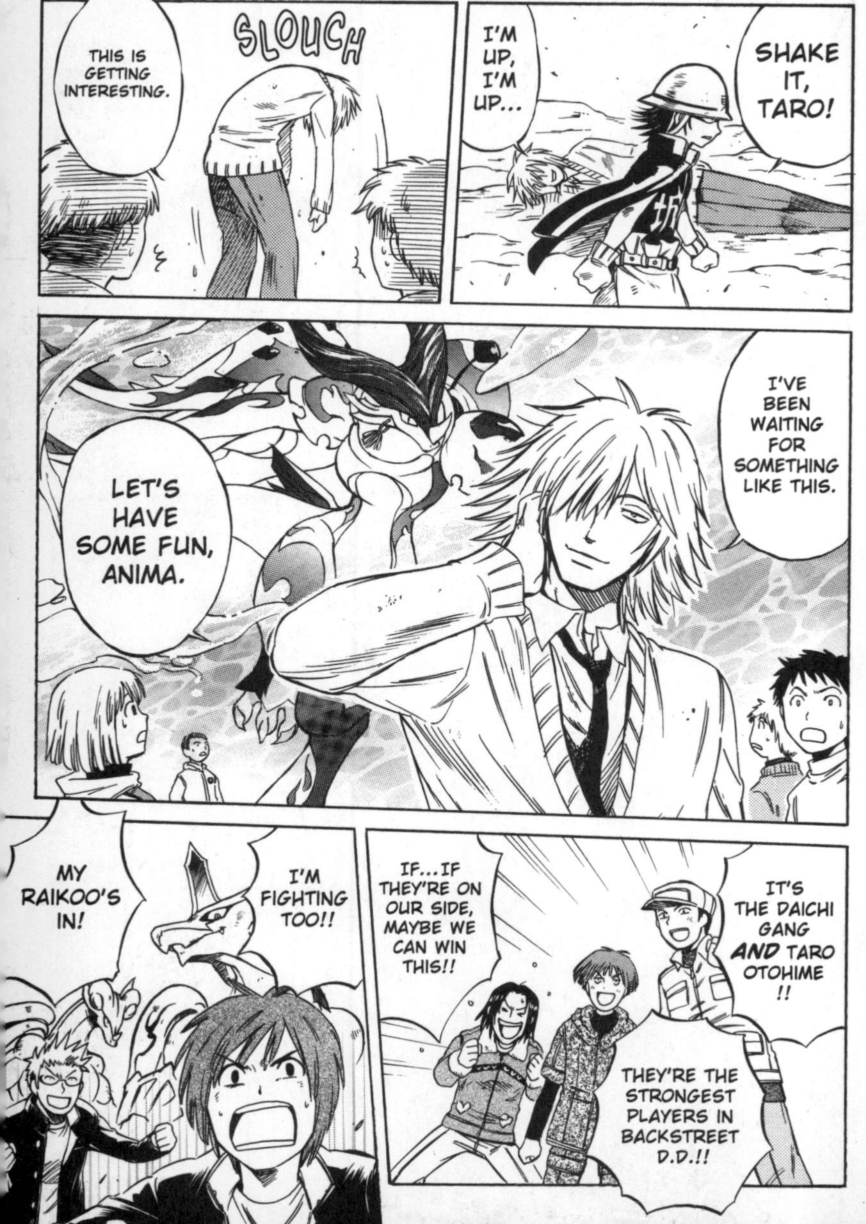
SHAKE IT, TARO!
I'M UP, I'M UP...
SLOUCH
THIS IS GETTING INTERESTING.
I'VE BEEN WAITING FOR SOMETHING LIKE THIS.
LET'S HAVE SOME FUN, ANIMA.
IT'S THE DAICHI GANG AND TARO OTOHIME !!
IF...IF THEY'RE ON OUR SIDE, MAYBE WE CAN WIN THIS!!
THEY'RE THE STRONGEST PLAYERS IN BACKSTREET D.D.!!
I'M FIGHTING TOO!!
MY RAIKOO'S IN!

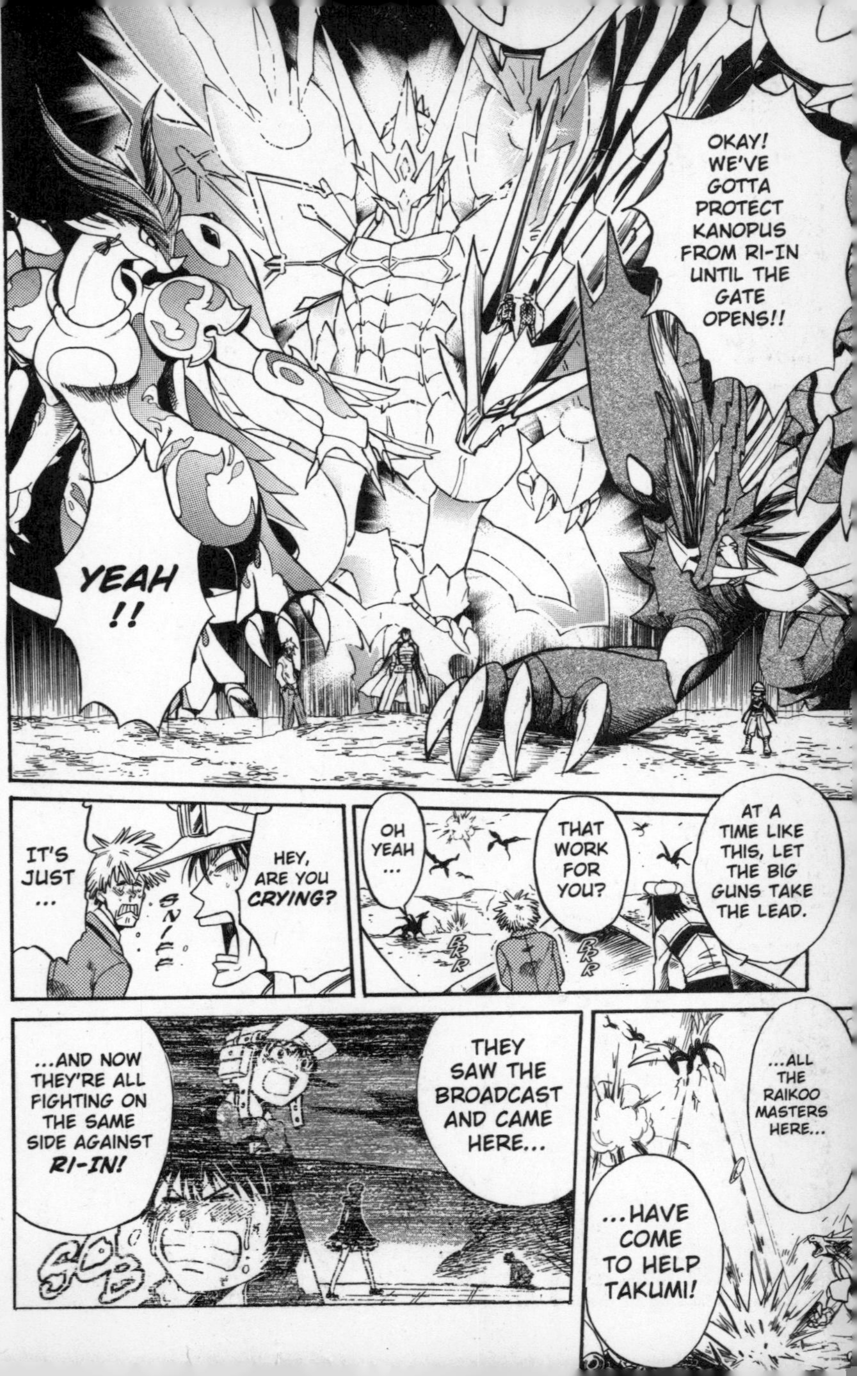
OKAY! WE'VE GOTTA PROTECT KANOPUS FROM RI-IN UNTIL THE GATE OPENS!!
YEAH !!
AT A TIME LIKE THIS, LET THE BIG GUNS TAKE THE LEAD.
THAT WORK FOR YOU?
OH YEAH ...
BRR
BRR
HEY, ARE YOU CRYING?
IT'S JUST ...
SNIFF
...ALL THE RAIKOO MASTERS HERE...
...HAVE COME TO HELP TAKUMI!
THEY SAW THE BROADCAST AND CAME HERE...
...AND NOW THEY'RE ALL FIGHTING ON THE SAME SIDE AGAINST RI-IN!
SOB

READ THIS WAY

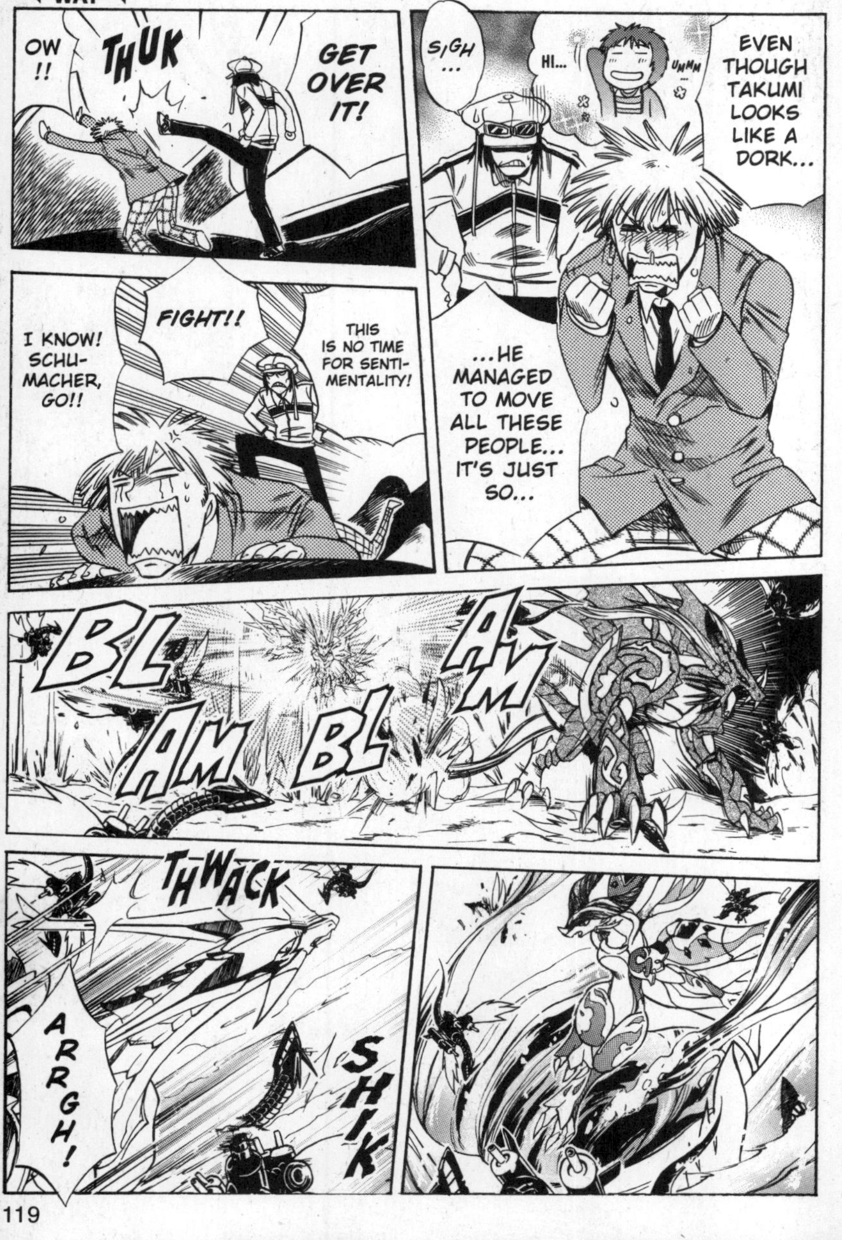
SIGH...
HI...
UMMM...
EVEN THOUGH TAKUMI LOOKS LIKE A DORK...
...HE MANAGED TO MOVE ALL THESE PEOPLE... IT'S JUST SO...
GET OVER IT!
THUK
OW!!
FIGHT!!
THIS IS NO TIME FOR SENTIMENTALITY!
I KNOW! SCHUMACHER, GO!!
BLAM BLAM
THWACK
SHIK
ARRGH!

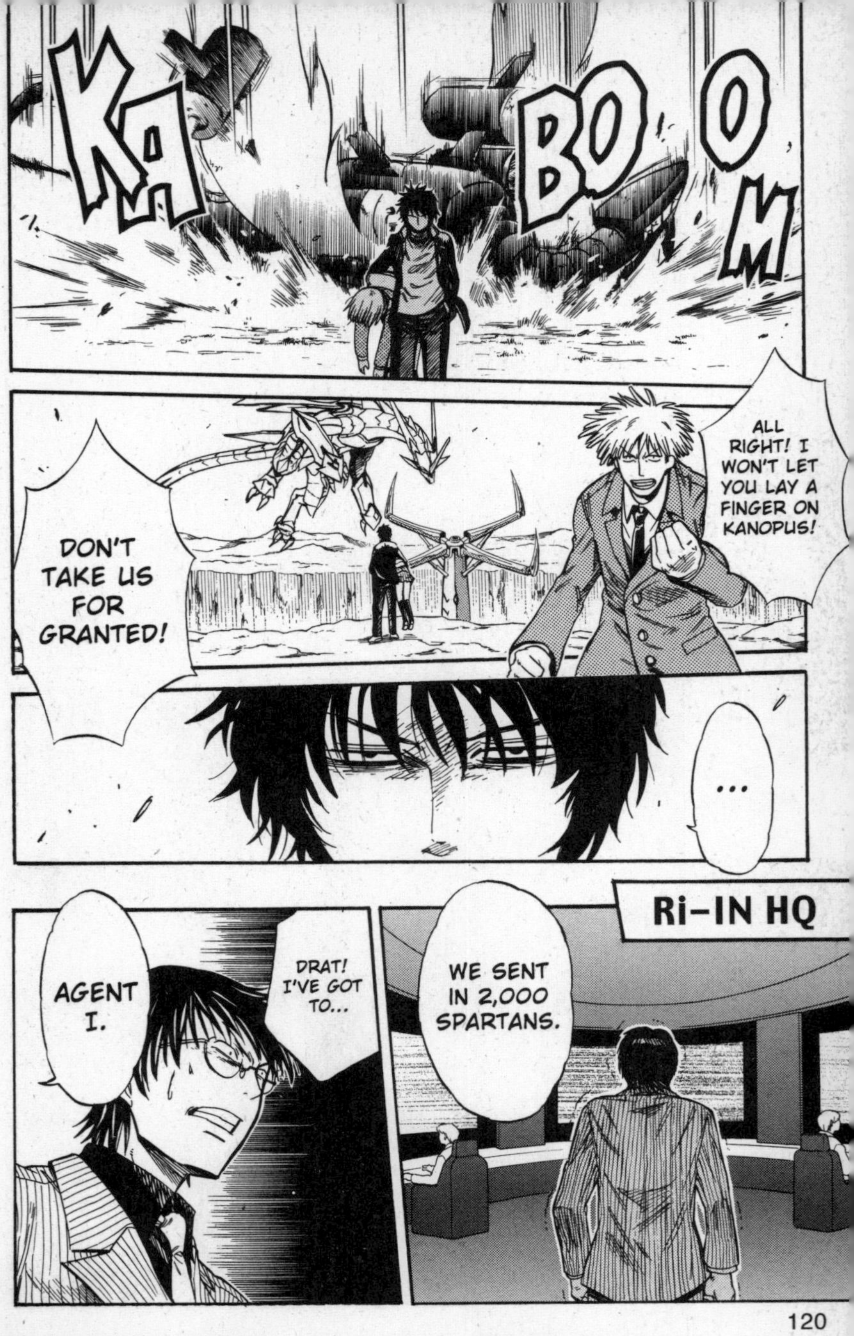
KA-BOOOM
ALL RIGHT! I WON'T LET YOU LAY A FINGER ON KANOPUS!
DON'T TAKE US FOR GRANTED!
...
Ri-IN HQ
WE SENT IN 2,000 SPARTANS.
DRAT! I'VE GOT TO...
AGENT I.

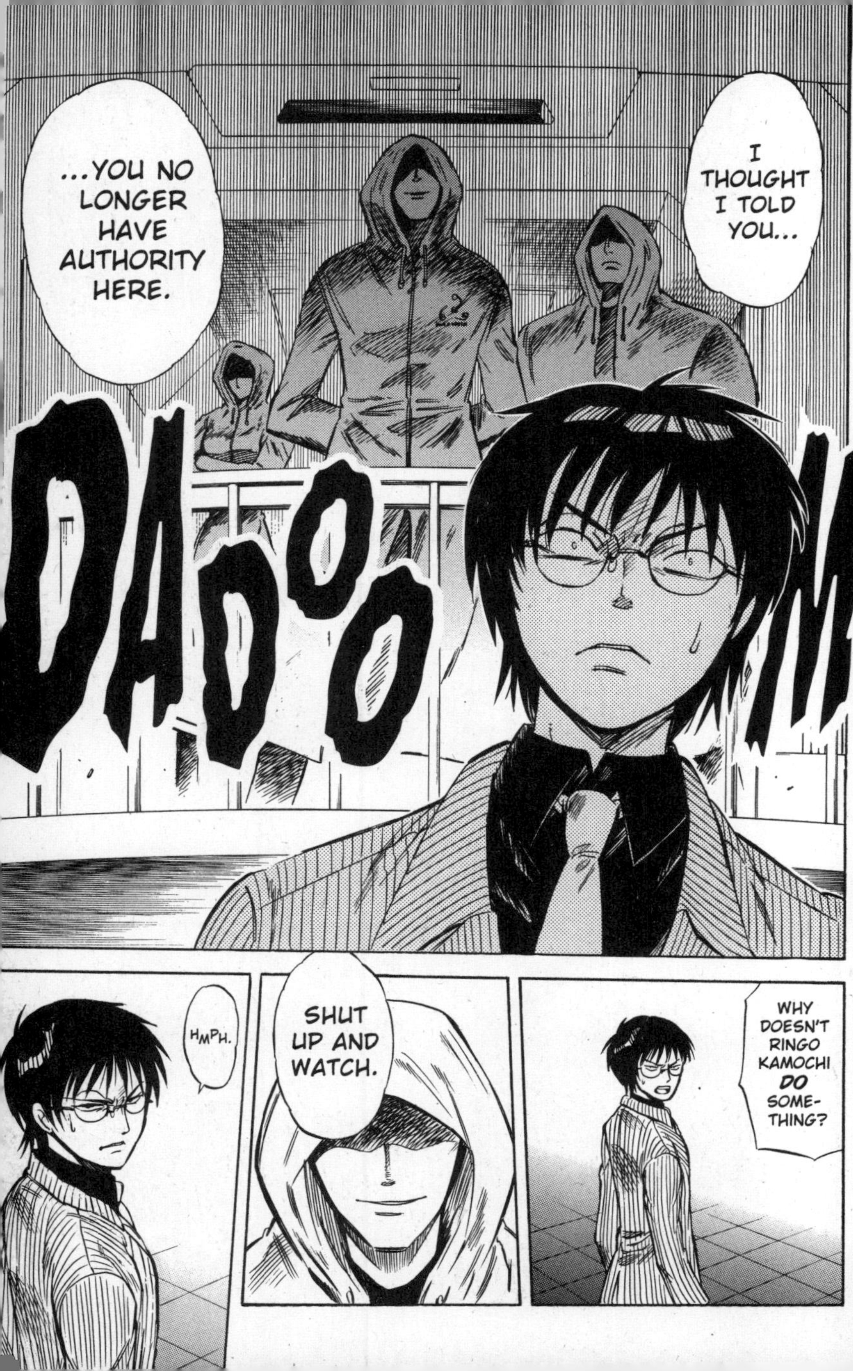
I THOUGHT I TOLD YOU...
...YOU NO LONGER HAVE AUTHORITY HERE.
DADOOOM
WHY DOESN'T RINGO KAMOCHI DO SOMETHING?
SHUT UP AND WATCH.
HMPH.

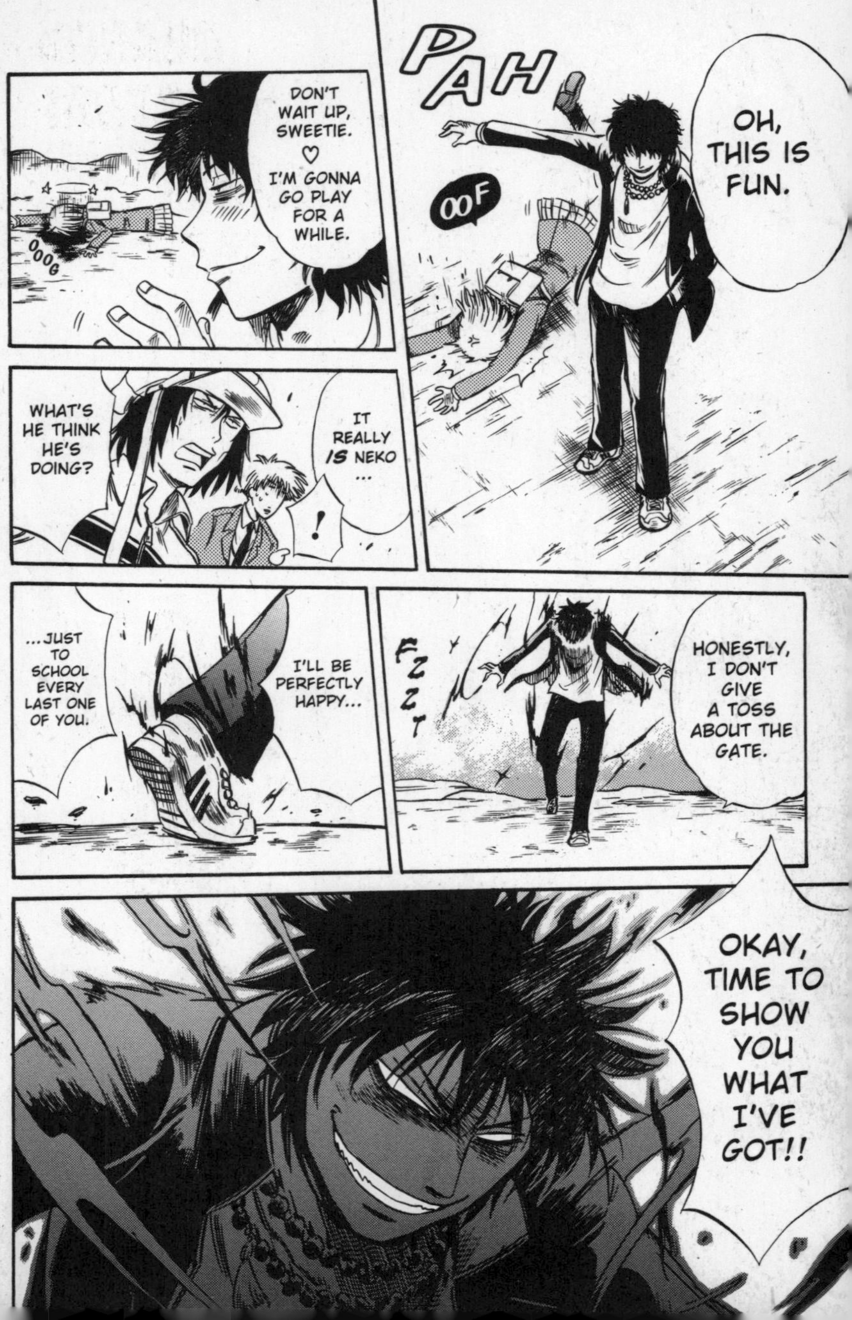
PAH
OH, THIS IS FUN.
OOF
DON'T WAIT UP, SWEETIE. ♡ I'M GONNA GO PLAY FOR A WHILE.
OOOG
IT REALLY IS NEKO...
!
WHAT'S HE THINK HE'S DOING?
FZZT
HONESTLY, I DON'T GIVE A TOSS ABOUT THE GATE.
I'LL BE PERFECTLY HAPPY...
...JUST TO SCHOOL EVERY LAST ONE OF YOU.
OKAY, TIME TO SHOW YOU WHAT I'VE GOT!!

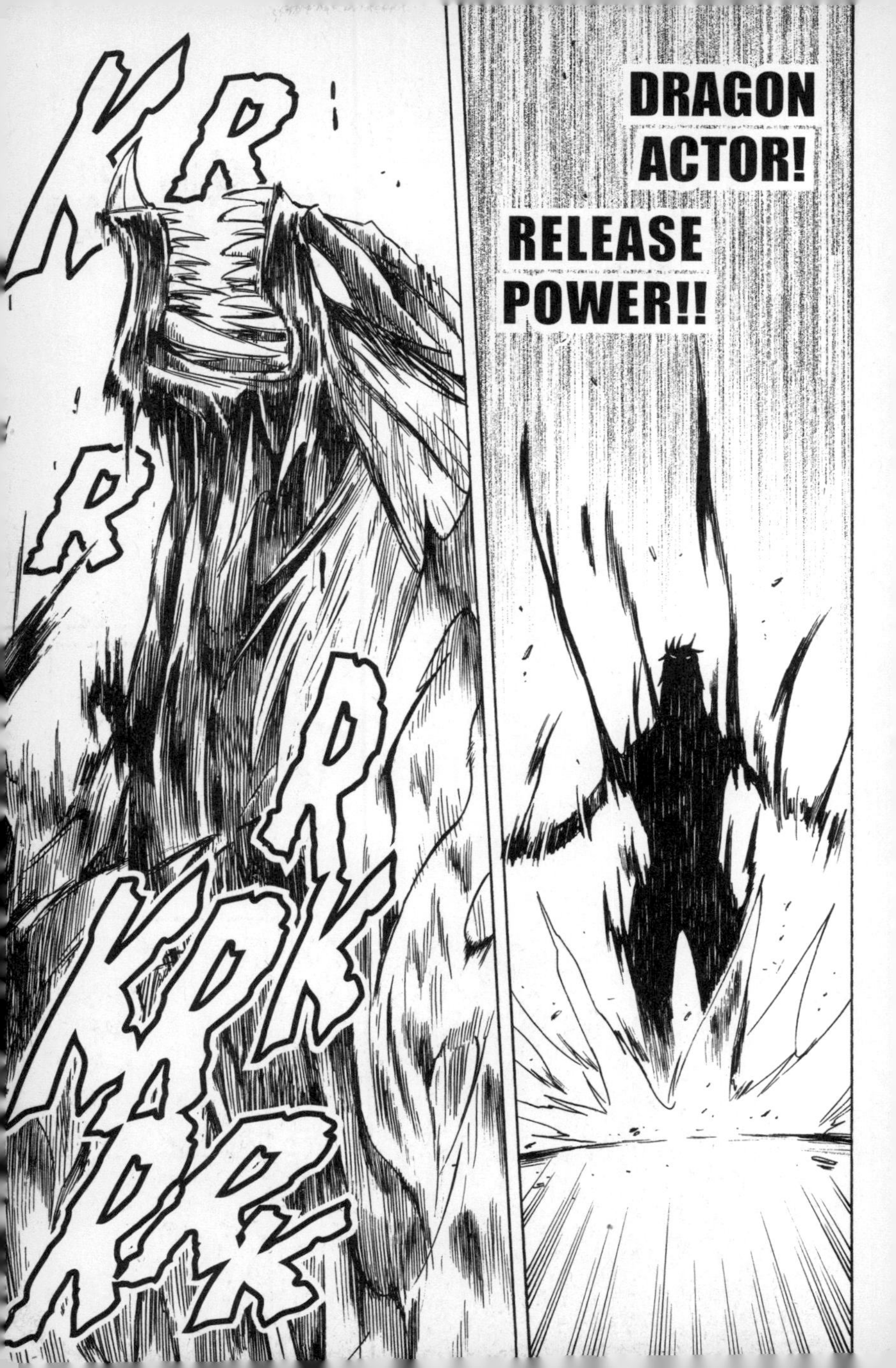
DRAGON ACTOR!
RELEASE POWER!!

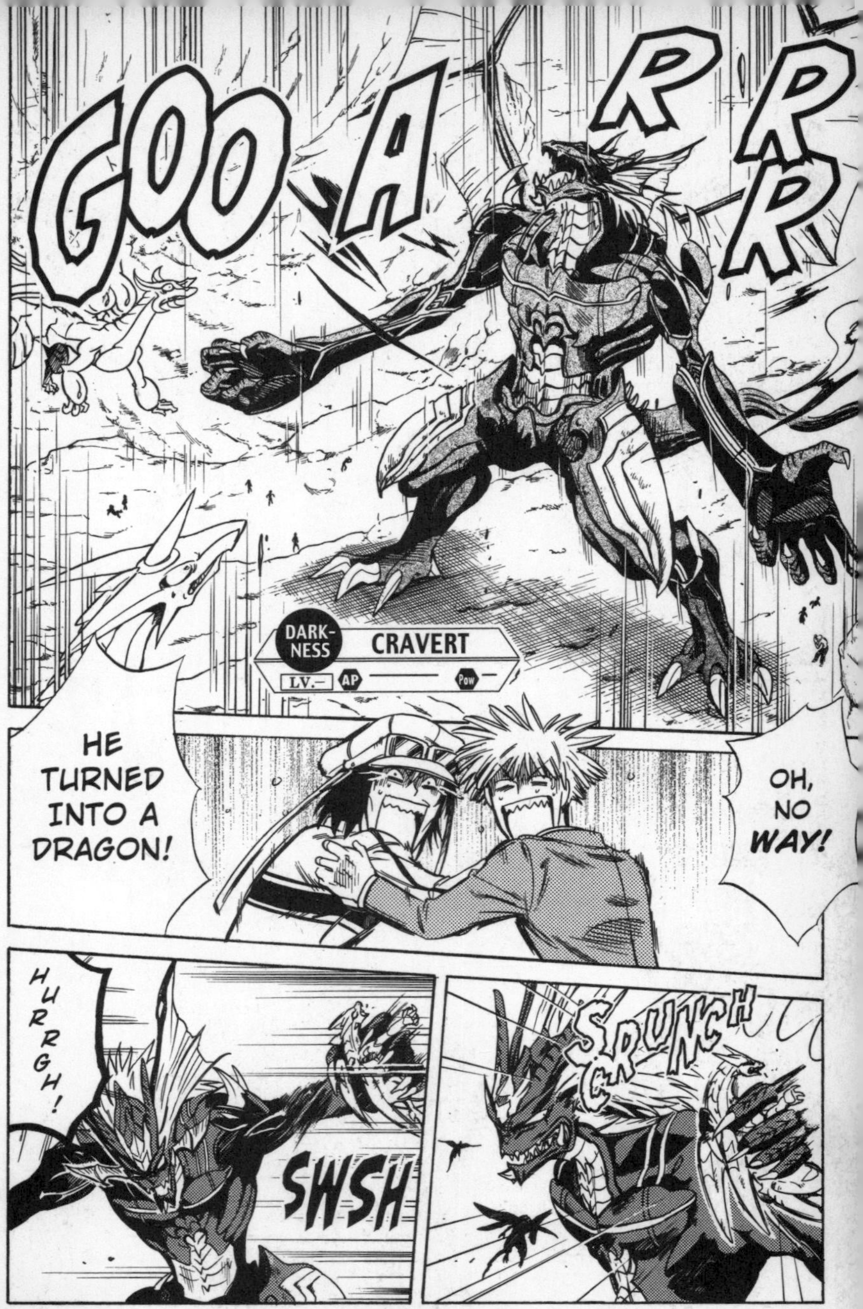
GOO-A RRRR
DARK-NESS
CRAVERT
LV.–
AP
Pow
OH, NO WAY!
HE TURNED INTO A DRAGON!
SCRUNCH
HURRGH!
SWSH

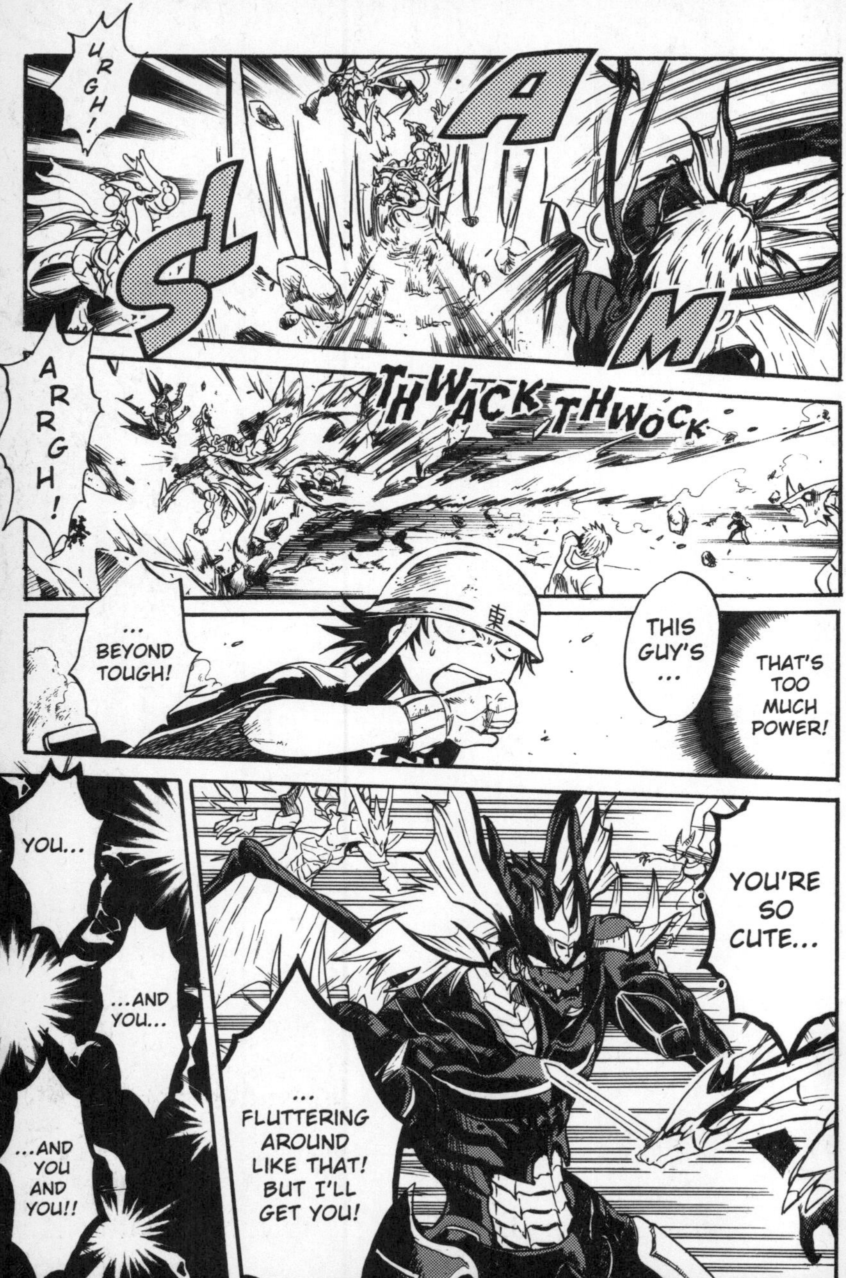
SLAM
URGH!
THWACK THWOCK
ARRGH!
THIS GUY'S...
THAT'S TOO MUCH POWER!
...BEYOND TOUGH!
YOU'RE SO CUTE...
...FLUTTERING AROUND LIKE THAT! BUT I'LL GET YOU!
YOU...
...AND YOU...
...AND YOU AND YOU!!

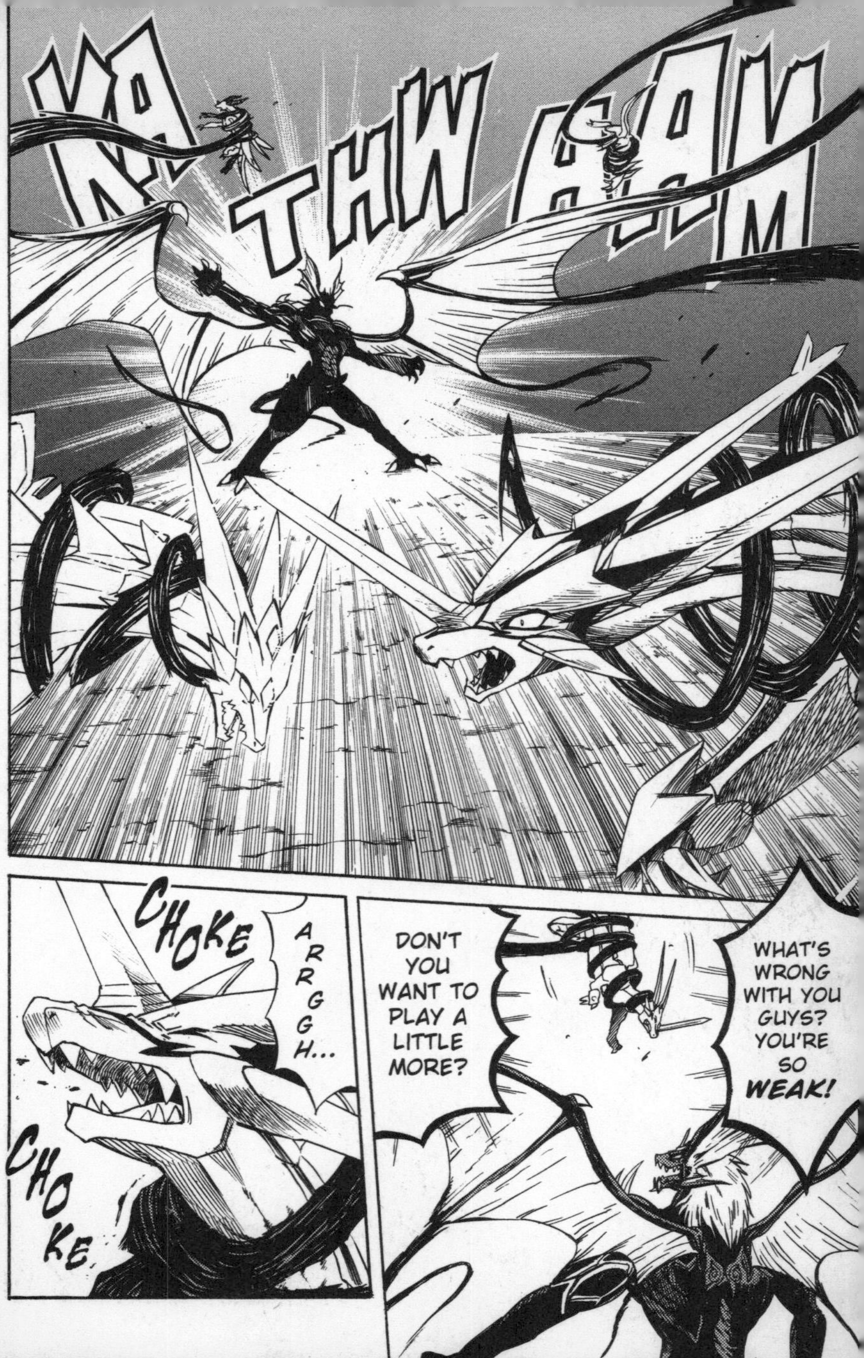
KATHWAAM
WHAT'S WRONG WITH YOU GUYS? YOU'RE SO WEAK!
DON'T YOU WANT TO PLAY A LITTLE MORE?
ARRGGH...
CHOKE
CHOKE

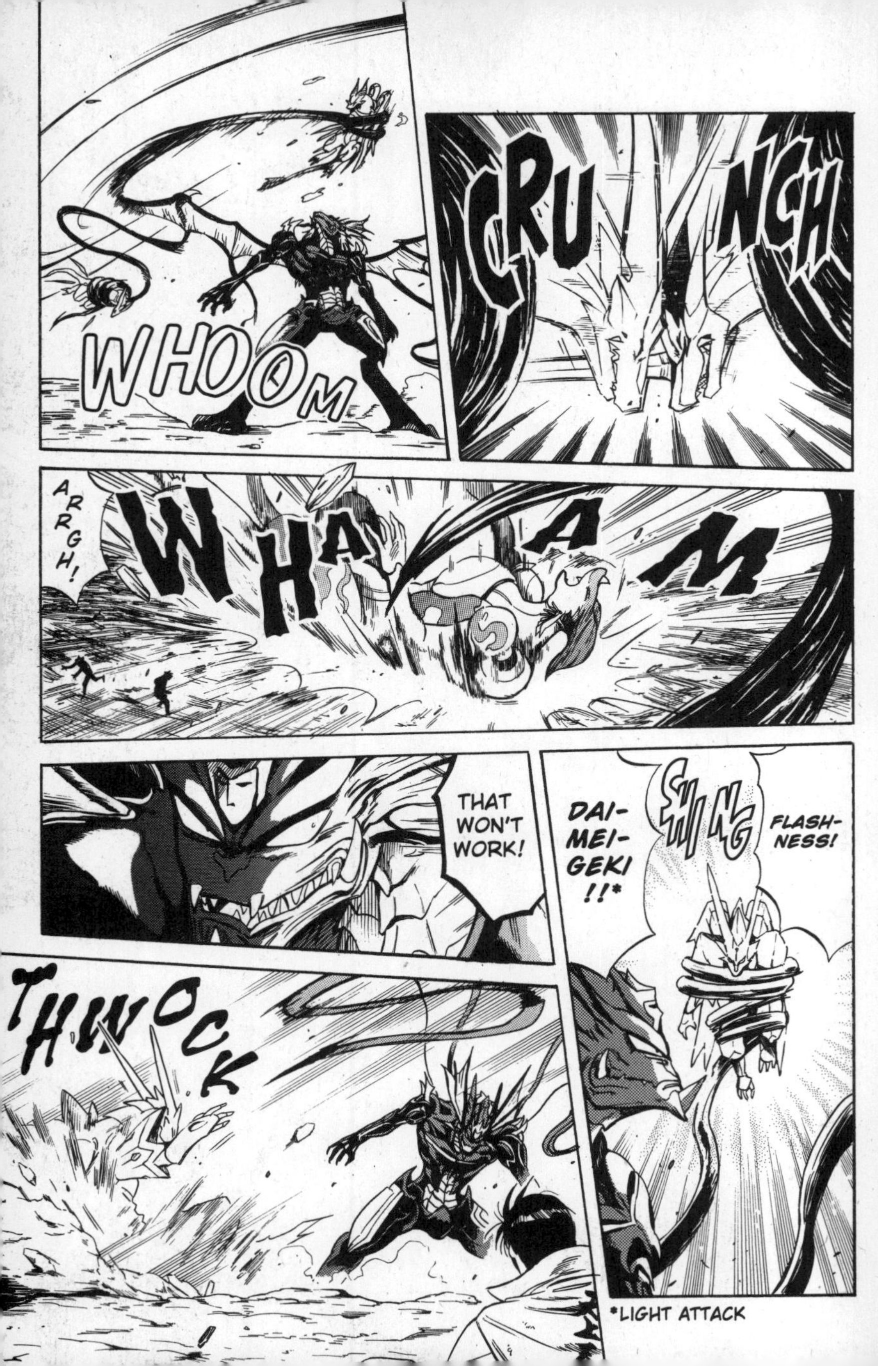
CRUNCH
WHOOM
WHAM
ARGH!
FLASHNESS!
SHING
DAI-MEI-GEKI!!*
THAT WON'T WORK!
THWOCK

*LIGHT ATTACK

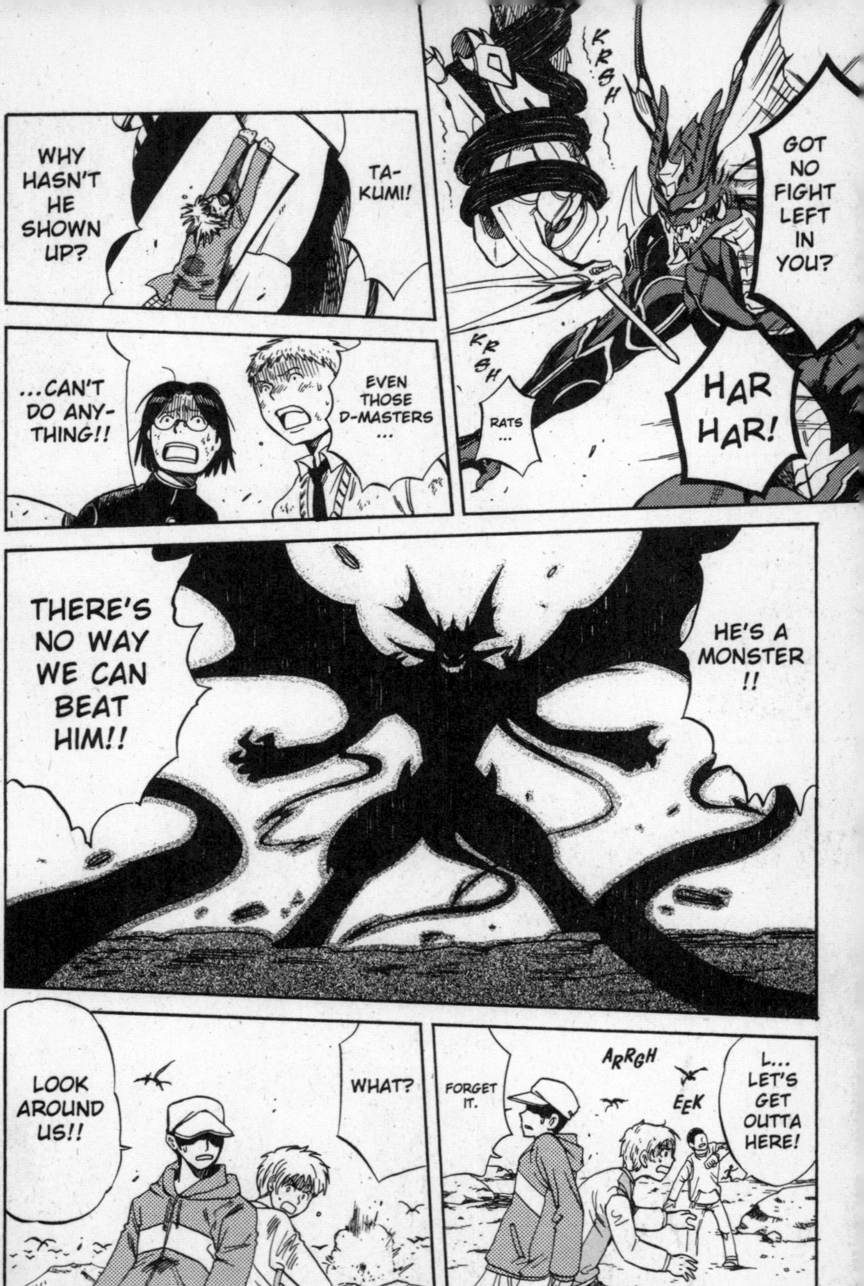
KRSH
GOT NO FIGHT LEFT IN YOU?
KRSH
RATS...
HAR HAR!
TA-KUMI!
WHY HASN'T HE SHOWN UP?
EVEN THOSE D-MASTERS...
...CAN'T DO ANY-THING!!
HE'S A MONSTER!!
THERE'S NO WAY WE CAN BEAT HIM!!
L... LET'S GET OUTTA HERE!
EEK
ARRGH
FORGET IT.
WHAT?
LOOK AROUND US!!

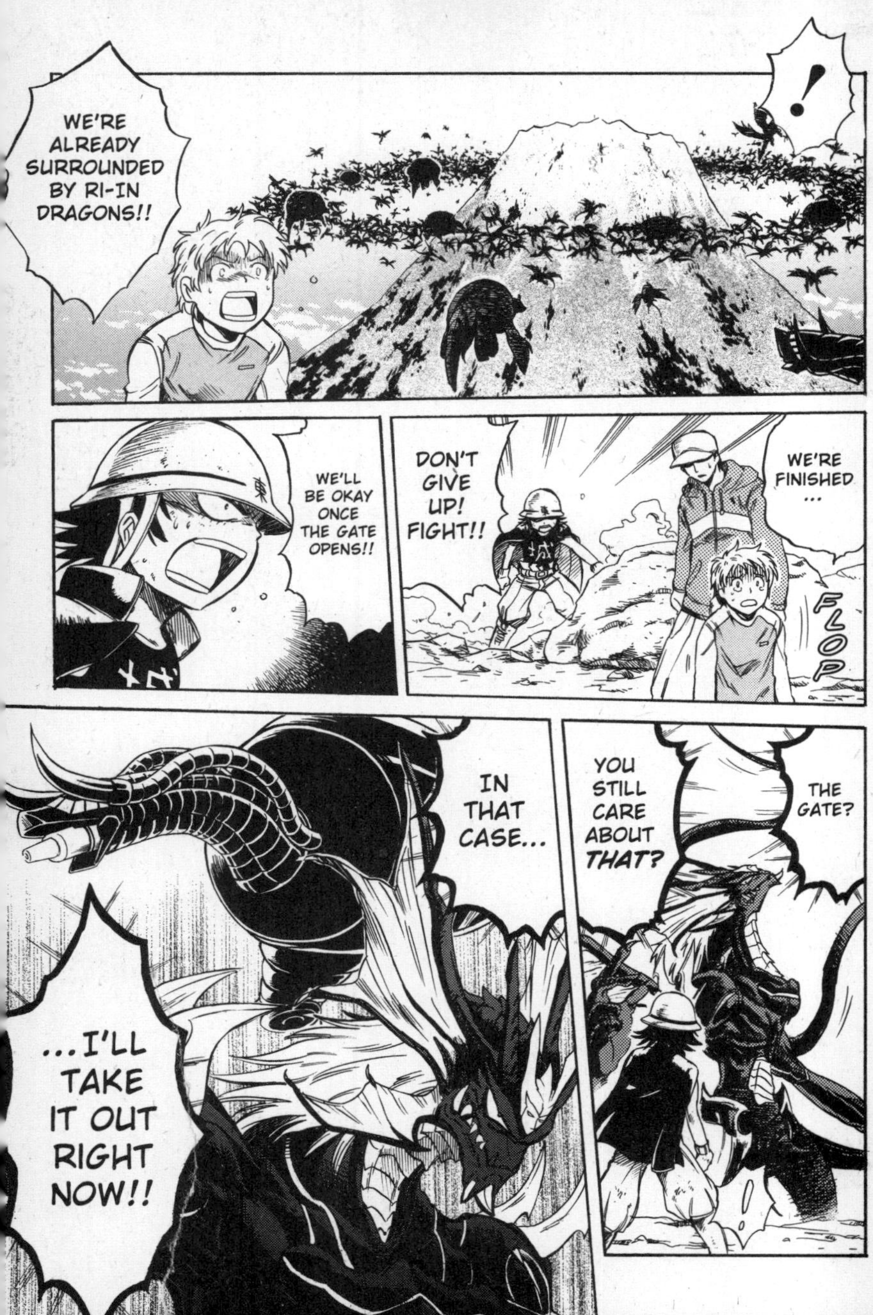
!
WE'RE ALREADY SURROUNDED BY RI-IN DRAGONS!!
WE'RE FINISHED...
FLOP
DON'T GIVE UP! FIGHT!!
WE'LL BE OKAY ONCE THE GATE OPENS!!
THE GATE?
YOU STILL CARE ABOUT *THAT*?
!
IN THAT CASE...
...I'LL TAKE IT OUT RIGHT NOW!!

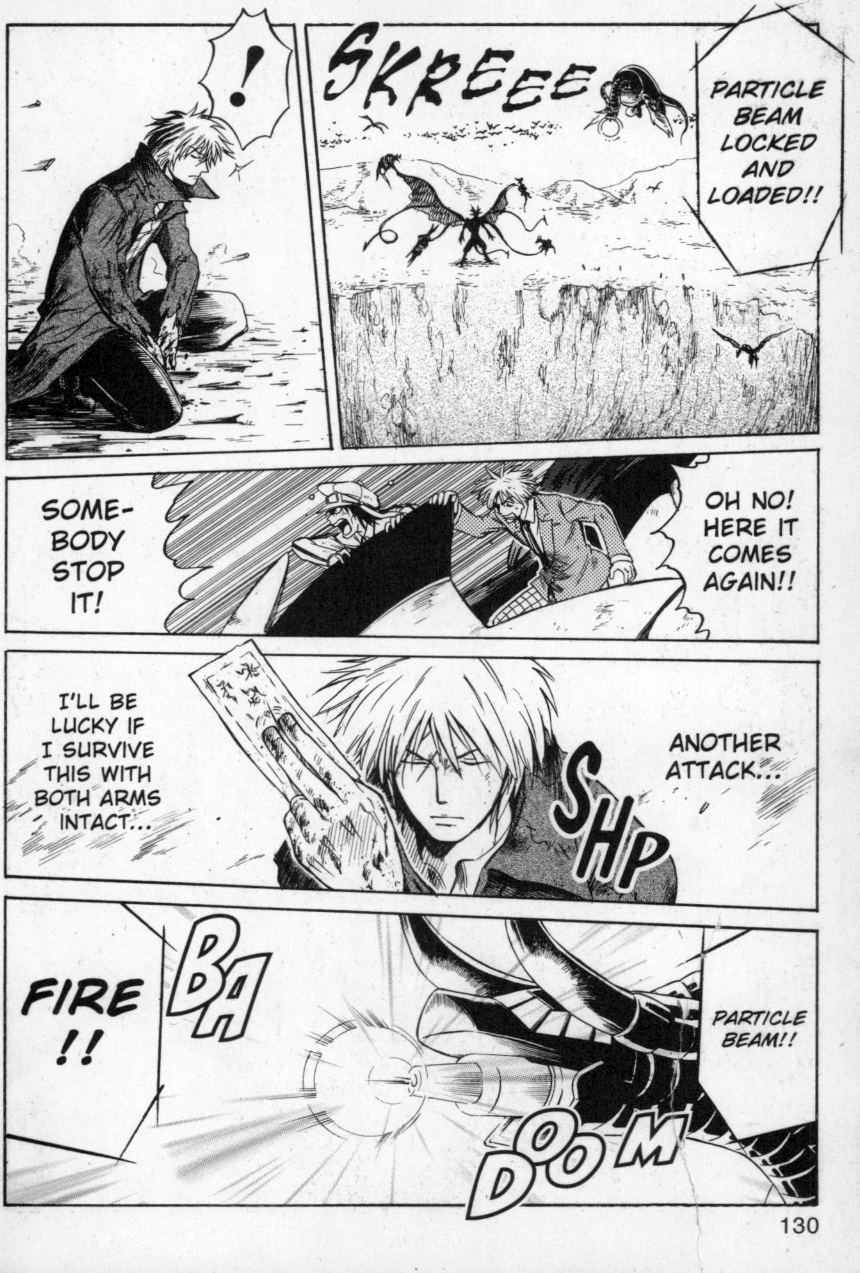
PARTICLE BEAM LOCKED AND LOADED!!
SKREEE
!
OH NO! HERE IT COMES AGAIN!!
SOME-BODY STOP IT!
ANOTHER ATTACK...
SHP
I'LL BE LUCKY IF I SURVIVE THIS WITH BOTH ARMS INTACT...
PARTICLE BEAM!!
BA
FIRE!!
DOOM

READ THIS WAY

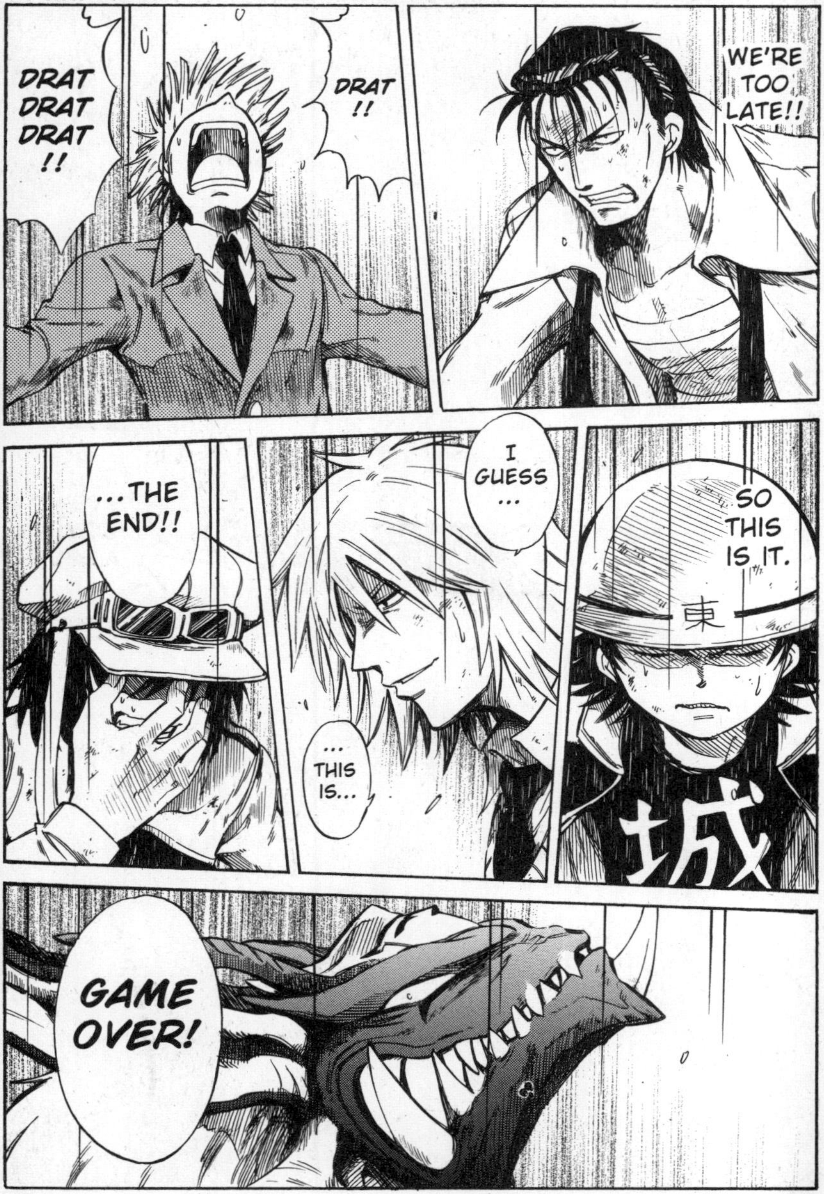
WE'RE TOO LATE!!
DRAT !!
DRAT DRAT DRAT !!
SO THIS IS IT.
I GUESS ...
... THIS IS...
...THE END!!
GAME OVER!

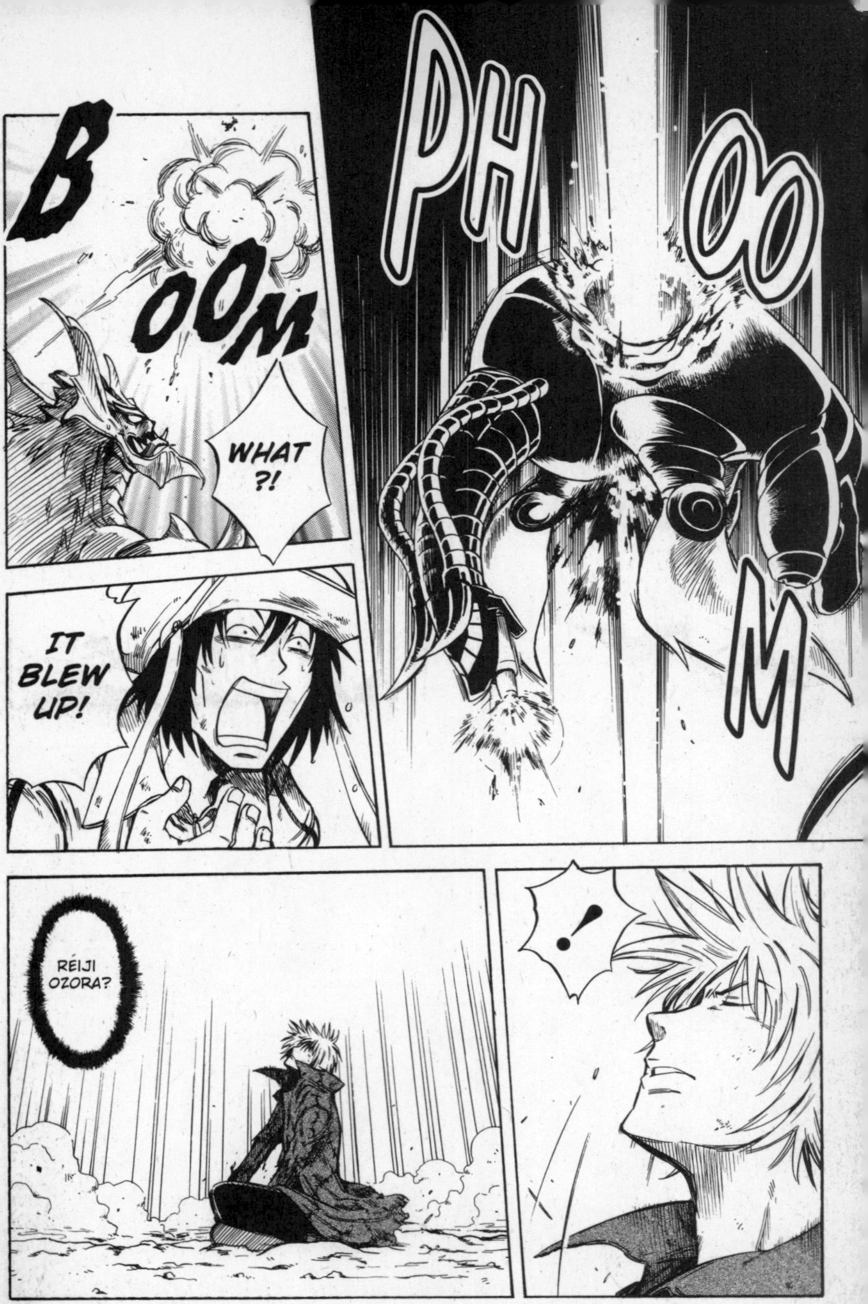
PHOOM
BOOM
WHAT ?!
IT BLEW UP!
!
RÉIJI OZORA?

READ THIS WAY

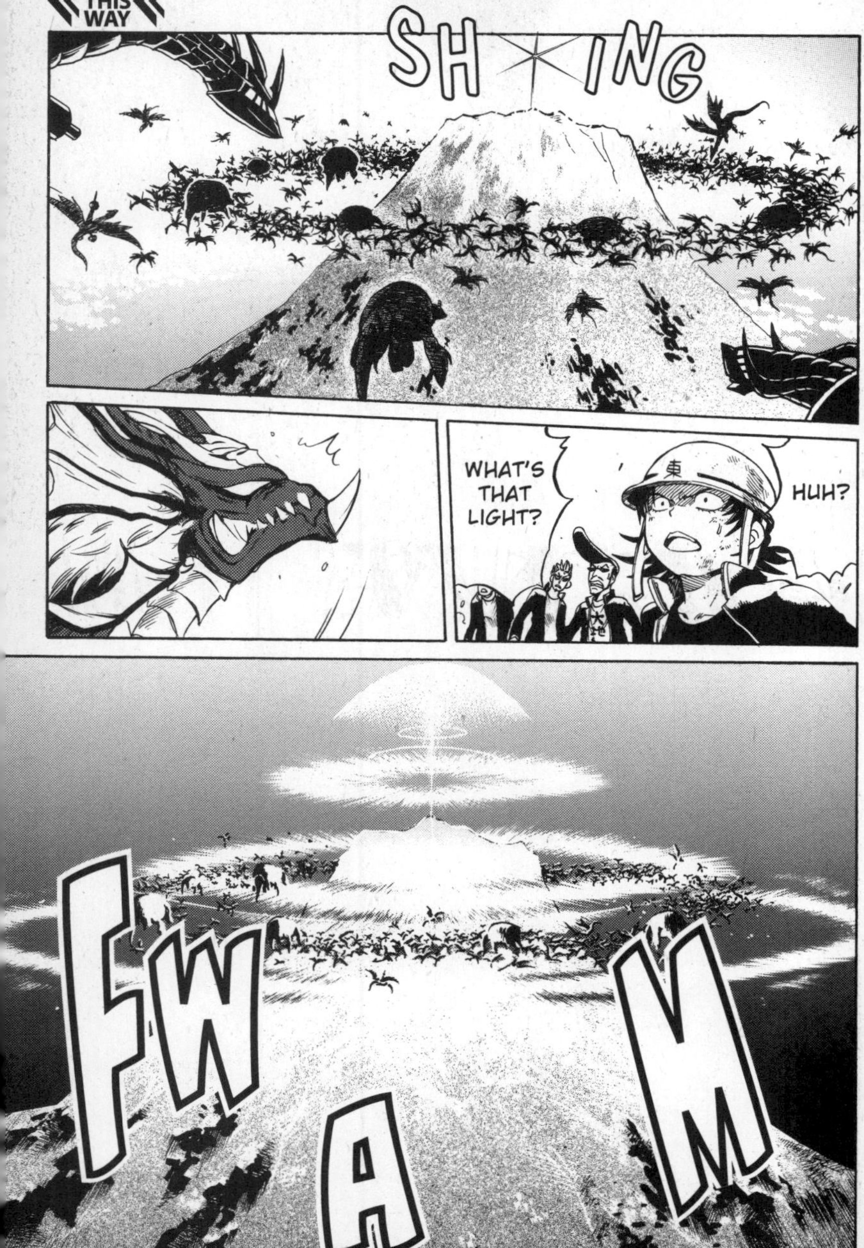
SHING
HUH?
WHAT'S THAT LIGHT?
FWAM

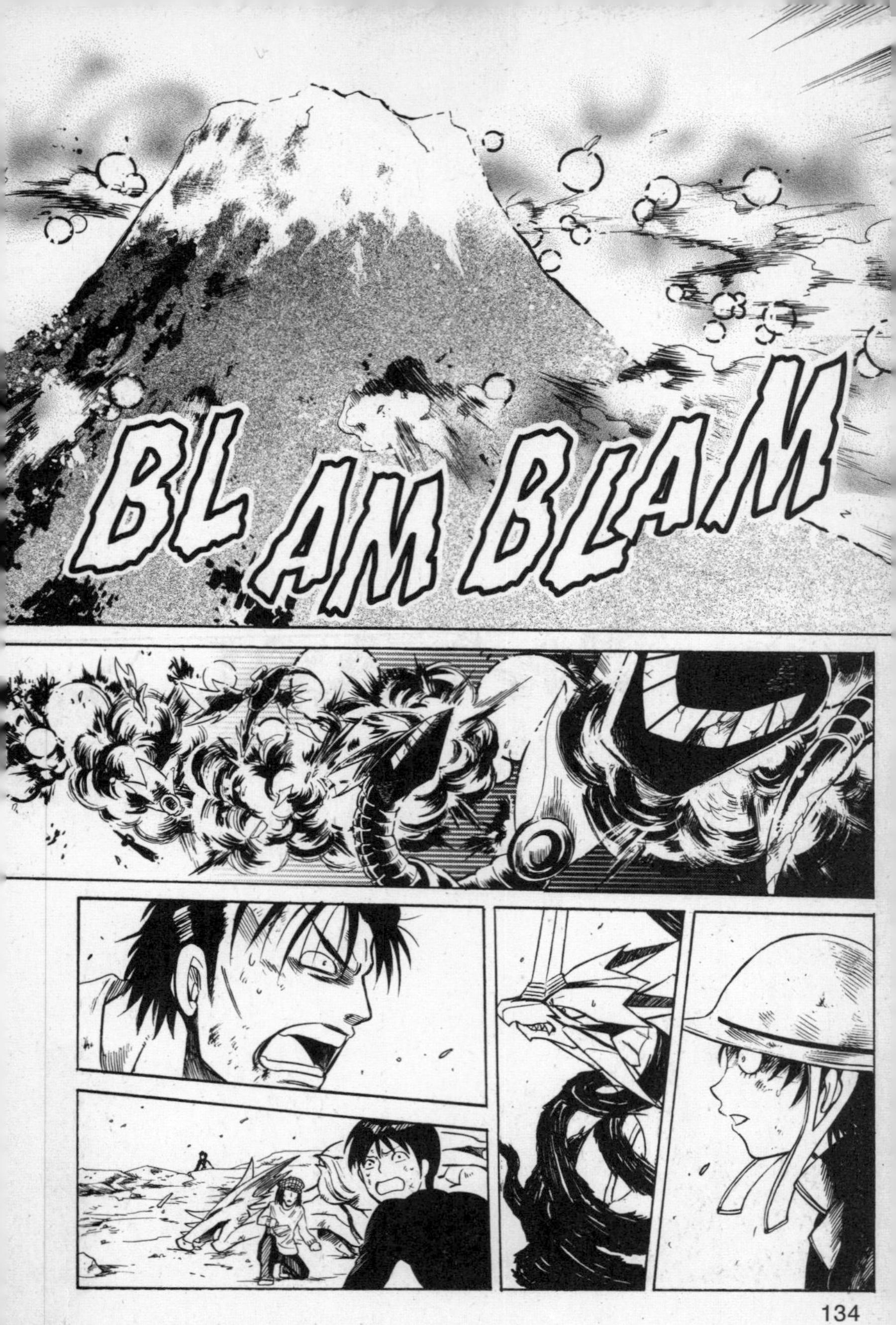
BLAM BLAM

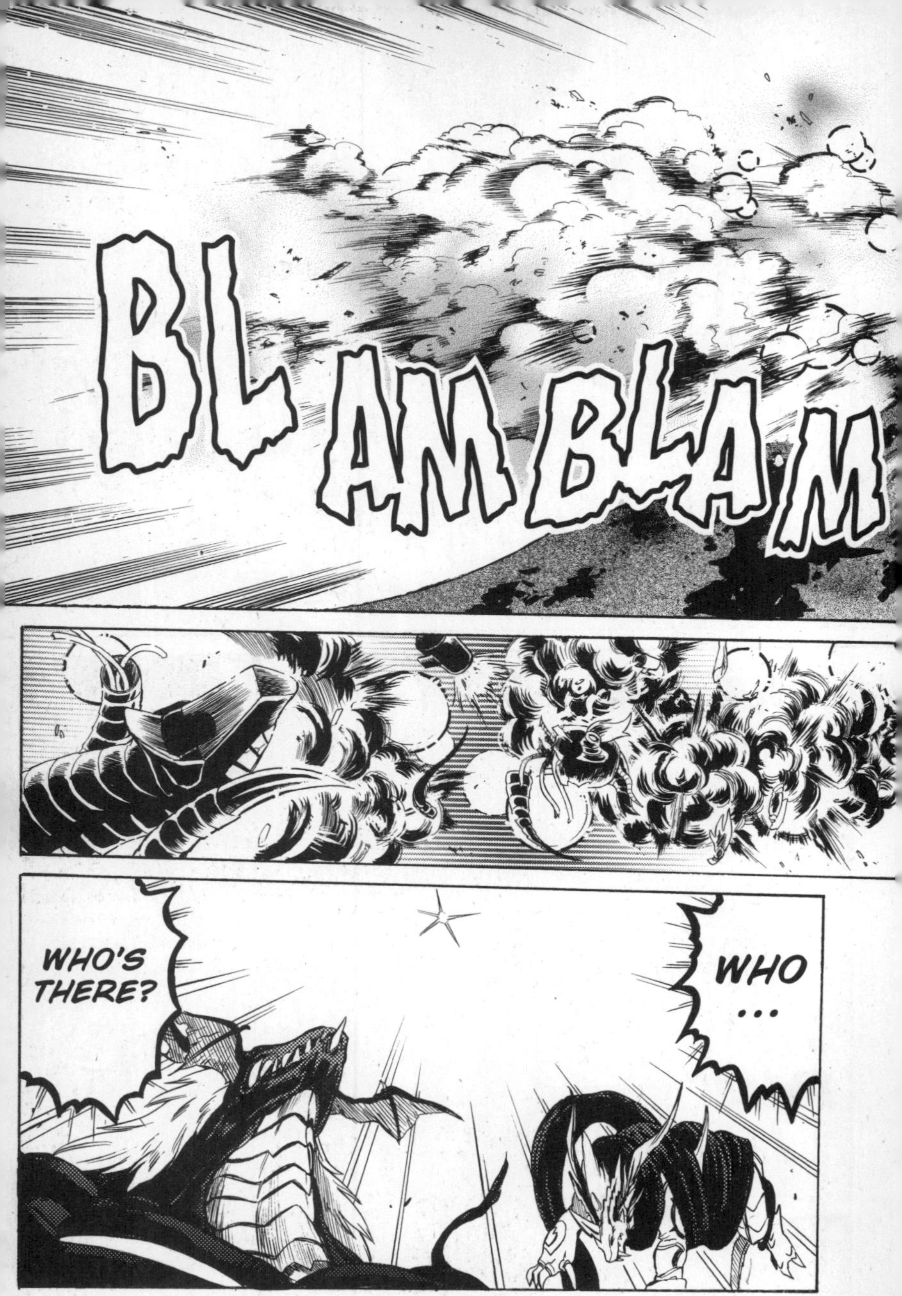
BLAM BLAM
WHO ...
WHO'S THERE?

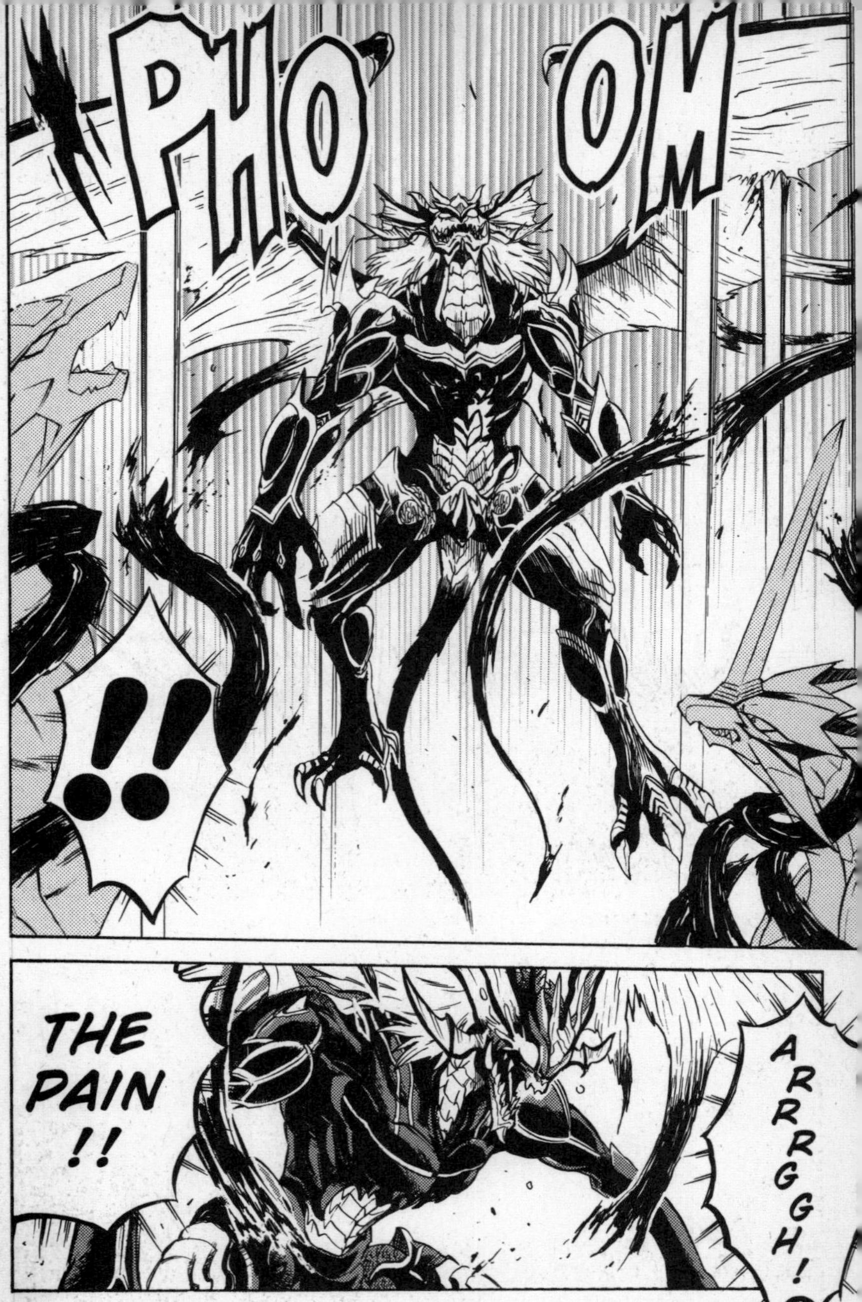
PHO OM
!!
ARRRGGH!
THE PAIN !!

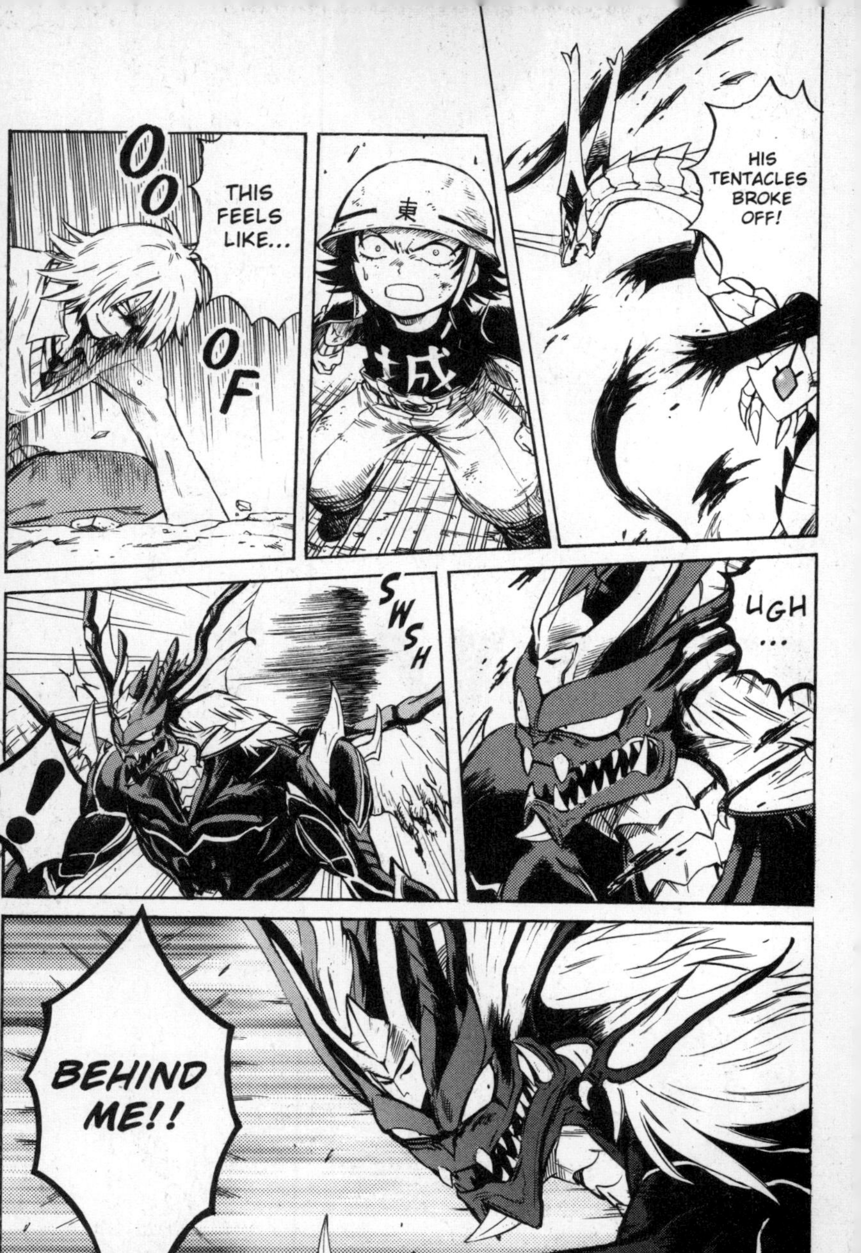
HIS TENTACLES BROKE OFF!
東
成
THIS FEELS LIKE...
OOOF
UGH ...
SWSH
!!
BEHIND ME!!

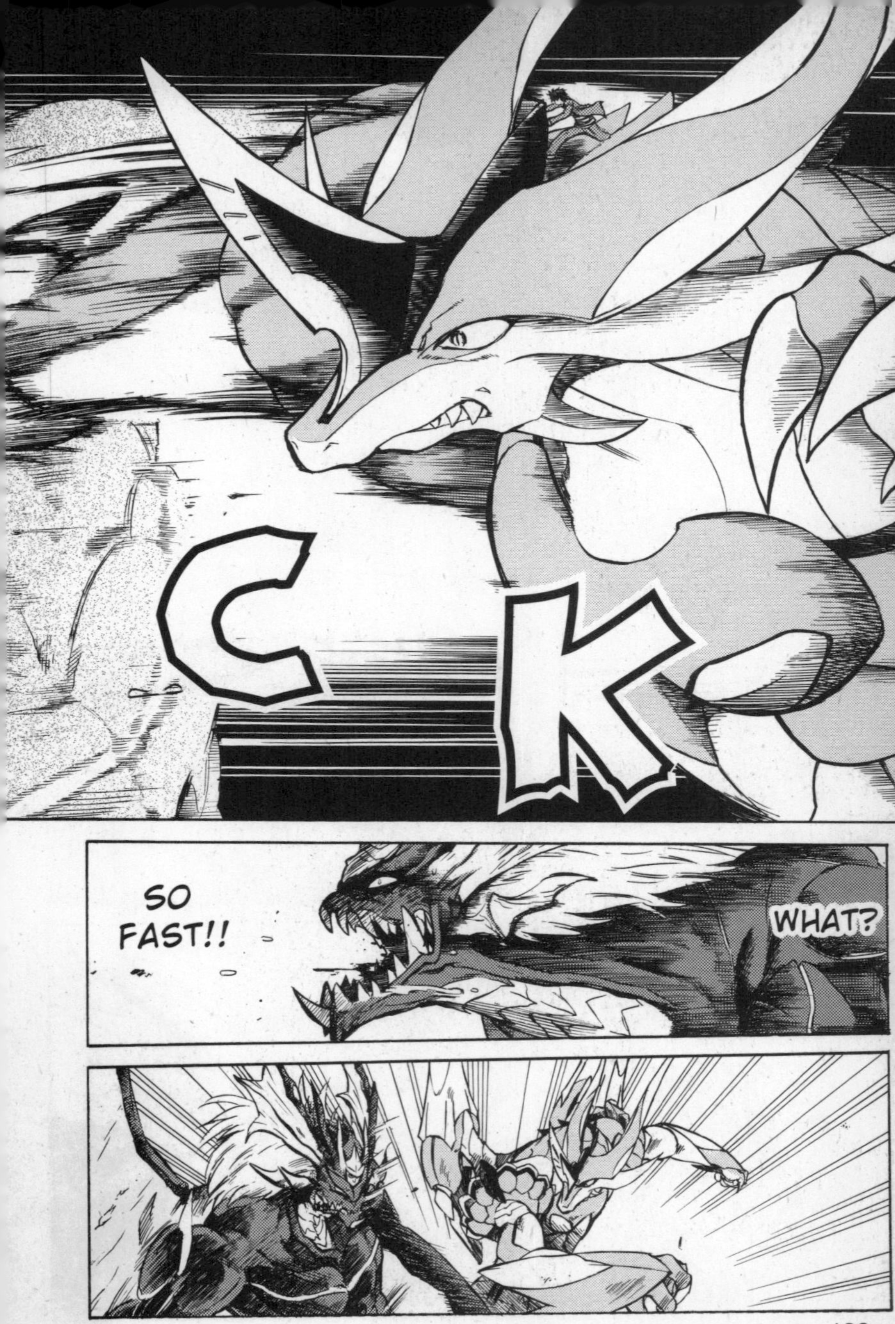
CK
WHAT?
SO FAST!!

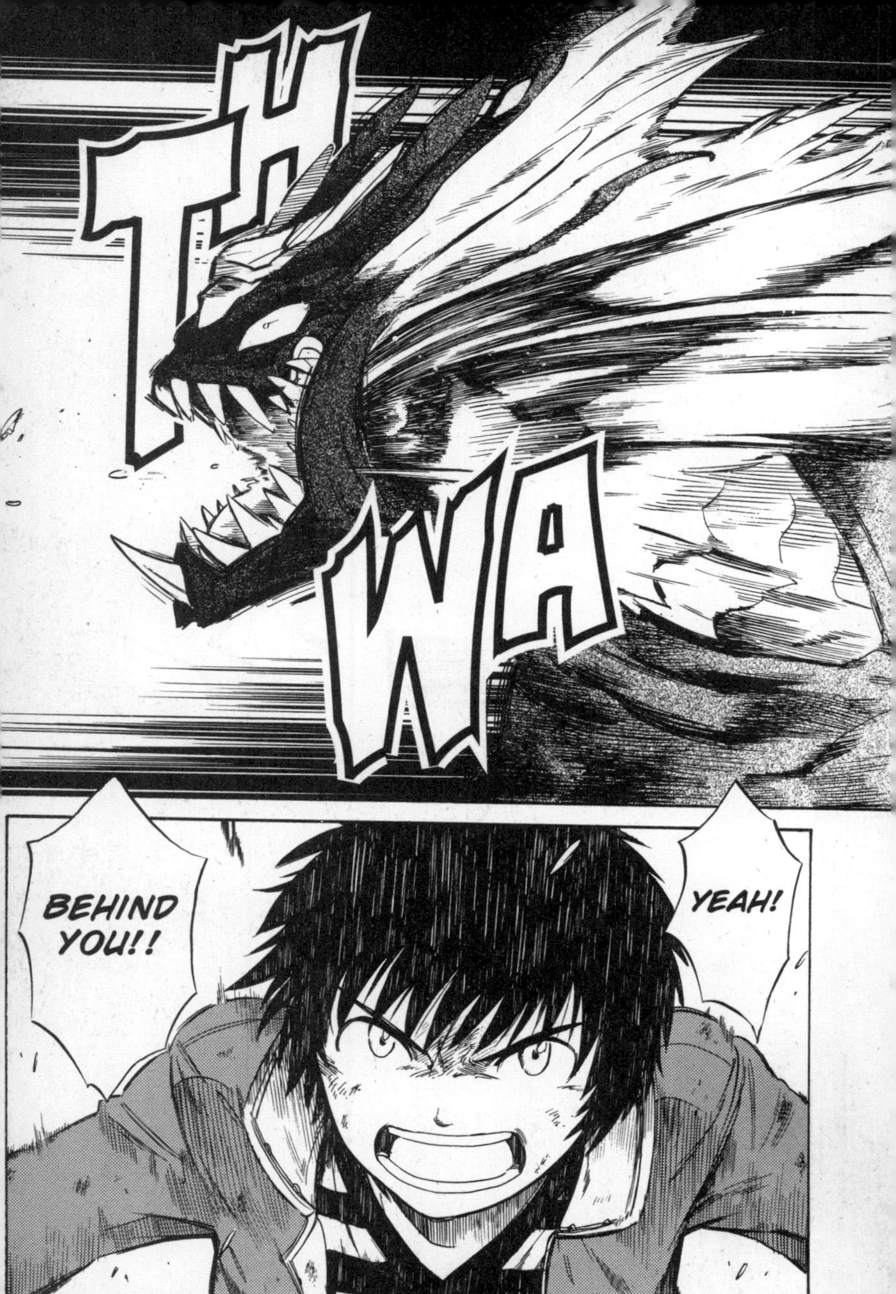
THWA
YEAH!
BEHIND YOU!!

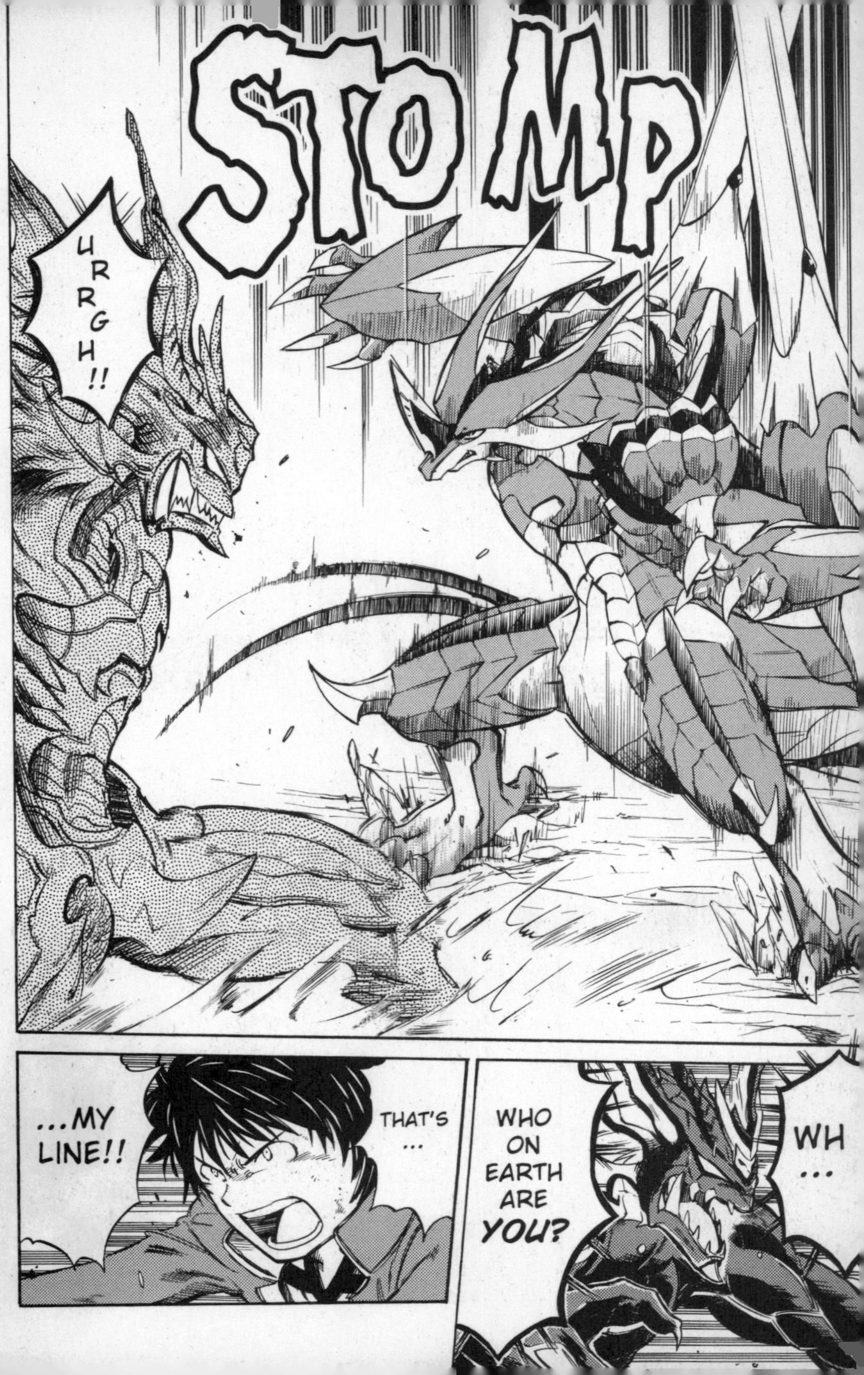
STOMP
URRGH!!
WH...
WHO ON EARTH ARE YOU?
THAT'S...
...MY LINE!!

READ THIS WAY

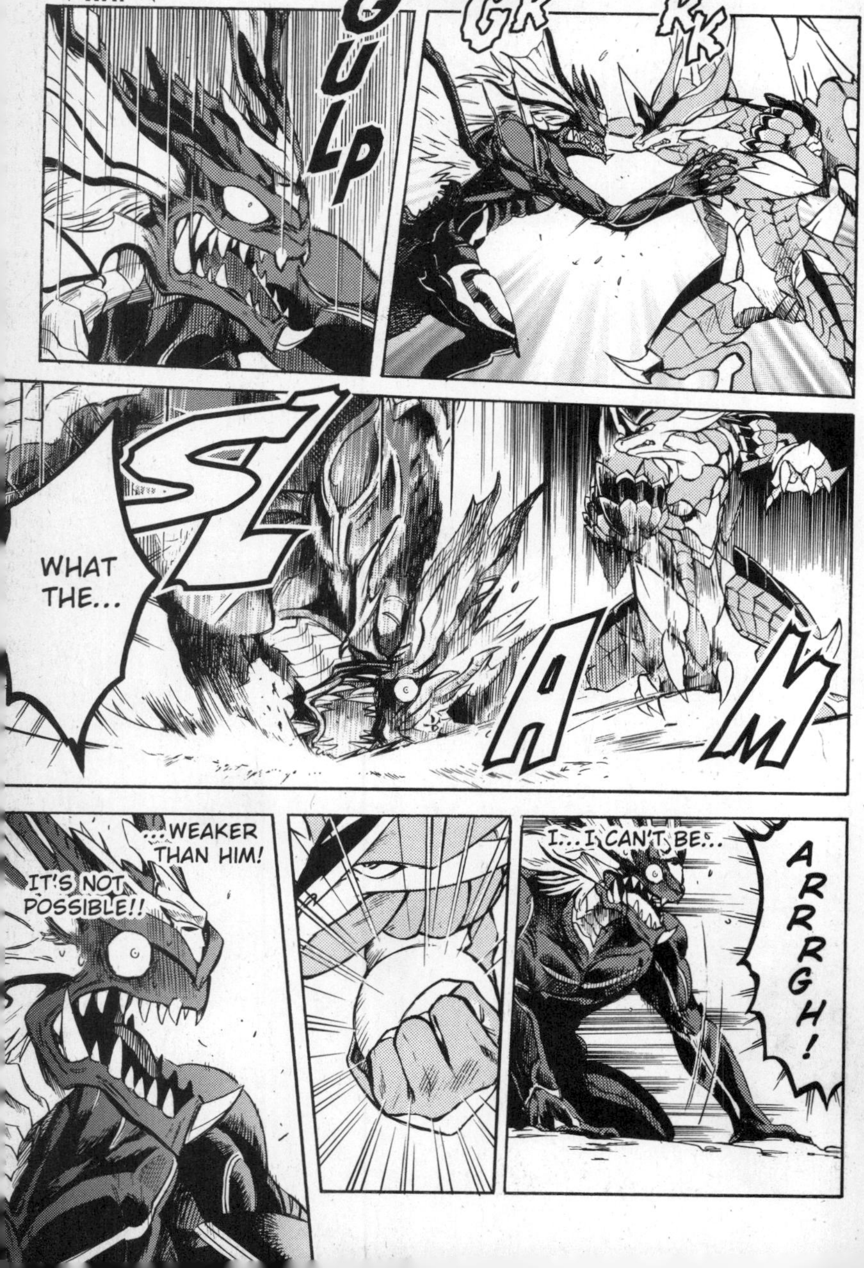
GR
RK
GULP
SLAM
WHAT THE...
I... I CAN'T BE...
ARRRGH!
...WEAKER THAN HIM!
IT'S NOT POSSIBLE!!

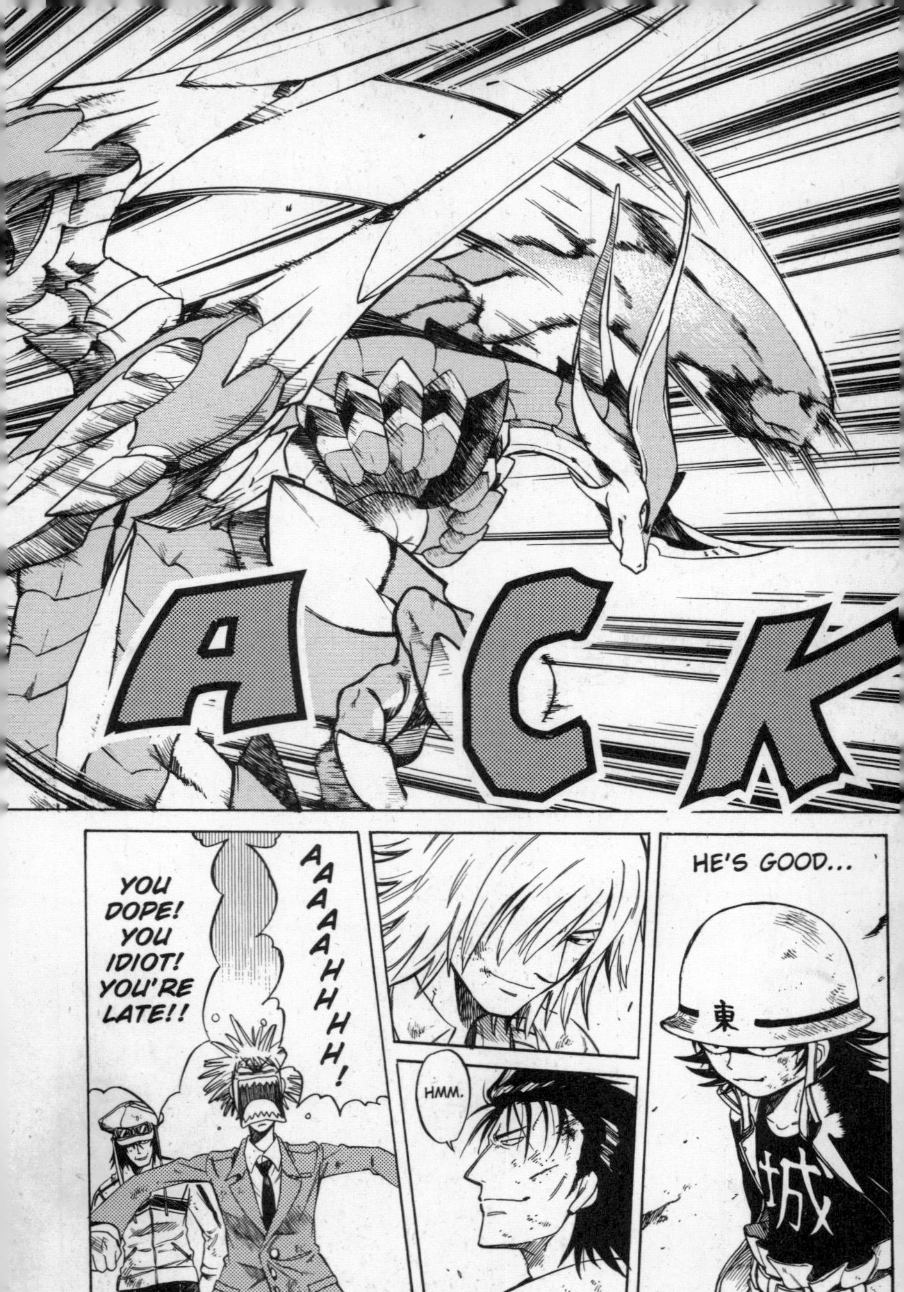
ACK
HE'S GOOD...
HMM.
AAAAAHHHH!
YOU DOPE! YOU IDIOT! YOU'RE LATE!!

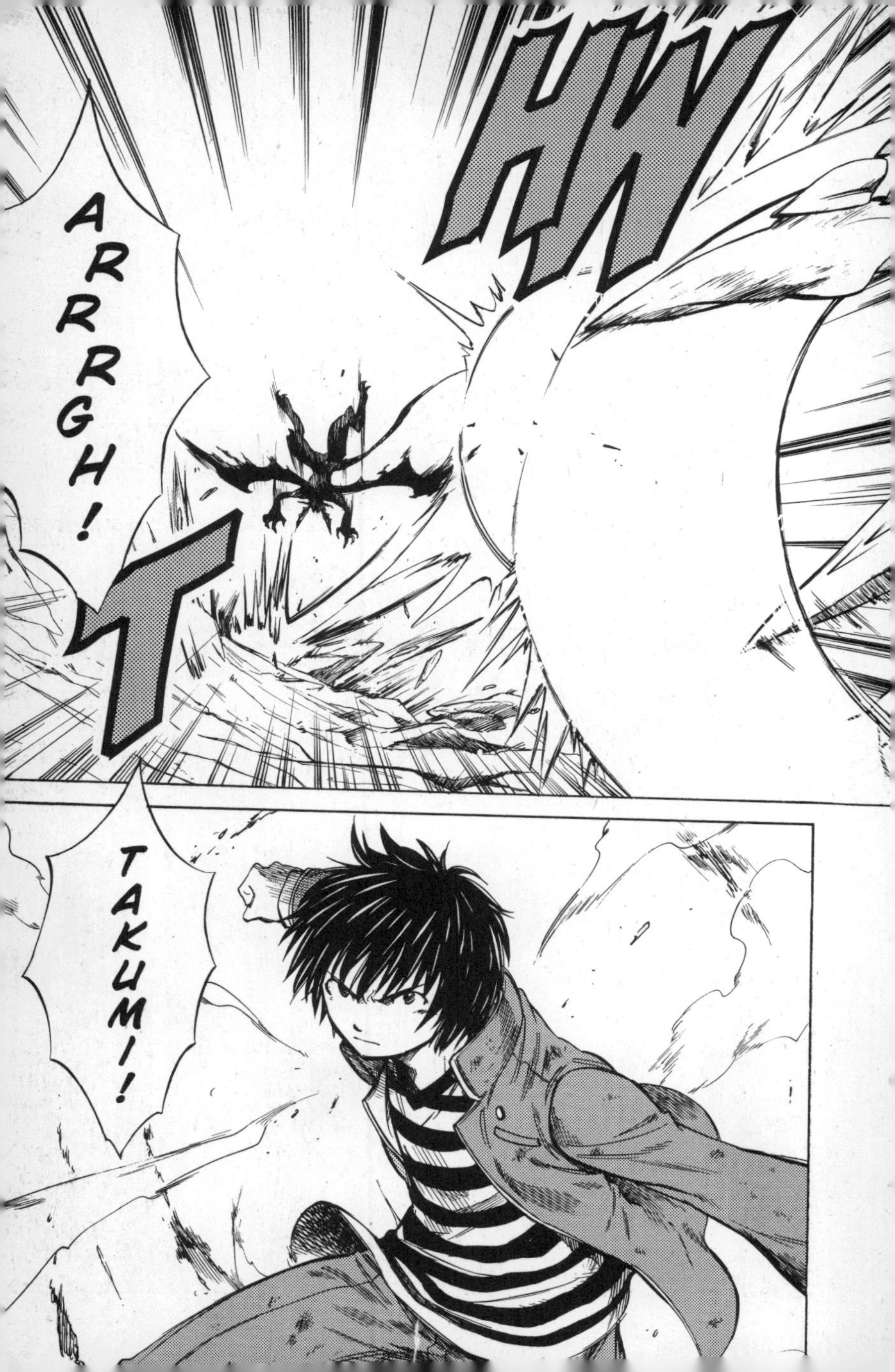
ARRRGH!
TAKUMI!!

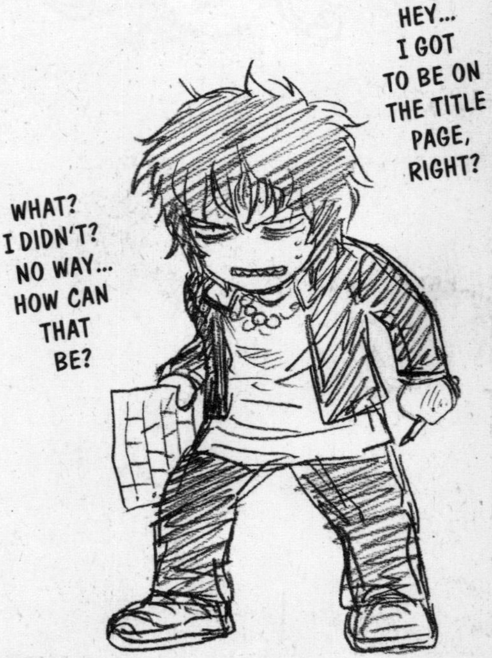
HEY... I GOT TO BE ON THE TITLE PAGE, RIGHT?
WHAT? I DIDN'T? NO WAY... HOW CAN THAT BE?

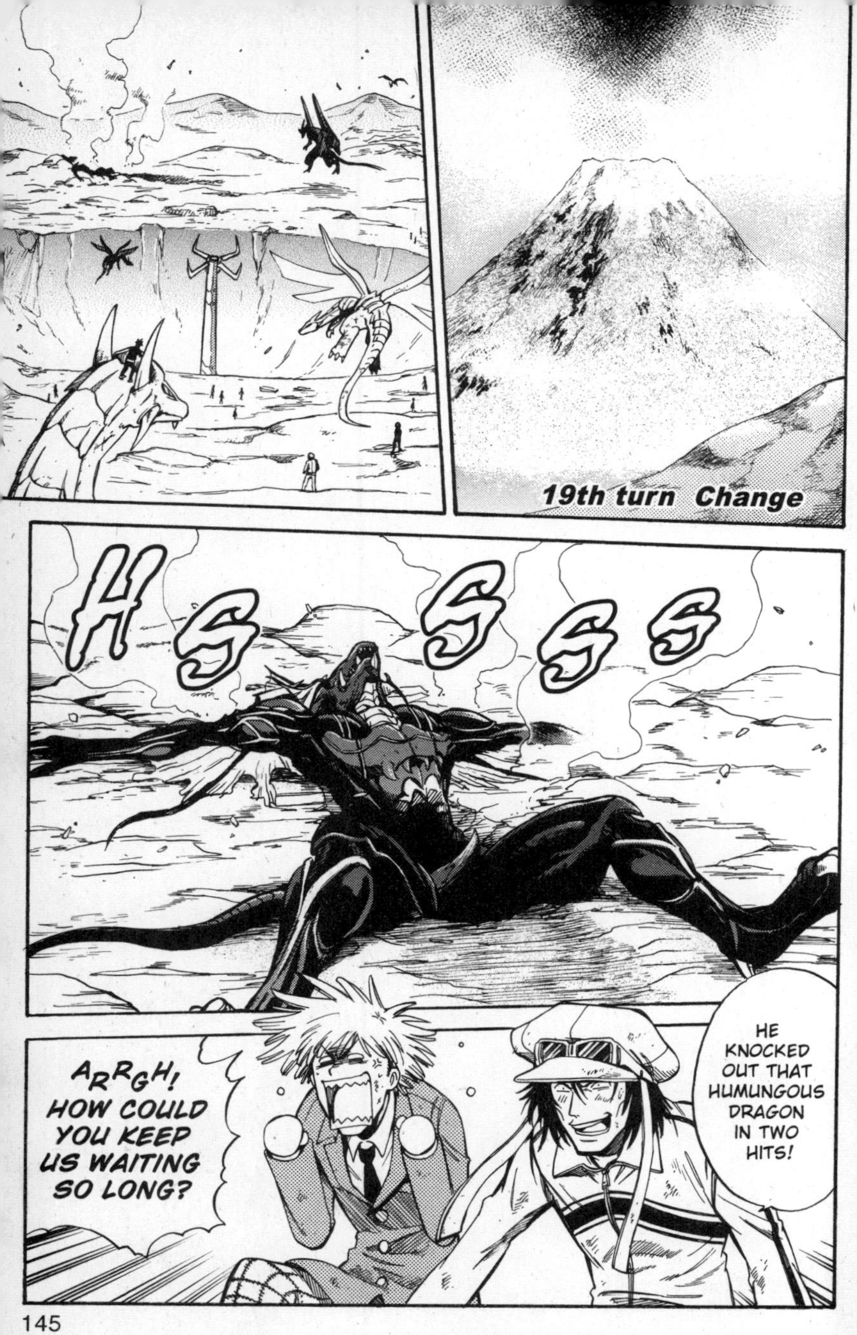
19th turn Change
HSSSS
HE KNOCKED OUT THAT HUMUNGOUS DRAGON IN TWO HITS!
ARRGH! HOW COULD YOU KEEP US WAITING SO LONG?

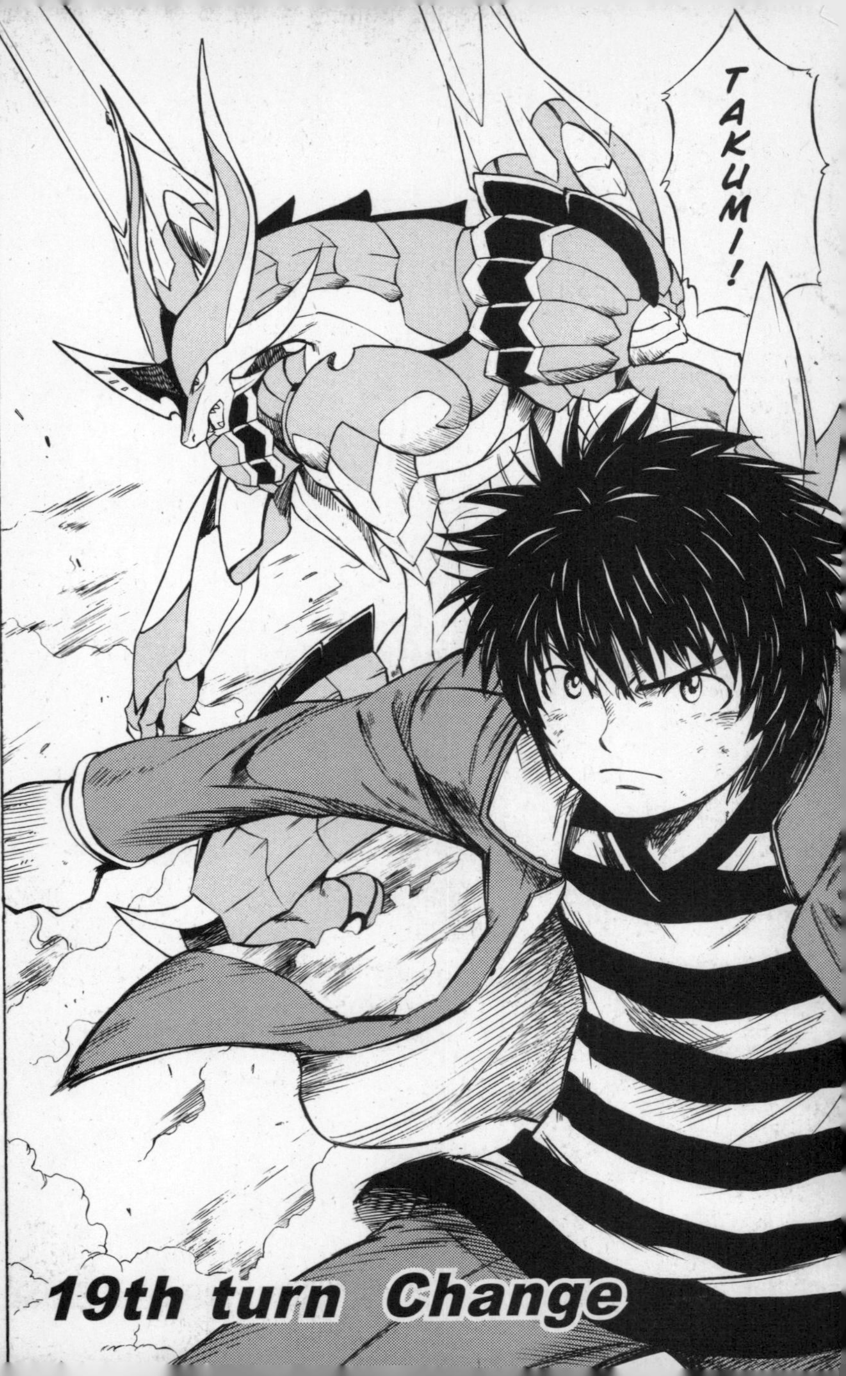
TAKUMI!
19th turn Change

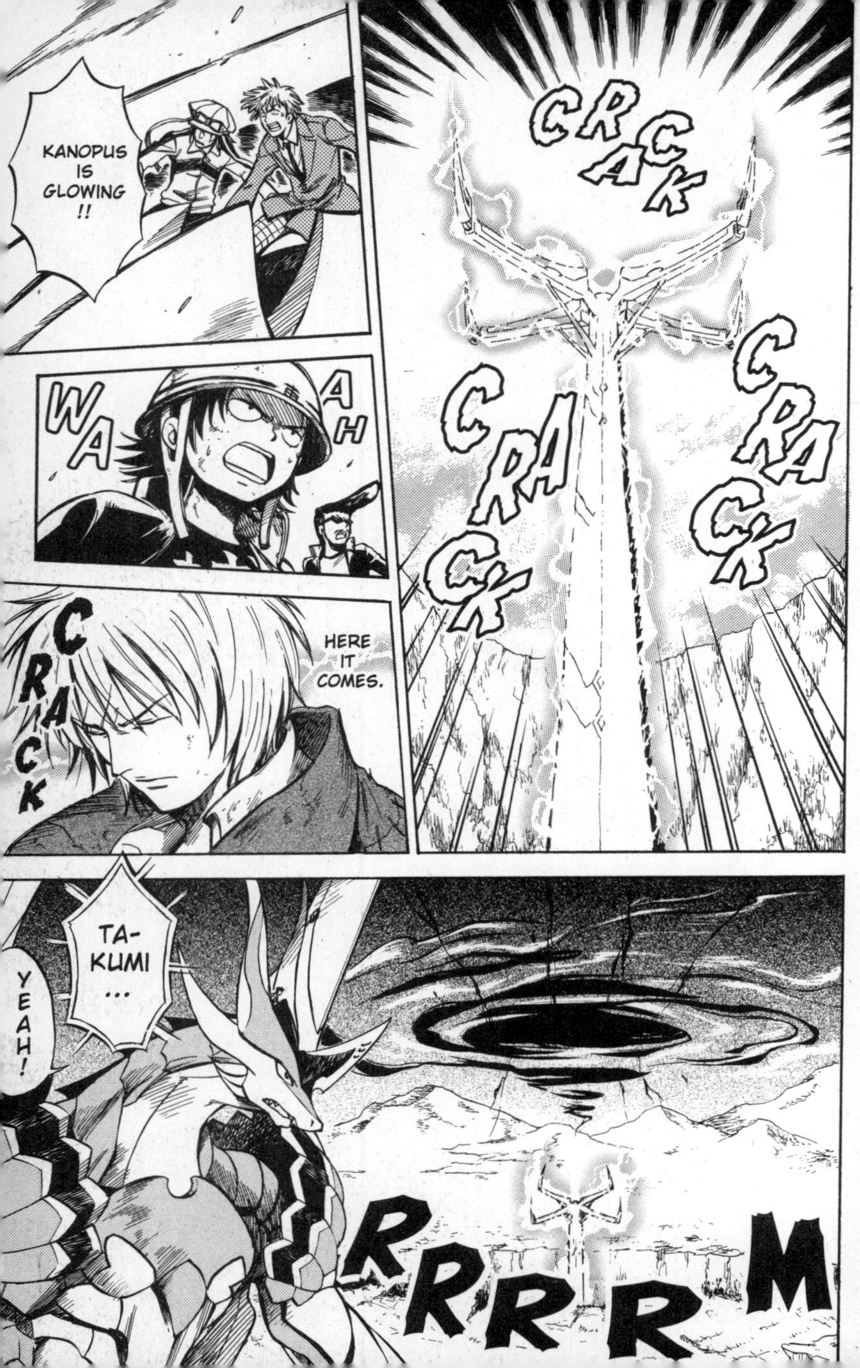
CRACK
CRACK
CRACK
KANOPUS IS GLOWING!!
WAAH
HERE IT COMES.
CRACK
TA-KUMI...
YEAH!
RRRRRM

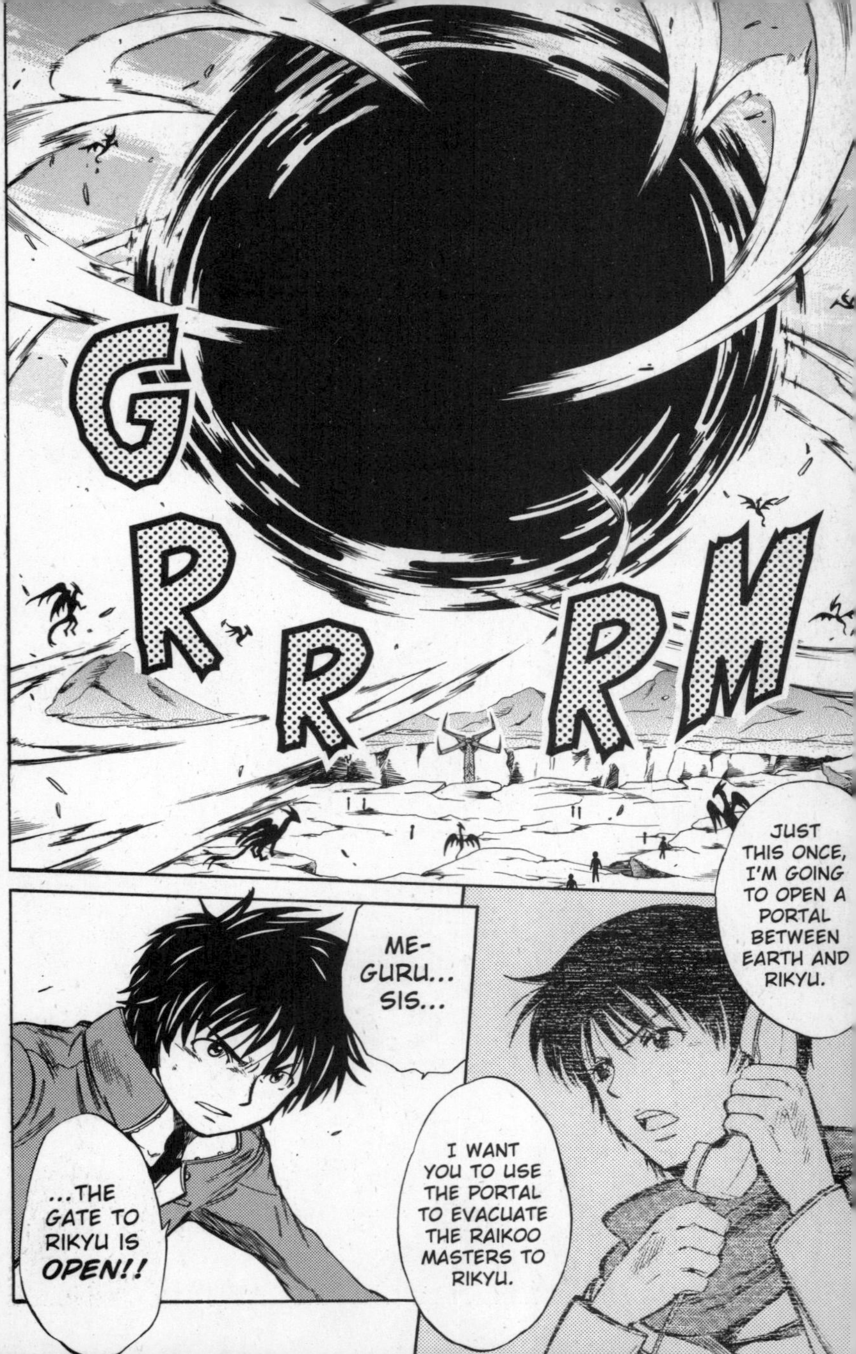
GRRRM
JUST THIS ONCE, I'M GOING TO OPEN A PORTAL BETWEEN EARTH AND RIKYU.
I WANT YOU TO USE THE PORTAL TO EVACUATE THE RAIKOO MASTERS TO RIKYU.
ME-GURU... SIS...
...THE GATE TO RIKYU IS ***OPEN!!***

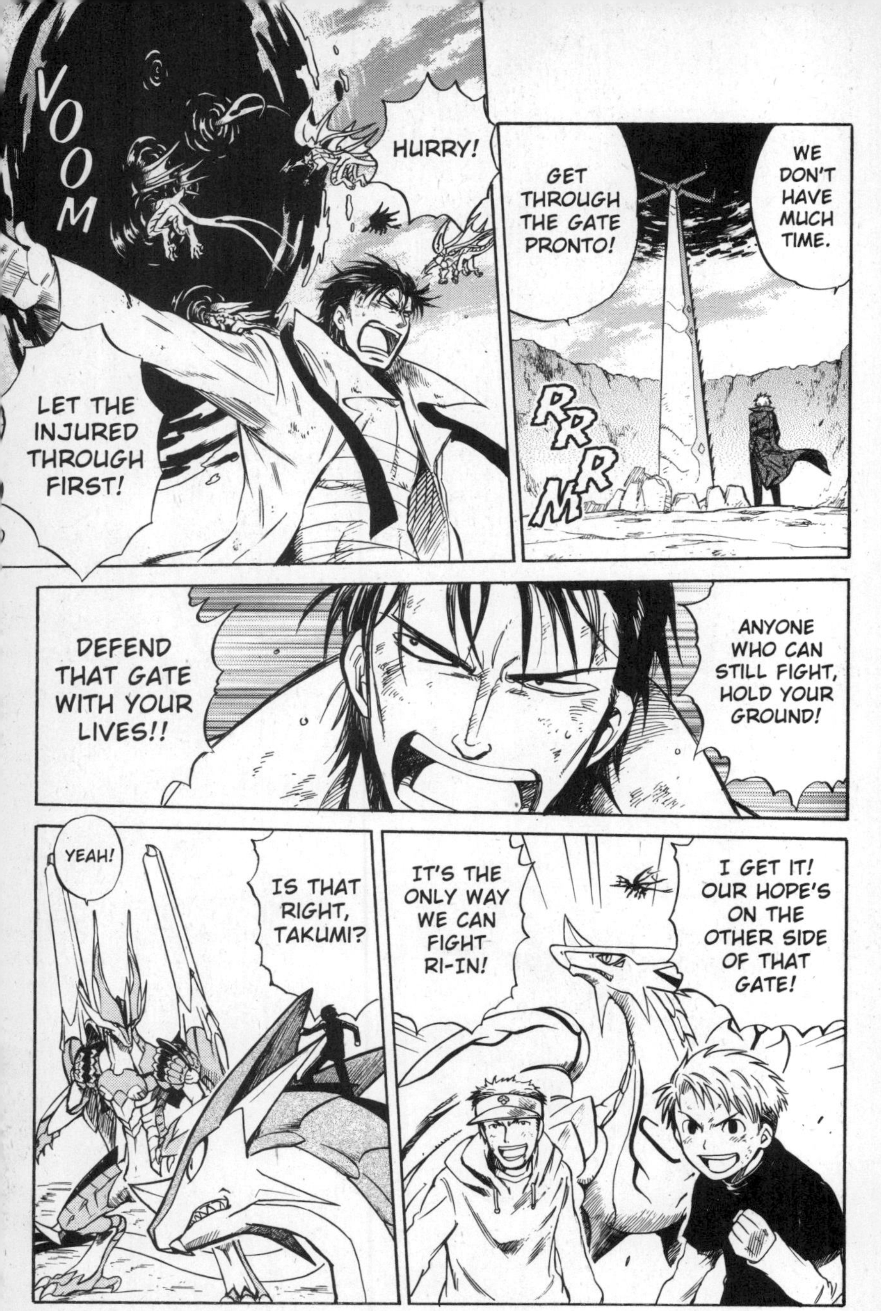

WE DON'T HAVE MUCH TIME.
GET THROUGH THE GATE PRONTO!
RRRM
HURRY!
VOOM
LET THE INJURED THROUGH FIRST!
ANYONE WHO CAN STILL FIGHT, HOLD YOUR GROUND!
DEFEND THAT GATE WITH YOUR LIVES!!
I GET IT! OUR HOPE'S ON THE OTHER SIDE OF THAT GATE!
IT'S THE ONLY WAY WE CAN FIGHT RI-IN!
IS THAT RIGHT, TAKUMI?
YEAH!

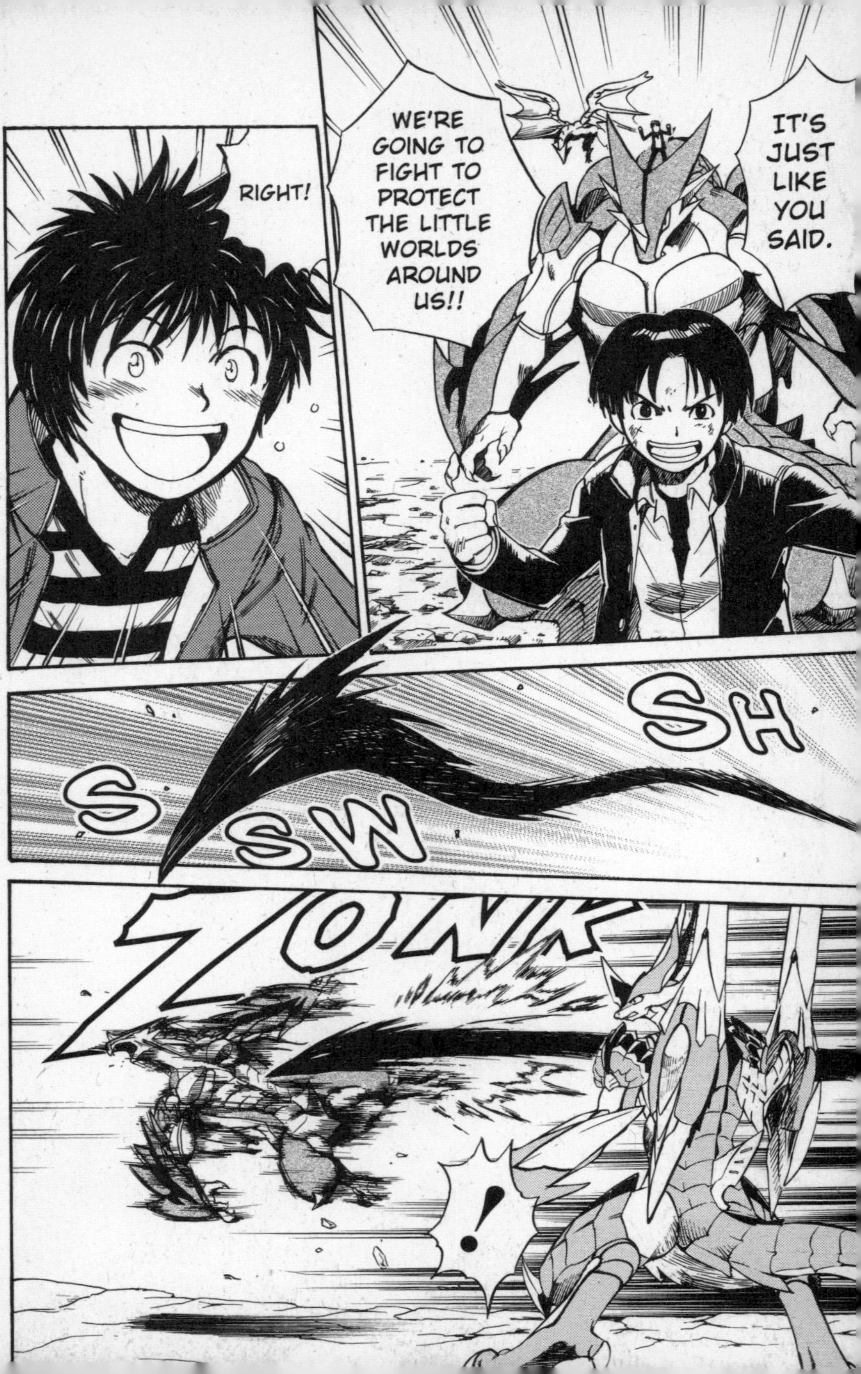
IT'S JUST LIKE YOU SAID.
WE'RE GOING TO FIGHT TO PROTECT THE LITTLE WORLDS AROUND US!!
RIGHT!
S SW SH
ZONK
!

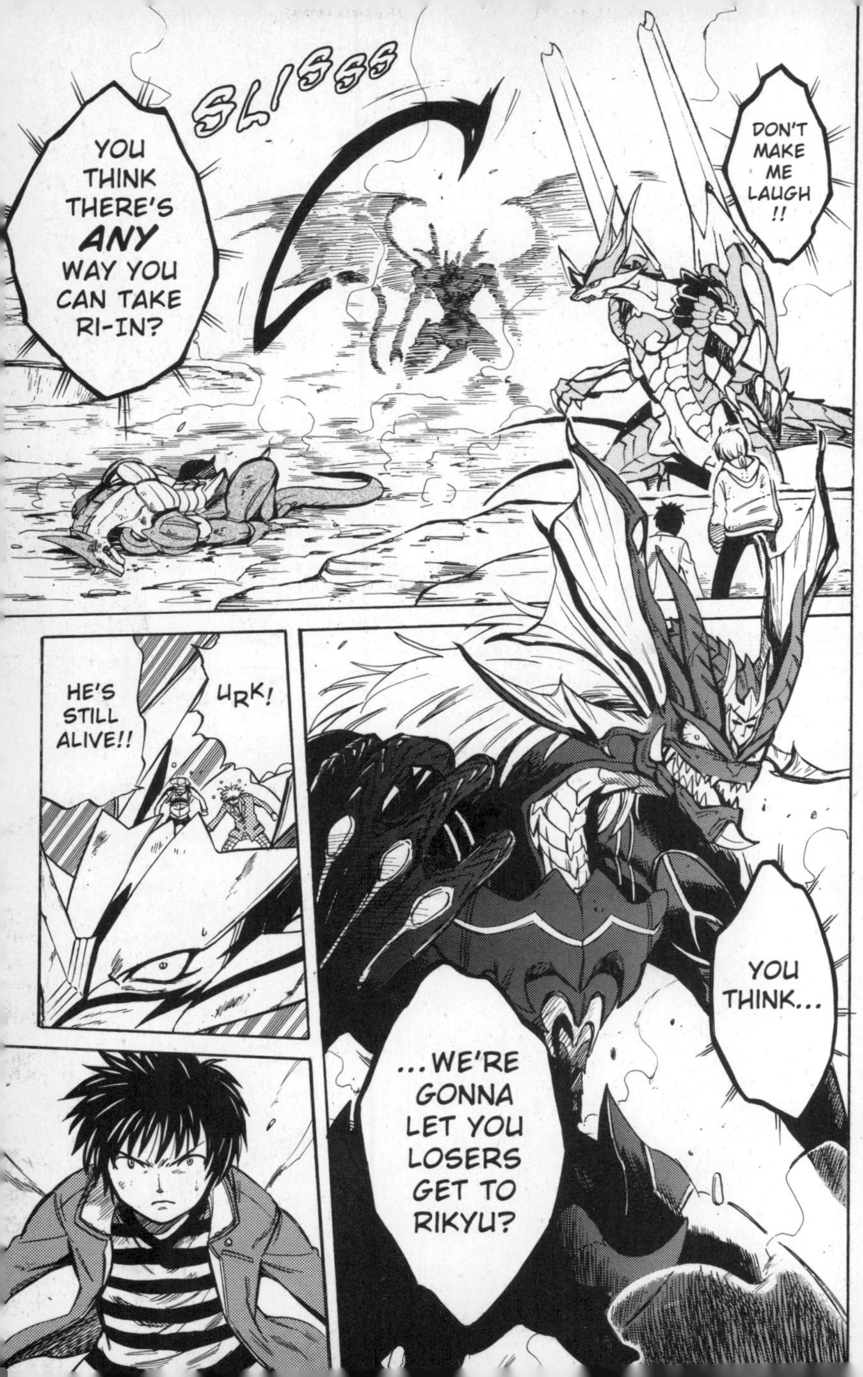
DON'T MAKE ME LAUGH!!
SLISSS
YOU THINK THERE'S ANY WAY YOU CAN TAKE RI-IN?
YOU THINK...
...WE'RE GONNA LET YOU LOSERS GET TO RIKYU?
URK!
HE'S STILL ALIVE!!

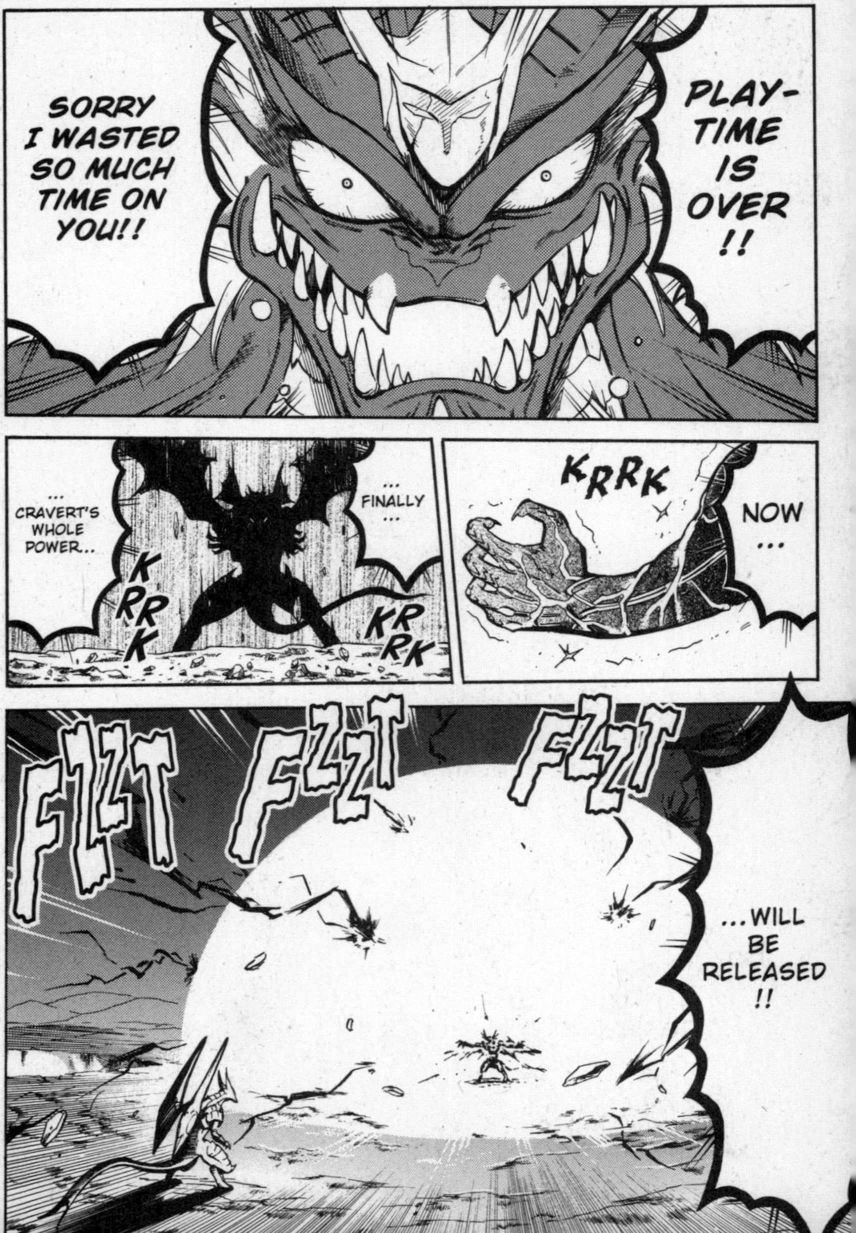
PLAY-TIME IS OVER!!
SORRY I WASTED SO MUCH TIME ON YOU!!
KRRK
NOW...
...FINALLY...
...CRAVERT'S WHOLE POWER...
KRRK
KRRK
FZZT
FZZT
FZZT
...WILL BE RELEASED!!

READ THIS WAY

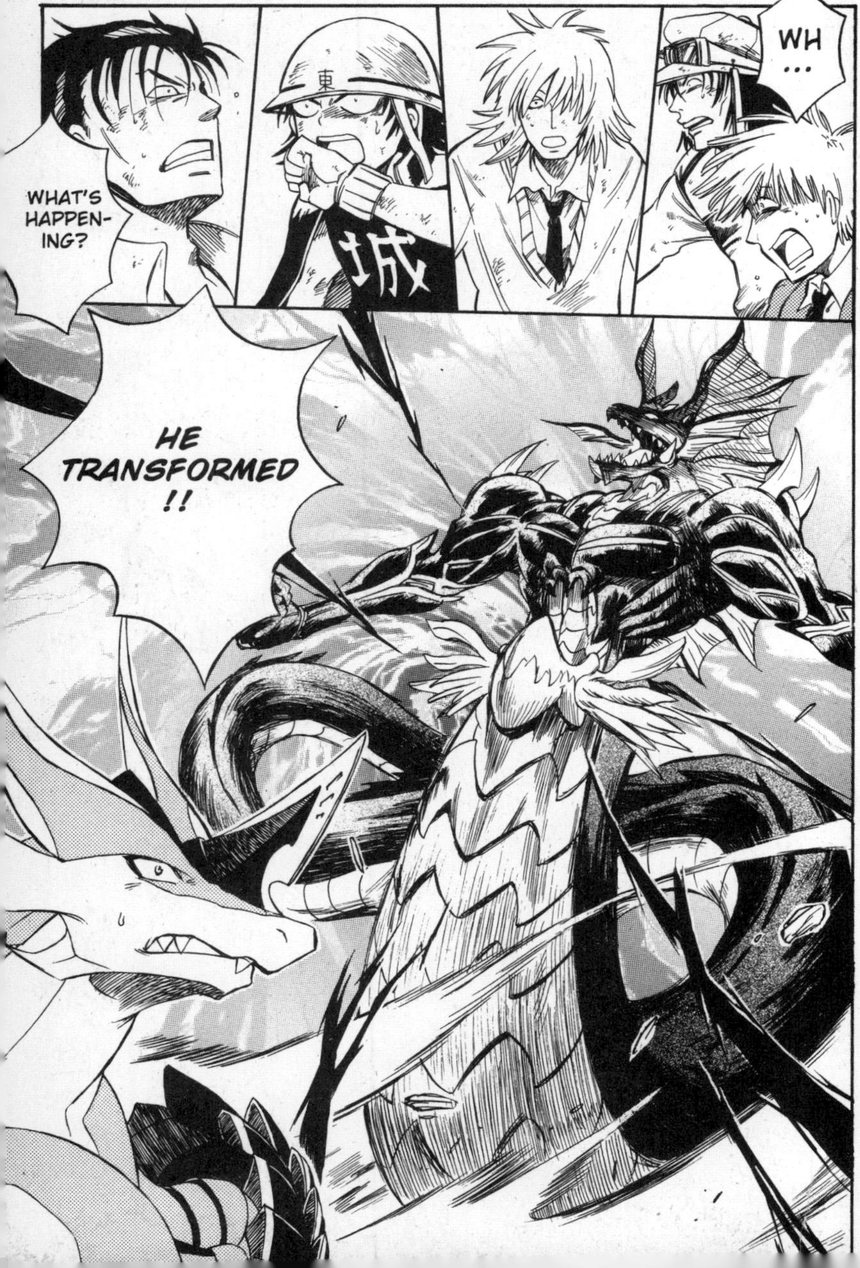
WH ...
WHAT'S HAPPEN-ING?
HE TRANSFORMED !!

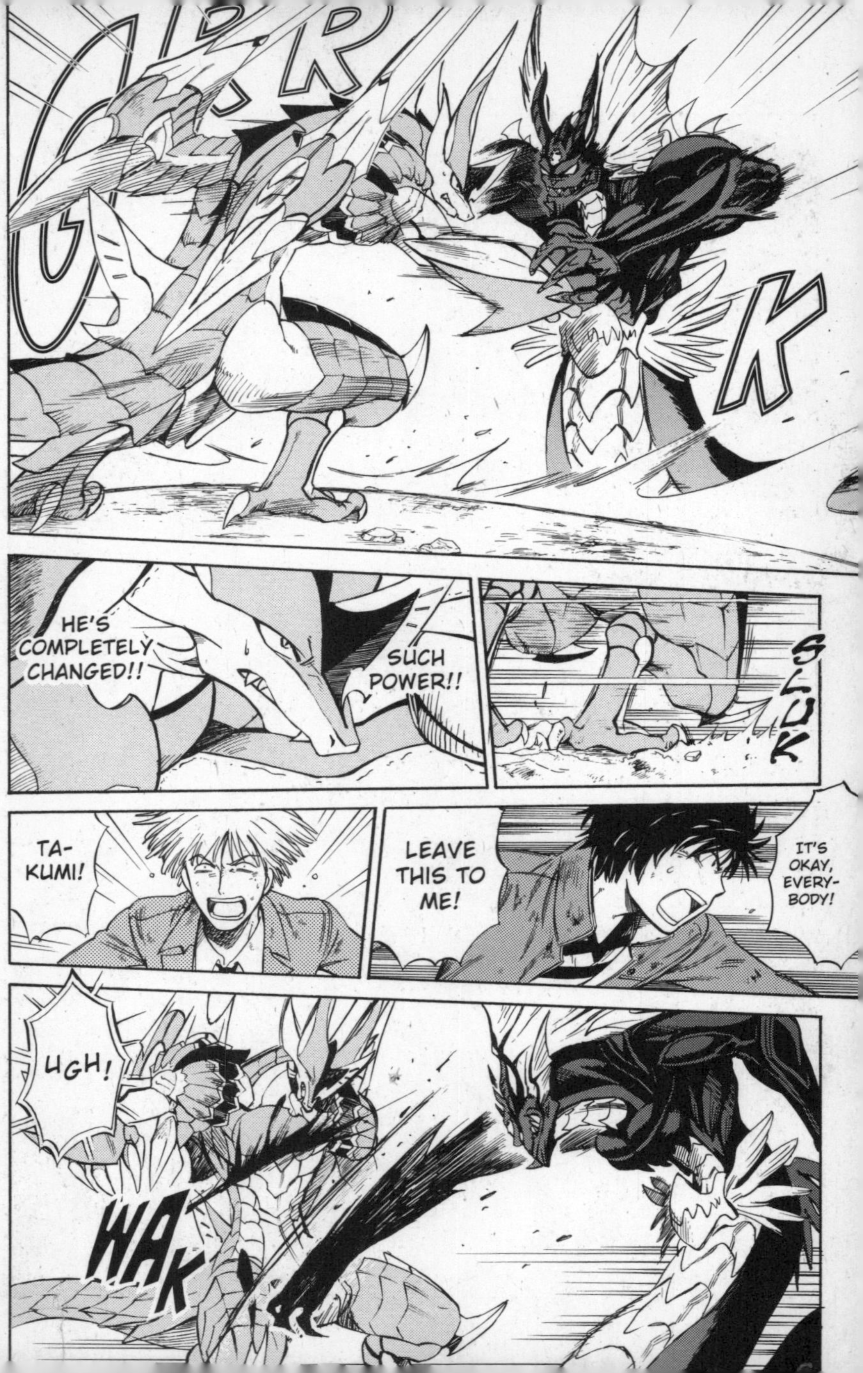
SLUK
SUCH POWER!!
HE'S COMPLETELY CHANGED!!
IT'S OKAY, EVERY-BODY!
LEAVE THIS TO ME!
TA-KUMI!
UGH!
WAK

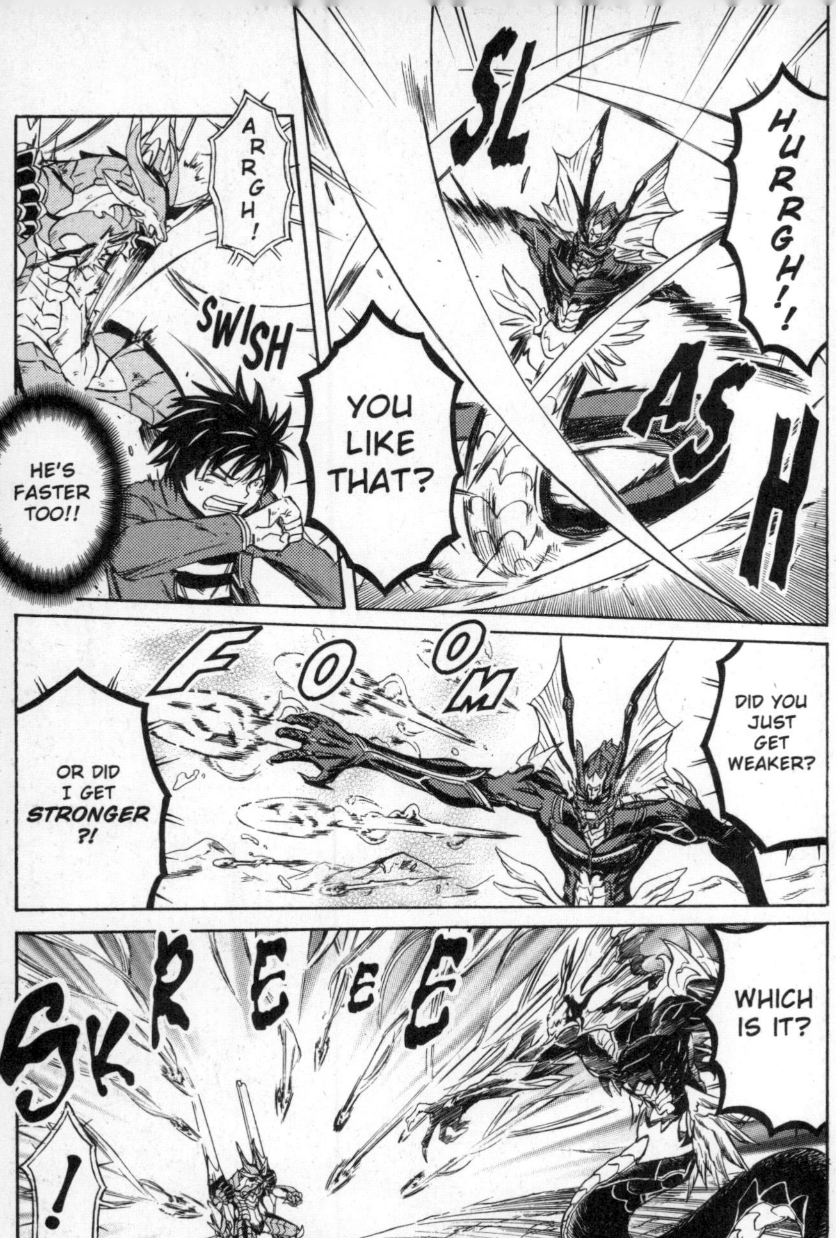
SLASH
HURRGH!!
ARGH!
SWISH
YOU LIKE THAT?
HE'S FASTER TOO!!
FOOM
DID YOU JUST GET WEAKER?
OR DID I GET STRONGER?!
SKREEE
WHICH IS IT?
!

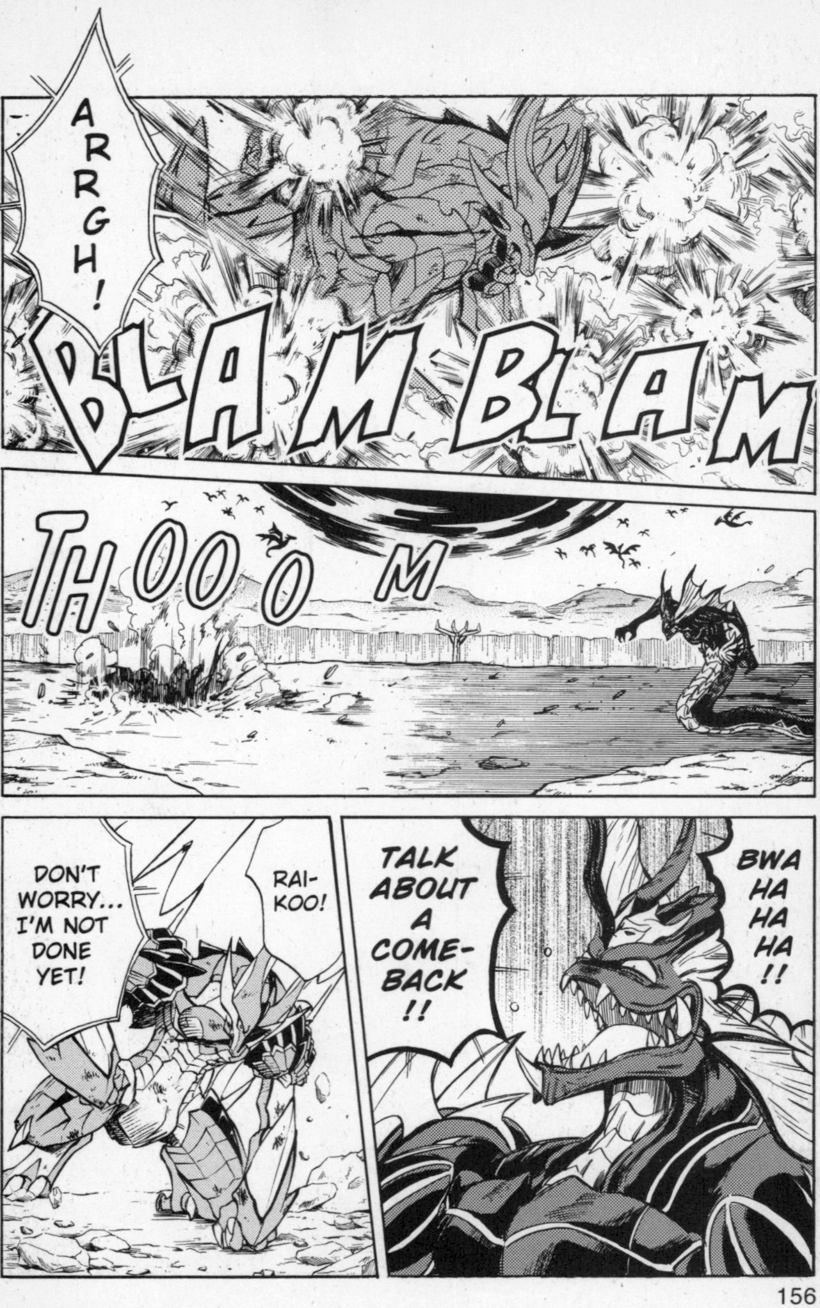
ARRGH!
BLAM BLAM
THOOOM
BWA HA HA HA!!
TALK ABOUT A COMEBACK!!
RAIKOO!
DON'T WORRY... I'M NOT DONE YET!

READ THIS WAY

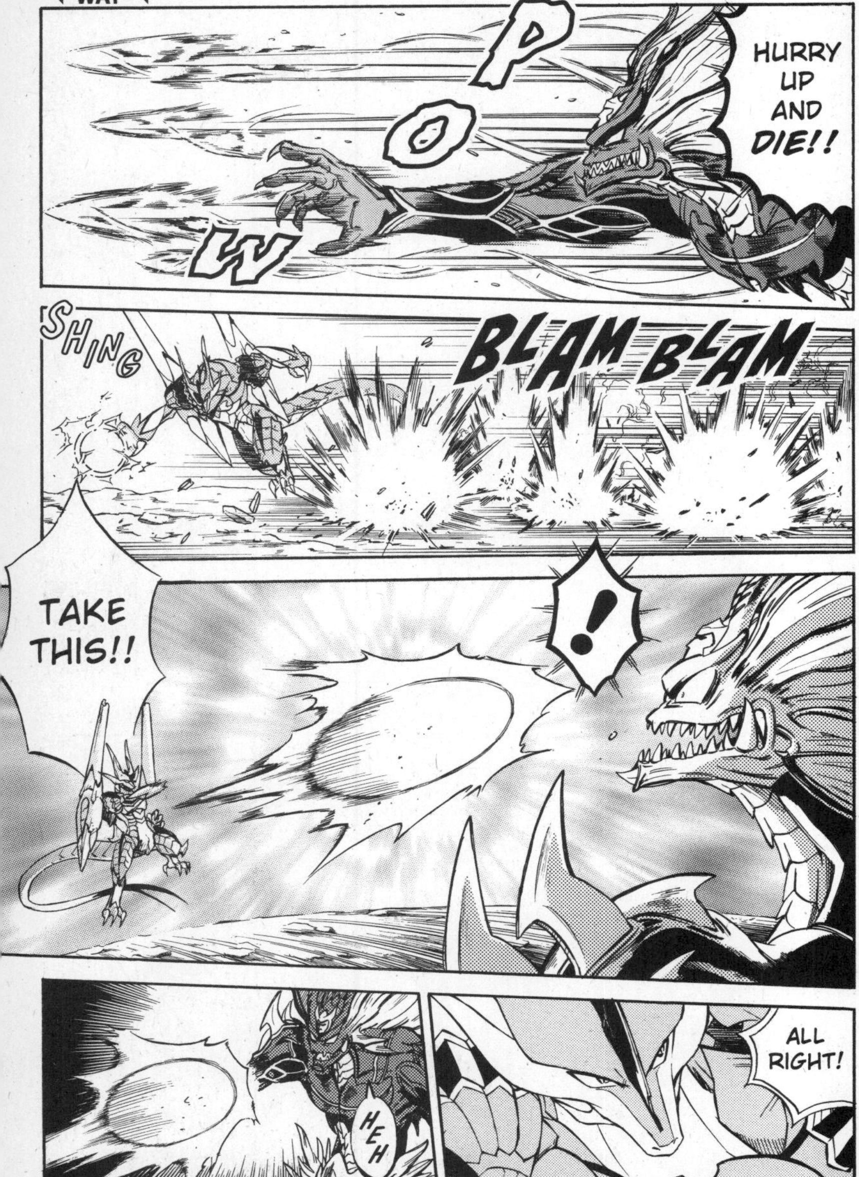
HURRY UP AND DIE!!
POW
BLAM BLAM
SHING
!
TAKE THIS!!
ALL RIGHT!
HEH

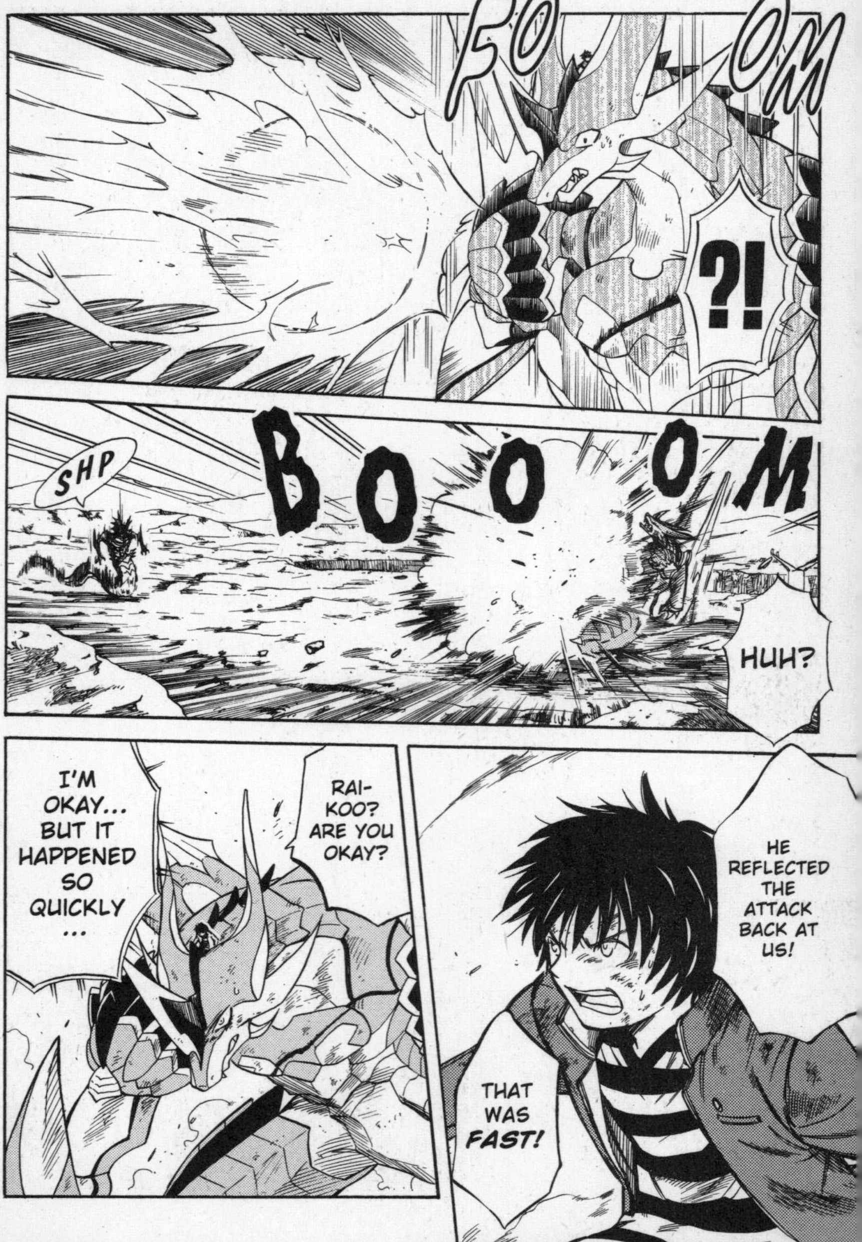
FO-OM
?!
BOOOM
SHP
HUH?
HE REFLECTED THE ATTACK BACK AT US!
THAT WAS FAST!
RAI-KOO? ARE YOU OKAY?
I'M OKAY... BUT IT HAPPENED SO QUICKLY...

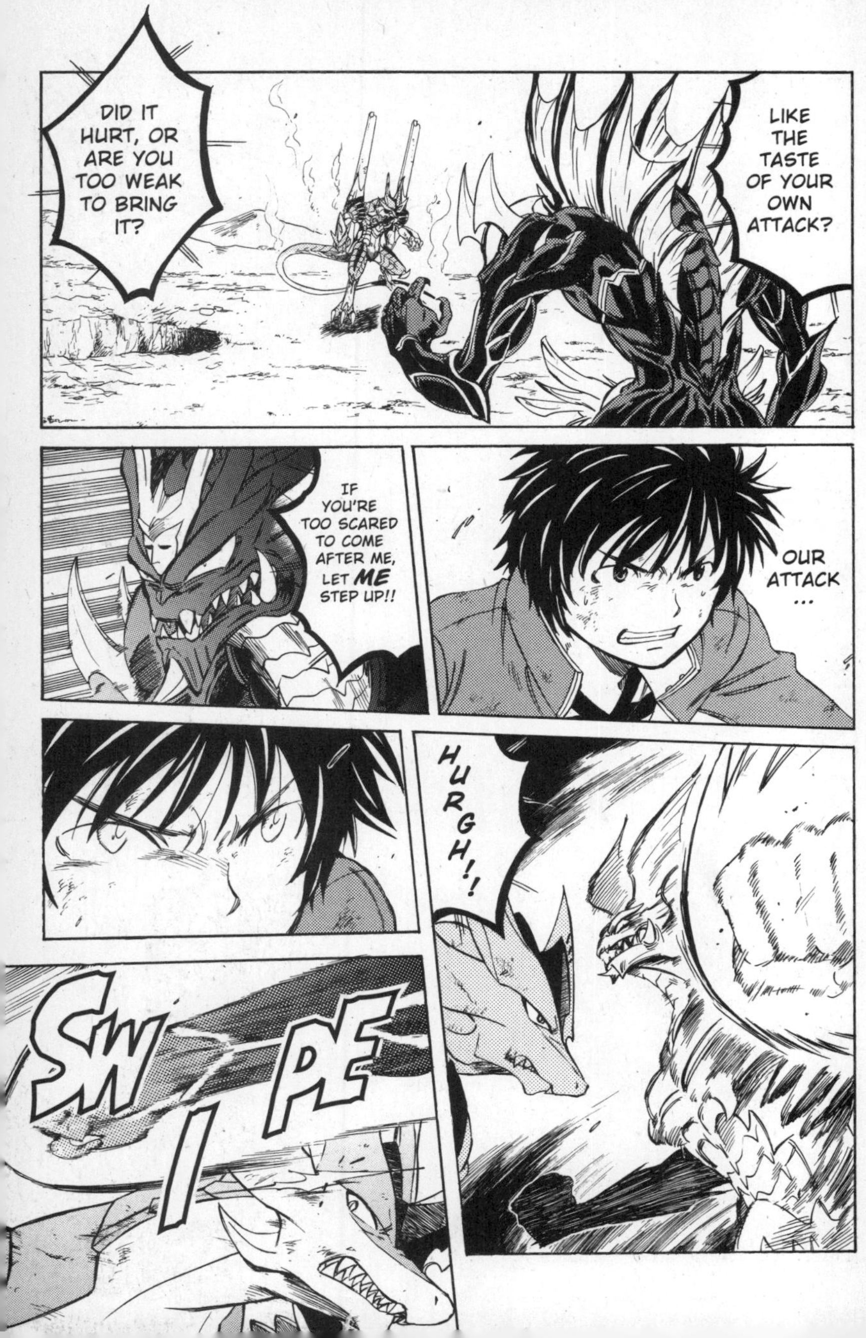
LIKE THE TASTE OF YOUR OWN ATTACK?
DID IT HURT, OR ARE YOU TOO WEAK TO BRING IT?
OUR ATTACK...
IF YOU'RE TOO SCARED TO COME AFTER ME, LET *ME* STEP UP!!
HURGH!!
SWIPE

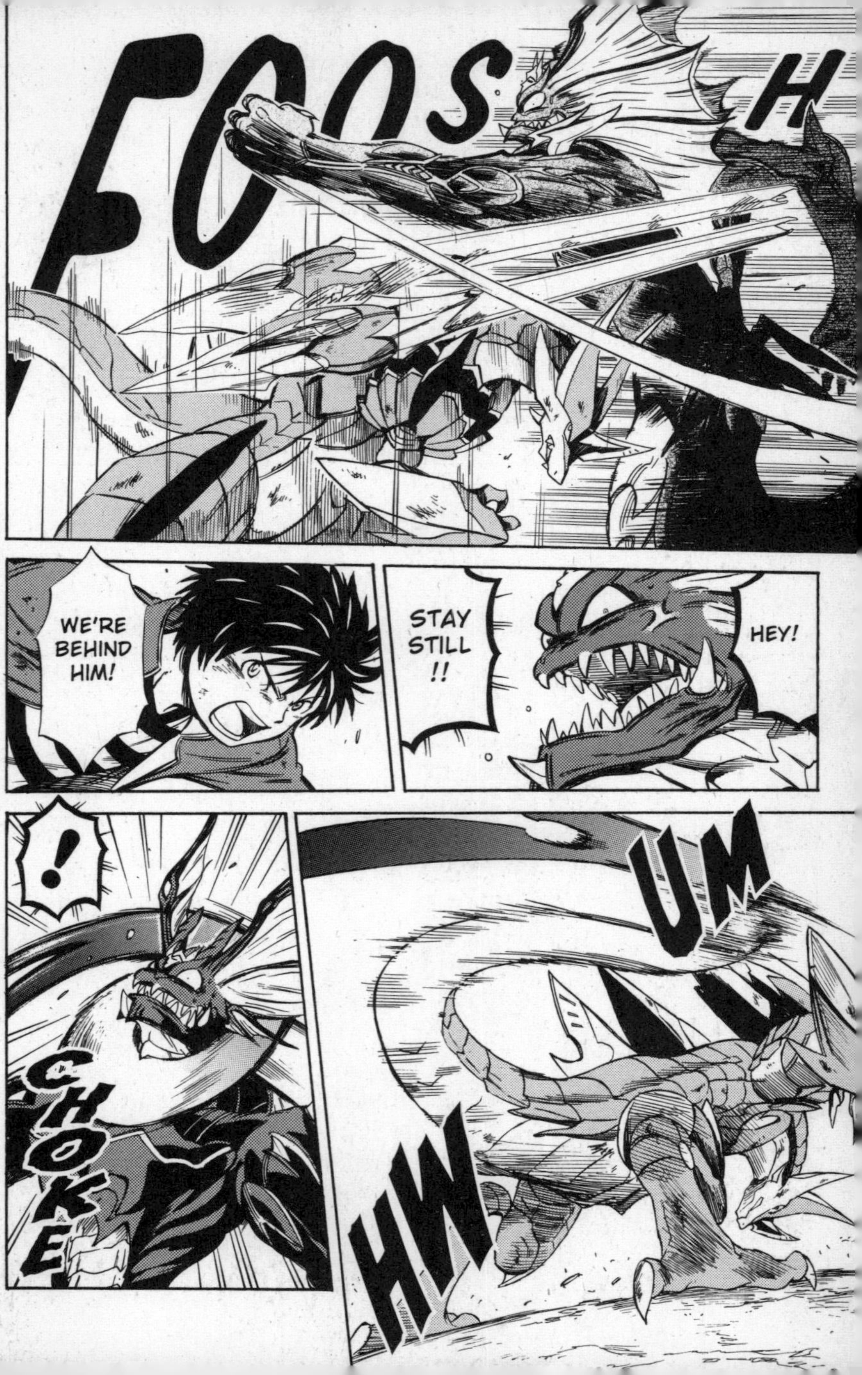
FOOSH
HEY!
STAY STILL !!
WE'RE BEHIND HIM!
WHUM
!
CHOKE

READ THIS WAY

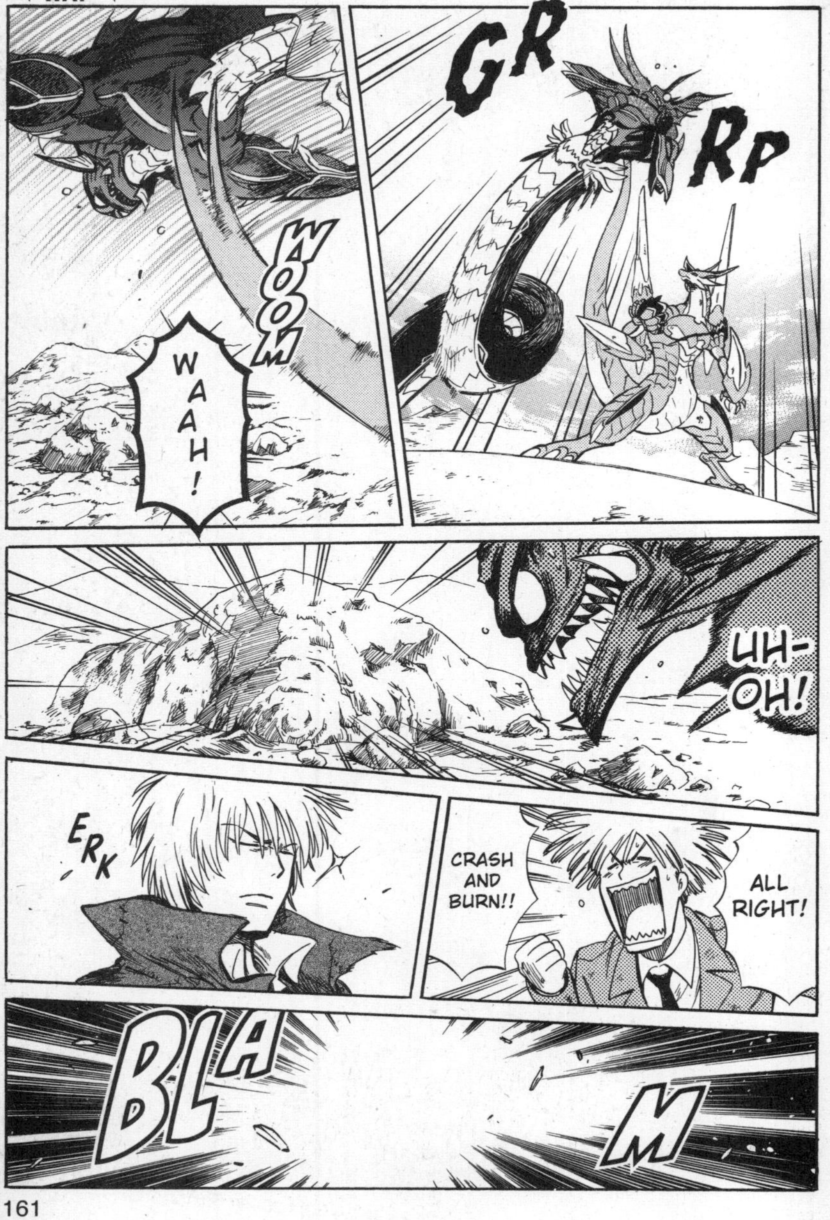
GR
RP
WOOOM
WAAAH!
UH-OH!
ALL RIGHT!
CRASH AND BURN!!
ERK
BLAM

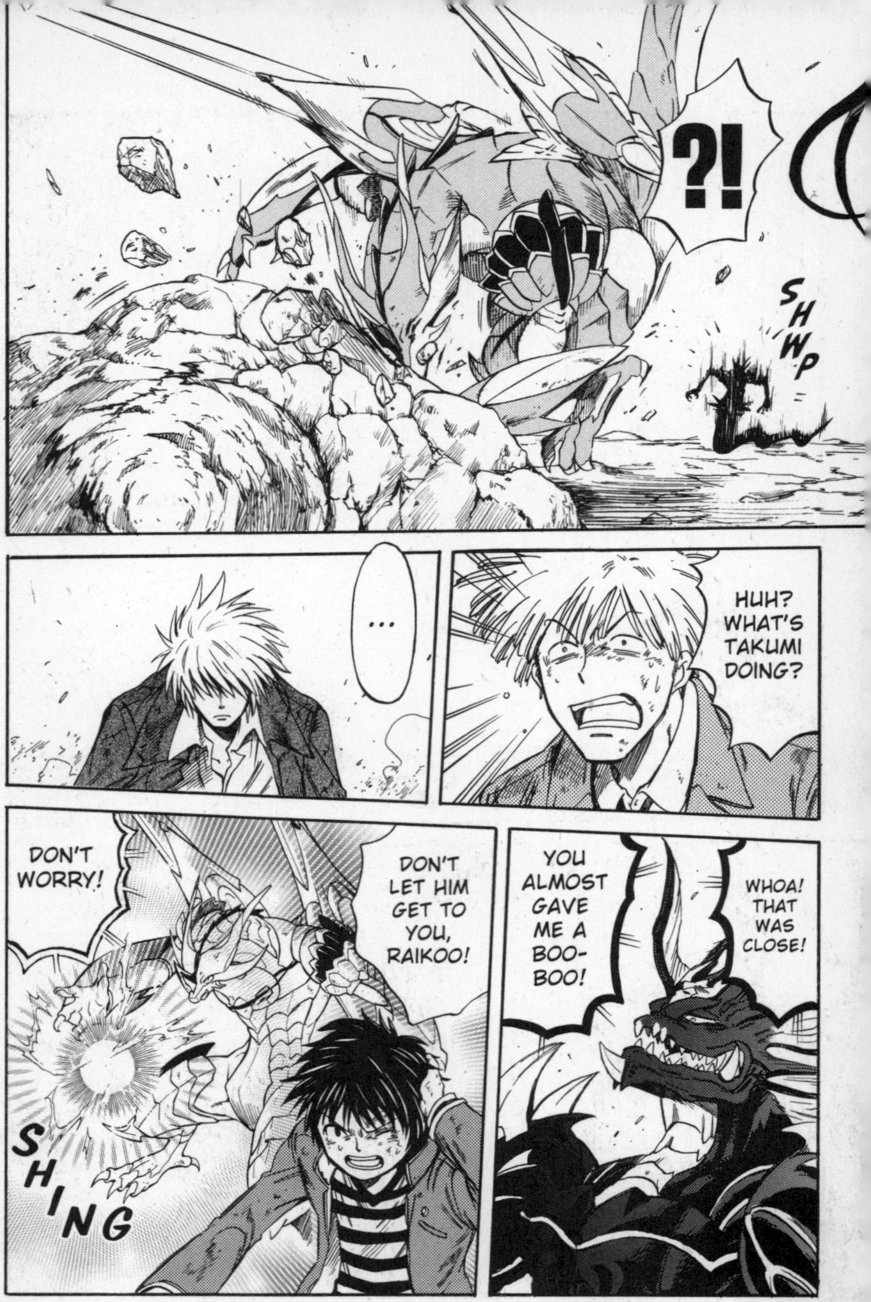
?!
SHWP
HUH? WHAT'S TAKUMI DOING?
...
WHOA! THAT WAS CLOSE!
YOU ALMOST GAVE ME A BOO-BOO!
DON'T LET HIM GET TO YOU, RAIKOO!
DON'T WORRY!
SHING

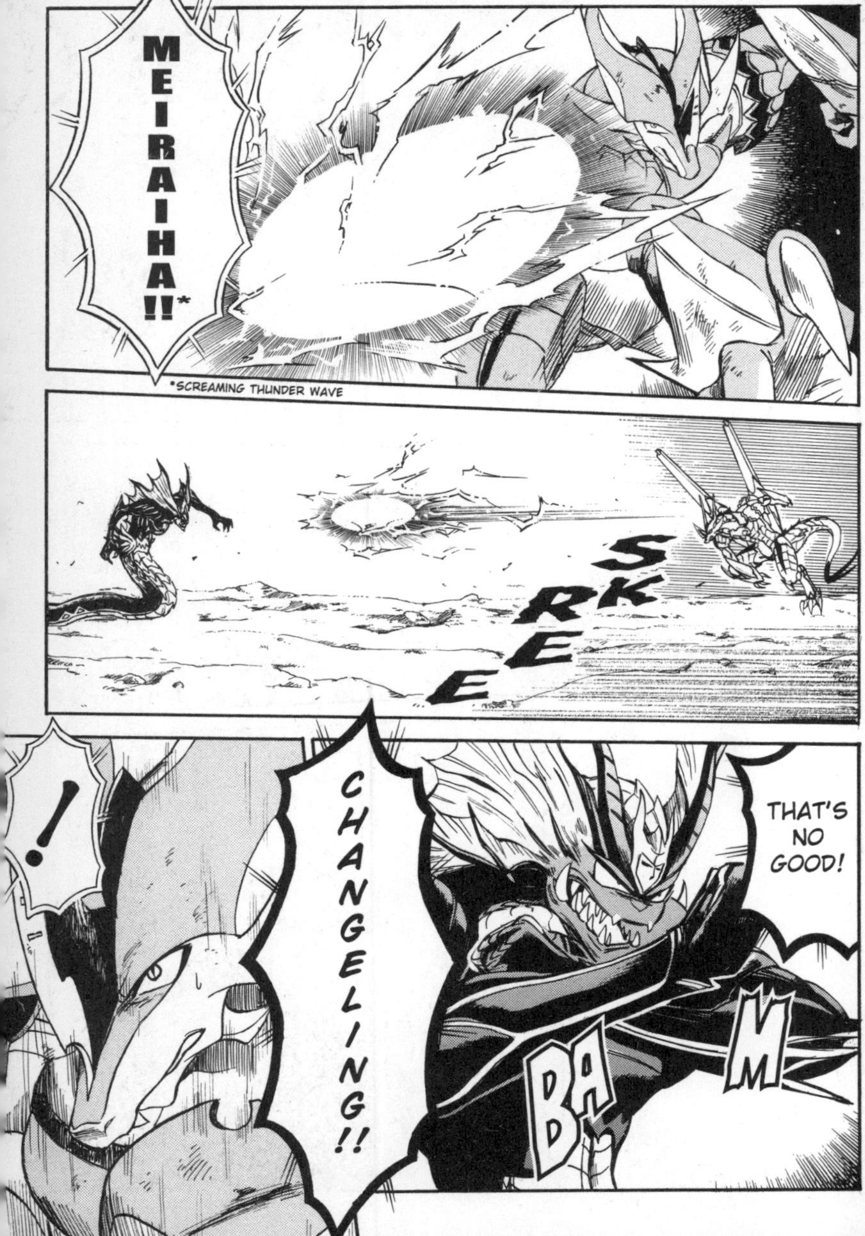
MEIRAIHA!!*
*SCREAMING THUNDER WAVE
SKREE
THAT'S NO GOOD!
BAM
CHANGELING!!
!

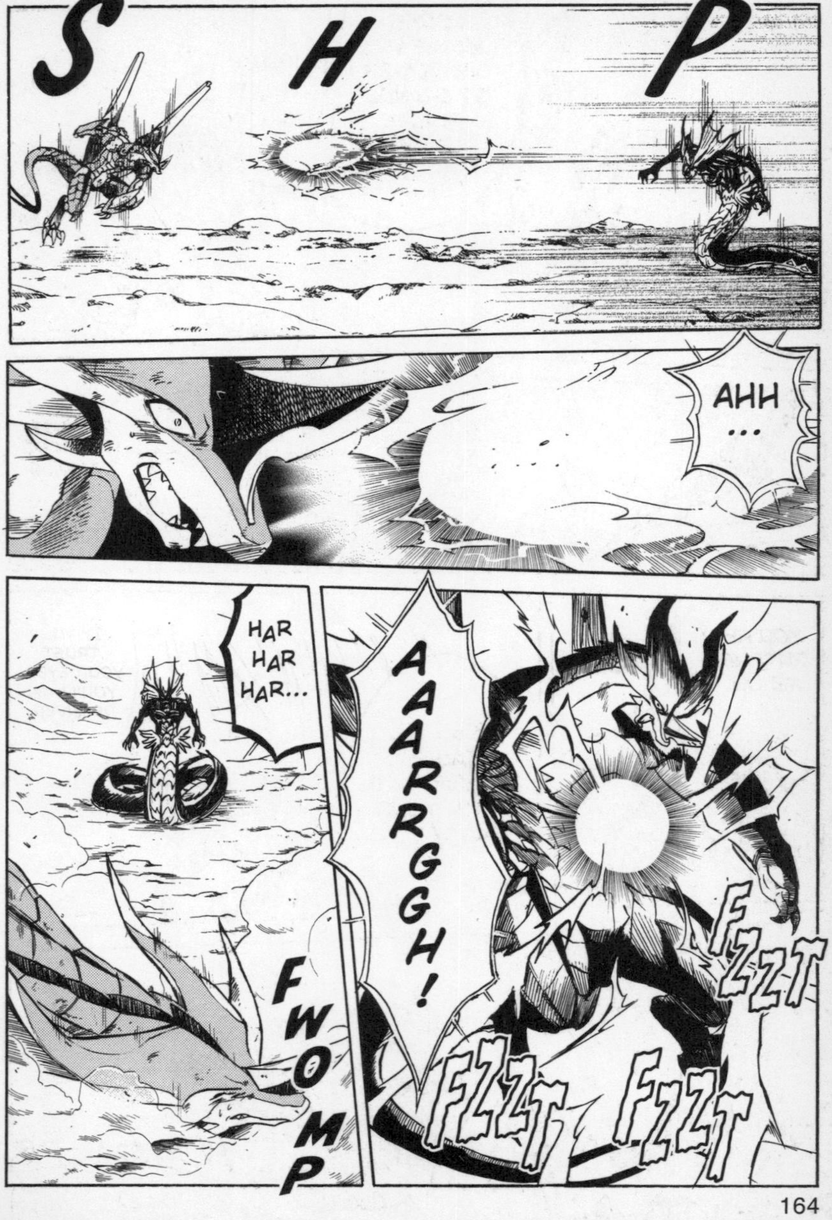
SHP
AHH...
AAARRGGH!
FZZT
FZZT
FZZT
HAR HAR HAR...
FWOMP

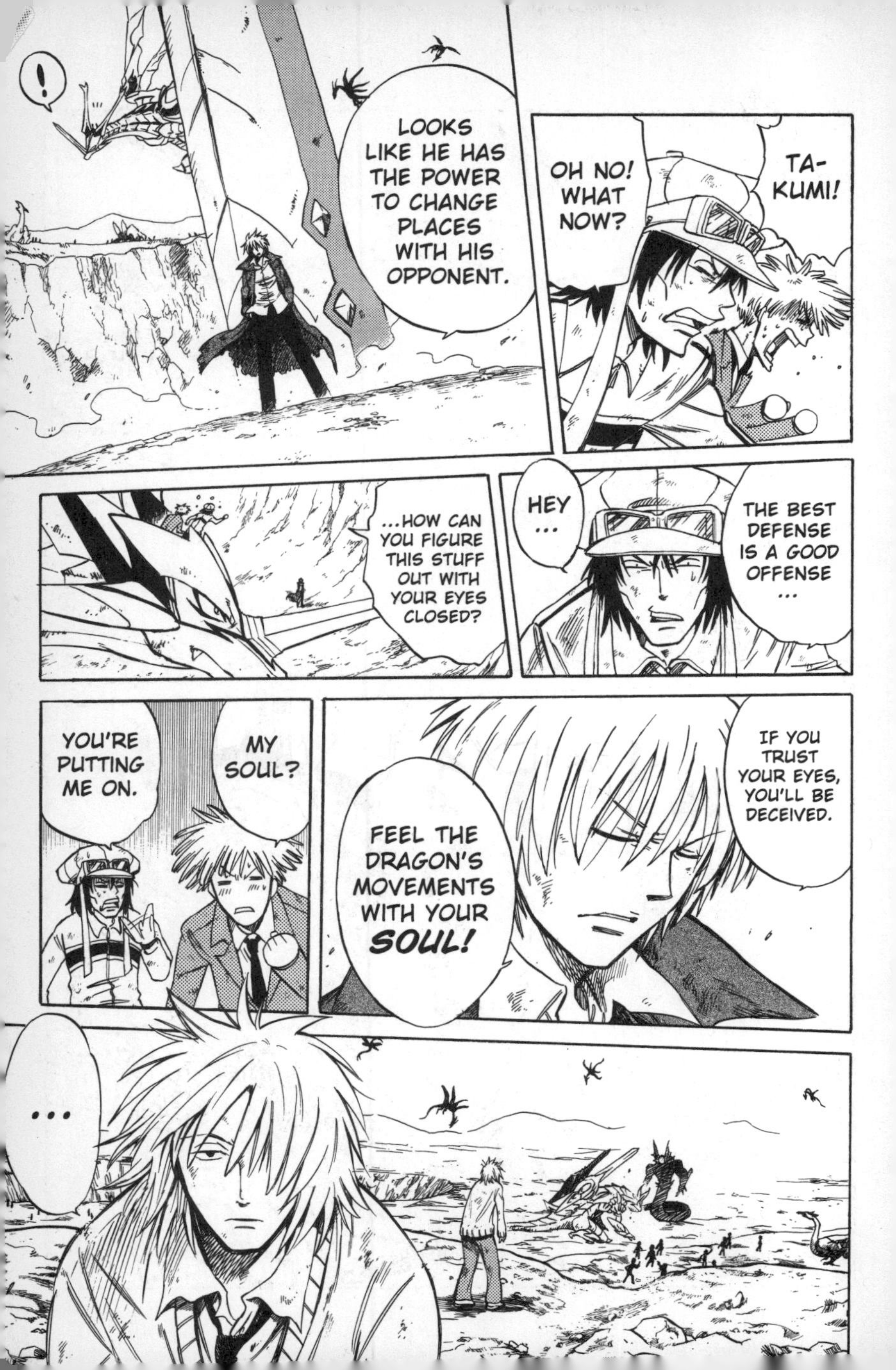
TA-KUMI!
OH NO! WHAT NOW?
LOOKS LIKE HE HAS THE POWER TO CHANGE PLACES WITH HIS OPPONENT.
!
THE BEST DEFENSE IS A GOOD OFFENSE...
HEY...
...HOW CAN YOU FIGURE THIS STUFF OUT WITH YOUR EYES CLOSED?
IF YOU TRUST YOUR EYES, YOU'LL BE DECEIVED.
FEEL THE DRAGON'S MOVEMENTS WITH YOUR **SOUL!**
MY SOUL?
YOU'RE PUTTING ME ON.
...

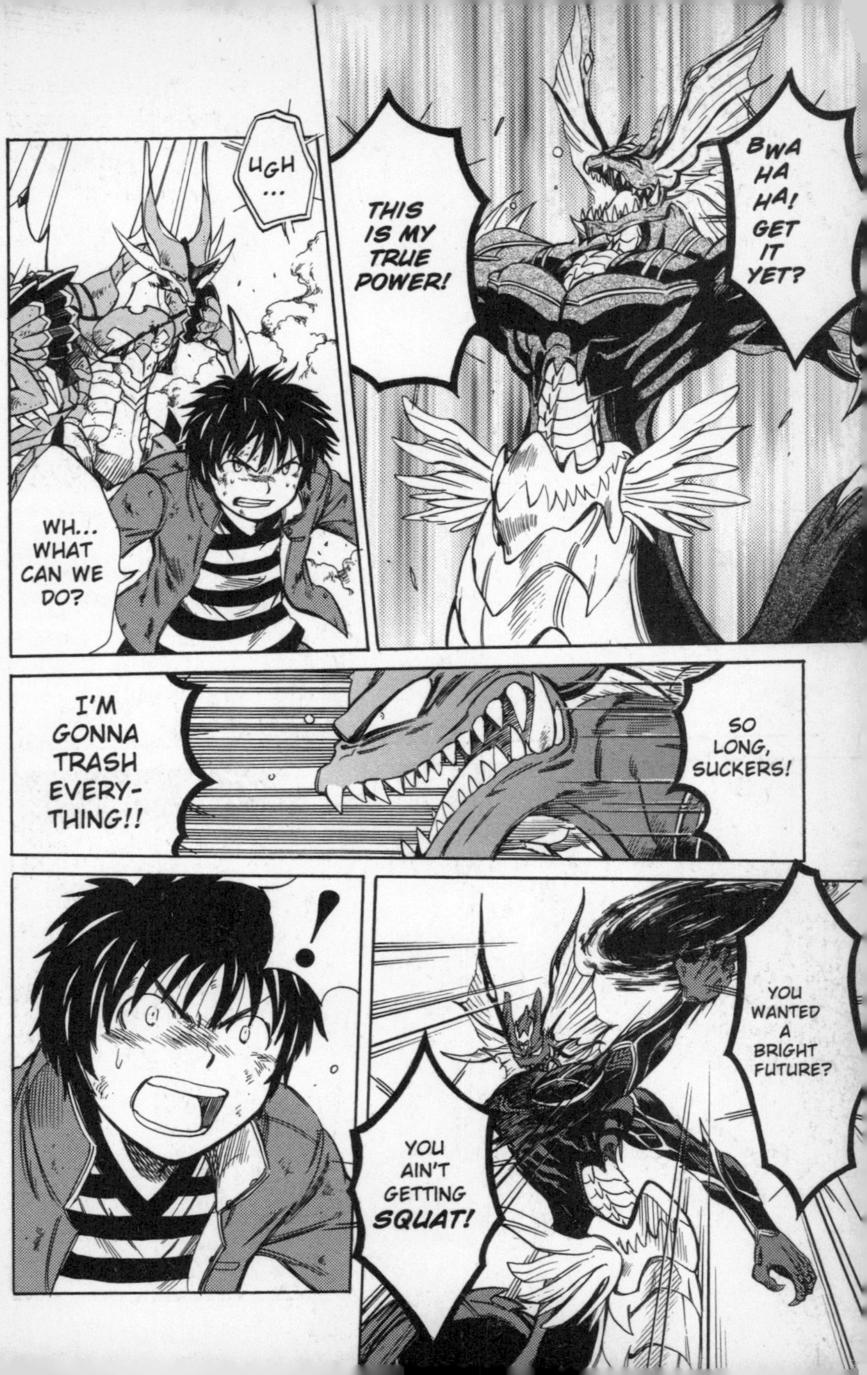
BWA HA HA! GET IT YET?
THIS IS MY TRUE POWER!
UGH...
WH... WHAT CAN WE DO?
SO LONG, SUCKERS!
I'M GONNA TRASH EVERYTHING!!
YOU WANTED A BRIGHT FUTURE?
YOU AIN'T GETTING SQUAT!
!

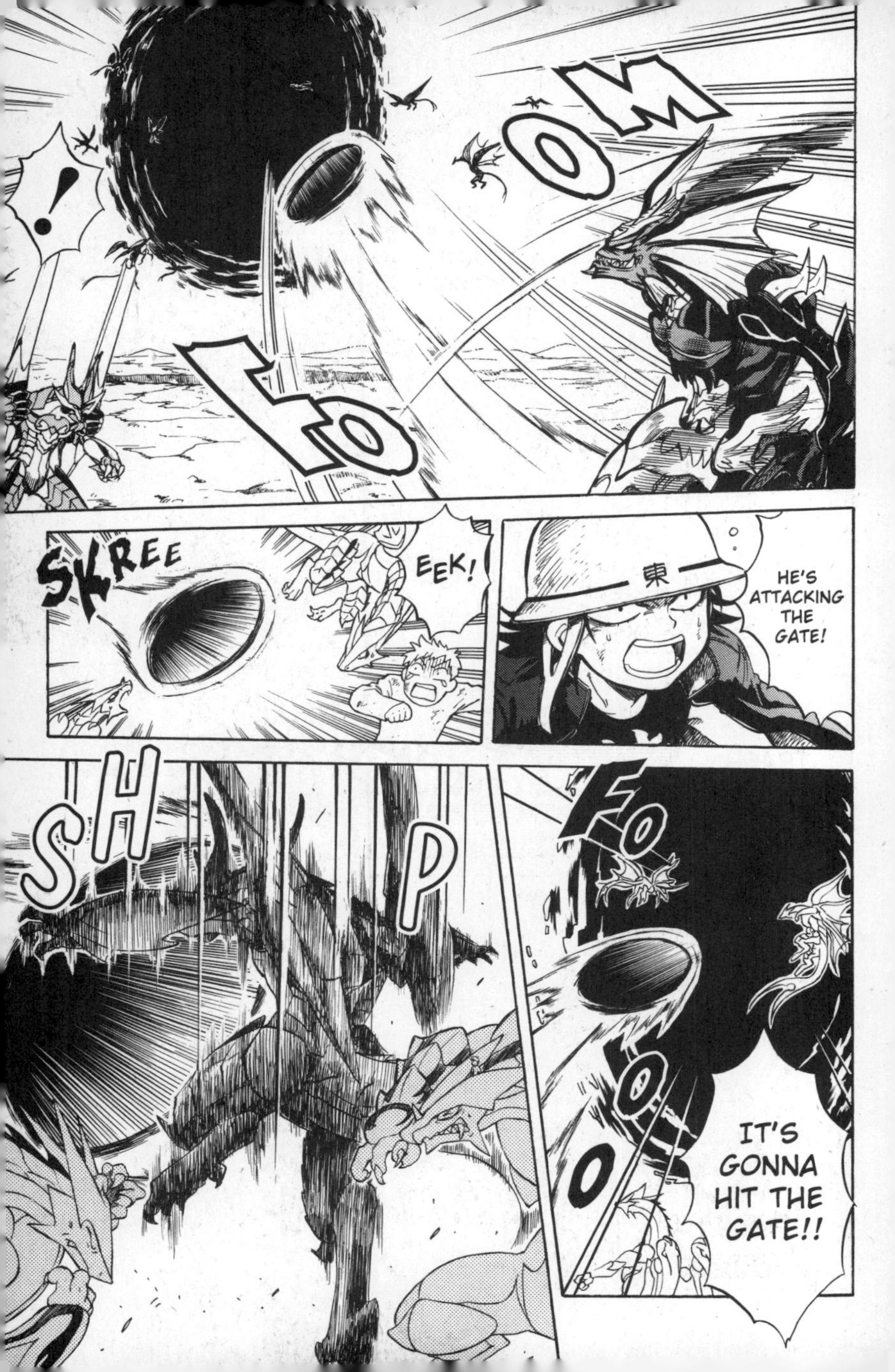
FOOM
!
HE'S ATTACKING THE GATE!
EEK!
SKREE
IT'S GONNA HIT THE GATE!!
FOOOOO
SHP

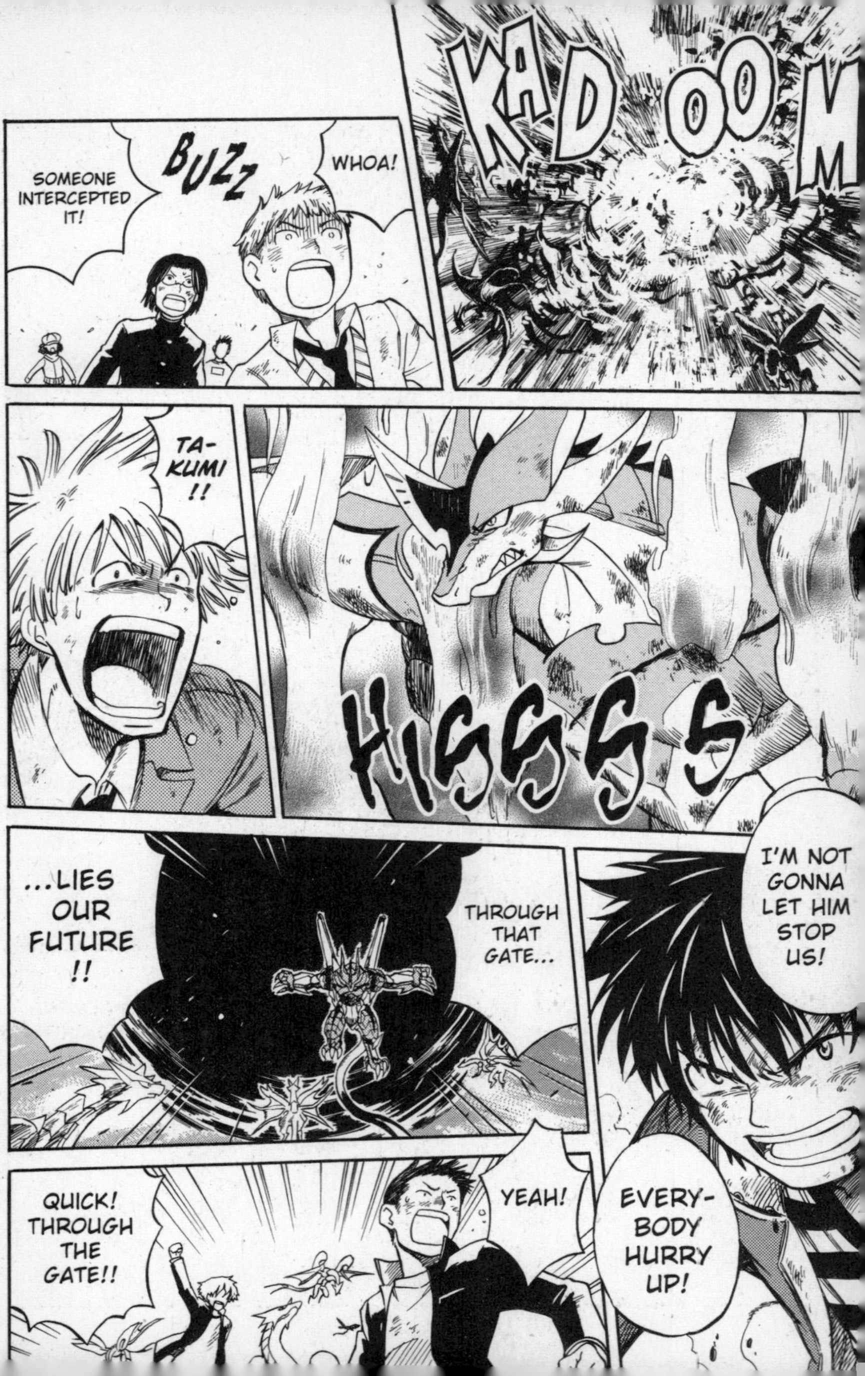
KADOOM
WHOA!
BUZZ
SOMEONE INTERCEPTED IT!
HISSSS
TA-KUMI!!
I'M NOT GONNA LET HIM STOP US!
THROUGH THAT GATE...
...LIES OUR FUTURE!!
EVERY-BODY HURRY UP!
YEAH!
QUICK! THROUGH THE GATE!!

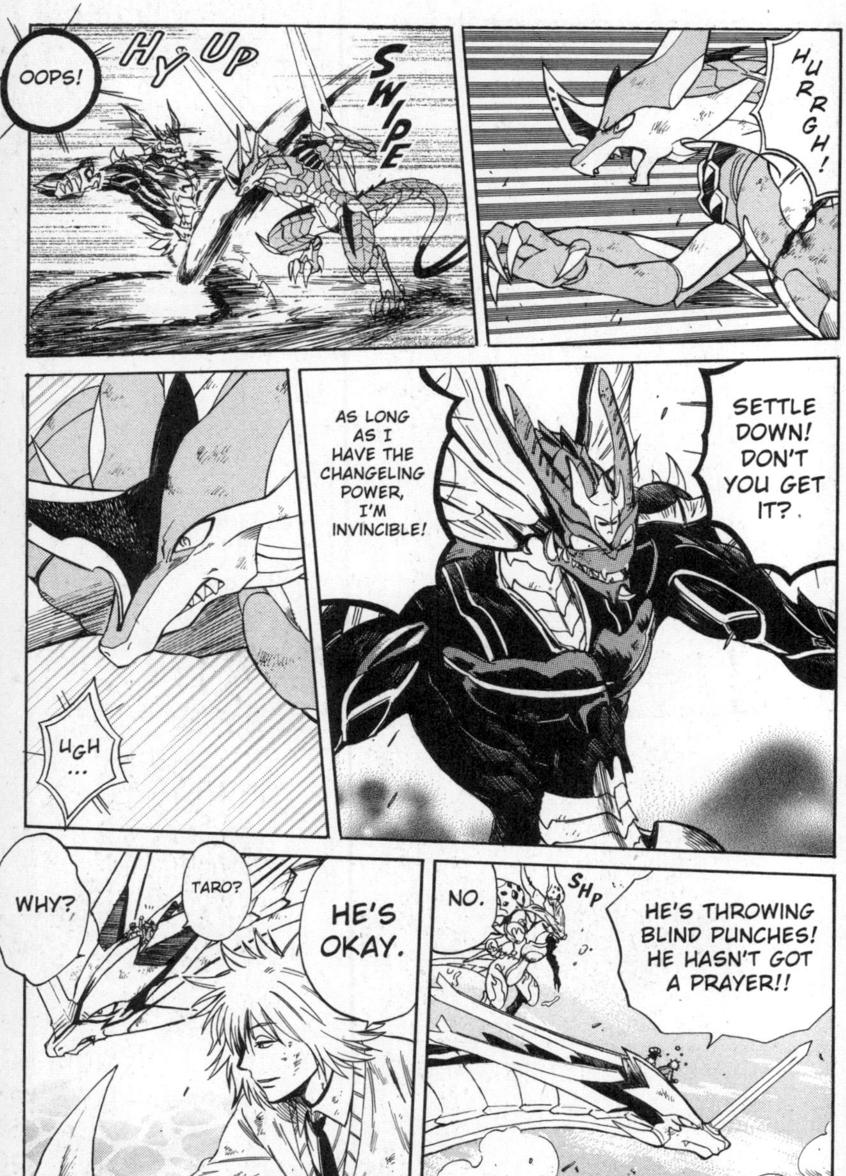
HURRGH!
SWIPE
HYUP
OOPS!
SETTLE DOWN! DON'T YOU GET IT?
AS LONG AS I HAVE THE CHANGELING POWER, I'M INVINCIBLE!
UGH...
HE'S THROWING BLIND PUNCHES! HE HASN'T GOT A PRAYER!!
SHP
NO.
HE'S OKAY.
TARO?
WHY?

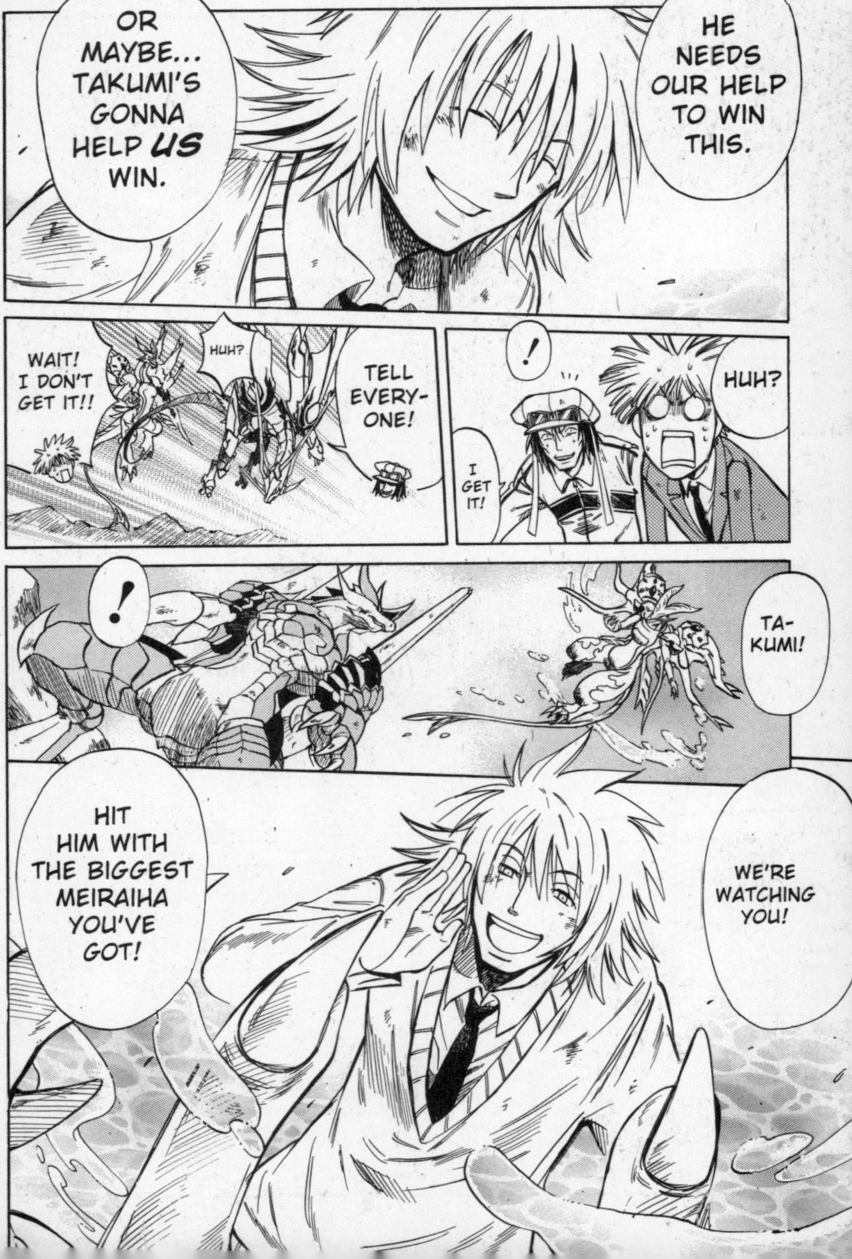
HE NEEDS OUR HELP TO WIN THIS.
OR MAYBE... TAKUMI'S GONNA HELP US WIN.
!
HUH?
I GET IT!
TELL EVERY-ONE!
HUH?
WAIT! I DON'T GET IT!!
TA-KUMI!
!
WE'RE WATCHING YOU!
HIT HIM WITH THE BIGGEST MEIRAIHA YOU'VE GOT!

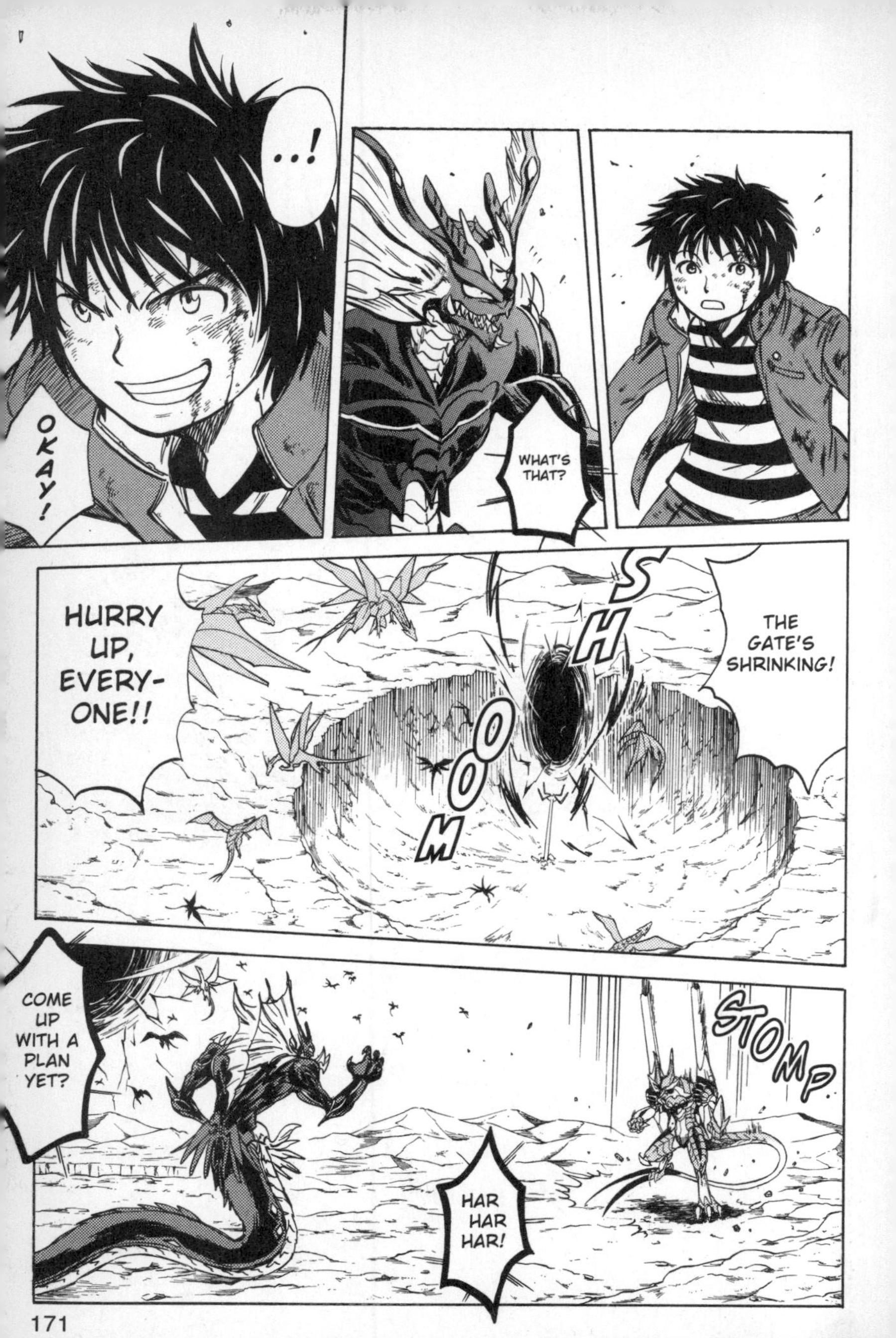
WHAT'S THAT?
...!
OKAY!
THE GATE'S SHRINKING!
SHOOOM
HURRY UP, EVERYONE!!
STOMP
COME UP WITH A PLAN YET?
HAR HAR HAR!

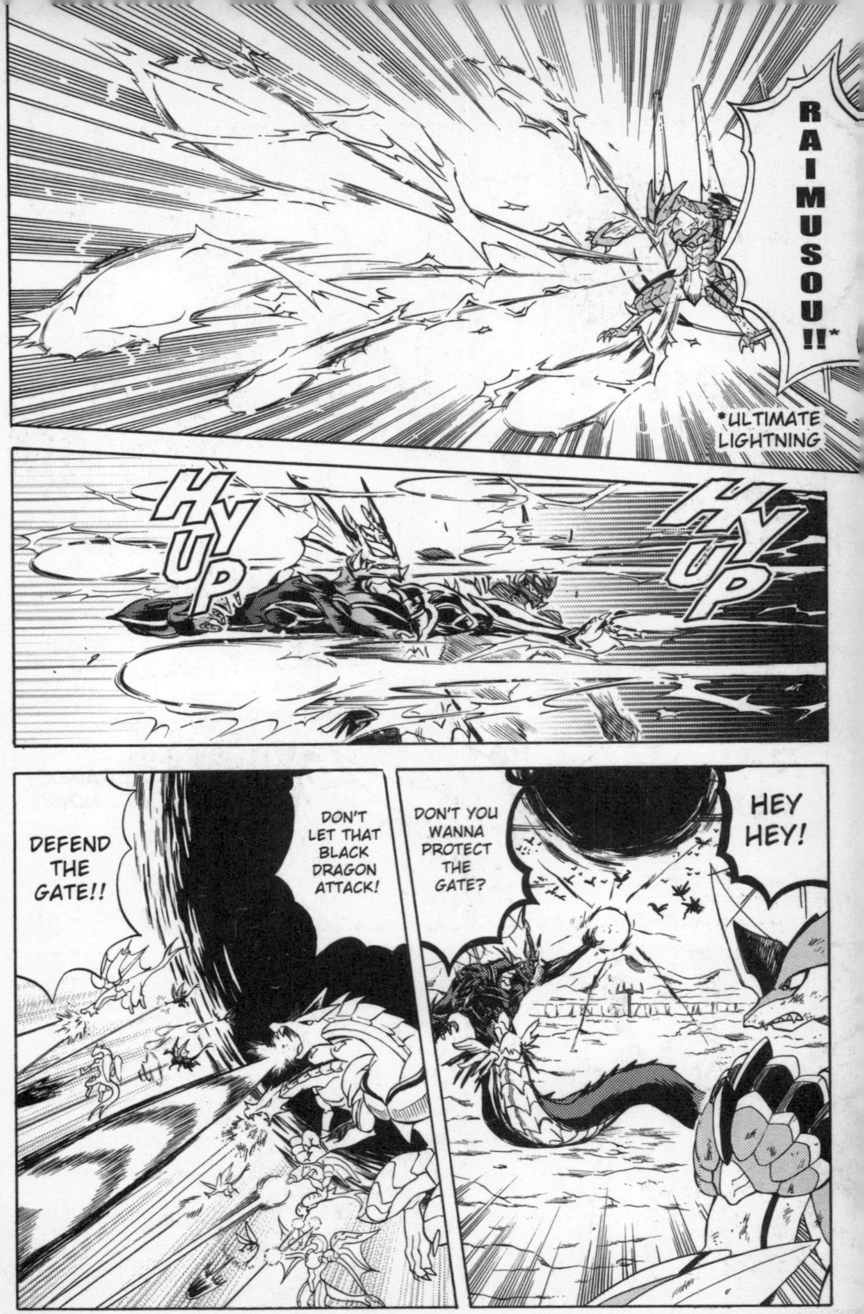
RAIMUSOU!!*
*ULTIMATE LIGHTNING
HYUP
HYUP
HEY HEY!
DON'T YOU WANNA PROTECT THE GATE?
DON'T LET THAT BLACK DRAGON ATTACK!
DEFEND THE GATE!!

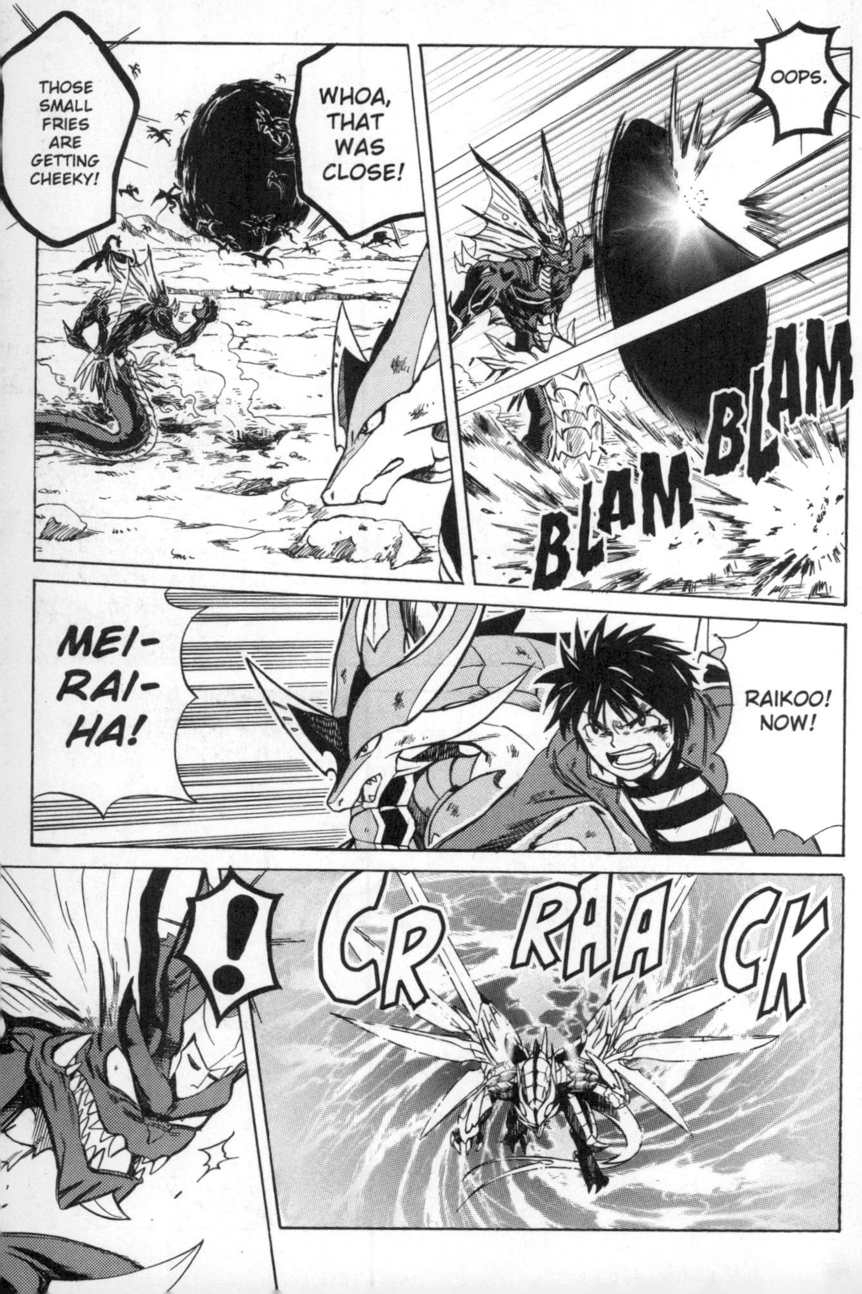
OOPS.
BLAM BLAM BLAM
WHOA, THAT WAS CLOSE!
THOSE SMALL FRIES ARE GETTING CHEEKY!
RAIKOO! NOW!
MEI-RAI-HA!
CRRAACK
!

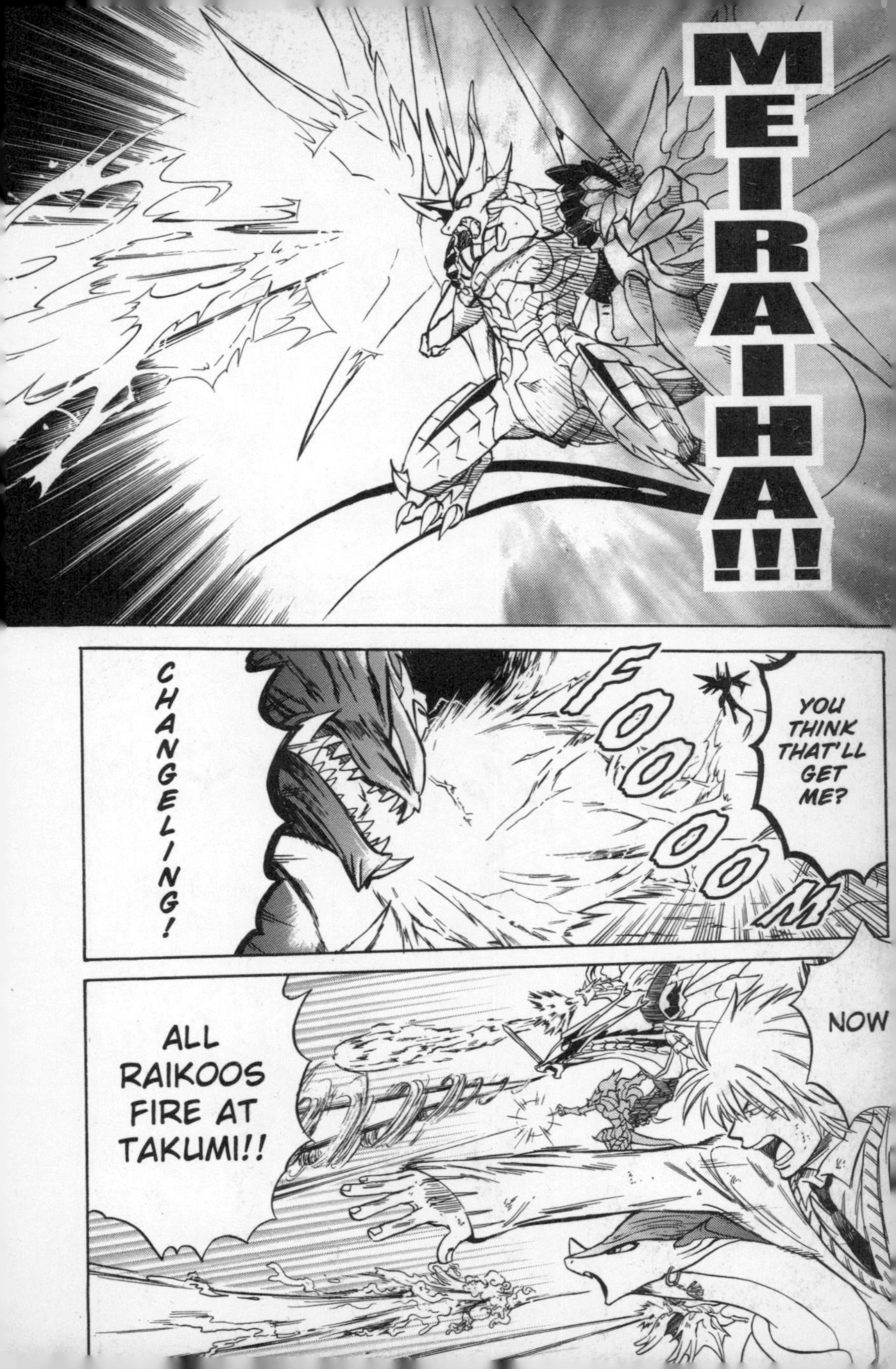
MEIRAIHA!!!
YOU THINK THAT'LL GET ME?
FOOOOOM
CHANGELING!
NOW
ALL RAIKOOS FIRE AT TAKUMI!!

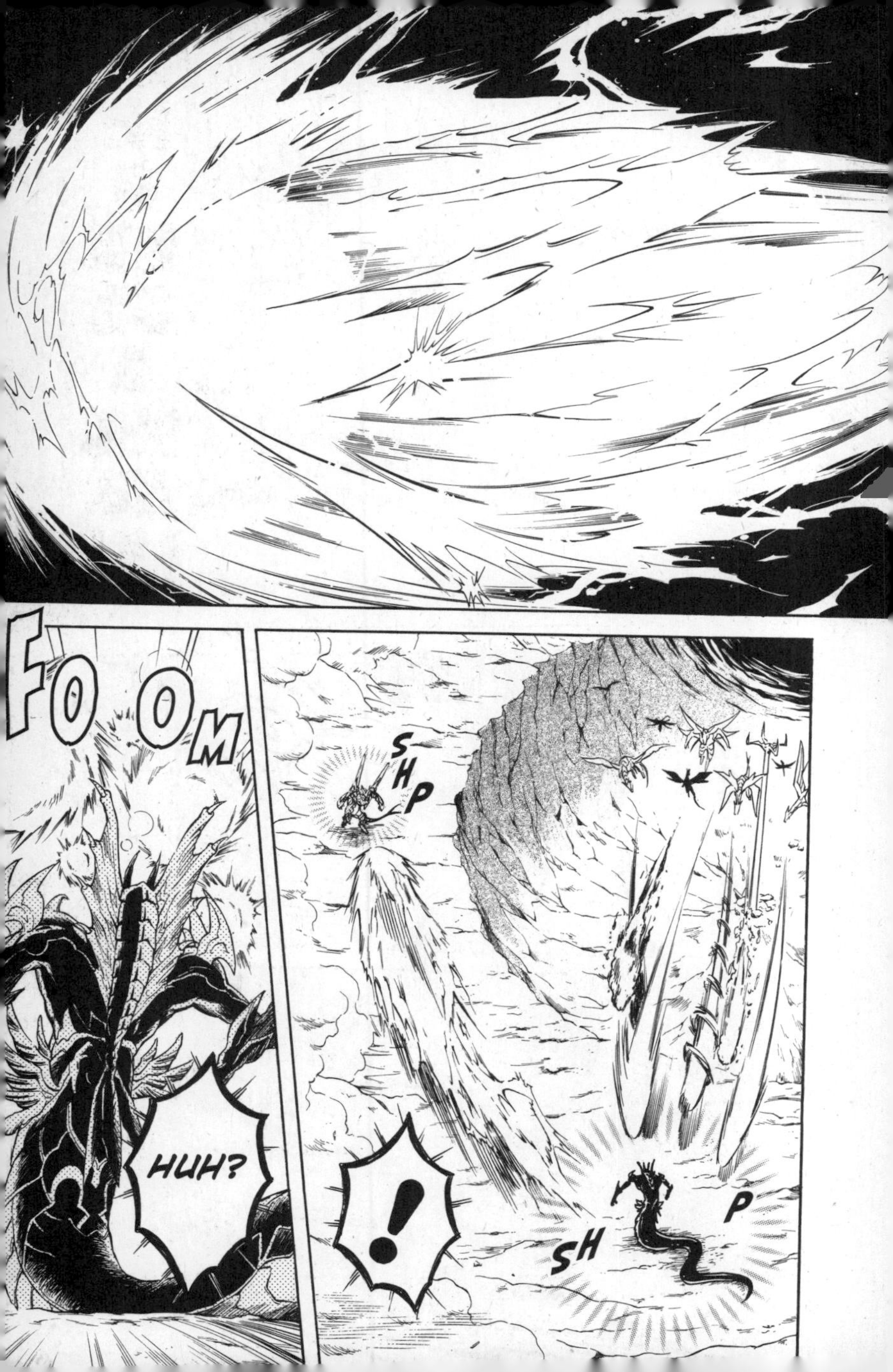
SHP
SHP
!
FOOM
HUH?

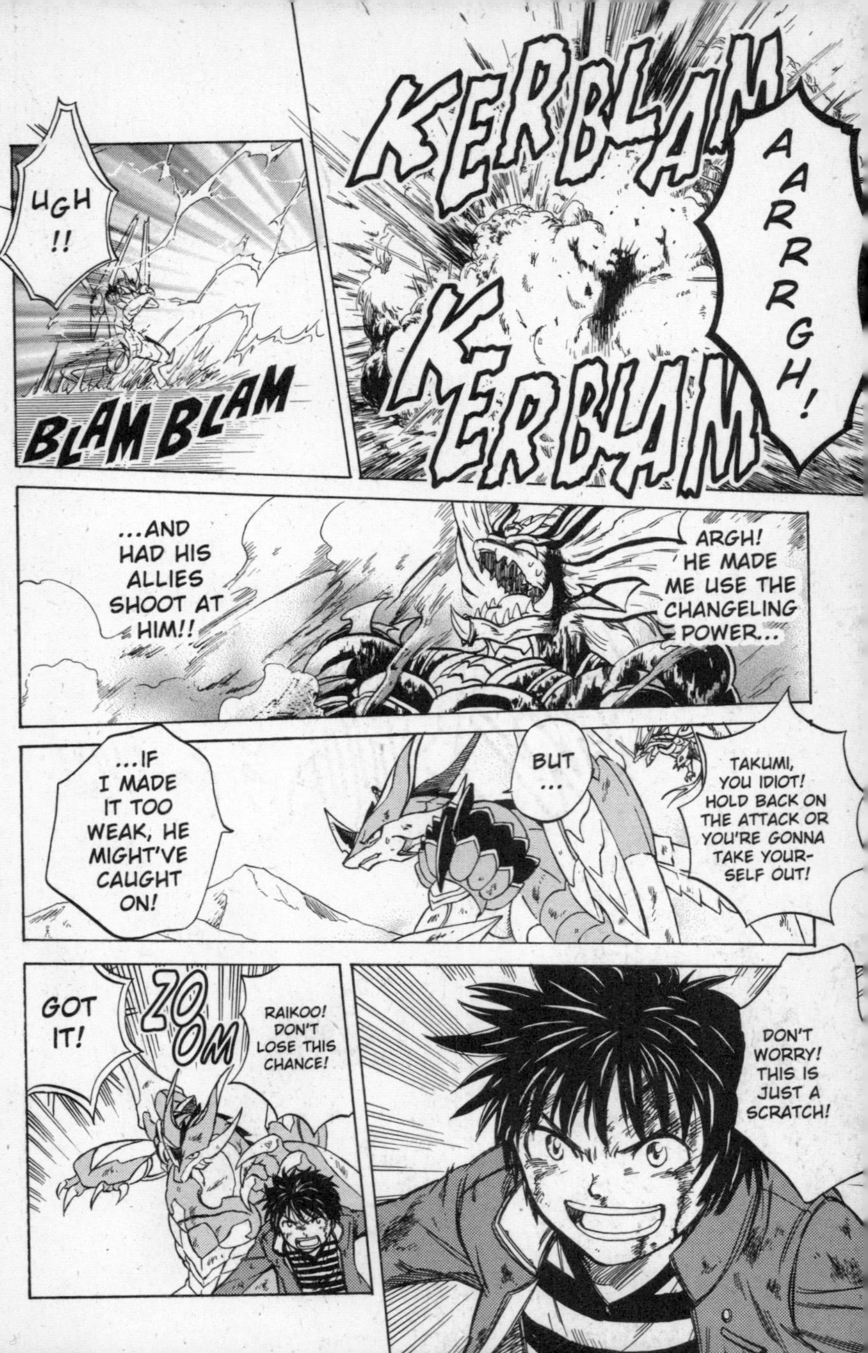
KERBLAM
AARRRGH!
KERBLAM
UGH!!
BLAM BLAM
ARGH! HE MADE ME USE THE CHANGELING POWER...
...AND HAD HIS ALLIES SHOOT AT HIM!!
TAKUMI, YOU IDIOT! HOLD BACK ON THE ATTACK OR YOU'RE GONNA TAKE YOURSELF OUT!
BUT...
...IF I MADE IT TOO WEAK, HE MIGHT'VE CAUGHT ON!
DON'T WORRY! THIS IS JUST A SCRATCH!
RAIKOO! DON'T LOSE THIS CHANCE!
ZOOM
GOT IT!

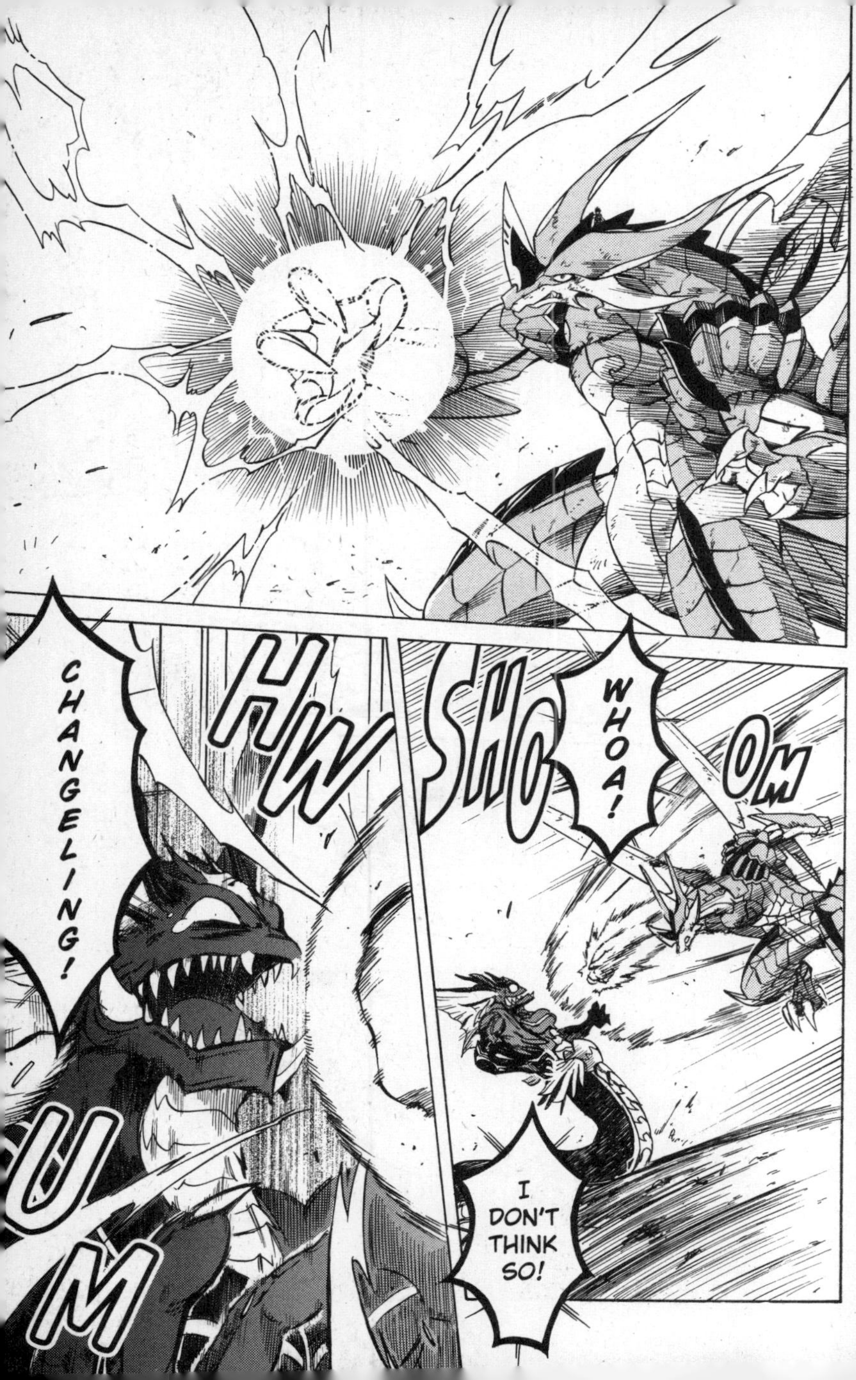
SHO
WHOA!
OM
I DON'T THINK SO!
CHANGELING!
HW
UM

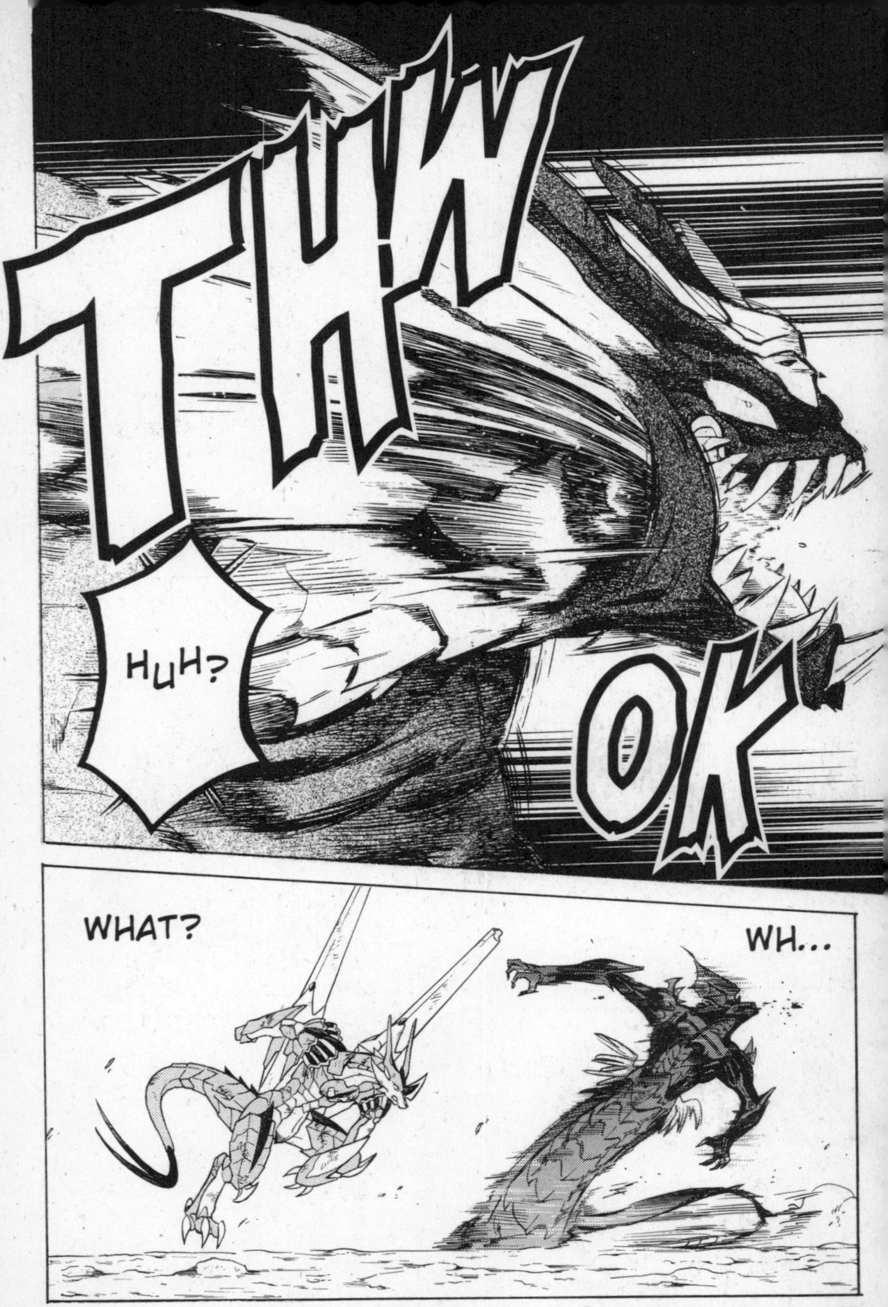
THWOK
HUH?
WH...
WHAT?

READ THIS WAY

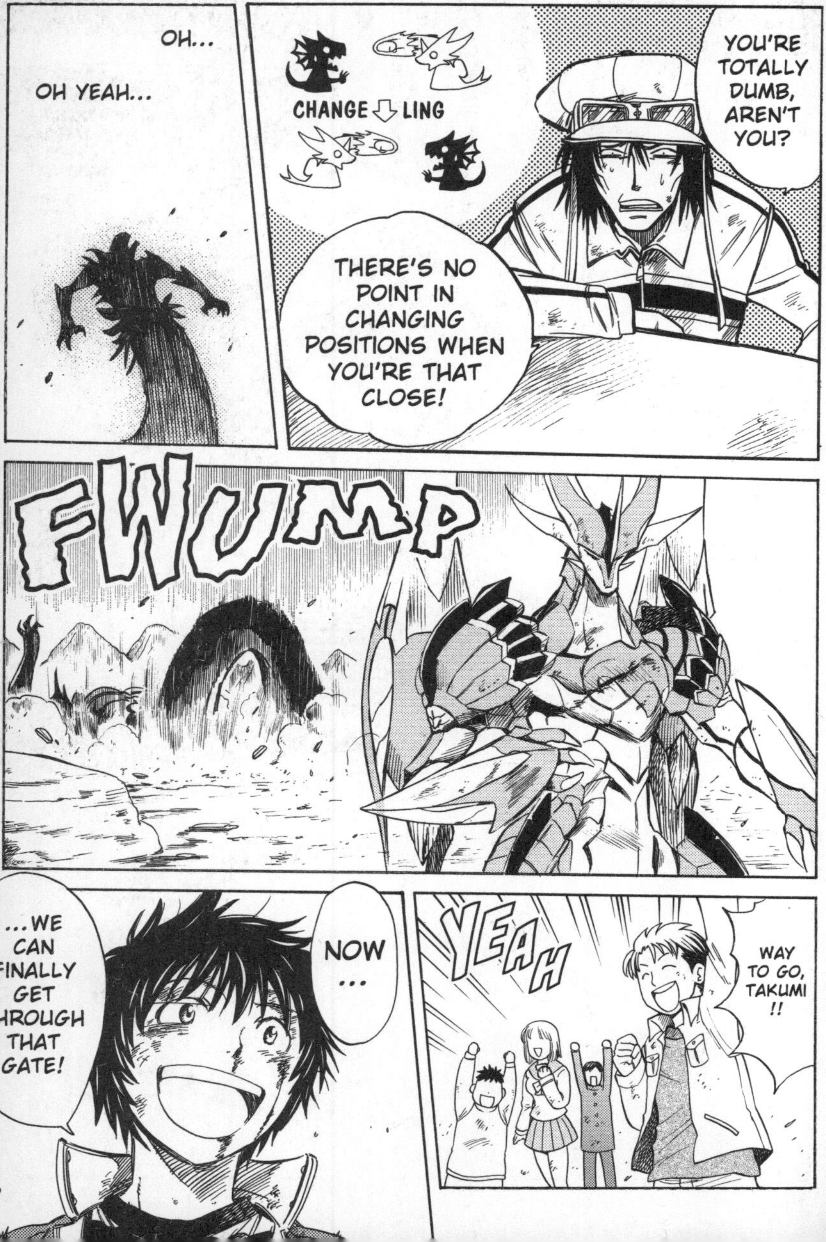
YOU'RE TOTALLY DUMB, AREN'T YOU?
CHANGE LING
THERE'S NO POINT IN CHANGING POSITIONS WHEN YOU'RE THAT CLOSE!
OH...
OH YEAH...
FWUMP
YEAH
WAY TO GO, TAKUMI!!
NOW...
...WE CAN FINALLY GET THROUGH THAT GATE!

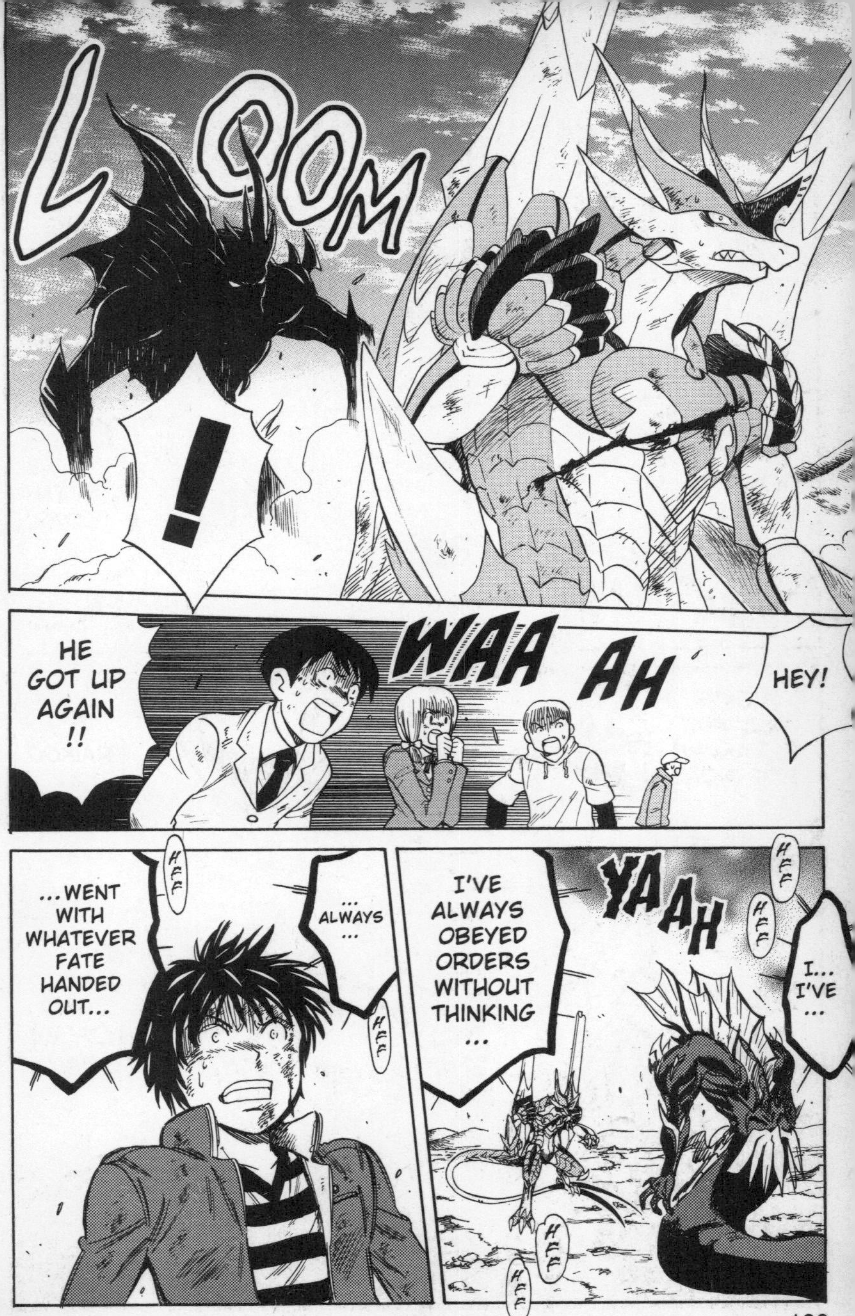
LOOOM
!
HEY!
WAA AH
HE GOT UP AGAIN !!
I... I'VE ...
HEFF
HEFF
YAAAH
I'VE ALWAYS OBEYED ORDERS WITHOUT THINKING ...
HEFF
HEFF
... ALWAYS ...
HEFF
...WENT WITH WHATEVER FATE HANDED OUT...
HEFF

READ THIS WAY

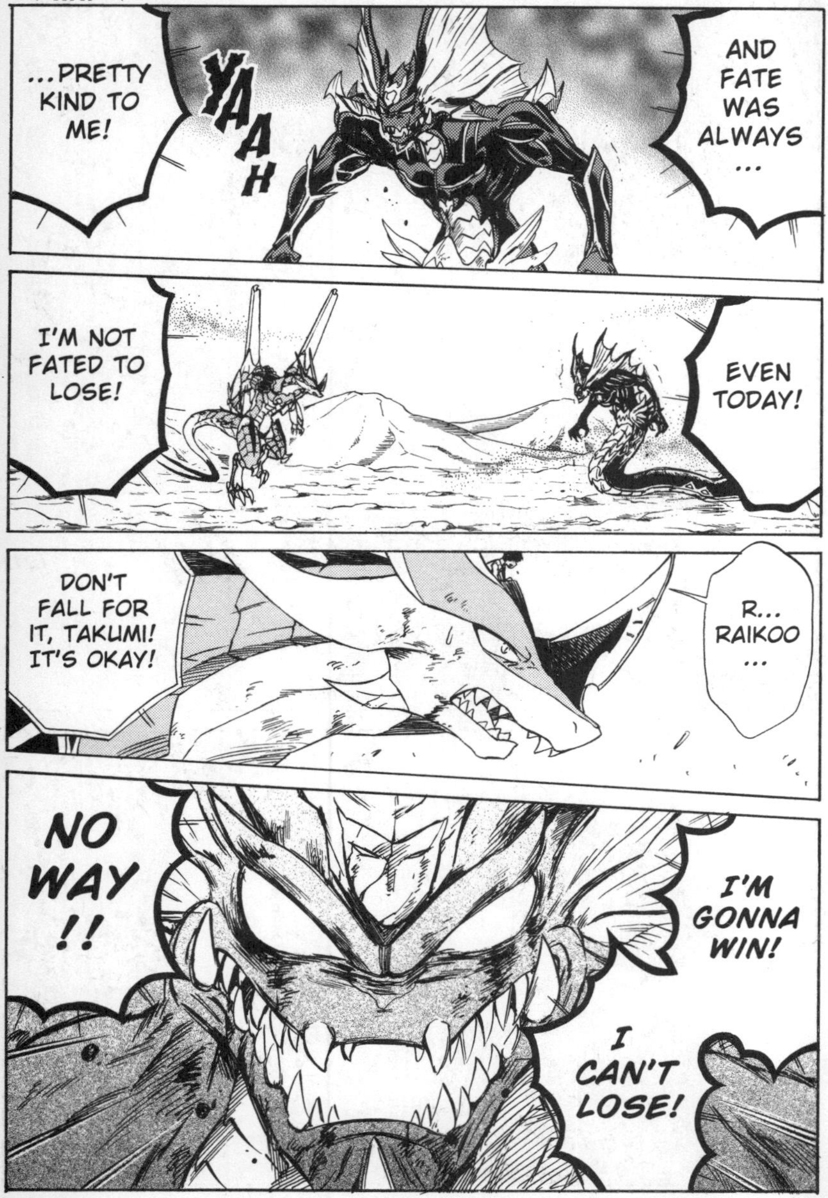
AND FATE WAS ALWAYS ...
YAAH
...PRETTY KIND TO ME!
EVEN TODAY!
I'M NOT FATED TO LOSE!
R... RAIKOO ...
DON'T FALL FOR IT, TAKUMI! IT'S OKAY!
NO WAY !!
I'M GONNA WIN!
I CAN'T LOSE!

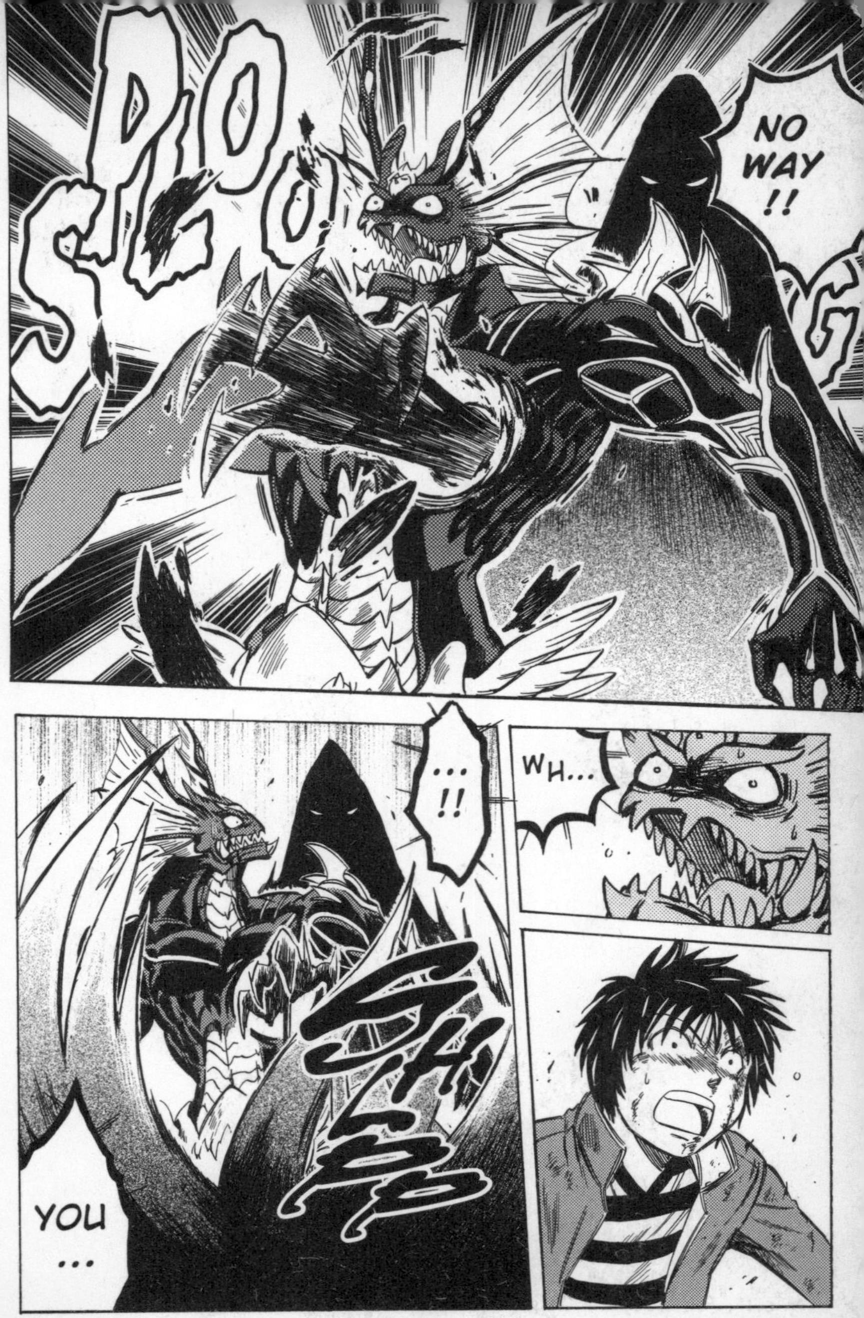
NO WAY !!
WH...
... !!
YOU ...

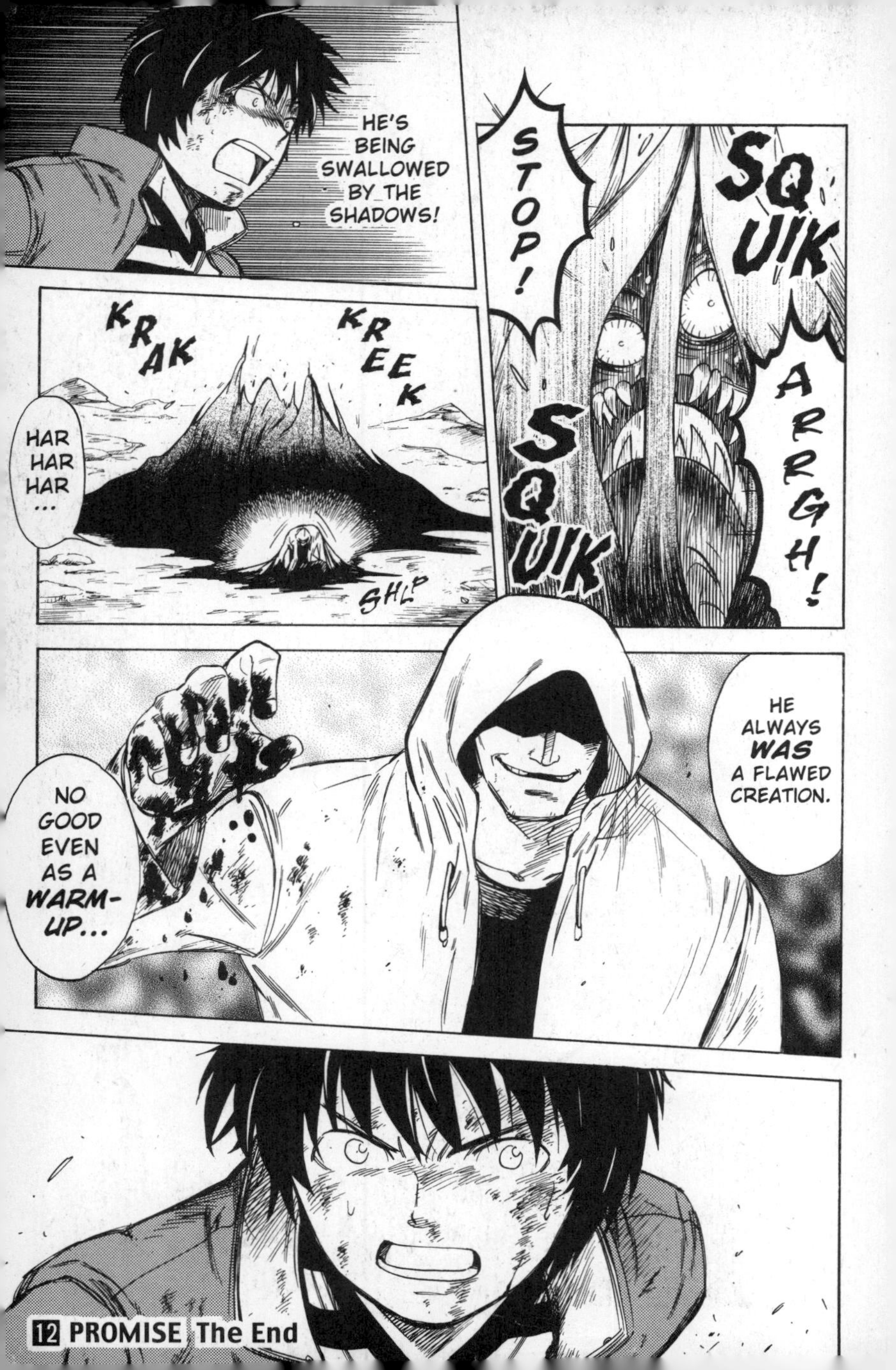
SQUIK
STOP!
ARRGH!
SQUIK
HE'S BEING SWALLOWED BY THE SHADOWS!
KREEK
KRAK
HAR HAR HAR...
SHLP
HE ALWAYS WAS A FLAWED CREATION.
NO GOOD EVEN AS A WARM-UP...

12 PROMISE The End

GO TEAM
SAKEN!

KIDOCCHI

NAGI

SAKEN

MOTSU

TORA

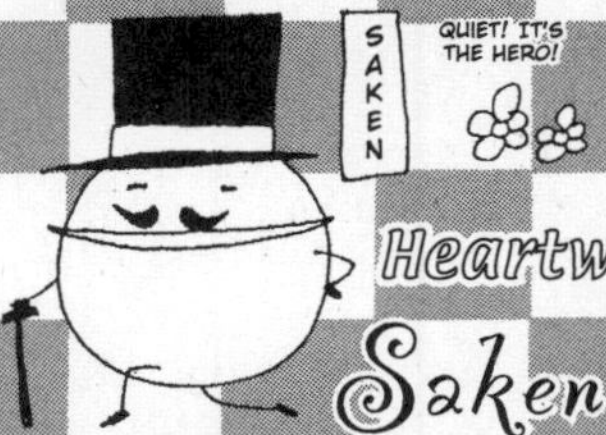
SAKEN
QUIET! IT'S THE HERO!

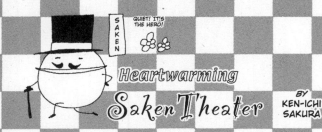

Heartwarming Saken Theater

BY KEN-ICHI SAKURA

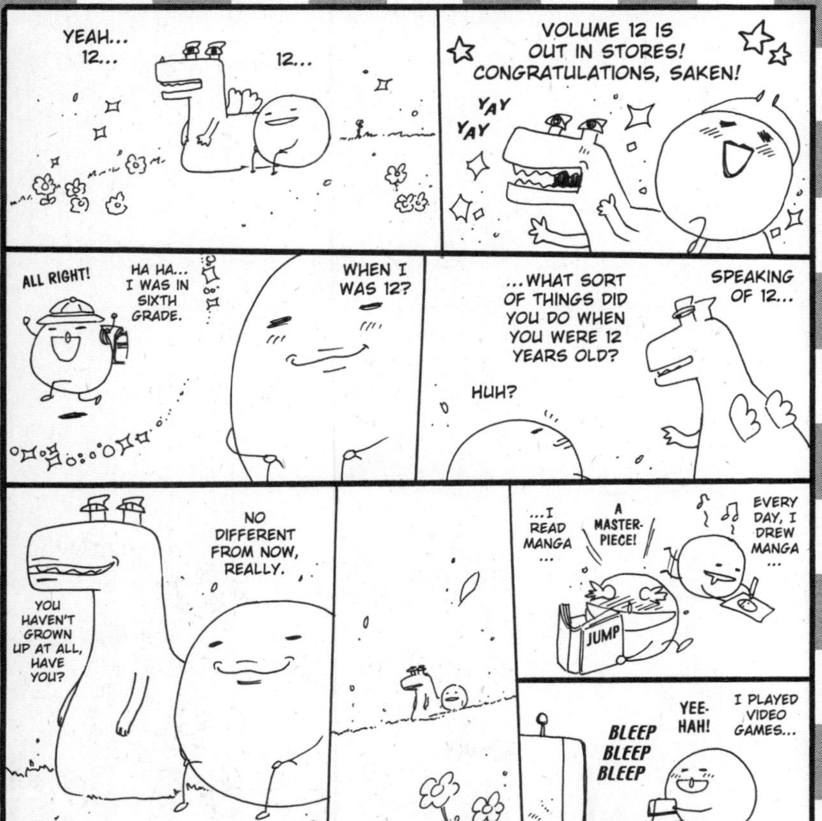
VOLUME 12 IS OUT IN STORES! CONGRATULATIONS, SAKEN!
YAY YAY
12...
YEAH... 12...
SPEAKING OF 12...
...WHAT SORT OF THINGS DID YOU DO WHEN YOU WERE 12 YEARS OLD?
HUH?
WHEN I WAS 12?
HA HA... I WAS IN SIXTH GRADE.
ALL RIGHT!
EVERY DAY, I DREW MANGA...
A MASTER-PIECE!
...I READ MANGA...
JUMP
I PLAYED VIDEO GAMES...
YEE-HAH!
BLEEP BLEEP BLEEP
NO DIFFERENT FROM NOW, REALLY.
YOU HAVEN'T GROWN UP AT ALL, HAVE YOU?

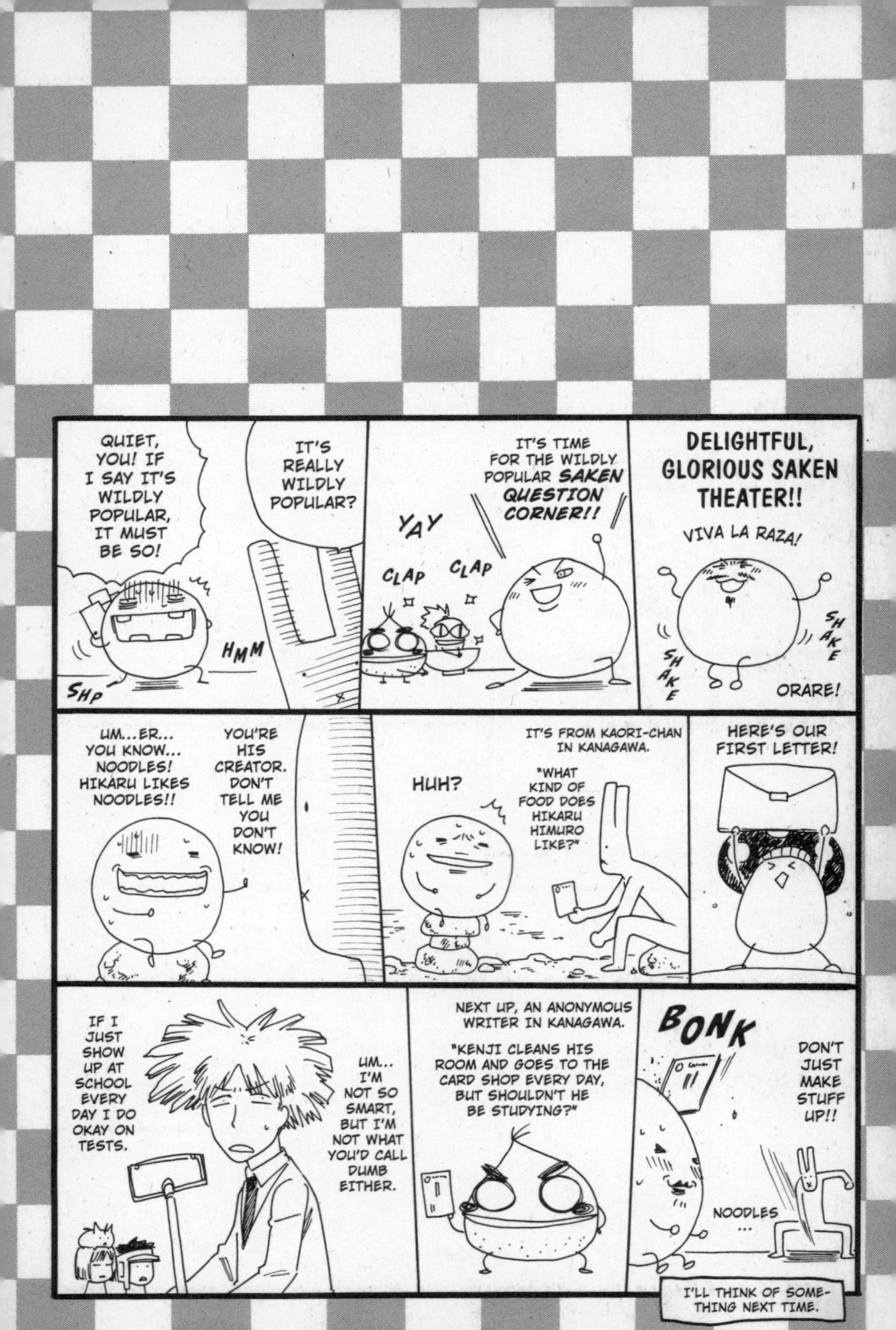
DELIGHTFUL, GLORIOUS SAKEN THEATER!!
VIVA LA RAZA!
SHAKE
SHAKE
ORARE!
IT'S TIME FOR THE WILDLY POPULAR SAKEN QUESTION CORNER!!
YAY
CLAP
CLAP
IT'S REALLY WILDLY POPULAR?
QUIET, YOU! IF I SAY IT'S WILDLY POPULAR, IT MUST BE SO!
HMM
SHP
HERE'S OUR FIRST LETTER!
IT'S FROM KAORI-CHAN IN KANAGAWA.
"WHAT KIND OF FOOD DOES HIKARU HIMURO LIKE?"
HUH?
YOU'RE HIS CREATOR. DON'T TELL ME YOU DON'T KNOW!
UM...ER... YOU KNOW... NOODLES! HIKARU LIKES NOODLES!!
BONK
DON'T JUST MAKE STUFF UP!!
NOODLES ...
I'LL THINK OF SOME-THING NEXT TIME.
NEXT UP, AN ANONYMOUS WRITER IN KANAGAWA.
"KENJI CLEANS HIS ROOM AND GOES TO THE CARD SHOP EVERY DAY, BUT SHOULDN'T HE BE STUDYING?"
IF I JUST SHOW UP AT SCHOOL EVERY DAY I DO OKAY ON TESTS.
UM... I'M NOT SO SMART, BUT I'M NOT WHAT YOU'D CALL DUMB EITHER.

Heartwarming

Saken Theater

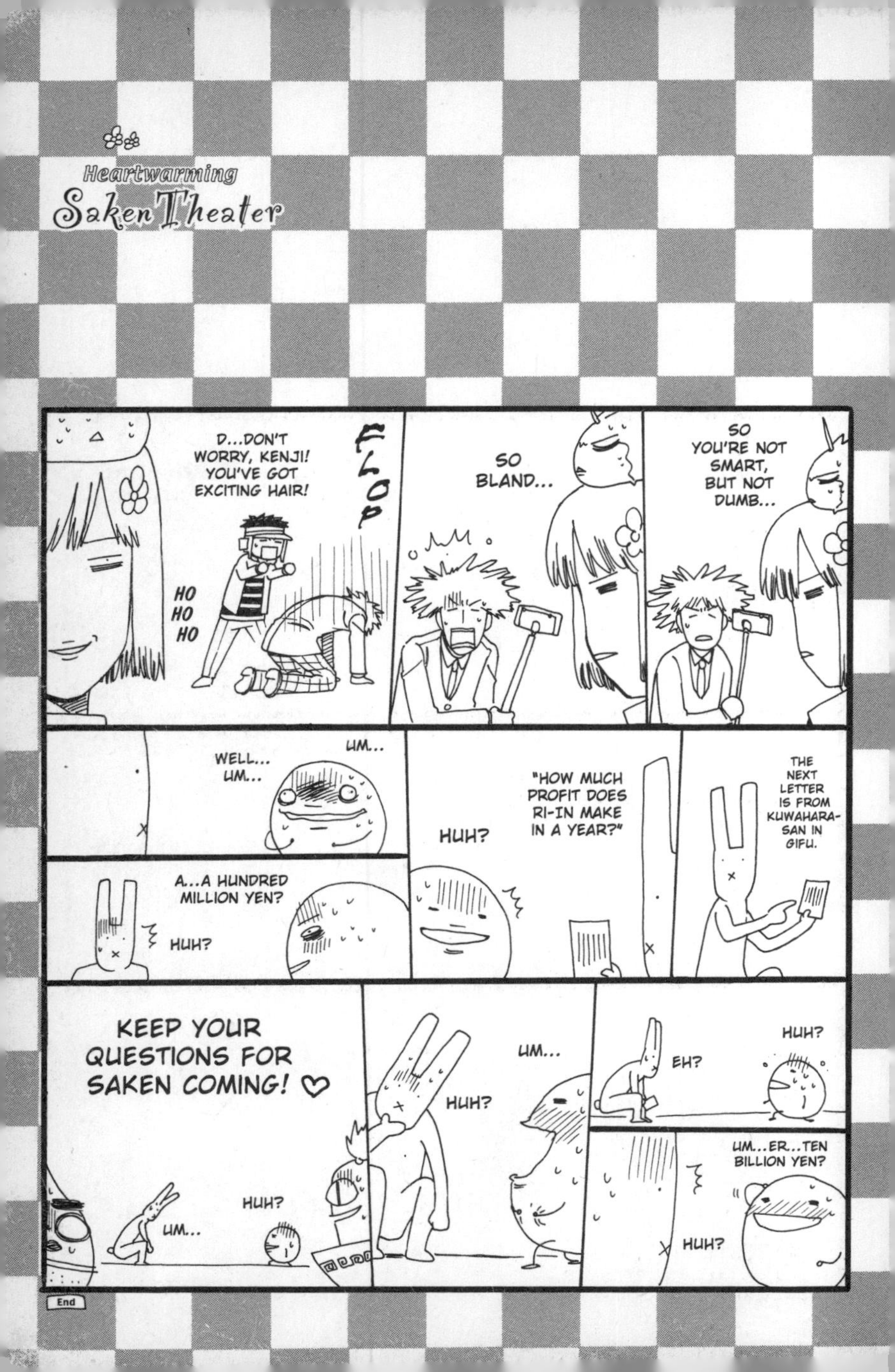
SO YOU'RE NOT SMART, BUT NOT DUMB...
SO BLAND...
FLOP
D...DON'T WORRY, KENJI! YOU'VE GOT EXCITING HAIR!
HO HO HO
THE NEXT LETTER IS FROM KUWAHARA-SAN IN GIFU.
"HOW MUCH PROFIT DOES RI-IN MAKE IN A YEAR?"
HUH?
UM...
WELL... UM...
A...A HUNDRED MILLION YEN?
HUH?
HUH?
EH?
UM...ER...TEN BILLION YEN?
HUH?
UM...
HUH?
KEEP YOUR QUESTIONS FOR SAKEN COMING! ♡
HUH?
UM...

End

COMING NEXT VOLUME...

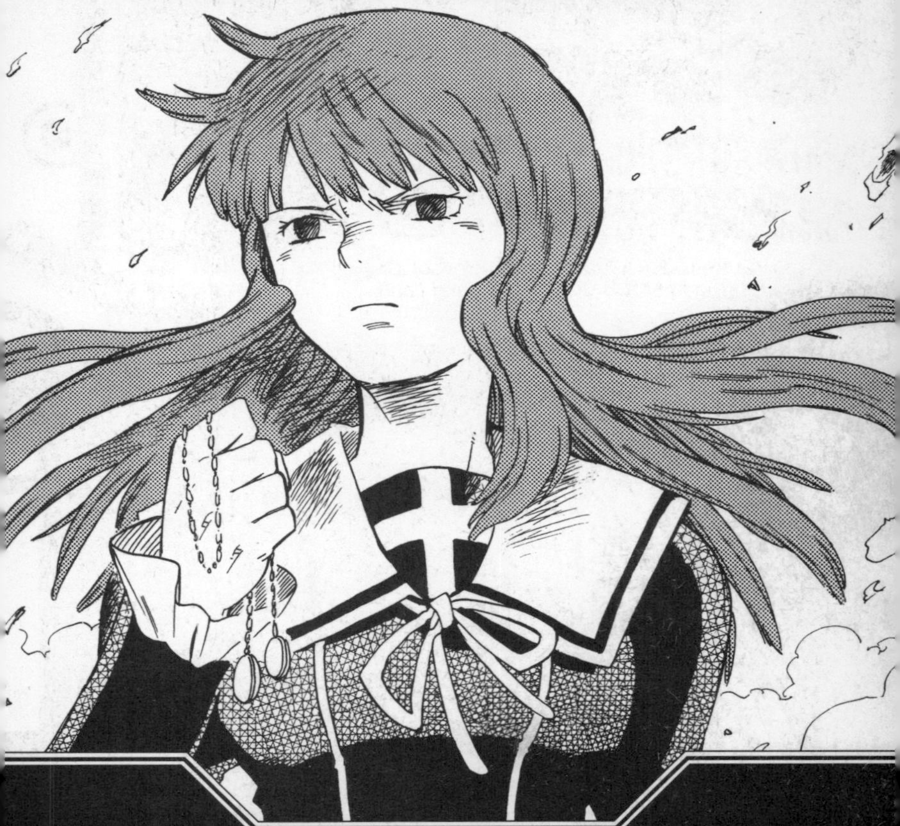

While the world's Raikoo masters escape to Rikyu, Takumi decides to stay behind and fight. Together, he and Arisa discover the purpose of the bizarre experiments Ri-IN has been performing on humans and dragons...and the full extent of Ri-IN's plans. This is more than one dragon master can handle. It's time for Takumi to meet an old hand named Reiji Ozora!

AVAILABLE IN APRIL 2009!

Save ... ...r price!

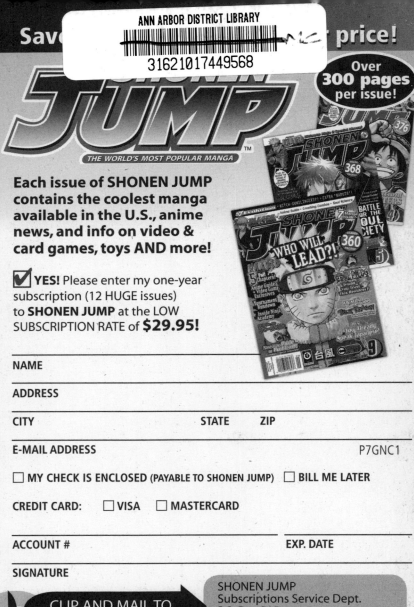

Over **300 pages** per issue!

Each issue of SHONEN JUMP contains the coolest manga available in the U.S., anime news, and info on video & card games, toys AND more!

☑ **YES!** Please enter my one-year subscription (12 HUGE issues) to **SHONEN JUMP** at the LOW SUBSCRIPTION RATE of **$29.95!**

NAME

ADDRESS

CITY   STATE   ZIP

E-MAIL ADDRESS   P7GNC1

☐ MY CHECK IS ENCLOSED (PAYABLE TO SHONEN JUMP)   ☐ BILL ME LATER

CREDIT CARD: ☐ VISA   ☐ MASTERCARD

ACCOUNT #   EXP. DATE

SIGNATURE

CLIP AND MAIL TO ➤   SHONEN JUMP
Subscriptions Service Dept.
P.O. Box 515
Mount Morris, IL 61054-0515

Make checks payable to: **SHONEN JUMP**. Canada price for 12 issues: $41.95 USD, including GST, HST and QST. US/CAN orders only. Allow 6-8 weeks for delivery.

RATED **T** TEEN
ratings.viz.com

BLEACH © 2001 by Tite Kubo/SHUEISHA Inc. NARUTO © 1999 by Masashi Kishimoto/SHUEISHA Inc.
ONE PIECE © 1997 by Eiichiro Oda/SHUEISHA Inc.